ABORTION PARLEY

ABORTION PARLEY

Edited by

James Tunstead Burtchaell, C.S.C.

with a Foreword by

Theodore M. Hesburgh, C.S.C.

Papers Delivered at the National Conference on Abortion
Held at the University of Notre Dame in October 1979

ANDREWS AND MCMEEL, INC.
A Universal Press Syndicate Company
KANSAS CITY • NEW YORK • WASHINGTON

Library of Congress Cataloging in Publication Data
National Conference on Abortion, University of Notre
  Dame, 1979.
  Abortion parley.

  Includes bibliographical references.
  1. Abortion—Congresses. 2. Abortion—United
States—Congresses. 3. Abortion—Moral and religious
aspects—Congresses. 4. Abortion—Moral and religious
aspects—Catholic Church—Congresses. I. Burtchaell,
James Tunstead. II. Title.
HQ767.5.U5N38 1979   363.4'6   80-19229
ISBN 0-8362-3600-9

CONTENTS

FOREWORD

Three years ago, during the presidential campaign, candidate Jimmy Carter spoke at Notre Dame. He had been under extraordinary pressure because of the abortion issue. He had declared himself personally against abortion. However, he was ambiguous, questioning, about the prudence of a Constitutional amendment. I told him at the time that this was really not his direct responsibility, since if the Congress passed a Constitutional amendment—a difficult passage—it would go directly to the states for their approval or disapproval.

Jimmy Carter came to Notre Dame that day in October to talk about human rights. When introducing him, I also said a few words on human rights in America. I stated my own belief in the absolutely fundamental human right—the right to life, once begun. I alluded to the fact that the issue of abortion was greatly distorting the electoral process in America, and that there was much confusion and emotion clouding the issue. I said that Notre Dame was prepared to hold a conference on the matter, in a university attempt to clarify the issue, to establish the facts, and, I hoped, to elevate the discussion from inflammatory rhetoric on both sides to more sober and reasoned positions.

Our stance is clear: we are against abortion. There is at least one condition under which Catholic theology would find it justified, namely, ectopic gestation. We have the impression that the present legal position of abortion is considered untenable by most Americans, for Americans have too high a regard for the right to life to permit abortion. Thus, we trust that open discussion of the kind congenial to the university environment might lead us from where we presently are to where we ought to be.

After candidate Carter's appearance, I asked our then provost, Father James Burtchaell, if he would arrange such an open and honorable discussion. We would ask only that the participants be honest and sincere, not that they should agree with us, although our own position is clear. We, on our part, would listen to them and declare ourselves committed to do this in the humane and reasonable fashion characteristic of university discourse. Naturally, we would hope that from this exercise we might elevate the present state of affairs from a strident shouting match to a serious discussion of fact and principle.

Even in proposing to do this we opened ourselves to recrimination and abuse. No matter. The issue is enormously important to the moral level of human policy in pluralistic America and the world, for one cannot deny the fact that very sincere people differ at present. What some see as of mild concern is monumentally important to others. We have witnessed the fact that political candidates who agree 95 percent with Catholic principles of social justice in most issues of public policy have been defeated by their opposition on this one issue and have been replaced by candidates who, agreeing superficially on this issue of abortion, disagree with us on almost every other issue bearing on justice and equality. Even worse, many candidates who agree with our position on abortion in this country advocate foreign policy positions that increase the likelihood that women in Third World countries will seek abortion. A life is a life—whether it be in the United States, Colombia, or Sri Lanka.

This conference is for us an occasion for hope: that the issue might be elucidated, that misunderstandings might be dispelled, that our position might be better understood, that the present conviction of most Americans might be clarified, and, especially, that a better scenario for the future might be envisioned.

This is no small hope. It is large enough to persuade us to take the chance, as universities do, to cast a bit of light into the gathering darkness. The issue itself is too important to be resolved by pressure politics alone. This university has confidence in the salutary effect of reason and faith when applied to the human condition. I am personally grateful to all who participated—pro or con—for joining us in this endeavor. I am especially grateful to Father Jim Burtchaell and to our university colleagues who have volunteered to join him in opening this dialogue. May it continue on a high level.

THEODORE M. HESBURGH, C.S.C.
President, University of Notre Dame

PREFACE

The essays in this book were prepared for the National Conference on Abortion convened in October 1979 at the University of Notre Dame. Each essay stands on its own legs; nothing said by way of preface can augment or diminish the sturdiness of their scholarship and their argumentation. Some word about the conference itself, however, may be worthy of the written record, for to our knowledge it is the first colloquy to which speakers and conferees were invited publicly from across the nation to discuss abortion—regardless of their moral judgment on it—since abortion-on-demand was made lawful throughout America in 1973, or, indeed, since it was first allowed in any jurisdiction in 1967.

The level of public discourse on abortion in our land has often seemed unworthy of the subject, considering the magnitude of what is at stake. Many individuals for whom this is a heartfelt concern have held themselves remote from public involvement simply because they recoiled from the coarse and partisan scuffling. One supposes that a similar wariness of being scorched explains the virtually total reluctance of academic institutions to sponsor symposia on abortion.

Nineteen seventy-six was the first presidential election year since the abortion decisions of 1973. The debate flared up then, and the two leading candidates were made to declare themselves on this as one of the sharper issues of the campaign. Representatives of the Roman Catholics in the United States were among those who interrogated Messrs. Carter and Ford. This seemed to be a wholesome right of citizen interest. Although abortion and governmental subsidies for abortion were legitimate topics for political debate, the entire issue also seemed to invite another sort of discussion, one less immediately political and more reflective: the sort of discussion a university might best initiate. It was during that campaign, when Jimmy Carter was on our campus to address the Center for Civil Rights, that Father Theodore Hesburgh, president of the university, announced publicly that we meant to sponsor such a conference at Notre Dame.

We decided, at the start of our undertaking, that we wanted a conference, not a rally: interested persons of whatever moral conviction would be invited. We wanted in fact to enlarge people's ethical perspective—not so much by provoking them to reconsider their overall judgment that abortion is right or wrong (an unrealistic ambition for a single conference), as by reminding them that alongside this enormous issue lie many questions that also deserve serious moral inquiry, questions about family and childbearing and adoption and public welfare and political freedom. We wanted speakers who could address those subjects honestly and knowledgeably: competence was sought rather than a past record of advocacy alone. And we wanted speakers to spend the full time of the conference here, as equal participants in the acquaintanceship and discussion, rather than flying in for brief and separate appearances.

With the help of four research associates—one each in the fields of law, ethics, social science, and medicine—I reviewed the span of scholarly literature on abortion, and over the course of two years carefully located a roster of speakers who could, we hoped, help us all to think more clearly on this troubled and troubling topic.

After agreeing upon and with those speakers, we made public our intention to sponsor the meeting. Our explanation was as follows:

The abortion question entails issues of social welfare, human and civil rights, ethical value, public funding policy, emotional integration, professional probity, health care and political dissent. The debate about abortion has at times been shrill and intemperate. But in a certain sense it has been timely and, in a good way, provocative. We are pushed by it to consider and to negotiate some issues close to personal conscience and the national welfare that we might otherwise be tempted to ignore.

Notre Dame's Center for the Study of Man in Contemporary Society is, for this reason, convening a conference on abortion. Speakers at the conference have been invited with two purposes in mind: first, to provide information or interpretation that might help to unclutter the national debate of unfounded assumptions or misconstrued facts; second, to address some important policy issues that the abortion debate stirs up but cannot resolve.

What are the circumstances and given motives of women and

couples who secure abortions? What is known psychologically about these women, and about others who experience unwanted pregnancy but do not choose abortion? About child adoption in America: how many children are sought and given in adoption, who are these children, what are the outcomes for all parties involved, what abuses are known? What is the reliability of reports—abundant but conflicting—of social science research regarding abortion? Has legalization effected any changes for medical professionals involved? Amid different polls and conclusions, what is the best verifiable sense of public opinion regarding the morality, the legality, or the funding of abortion? What principles should govern public policy in funding any service that is a lawful right? What implications arise from United States support of population programs in developing nations? What is to be learned from analyzing the course of the debate itself? The clash of opinions on abortion is often attributed to religious doctrine; what difference ought this make to either ethical judgment or government policy? Is there any avenue of ethical inquiry down which parties on opposing sides might journey together? These are some of the questions that conference speakers will address.

The speakers hold a variety of personal and political positions on the acceptability of abortion. They were not selected, however, in order to defend one or a variety of positions. Each has been invited because he or she has cogent and articulate things to say which can contribute professionally to anyone's thinking on abortion, from whatever perspective.

We sent invitations to about two thousand individuals: doctors, prolife and prochoice advocates, law professors, church executives, members of Congress, and others. Advertisements were run in the *New York Times*, the *Washington Post*, the *Chicago Tribune*, and the *Los Angeles Times*. Announcements were placed in journals devoted to bioethical inquiry. Two results flowed from this advertising: we were widely criticized for having such a conference at all, and far fewer persons came to it than we had anticipated.

Our advertising brought in a jumble of letters that reminded us of the nerve we were twanging. Some correspondents were supportive of abortion choice. One woman from Flushing, New York, who signed as "Wife, Mother, and Grandmother and Christian" wrote of her own experience:

> I had an illegal abortion 31 yrs. ago. I have never regretted it nor have I ever suffered the least bit of remorse or guilt. It was clearly the best decision I could have made for I would not have

survived otherwise.

Who amongst us know what's best for another person? Let each decide for her/himself. [All letters are cited without alteration.]

A man in Brooklyn wrote in an open letter to the conferees:

Legally, the Supreme Court has upheld the long-established constitutional right of a person to make such a basic decision as to whether she should bear an unwanted child. But how depressing it is to see how easily judges, district attorneys, and legislators, as well as doctors and hospital administrators can be intimidated by outright threats to withhold votes, financial support, and even physical violence. And I am amazed to hear from the highest officer in the land that such a legal right mandated by the highest court should apply only to those wealthy enough to buy the best possible medical treatment.

I have been involved for all my adult life in community activities—local planning boards, hospital advisory committees, Health Service Agency groups. How insulting to be told that I cannot tell the difference between murder and morality.

Another man, from Larchmont, New York, whose letterhead reads "Non-Sectarian Committee for Life," wrote:

I have been spending about $25,000. of my own money per year over the past 10 years in the defense of the meaning of man.

I belong to no churches or clubs. My wife calls me a "nothing at all."

A lady in Detroit, whose husband cosigned her letter, had this to say:

Re: Amniocentesis and its search and destroy philosophy, as proven by the March of Dimes booklet, purchased by myself some three or four years ago, we cannot emphasize too strongly the evil of destroying an unborn child who may be deformed. I can give personal witness to the fact that such unborn sick children do want to live. I am a Marfan's Syndrome and Spina Bifida person, happy that my parents loved me enough 56 years ago to give me my right to live and be a Catholic. Though both diseases cause me only mild problems, I would still want to live if I had been a more severe case. When I did volunteer work in a local nursing home, I was struck by the cheerfulness and will to live of the patients there, all poor, many black, whom many would say should never have been born—how un-Christian and hard-of-heart we as a nation are.

From Chicago a friend of the university expressed displeasure:

I see the press characterizing the conference as one held by enlightened and far-seeing members of the Church. To those of us who have been characterized as "bigots" because of our opposition to abortion, your conference will provide the media with additional material to be used against us.

Another very personal letter came from a woman in New Jersey:

I am 38, mother of 3, wife of a clergyman, had 4½ years of grad. work in Philosophy, Religion and Psychiatry, author of a philosophy textbook for children.

I had an ektopic pregnancy in 1972 which was not discovered until surgery 7 weeks after conception. When I awoke, the intern informed me that I had been pregnant, which none of us suspected since I had a loop. I was flooded with awe and amazement during my hospital stay. When I got home, the thing began to sink in: *What happened to the child?*, for I truly believe that the moment of conception introduces a new life.

No one told me, but I'm sure it was put into a plastic bag and incinerated: devastating to a woman who felt love and responsibility toward that life. There was no way to assuage the love and committment I as a mother needed to exert for her child. After a year of grieving for the child, something my husband and no one else I talked to could understand, a priest prayed with me for the child, the only thing I could do to bestow the love, dignity of life and honor of God's miracle that that child was entitled to.

The mail also included a bundle of letters that were quite personal, but in a different way. A South Bend couple wrote indignantly:

So! the conference director on abortion and former provost who is now professor of theology will be host to the baby killers! . . . Now that Father Hesburgh has endorsed ERA which locks in abortion on demand, promotes homosexuality, and is against the home and family, you are making a mockery of the former Christian religious institution called Notre Dame. . . . With the sex perverts roaming your campus and a part of it, how can you call your institution Christian? Perhaps, this explains why so many are leaving the Catholic Church. . . .
For God and Country, (and former Catholics). . . .

A man in Chicago sent copies of a duplicated sheet entitled *"Contraception:* A Suggested Cause of Genitals Malignancy and Subnormal Progeny," which had presumably been prepared for wider distribution. It explained:

—The sole and only function and purpose of coition is to achieve the conception and birth of a child or children.

When a couple engage in coitus, various glandular secretions and nerve forces are generated in the processes of procreation. If these are obstructed the result is similar to damming a river,—these secretions and forces seek outlets,—and appear to do so in the forms of polyps, tumors, cancers, neuroses and nervous disorders.

NOTE: If, despite efforts at contraception, a birth results, it seems that probably such offspring, generally, would be physically defective and/or mentally retarded.

A "Rev." correspondent reached us from California:

Dear Sir's, I like more information on abortion.

I would like to know all about abortion, you see I would like to preach and explain it to the public.

The Bible states that at the point of conception, or when the ovum is being fertilized by the man's Spermatozoa, Psalm 139: At that very moment it becomes a zagote, takes from three to five days.

The other point is: the baby has no life till after it emerges from the uterus, thats when God's life enters the baby's body, and started crying.

Another Californian had a different sort of message:

I am writing to inform you that I know a special method of protection and which I practised myself.

I had three children in first 5 years and wishing not to have more soon, consulted doctors who suggested operations which then was against the law. Consulted friends, one of them was an old doctor and in several talks he gave an idea. After serious thought I adopted the practice which is safe, sound and painless and marriage activities continued without fear of pregnancy.

After 9 years of practice I suddenly found my wife to have a new baby and I suggested to her to go to doctor but she refused and exactly after 10 years we had a baby boy.

I would like to give the information of this method but first I must be paid because I am a poor man and need money to carry on because I cannot work to earn at my present age of 83 years.

Send your representative with whatever good offer you think I deserve and shall only talk when good cash is paid.

A woman in Detroit was brief:

The Popes have all said abortion is murder. If you don't believe it—get out of the Church and stop using the "Father."

We hoped that our conference would find coverage by the communications media. Our first lesson came from the *Los Angeles Times*, which lost our ad copy for a whole month. A minor clerk in the advertising department had simply thrown it away when he noted mention of "abortion," a word the paper's editorial policy had embargoed. After long-distance explaining we succeeded in having our ad exhumed and printed. Then, after a succession of preliminary releases to major newspapers elicited no interest, we found that virtually every major newspaper had shunted the information to its religion editor. Every religion editor in the country that week had gone to ground, exhausted from covering the pope's recent visit. No general editor could be persuaded that a conference on abortion among psychiatrists, lawyers, obstetricians, ethicists, sociologists, and political scientists could be anything but religious news. Locally, one television channel came and interviewed a number of participants, but we received no coverage at all from the TV station owned by the university and located on campus.

People came to the conference from all over the land. We had national representatives from the Population Department, United Methodist Board of Church and Society; the Pro-Life Activities Committee of the National Conference of Catholic Bishops; the March of Dimes; the National Committee for a Human Life Amendment; the Alan Guttmacher Institute; the Religious Coalition for Abortion Rights; the National Right to Life Committee; the Population Crisis Committee; Americans United for Life; the National Abortion Rights Action League; the Catholic Health Association; and the National Abortion Foundation. We had sisters from the pastoral care departments and administrative staffs of Catholic hospitals; we had staffers from large abortion facilities in Cleveland and Indianapolis and the director of a national chain of nine abortion clinics. We had the head of the American Association of Pro Life Obstetricians and Gynecologists alongside the doctor who performs all of South Bend's abortions (he was the only member of the local medical fraternity who chose to attend). We were Protestants, Jews, and Catholics together, and citizens of no religious interest too. There were law professors and housewives and corporation executives and psychologists and Jesuits and abortion counselors; people who cared for neonatal nurseries and others who defended the rights of the retarded; a black woman who works as a hot-line staffer, and our bishop. These were virtually all people who had staked enough interest in the abortion issue to have attended conferences on it before—yet now, for the first time, two opposite clans were literally breaking bread together.

We were about seventy-five persons in all, plus interested faculty and students from Notre Dame and St. Mary's College who sat in at this or that session. I had hoped for 350, but soon saw that had the larger number turned out, participants would have stood on the floor addressing mostly strangers, and we might well not have drawn together enough to look very closely into one another's eyes. With our smaller complement of people, we quickly became bound by personal acquaintance and spoke to one another with the respect and patience and precision that we are not so disposed to observe when talking behind someone's back or over someone's head. From Monday to Wednesday we sat together through twelve sessions, each lasting for at least two hours, with more of that time allocated to discussion than to delivery of papers. We all dined together, and had hours of time at refreshment breaks to further the exchanges begun on the conference floor. In those three days I never heard an uncivil word about abortion spoken, and I also heard no hedging.

Our purpose was not to hold a debate. Hence we did not line up speakers on the pro and con sides of various issues. That would have encouraged us to speak out mostly as partisans in a struggle. We were not even aiming at dialogue, for that too might have ranged us self-consciously as protagonists and antagonists. Our hope was to host a conversation, an earnest conversation which could at least begin without everyone assuming they knew each other's full mind. We had no expectation that any of those people, most of whom had spent themselves heavily on abortion-related endeavors for years, was going to reconsider his or her position. All that we hoped was to allow them to do their considering in the presence of one another, and in that way somehow to initiate a more humane style of disembittered discourse among those who care the most but have not always spoken the best. Our hopes were satisfied. We came away better for having met and listened and talked.

Reactions to the conference included some that were negative. After the end of the first session a professor of psychiatry walked out and returned to Cleveland. A corporation executive, in a published account of the event, was distressed at the civility of the sessions:

> King Solomon again sat in judgment, this time at the University of Notre Dame. Again the best interests of a mother and child were at issue. But last week the child didn't fare well.... one vividly formed impression is that for some, even of those convening the Conference, the elective abortion over the last six years of 7,700,000 unborn American children is an interesting intellectual question to be examined in an antiseptic, dispassionate and leisurely manner.

More hostile comment arrived from people who had not been present. A woman from Portland, Oregon, wrote:

> You say "it's the job of the university to promote discussion and interaction." It may be the secular university's job, but in the area of abortion it is not the Catholic university's job.

A man from the same city had a like objection:

> Recently I have noticed the repetition by various Catholic spokesmen of this idea: "Abortion is a complex matter." I beg to differ. Abortion is simple and crude. That it was considered worthy of serious intellectualizing on your campus only shows again that some are educated beyond their intelligence.

And from Maine:

> What a gigantic waste of money! Putting up the murderers of babies and giving 'em a forum! You ought to go into a monastery and do penance.... Vatican II labelled abortion an unspeakable, repeat *unspeakable* crime. Not to be discussed, Father.... Your Viet Cong pals, Father, invaded Cambodia, and are committing worse genocide, proportionately, than the Holocaust, yet I hear no peep from you, rich and comfortable at Notre Dame.

Persons who shared the days together were more positive

in their evaluations. One woman active in Right-to-Life work reflected:

> Perhaps the most important thing that happened is that we listened to each other.

> Personally I don't feel any myths on the topic of abortion were revealed, but for myself I recognized many prejudices I have that I wasn't aware of before.

> My stand against abortion has not lessened. In fact I feel stronger and more determined to have it ended. My tactic has changed hopefully from accusation to a helping hand. . . . While eating lunch with Dr. Hauerwas he mentioned working with some retarded children and how it would make us sick to see them and how few are responding to their needs. I respect his frustration and anger. For my many years in ———— County Right-To-Life work I have felt determination, frustration and anger.

> I thought of Mother Teresa and what she said is the one necessary ingredient needed of the young women joining her order— joy—if they are to survive the long hours of work and the injustices they witness.

> Perhaps for too long we've blinded ourselves to the individual because of the anger and frustration we experience in just seeing their needs.

A churchman was pleased:

> I left the Conference more deeply convinced than I have been about the urgent pastoral need to clarify our thinking on the sanctity of life, on the means to preserve the sanctity in a culture which is becoming increasing calloused toward the destruction of life. . . . In certain high quarters I have said and will continue to say that the Notre Dame conference made a solid contribution to scholarly research on a topic of crucial importance to our church.

One pediatrics professor, however, had a different view of it:

> The opportunity of speaking to individuals that participate, support or recommend abortion allowed me to realize even greater the frailty of their position. They are to be pitied and are in need of our prayers.

Possibly typical were the comments we received from two women who have been equally involved for years on opposite sides of the quarrel. One with Right-to-Life wrote:

> Although I know that the goal of the conference was not necessarily to change minds, you might like to know that at the close

of the Conference, one of the pro-abortion participants told the reporter from the *National Right To Life News* that she was re-examining her position. Since she is a counselor at a clinic, who knows how many lives might be saved as a result? And saving lives is really what the Right to Life movement is all about.

It is my hope, too, that the conference may have another side effect, and that is to establish better communication and understanding among the various pro-life individuals who participated and also between the groups they represent.

The other wrote:

As an abortion provider, I can assure you that I enrolled in the seminar with some hesitancy. I must also tell you that I felt extremely reinspired after the conference. To finally be in a position of exchanging dialogue as opposed to being on opposing picket lines was indeed a welcome change. I have worked in the field of abortion services for eight years, and felt that this meeting was one of the few positive efforts I have seen from either side in years. . . . Your roundtable discussions were excellent, and certainly forced people to communicate. I learned a great deal from these frank conversations, and would welcome more in the future.

I wanted to tell you how much I respect you for having initiated this type of gathering. I know that it is hard for people to understand how a group could feel that they are "helping people" by providing safe, legal abortions. It is hard for me to understand how people can feel they are "helpers" by denying reality. I can only hope that by bridging that lack of understanding we may eventually come to a solution that helps women to take more responsibility in their lives and avoid the traumatic condition of unwanted pregnancy.

There were scenes that remain as thought-provoking memories. Possibly the sharpest exchange during the three days was between a Methodist theologian and a Methodist Church executive, each of whom accused the other's stated position of being unfaithful to Christian principles. Then there was the observation by a Jewish child psychiatrist that he had met no one at the conference who really favored abortion, and no one who did not energetically want to help women and couples with distressful pregnancies. One cannot forget the two women at the last session who came during the discussion to tell of their distressed pregnancies years before: one quietly told the story of her abortion, and testified how it had dedicated her to sparing similarly trapped women similar indignities, by offering them decent abortion services; the other, more dramatic, recounted how bearing her child out of wedlock had turned her towards active work in Right-to-Life, to persuade other women to spare their children from destruction. Those were things it helped us all to hear, and to hear in one another's company.

In the aftermath of those October days we were reminded that not everyone thought it appropriate for those conversations to have taken place—or to have taken place here, at Notre Dame. One afternoon recently a close friend on the faculty ambled into my office, boring his pipe, and confessed that he just did not feel our university should have had a conference on abortion. Was it a subject, I asked, that we should never discuss aloud, or that he or I would do wrong to treat of in the classroom? No, he said, it was perfectly appropriate in the classroom. But to hold an open conference might give the impression that we were in doubt on the subject, that we might be neutral. What had people concluded, I asked him, about our conference on South Africa the preceding week: that we had gone soft on apartheid? And would a conference on God suggest that we were having second thoughts about him? At this point I could only barely see his Irish eyes behind billows of troubled smoke. I asked him, in some heat, to draw me up a list of subjects he really thought should be embargoed from open discussion at this university. I added that I was hardly surprised at remarks like this from people who had no idea what a university was, but that I had no stomach for it from a fellow professor. At that point he took exception at being called a know–nothing, slipped anchor, and sailed, under a full funnel, back to his own office.

That same day I received a telephone call from a former Notre Dame colleague now serving a small Catholic college as vice-president. The new bishop in their town, he explained, was angry that Betty Friedan had been invited to speak on their campus (he cited her stand in favor of abortion, though that was not to be the topic of her talk), and had threatened all manner of reprisals unless her speech was canceled. What, my friend asked, should they tell the bishop?

My memory conveniently blurs my reply to him, but those two conversations reminded me that many people—some of whom ought to know better—do not understand what the work of a university is. A university is a place where men and women try to learn together. We study what others say— mostly through their publications and, if they are our contemporaries, by hearing them out in person. Whom we read, whom we listen to—is not decided by allegiance. Some of the best that we know has been shared with us by the most brilliant minds, the most disciplined workers, the wisest thinkers. But we also owe a great deal to those we judge to be mistaken, or deceptive, or dishonest. In my own time I have learned from great speakers, like Jacques Maritain, Josef Pieper, John Courtney Murray, and Rosemary Haughton. But I have also been provoked to learn much by George Wallace and James Pike and Francis Crick: a charlatan, a buffoon, and a bigot. I could not now say whether my mind has been stirred to its best work by those whose conclusions I came to endorse or by those whose views I worked to controvert. Whichever it be, I know I could not have become a learned man had I not been given an appetite to seek out those I most deplored along with those I most admired. The former are triply important to us: because we are more likely, through antipathy, to misrepresent their evidence and arguments, to miss matters of value they are advocating; because they oblige us to explain again to ourselves why we stand where we do; and because they sometimes show us we were wrong. My education had me read Augustine's *Confessions* and Marx and Engel's *Manifesto*—both exciting, and challenging, and worth my study.

So it is that, at a university, the more severe the controversy, the more the need to read one's adversary, or even to hear him or her out at first hand. And it must be done with dignity. A university is a sort of trucial territory, a demilitarized zone where the spite and hostility that afflict partisan struggles must be laid aside. Those who are active in struggle may turn an impatient ear on academic disengagement and restraint, but we must still persevere in the work and service that is ours. It is not all that the world needs, but it is something special we have to give.

Some constituents of the university have berated our Board of Trustees because they have never passed a resolution condemning abortion. How, they ask, can we be Catholic and not take a stand?

A Catholic institution such as the University of Notre Dame has no business issuing moral condemnations of abortion, any more than it would endorsing a presidential candidate or sponsoring a theory of biogenetics or ratifying a certain school of philosophical thought or favoring a method of financial accounting. To the extent that its chartered responsibilities and welfare require, a university may choose a certain accounting method for its own bookkeeping, or exclude abortion from its student health program. But for the world at large it has no teaching on these or other matters. Its service to the church and to the world is not to be a teacher but to harbor teachers, to let us scholars learn and expound ethics and politics and genetics and philosophy and accountancy. It is the institution's resolute aloofness from general issues that affords us the freedom to be committed and partisan. And in this haven we search freely and argue peaceably with anyone we wish. There is ancient precedent for it—in the Man who sat and supped and talked and puzzled with everyone who would abide it. It was, I do believe, in his Spirit that we gathered at Notre Dame October last to consider together this sad matter of so many children never to be born.

Thanks are due first of all to Father Theodore M. Hesburgh, C.S.C., president of the University of Notre Dame, who asked that this conference be held, encouraged the work which led to it, and subsidized its expenses. We are also grateful to Prof. David Leege, director of the Center for the Study of Man in Contemporary Society, under whose direct sponsorship the conference was held. Valuable research work was done by Dr. Mary Ann Lamanna; Rev. Edward Malloy, C.S.C.; William Fiorini, M.D.; and Stephen Squeri, Esq. Especially helpful support was provided from Notre Dame's Office of Public Information, by Richard Conklin and Diane Wilson. Robert Gordon and Terence Keeley helped with arrangements. Jim Andrews believed in our undertaking enough to agree to publish it sight unseen. And, most of all, thanks are due to Sparky Tavis, who so kindly and indefatigably saw to all the conference arrangements.

JAMES TUNSTEAD BURTCHAELL, C.S.C.

ABOUT THE AUTHORS

VIRGINIA DEANE ABERNETHY is associate professor of psychiatry (anthropology) and director, Division of Human Behavior, Department of Psychiatry, in the Vanderbilt University School of Medicine. Since her years of education at Wellesley and Harvard, she has studied female motivation and attitudes with respect to sexual relations, contraception, unwanted pregnancy, abortion, childbearing, and divorce.

RAYMOND J. ADAMEK, trained as a sociologist at Purdue, is professor at Kent State University. His research has included attitudinal and behavioral studies of delinquent teenagers, student radicals, parent-child relations, and steelworkers.

HADLEY ARKES, a political scientist from the University of Chicago, is professor and chairman of his department at Amherst College. His interests and writings have dwelt on constitutional law and political philosophy, and on the connections between morals and law, with special attention given to racial defamation, legal redress of discrimination, and abortion.

JUDITH BLAKE, after studies at Columbia University and a decade of service at the University of California, Berkeley, has become Fred H. Bixby Professor of Population Policy, School of Public Health and Department of Sociology, UCLA. Her principal work has been in the areas of childbearing and fertility control, the status of women, and population growth. She is the foremost analyst of surveys of American public opinion on abortion. Jorge H. del Pinal is her research assistant at UCLA.

ELIZABETH S. COLE is director of the North American Center on Adoption, associated with the Child Welfare League of

America. Her career as a social worker has been devoted mostly to child welfare and adoption. As chief of the Bureau of Resource Development in the New Jersey Division of Youth and Family Services, she influenced, on state and national levels, model legislation and new subsidized adoption programs.

HENRY P. DAVID is director of the Transnational Family Research Institute and associate clinical professor of psychology in the University of Maryland School of Medicine. An early career as a clinical psychologist was followed by extensive international research on contraception and abortion and the psychological factors in fertility regulation.

STANLEY MARTIN HAUERWAS, professor of theology at the University of Notre Dame, works in the discipline of Christian ethics. His graduate education was at Yale, and his publications are concerned with the care of the retarded, euthanasia, abortion, political ethics, marriage and family, and virtue and character.

ARTHUR KORNHABER is medical director of Pediatric Neuropsychiatric Associates in Mt. Kisco, New York. Trained as a physician at the University of Paris and as a psychiatrist at the University of Florida, he works particularly with children and adolescents and their families. Past research interests have included obesity, television violence, and the effects of marijuana on adolescents. Presently he is writing a book on child / grandparent relations.

MARY ANN LAMANNA is assistant professor of sociology in the University of Nebraska at Omaha. She was educated at many universities: Washington (St. Louis), Strasbourg, North Carolina, Notre Dame, and Michigan. Her areas of interest have been marriage, family and sex roles, medical sociology, and social psychology. She has particularly studied the value of children to biological and adoptive parents.

KATHLEEN ASSINI PERRY and JUDITH YOUNG PETERSON are, respectively, president and executive director of B*E*T*A* (Birth*Education*Training*Acceptance), a service in Orlando, Florida, for women with distressful pregnancies. A Catholic home economist and a Jewish dentistry management consultant, the two have founded and managed an innovative total support program for pregnant teenagers that has attracted national awards. Diane Wilson is assistant director of Information Services at Notre Dame.

MARY C. SEGERS is associate professor of political science at the Newark College of Rutgers University. Since her graduate studies at Columbia University, she has turned her interests to contemporary political theory on equality, theories of natural law and natural rights, and ethical issues attached to abortion policy.

DONALD P. WARWICK is professor at the Harvard Institute for International Development. Trained in social psychology and sociology at the University of Michigan, he has taught at Oberlin College and Michigan, San Marcos (Lima), York, and Harvard universities, and has done extensive resident research in Indonesia, Paraguay, El Salvador, Mexico, and Peru. In the field of international development, he has studied the ethical, cultural, and political impact of social intervention on developing countries.

JAMES TUNSTEAD BURTCHAELL, C.S.C., the editor, is professor of theology at the University of Notre Dame. His graduate studies were in Rome, Washington, Jerusalem, and Cambridge. His research interests have included constitutional issues about religious freedom and establishment, marriage and childbearing, and abortion. His own book on abortion, *Rachel Weeping*, will soon be published by Andrews & McMeel.

1

ABORTION POLICY: TIME FOR REASSESSMENT

RAYMOND J. ADAMEK

A S THE RESULT of the Supreme Court's decision of
January 22, 1973, we have now had a permissive abortion policy nationwide for over seven years. From 1973
through 1978, approximately 5.3 million American women
had 6.6 million legal abortions (cf. Forrest, Tietze, and Sullivan 1978, and Tietze 1978). Although any policy affecting so
many individuals should be reviewed periodically, this
would appear to be especially true of abortion policy, for the
following reasons. First, even though this policy has been in
effect for over seven years, it operates with very little general
consensus—our society is still deeply divided over its desirability and efficacy. Second, as it has developed in the
courts and legislatures, our abortion policy has legal implications for the family and family relationships which reach
far beyond the question of abortion itself. Third, in several
areas, it is doubtful that our present policy is working as it
was intended to work. Fourth, some evidence suggests that
in the effort to change past public policy, the medical benefits and safety of legal abortion were emphasized while the
disadvantages and dangers were soft-pedaled. Given our
recent experience with "the pill," a reassessment of our
abortion policy seems called for to ensure a more balanced
view.

Before undertaking a discussion of these points, we should
briefly note the nature of the Court's 1973 decisions, which
outline the basic structure of our present policy. The Court's
ruling was both prohibitive and permissive. That is, it prohibited the states or any other legal entity in the nation from
outlawing abortion during the first two trimesters of pregnancy (or more accurately, prior to viability), while it permitted them, if they so chose, to outlaw abortion after viability, i.e., in the last trimester (U.S. Supreme Court 1973).
Even if a legislative body chose to outlaw abortion in the
third trimester, however, the Court noted that abortion
could not be proscribed "where it is necessary, in appropriate medical judgment, for the preservation of the life or
health of the mother" (1973:184). It further went on to note
that in determining whether an abortion was necessary to
preserve the mother's health, "medical judgment may be
exercised in the light of all factors—physical, emotional,

psychological, familial, and the woman's age—relevant to the well-being of the patient" (1973:212). Given this broad definition of the components of health, our society's present norms, and the fact that its ruling regarding the prohibition of abortion during the third trimester was permissive, the Court in effect legalized abortion throughout the nine months of pregnancy for virtually any reason.

LACK OF CONSENSUS

Many hoped that the Supreme Court's abortion decisions would firmly establish the legitimacy of legalized abortion in the United States, and that subsequent to the January, 1973, decision, the major problem to be faced would be the practical implementation of the decision: making abortion facilities readily available to every female of childbearing age. Subsequent developments suggest, however, that a coherent, comprehensive social policy on abortion has not been achieved as yet, and that the various segments of society concerned with abortion policy (e.g., the Supreme Court, the Congress, the Carter administration, state and local governments, private organizations, and the public itself) are at odds with each other, and themselves, regarding just what our policy toward legalized abortion should be.

Although the Court's vote in January of 1973 was 7–2, the closest it has come to unanimity in its early abortion decisions, Justice White's dissenting opinion, concurred in by Justice Rehnquist, presaged the deep differences which were to characterize discussions on abortion policy at all levels and in all sectors of the society. Justice White wrote:

> I find nothing in the language or history of the Constitution to support the Court's judgment. The Court simply fashions and announces a new constitutional right for pregnant mothers and, with scarcely any reason or authority for its action, invests that right with sufficient substance to override most existing state abortion statutes. The upshot is that the people and the legislatures of the 50 States are constitutionally disentitled to weigh the relative importance of the continued existence and development of the fetus on the one hand against a spectrum of possible impacts on the mother on the other hand. As an exercise of raw judicial power, the Court perhaps has authority to do what it does today; but in my view its judgment is an improvi-

dent and extravagant exercise of the power of judicial review which the Constitution extends to this Court. (1973:195–96)

In *Planned Parenthood* v. *Danforth*, the Court (1976) extended abortion rights by declaring in a 6–3 vote that a pregnant married woman could not be required to obtain her husband's consent before undergoing an abortion, and in a 5–4 vote that minors could not be required to obtain their parents' consent before undergoing an abortion. The major reason for these decisions, the Court stated, was that "since the State cannot regulate or proscribe abortion during the first stage, when the physician and his patient make that decision, the State cannot delegate authority to any particular person . . . to prevent abortion during that same period" (1976:805). Noting that this line of reasoning suggests that spousal and parental rights are granted to individuals by the State, rather than inherently existing in individuals, a formulation which would have consequences for family policy far beyond the issue of abortion, Justice White and others again dissented.

In *Beal* v. *Doe* and *Maher* v. *Roe*, the Court (1977a) by a 6–3 vote decided that although women had a right to an abortion, neither federal nor state governments had to provide tax money to pay for elective abortions, and that, in fact, these bodies could favor birth over abortion in their funding of welfare services. By a similar 6–3 vote in *Poelker* v. *Doe*, the Court (1977b) ruled that publicly financed hospitals need not make their facilities available for nontherapeutic abortions. Some observers considered these decisions as signaling a definite retreat by the Court from its earlier liberal positions, and dissenting Justices Blackmun, Brennan, and Marshall criticized them in strong language rivaling that of Justice White's critique of the 1973 decisions. Both as individuals and as a body, therefore, the Court has manifested different positions on abortion policy.

Congress has likewise manifested deep divisions on abortion policy, both within and between the two houses. The most notable example here is the 1977 debate on the Hyde Amendment, which held up a $60.2 billion Department of Health, Education, and Welfare (DHEW) budget for over five months, and involved some fifteen roll call votes. Deadlocked over the conditions under which the federal government should pay for Medicaid abortions, the House majority voted consistently to restrict payment to "life of the mother" circumstances, while the Senate consistently held out for a more liberal policy. A reading of the *Congressional Record* for the many days of debate again illustrates the depth of feelings and division on this issue within each chamber, as well as between houses.

The Carter administration also exhibits ambivalence on the abortion issue. Top aides, such as Midge Costanza, and later Sarah Weddington, have appeared to be militantly proabortion, in contrast to President Carter's statements indicating he believes federal policies should favor contraception, sex education, and financial support for adoptions as a means of dealing with unwanted pregnancies (*Akron Beacon Journal* 1977). Former DHEW Secretary Joseph Califano publicly concurred with Carter's views, while at the same time formulating rules for the application of the Hyde Amendment which were much more to the liking of the liberal Senate than they were to the more restrictive House (*Akron Beacon Journal* 1978).

Similarly, heated debates over abortion policy take place at the city, school district, county, and state levels as legislators, program administrators, and citizens argue over policies providing tax funds for welfare abortions, the inclusion of abortion counseling and services in family planning and sex education programs, and the regulation of abortion clinics.

In addition to the debates in various governmental bodies, there are also several private organizations which vigorously represent one or the other side of the issue nationwide. Two prominent examples are the National Right to Life Committee, whose ultimate goal is the passage of a constitutional amendment which would, in effect, nullify the Supreme Court's decision by defining the unborn as legal persons subject to the Constitution's protection, and the Planned Parenthood Federation of America. The latter organization, once thought of as simply a service organization offering nonjudgmental counseling to women regarding contraception and untimely pregnancies, has recently served notice that it will become a more vigorous advocate for abortion rights (*Kansas City Star* 1978). Indeed, as early as October of 1975, it stated that its mission was "to serve as the nation's foremost agent of social change in the area of reproductive health and well-being" (1975:5), and that it intended "to increase support for key national issues especially: keeping abortion legal" (1975:11). There are, of course, many other special interest groups urging that this or that abortion policy be adopted.

Finally, public opinion polls indicate that the public itself is divided on the abortion issue, and at odds with the Supreme Court's ruling. Thus, although the Court's 1973 decision in effect gave us a policy of elective abortion throughout the nine months of pregnancy, a careful reading of recent major polls (Davis 1978; Gallup 1978) indicates that a majority of Americans approve of legal abortion only for three "hard" reasons (life / health of the mother seriously endangered, fetal defect, rape or incest), and then generally only in the first trimester (the one exception to the first trimester restriction in the public's mind is the life-of-the-mother justification, which has majority approval throughout the pregnancy). Currently, then, it would appear that a majority of the public approves of only about 5 percent of the legal abortions being performed in the United States, since this is approximately the percentage being performed for the three "hard" reasons (Kahn et al. 1971; U.S. DHEW 1971).

One reason for this disagreement between the public and the Court seems to be clear: a different evaluation of the crucial questions of when human life begins and when the human being may be considered to be a "person." On the first question, the Court's explicit position was that it did not know when human life began:

> We need not resolve the difficult question of when life begins. When those trained in the respective disciplines of medicine, philosophy, and theology are unable to arrive at any consensus, the judiciary, at this point in the development of man's knowledge, is not in a position to speculate as to the answer. (1973:181)

Implicitly, however, the Court's ruling favored the "viability" or "birth" answers to the question of when human life

7

begins, since while it stated that prior to viability the state had no "compelling interest" in protecting "potential human life," it did allow the state to prohibit abortion after viability in some circumstances, and indicated that after birth the Constitution protected the individual. In a special Gallup poll conducted one week after the Court's decision, however, Judith Blake (1977) found that only 15 percent of American men and 12 percent of American women thought that human life begins at viability, and only 19 percent of the men and 8 percent of the women thought human life begins "only at birth." Thirty-six percent of the men and 50 percent of the women, on the other hand, believed that human life "begins at conception."

On the issue of personhood, the Court noted that as used in the Constitution, the word *person* "has application only postnatally" (1973:179), and concluded that the Constitution's protection of rights guaranteed to persons begins only at birth. Repeating her poll in 1975, Blake (1977) added a question asking the American public when they thought the unborn "may be considered a human person." Only 18 percent of the men and 8 percent of the women adopted the Court's position by responding "at birth," while 33 percent of the men and 51 percent of the women responded "at conception."

With such basic disagreement on abortion policy evident at all levels and in all spheres of American life, and with so little public support evident for current policy, a major reassessment of our abortion policy seems called for.

FAMILY LAW

One of the effects of the Court's 1973 decision was to extend the legal power of individuals to control family size through active intervention in the reproductive process, a legal power first established on a nationwide basis by various contraception cases beginning in the mid-1960s. A second effect was to give women legal access to a wider variety of means to control their reproductive histories. Both of these effects obviously have ramifications for the structure and functioning of individual families and the American family system far beyond the issue of abortion.

While many view these developments in a positive light, suggesting that they afford both families and individuals greater opportunities to be self-directing, others wonder whether they may not also serve to undermine the family as a unit of society. This issue comes up most directly, perhaps, in the *Planned Parenthood* v. *Danforth* decision (U.S. Supreme Court 1976). In this decision, the Court exhibited a growing tendency to focus upon members of the family as individuals with competing interests, rather than upon the family as a natural community with interests of its own, to be protected by the state as a basic unit of society. This tendency was first noted in the contraception cases of the mid-1960s. Thus, whereas in *Griswold* v. *Connecticut* (1965), the Court talked about a zone of *family* privacy and noted that empowering the state to search "marital bedrooms for telltale signs of the use of contraceptives" would be "repulsive to the notions of privacy surrounding the marital *relationship*" (1965:516, italics added), in *Eisenstadt* v. *Baird* (1972:438) it extended the right of privacy in matters of reproduction to *individuals*, married or unmarried. Having based a woman's right to have an abortion on the right to privacy in *Roe* v. *Wade* (1973), the Court in *Planned Parenthood* v. *Danforth* (1976) then went on to allow the wife, in consultation with her physician, to reach and effectuate an abortion decision in the first twelve weeks of pregnancy unbeknownst to her husband, even though it was aware of "the deep and proper concern and interest that a devoted and protective husband has in his wife's pregnancy and in the growth and development of the fetus she is carrying" (1976:805). Rejecting the reasoning of the State of Missouri that requiring the joint consent of husband and wife for an abortion would serve to protect the institution of marriage and that "any major change in family status is a decision to be made jointly by the partners," the Court concluded that the wife could act unilaterally in this matter, "since it is the woman who physically bears the child and who is the more directly and immediately affected by the pregnancy" (1976:804;806). Thus, the Court opted to emphasize the interests of an individual in the family relationship, rather than those of the family relationship itself.

It did this even more dramatically in the same *Planned Parenthood* v. *Danforth* case when it ruled that a legislative body may not require parental consent before a minor, unmarried daughter may obtain a first trimester abortion. Again rejecting the argument that such a requirement would safeguard parental authority and the family unit, the Court stated that "any independent interest the parent may have in the termination of the minor daughter's pregnancy is no more weighty than the right of privacy of the competent minor mature enough to have become pregnant" (1976:808). Thus again the Court asserted the interests of an individual family member over the interests of the family as a unit, and what had started out as a zone of *family* privacy now became an area of *personal* privacy shutting out familial concerns.

The Court's major justification for its rulings in both the parental and spousal consent instances was that the state could not delegate to individuals that authority which it itself lacked (to proscribe abortion in the first trimester). This justification is looked upon by some as an ominous one, since it implies that the state confers spousal or parental rights upon individuals, rather than recognizing that husbands have inherent interests in their unborn children and that parents have inherent interests in the destiny and upbringing of their child which ought to be protected by the state. The ramifications of these aspects of abortion policy for the structure and functioning of families deserves more thorough consideration in the future.

POLICY IMPLEMENTATION

Another reason to reassess our abortion policy is that in several areas it does not appear to have been implemented as was originally intended. It is clear, for example, from a reading of the various Supreme Court decisions, that in giving the woman a right to make an abortion decision unhampered by state regulation, the Court expected the abortion decision to be made in consultation with her physician. Indeed, in *Roe* v. *Wade*, the Court stated: "The abortion decision in all its aspects is inherently, and primarily, a medical decision, and basic responsibility for it must rest with the physician" (1973:184). From its discussion in *Doe* v.

Bolton, the companion 1973 case, it is clear that the Court envisaged a rather thorough consultation between patient and physician, in which "all factors—physical, emotional, psychological, familial, and the woman's age—relevant to the well being of the patient" (1973:212) would be taken into account. Given the gravity of the abortion decision, and the ambivalence which accompanies it for many women (Denes 1976; Francke 1978), this would appear to be a reasonable expectation. Various studies suggest, however, that this type of consultation process is the exception, rather than the rule.

For example, polling 940 Michigan women who had had legal abortions and who answered "Yes" to the question: "Do you have a regular doctor to whom you usually go when you need medical care?" Rosen (1977:863) found that "only 17 percent turned to their physician for advice when they first thought they might be pregnant. Only 41 percent went to their physician to find out whether they were pregnant," and 88 percent said their physician had no influence on their decision to abort. Another study (Jain 1977) of twelve abortion clinics in Ohio and 276 of their patients indicated that only about 24 percent consulted private physicians before contacting an abortion clinic, while another 20 percent were referred to clinics by family planning agencies, where they may or may not have consulted with a physician.

Little, if any, consultation with physicians appears to take place in the typical abortion clinic itself, the patient often first seeing the doctor in the procedure room, perhaps even only after being helped on the table. Indeed, little consultation about the abortion decision itself may take place at all. Counseling in abortion clinics tends to be conducted by nonprofessionals. Jain (1977) found that only 20 of the 102 staff members in the twelve Ohio clinics had professional degrees, and 16 of these were R.N.'s. Moreover, the majority of the time in "counseling" sessions in clinics is spent instructing patients in abortion procedures, aftercare, and birth control methods, not in exploring the abortion decision and its alternatives. In the worst cases, the "counselor's" main function is to sell abortion to the client (*Time* 1978).

Jain (1977) found that the main qualification for prospective counselors was not formal training, but an ability to relate to people and a profeminist, proabortion ideology. To what extent the ideal of objective, nonjudgmental counseling can be achieved in these circumstances is questionable. It seems obvious, therefore, that our present abortion policy is not being implemented in a way which those who legitimized a woman's right to choose would endorse, and that many women and young girls in desperate situations receive less than adequate counseling about their decisions.

The phenomenal growth of specialized, nonhospital abortion clinics from 178 in 1973 to 448 in 1976 is also of concern to some and is viewed as a consequence of the failure of the medical profession to respond adequately to the Court's decision. Thus, Forrest, Tietze, and Sullivan (1978:276) report that "four years after the 1973 Supreme Court decisions legalizing abortion, only one in five public hospitals and fewer than two in five non-Catholic private hospitals provided any abortion services." They note that some 61.3 percent of the legal abortions performed in 1976 were done in nonhospital clinics. The reluctance of the established medical system to provide this new service speaks to the deep divisions within the medical community over this issue and, again, to the lack of consensus in our society over abortion policy.

PUBLIC HEALTH

It is time to reassess our abortion policy also because of the natural tendency of those seeking to initiate and implement a new policy, particularly in the face of opposition, to emphasize the public health benefits of that policy and to downplay its negative aspects. A review of the major physical health complications of legal abortion may assist us in attaining a more balanced view prior to reconsidering our present policy. Although we might also consider mental health, we focus here only on physical health, since this area yields a larger body of hard data gathered in larger-scale studies which yield less equivocal findings.

Short-term Complications
Although, in general, it is true that the earlier an abortion is

performed the safer it is for the mother, abortion is a procedure which always involves some risk. The m mon early complications of legal abortion include infection, hemorrhage, perforation or other damage to the walls of the uterus, and laceration of the cervix. There is some evidence that these complications are more frequent in young women pregnant for the first time, since their organs are more rigid. Studies by those who favor permissive abortion policies as well as by those who favor more restrictive policies tend to agree that the overall short-term complication rate for legal abortion is about 10 percent. To cite some specific studies, Pakter and Nelson (1971) report a short-term complication rate of 10 percent in New York City's first nine months' experience with its permissive law. Tietze and Lewit (1971), reporting on 42,598 abortions performed in sixty-four hospitals and clinics in twelve states, also report a 10.1 percent complication rate overall, and a more conservative 1.2 percent for major complications. Hilgers (1972) cites eleven studies in Europe and the U.S. reporting similar or higher short-term complication rates.

TABLE 1

LEGAL ABORTION MATERNAL COMPLICATION RATES AND
MATERNAL MORTALITY RATES, BY TYPE OF ABORTION PROCEDURE

| Procedure | Complication Rates* | | Deaths 1972–77** | |
	Total	Major	N	Rate
Suction	5	.4	51 ⎱	1.5
Sharp D&C	11	.9	15 ⎰	
Intrauterine instillation	43	1.9	48	13.5
Hysterotomy	49	15.0	—	—
Hysterectomy	53	16.0	—	—
Hysterotomy/Hysterectomy	—	—	9	43.6
Other/Unknown	—	—	6	10.4

*Complication rates in percent. Based on 80,437 legal abortions reported between September 1971 and June 1975 by 32 institutions. SOURCE: Adapted from *Family Planning Perspectives* (1976:71).
**Death rate is per 100,000 abortions. Based on 3,576,097 abortions with type of procedure known. SOURCE: Center for Disease Control, *Abortion Surveillance 1977* (1979:47–48).

TABLE 2

LEGAL ABORTION MATERNAL COMPLICATION RATES
BY WEEKS OF GESTATION, IN PERCENT

| Weeks of Gestation | Complication Rates* | |
	Total	Major
6 or less	7	—
7–8	5	.3
17–20	40	—
21–24	—	2.3

*Complete data are not reported. Study group same as in table 1. SOURCE: *Family Planning Perspectives* (1976).

TABLE 3

NUMBER OF LEGAL ABORTIONS AND ABORTION MATERNAL
MORTALITY RATE BY WEEKS OF GESTATION, 1972–1977

| Weeks of Gestation | No. of Abortions* | Maternal Deaths | |
		N	Rate**
8 or less	2,145,802	12	.6
9–10	1,393,551	23	1.7
11–12	741,536	20	2.7
13–15	253,890	19	7.5
16–20	295,196	43	14.6
21 or more	58,642	12	20.5
Total	4,888,617	129	2.6

*Based on distribution of 3,547,194 abortions reported with weeks of gestation known, or 72.6 percent of the total reported to the Center for Disease Control. The latter underestimates the total number of legal abortions in the U.S. by about 16 percent (cf. Forrest et al. 1978).
**Maternal death rate is per 100,000 abortions. SOURCE: Center for Disease Control, *Abortion Surveillance 1977* (1979:47).

Tables 1, 2, and 3 give a summary of more recent data on short-term complication rates. As these data indicate, from the mother's standpoint, legal abortion is safest when it is performed early in the pregnancy by the suction method.

The data in tables 1, 2, and 3 are for abortions performed in hospitals, free-standing clinics, and physicians' offices combined. In a study reporting on 7,885 abortions performed only in clinics ($N = 46$) in fourteen countries during 1973–75, Miller, Fortney, and Kessel (1976) focused on early vacuum aspiration procedures (the patients had reported being fourteen or less days late with their menses). This study reports a short-term complication rate of 9 percent overall, and 3 percent for major complications. (These findings, like all those from other countries, should be applied to the U.S. with caution, because of differences in the state of medical techniques and services, the different types of women typically served in abortion facilities, and differences in their reproductive histories. For more details on these points, see Belsey 1977). The same study reports even higher total and serious complication rates of 10.3 percent and 5.2 percent, respectively, for 536 additional women who reported being fifteen to twenty-one days late with their menses. Thus, even for the earliest period in pregnancy, and utilizing the least traumatic method (often called menstrual regulation), legal abortions in clinics can be expected to result in short-term complications for one in ten women.

Perhaps the most shocking statistic in the Miller, Fortney, and Kessel (1976) study is that although 46.5 percent of the women involved had negative pregnancy tests, vacuum aspirations were performed anyway, ostensibly to give the women peace of mind. Of the 7,885 aspirations performed, 32.4 percent were found to be unnecessary, as clinical examination of aspirated uterine contents established that the women were not pregnant. What other medical situation is there where a physician operates to treat a condition which has previously been diagnosed to be absent? One wonders about the motivation and clinical judgment prompting such procedures in abortion clinics.

Long-term Complications

Since large-scale legalized abortion is a relatively recent phenomenon in the U.S., relatively few studies on the long-term effects of legalized abortion have been done in this country. However, reviewing some seventy-two publications from twelve countries (including some from the U.S.), Wynn and Wynn (1972) report that having a legal abortion increases the probability of complications for the woman who subsequently bears a child, creating problems for both her and the child. Among other complications, they note that women who had undergone legal abortions experienced a 40 percent increase in premature births (incurring greater risk of handicap to the child), a doubling of the rate of stillbirths and infant deaths in the first week after birth, a 100–150 percent increase in ectopic pregnancies, a fourfold increase in pelvic inflammatory conditions, menstrual and other disorders, and increases in sterility. A more recent article by Richardson and Dixon (1976) reports a comparison between 211 patients who had undergone elective legal abortions and a control group of women, matched for parity, whose last pregnancy had ended in spontaneous abortion. The overall fetal loss in the subsequent pregnancy for the spontaneous abortion group was 7.5 percent. For those who had had a legal abortion, it was 17.5 percent. Among eleven women whose cervices had been lacerated during the legal abortion, fetal loss in the subsequent pregnancy was 45.5 percent.

A preliminary report of a current study funded by the National Institute of Child Health and Human Development underway in New York State (Health Research, Inc. 1978) states that there are "higher age-adjusted rates of adverse pregnancy outcomes among women with prior recorded induced abortions than among women with no prior induced abortions." These include: (1) an 85 percent higher spontaneous fetal death ratio; (2) a 32 percent higher rate of low birthweight infants; (3) a 67 percent higher rate of early gestation infants; (4) a 47 percent higher rate of labor complications; and (5) an 83 percent higher rate of delivery complications. The study authors note that more detailed analysis of the data may reduce the differences in adverse rates between the study and control groups ($N = 20,306$ each), but it seems unlikely that such analyses will completely explain away the differences, since the two groups were matched on several variables when they were selected for study.

Three other large-scale, carefully controlled studies

suggest that adverse effects in subsequent pregnancies are especially characteristic of legal abortions involving dilatation and curettage (D and C). A World Health Organization (1978) study was made of 7,194 women in eight European cities grouped into three clusters according to the predominant type of abortion procedure used. When maternal smoking, age, height and education, and infant sex and gestational age at entry into the study were controlled, regression analysis indicated that "a reduction of mean birth weight and mean gestation . . . could be ascribed to the effect of induced abortion," particularly in the cities where D and C was the main procedure. In the cities where D and C and vacuum aspiration (VA) were used with about equal frequency, "the data suggest that the adverse effect of D and C is expressed in terms of mid-trimester spontaneous abortion, whereas the adverse effect of vacuum aspiration is not expressed until the last trimester of pregnancy as a pre-term delivery and low birth weight. . . . In one city cluster where nearly all procedures were by VA, no effect could be observed." A second study (cf. *Family Planning Perspectives* 1978b) involving 6,105 women in Singapore found that even when race, economic status, maternal age, and year of delivery were controlled, women whose first pregnancies were terminated by the D and C procedure gave birth to infants who were 207 grams lighter, on the average, than those born to women whose first pregnancies were terminated by the suction procedure or who had never been pregnant before. Higher rates of spontaneous midtrimester abortion also were related to the D and C procedure, particularly where dilatation was relatively great.

Maine (1979) reported on a third study involving more than 31,000 members of the Kaiser-Permanente health plan who visited one of the plan's clinics in northern California during 1974–77 for prenatal care. Twelve percent of these women reported at least one prior legal abortion. "Nulliparous women who had had one or more abortions were 80 percent more likely to have a second-trimester miscarriage of a subsequent pregnancy than were nulliparous women who did not report a prior abortion. When the analysis was confined to nulliparous women who had terminated their *only* previous pregnancy by abortion, they also were found to have a significantly higher rate of subsequent second-trimester miscarriages than comparable women who had never been pregnant before" (Maine 1979:99). Controls for age, race, marital status, smoking, and alcohol consumption failed to nullify the findings. Although data were not gathered on type of abortion procedure used, Maine notes that these relationships held only for women receiving abortions before 1973, when D and C procedures predominated in California, but did not hold for women who had abortions subsequently, when vacuum aspirations predominated.

Not all studies have found an association between legal abortion and adverse long-term effects, however (cf. Trussell 1973; Hogue 1977; *Family Planning Perspectives* 1978a). While it may be true, therefore, that "the definitive studies on the consequences of induced abortion have yet to be reported" (Trussell 1973), and that because of faulty methodology, unequivocal causal linkages between induced abortion and subsequent fertility complications have yet to be established, common sense would suggest that this issue should be given more attention when our abortion policy is considered.

Maternal Death Rate

Those who favor a permissive abortion policy note that if performed in the first twelve weeks of pregnancy, abortion results in fewer maternal deaths than does carrying the baby to full term. Although the Supreme Court called this an "established medical fact" in its 1973 decision, whether or not it was at that time seems open to question. Geis (1972), Hilgers (1972), and Willke and Willke (1972) all cited data which ran contrary to that belief, and Hilgers severely criticized the reliability and validity of the data from New York City and Eastern European countries, which were the only sources cited by the Court. (Hilgers himself has subsequently been taken to task for paying too little attention to such variables as location, type of abortion procedure, stage of gestation, and maternal characteristics in making comparisons of the relative safety of legal abortion and childbirth—see Fulton 1973).

It is undoubtedly true that as abortion technology develops and as more medical experience is gained, legal abortion will become safer for the mother than it previously was. Recent U.S. figures do indicate that abortions result in fewer maternal deaths than do pregnancies: 3.4 / 100,000 vs. 12.8 / 100,000, respectively, for 1975 (cf. Center for Disease Control 1978:7; U.S. Bureau of the Census 1977:70). From the standpoint of the individual woman faced with an abortion decision, however, although mathematically one rate is 3.8 times higher than the other, as a practical matter, the chances of death from either abortion or childbirth are very low and quite similar, and the decision to abort or not to abort will be better made by giving much greater weight to factors other than mortality rates.

From the standpoint of public health and policy, two facts should be kept in mind in considering the relative safety of childbirth and legal abortion. First, because of the negative social evaluation which attends abortion, maternal deaths due to legal abortion are more likely to be intentionally misclassified—and thus underreported—than are maternal deaths due to pregnancy. The recent exposé (*Time* 1978) of abortion mills in Chicago, for example, uncovered twelve abortion-related deaths between 1973 and 1978 that were unknown to state health officials. Since this is only one jurisdiction of over fifty that report to the Center for Disease Control on such deaths, the true maternal death rate from legal abortion may be quite different from the reported rate. Second, in terms of the total loss of human life, abortion takes a far greater toll than pregnancy. Although mention of fetal deaths is typically omitted from discussions of legal abortion policy, there is no strictly empirical reason for doing so, and they are therefore included here. Thus, using the 1975 figures previously cited, the human death rate in 100,000 legal abortions is approximately 100,003 (100,000 human fetuses + 3 mothers), although in a few cases involving late-term abortions, the fetus may be born alive and survive. In 100,000 pregnancies, on the other hand, the human death rate after twenty weeks' gestation is approximately 2,233 (1,060 fetal deaths + 1,160 infant deaths within twenty-eight days of birth + 13 maternal deaths—cf. U.S.

Bureau of the Census 1977:70). Allowing for a spontaneous fetal loss rate of 22 percent (cf. Tietze, Bongaarts, and Schearer 1976:7) prior to twenty weeks would give us a total of 24,233 deaths. The human death rate is, therefore, approximately four times higher in 100,000 instances of legal abortion than it is in 100,000 pregnancies allowed to run their course.

Back-Alley Abortions

Even though legal abortions cause short- and long-term complications and multiply fetal deaths, some maintain that a permissive policy is desirable from a public health standpoint since it prevents women from resorting to "back-alley abortionists." This rationale makes at least three assumptions which should be evaluated more carefully. The first one is that all legal abortions become relatively safe abortions. The recent exposé of abortion mills in Chicago (*Time* 1978) indicates that this is not so—some people will abuse public policy no matter what it is. The second assumption is that all illegal abortions were unsafe. However, many of them were done by licensed physicians under conditions similar to those under which legal abortions take place today. The third assumption is that legal abortions replace illegal ones, which often entail greater risk to the mother. There is some evidence to indicate, however, that the legalization of abortion has no effect on illegal rates. Frederiksen and Brackett (1968) find this to be true in their review of data from seven Eastern European countries, Sweden, and Japan, and Hilgers and Shearin (1971) reach the same conclusion after reviewing sixteen studies of ten countries and the State of Colorado. They report that after abortion was legalized, the illegal rate remained the same in nine jurisdictions and actually increased in two.

Some authors favorable to a permissive policy do report that legal abortions replace illegal ones, at least in New York City. Pakter and Nelson (1971) report that only one maternal death from illegal abortion was recorded in New York City in the first six months of 1971, and that "all hospitals report a sharp drop in incomplete or 'septic' abortions since the liberalization of the law." Their data indicate, however, that the percent of maternal deaths due to abortions (both legal and illegal) had been steadily decreasing since 1964, so attributing the continuing decrease only to a permissive law which took effect in 1970 is unwarranted. Tietze (1973) maintains that in the first two years of New York City's experience, legal abortions replaced 100,000 illegal ones. He bases his estimate on the decrease in the number of births recorded in the city, assuming that half of the decrease was due to legal abortion. The process by which he determines the number of replaced illegal abortions is rather speculative, however, involving estimated values at four points where actual data are unavailable. Relying upon this chain of estimates, Tietze concludes that 70 percent of the legal abortions in New York City for the two-year period 1970–72 replaced illegal ones. In a subsequent report (Tietze et al. 1975), he projects his estimate for New York City to the U.S. as a whole. But a statistically questionable estimate developed for one city and then projected to the country as a whole produces an even more questionable estimate. The most honest thing that can be said about illegal abortions is that "the number of illegal abortions . . . were unknown before the legalization of abortion, and remain unknown after the fact" (Tietze et al. 1975:85). Hence, the number of illegal abortions replaced by legal abortions also remains unknown.

Similarly, the number of maternal deaths caused by illegal abortion has never been definitely known. Geis (1972) states that some estimates run as high as 10,000 per year, but notes that Tietze suggests the actual figure is closer to 500. Actually, the number of maternal deaths due to abortion of all types (spontaneous, legal, and illegal) and reported to the National Center for Health Statistics has not exceeded 500 per year since 1947, and had dropped quite steadily from 324 in 1961 to 160 in 1967, when the states first began to pass abortion reform laws. Much of the decline in maternal abortion deaths is attributable to the general improvement in medical care and other factors, then, not to the legalization of abortion.

Whatever the actual number of women who die from illegal abortion, it is a tragic figure, and few would oppose effective and humane measures to decrease it. Public health education emphasizing the dangers of such abortions and education for responsible sexuality might provide a start, but more far-reaching socioeconomic reforms are probably necessary so that women are not driven by social attitudes and neglect to take such drastic action. Some would suggest, however, that our present policy of permissive abortion creates as many problems as it resolves. Besides increasing fetal deaths, to the extent that legalizing abortion encourages women who would not break the law to have abortions, it increases the number of women who are exposed to the hazards of legal abortion. Tietze (1975:75), perhaps the foremost statistical authority on legal abortion in the U.S., agrees that "to the extent that unintended births are replaced by legal abortions, the *total* number of legal and illegal *induced abortions* increases subsequent to legalization." How great this increase is over the total number of legal and illegal abortions performed prior to abortion law reform is hard to say, since, as we have noted, no one can accurately state how many illegal abortions occurred. Earlier "guestimates" placed the number of illegal abortions in the U.S. at anywhere from 200,000 to 1.2 million (U.S. DHEW 1971). More recent estimates suggest that the latter figure is much too high, however. Tietze (1975), for example, has suggested that the illegal abortion maternal death rate in developed countries is approximately 40 per 100,000 cases. In 1966, the last year before the abortion reform movement began to have legislative impact, the National Center for Health Statistics reported a total of 189 maternal deaths due to abortions of all types—legal, illegal, and spontaneous. Even if we were to allow for underreporting of illegal abortion maternal deaths by assuming that all of these maternal deaths were due to illegal abortion, the total number of illegal abortions in the U.S. in 1966, at an outside maximum, would have been $189 / 40 \times 100,000 = 472,500$. Cates and Rochat (1976), utilizing a lower estimate of 30 maternal deaths per 100,000 illegal abortions, suggest that there were only about 130,000 illegal abortions in the U.S. in 1972, one year before the Supreme Court decisions, when access to legal abortion was limited to a few urban centers.

Contrasting either of the above estimates with the 1.4 million legal abortions projected for 1978 (Forrest, Sullivan, and Tietze 1979) should give us cause to ponder the wisdom of present policy. One result of this policy is that more women now die from legal abortions than from illegal ones in the U.S. The latest government figures (*Family Planning Perspectives* 1979b) indicate that during 1972–77, inclusive, 129 women died from legal abortions, whereas 74 died from illegal abortions. Furthermore, as legal abortion becomes more accepted as simply another medical procedure available to women to control their fertility, repeat abortions, with their attendant risks to the mother and to children carried subsequently, will become more prevalent. Tietze estimates that 23 percent of the legal abortions performed in 1976 were repeat abortions and concludes that "a repeat-abortion rate that is higher than the first-abortion rate is to be expected, without any decline—indeed, even in the face of improvement—in contraceptive practice" (1978:288). Three recent studies comparing the pregnancy outcomes of women who had had two or more legal abortions to those who had had only one or none indicate that repeated legal abortions increase the risk of miscarriage, premature births, and low birth weight babies in subsequent pregnancies. The first study of 240 women entering Boston Hospital for Women for spontaneous abortions and their matched controls found that "women who had had two or more induced abortions were 2.7 times more likely to have a future first-trimester spontaneous abortion—and 3.2 times more likely to have a second-trimester incomplete abortion—than were women with no history of induced abortions" (*Family Planning Perspectives* 1979a). Similarly, in the carefully controlled World Health Organization study previously discussed, it was found that in each of the study cities, "repeated abortion is associated with a two to two and a half fold increase in the rate of low birth weight and short gestation when compared with . . . either one abortion or one live birth" (*Family Planning Perspectives* 1979a). The Kaiser-Permanente study (Maine 1979) found that 6 percent of women who had had two or more induced abortions miscarried in the second trimester of the study pregnancy, compared to 3.4 percent of those who had had one abortion, and 2.1 percent of those who had had no induced abortion. These rates reflected adjustments to take the women's age, race, number of prior miscarriages, alcohol and tobacco use, and marital status into account.

CONCLUSION

Our present abortion policy, now in effect for over seven years, is one which has resulted in deep divisions in our society and which operates with relatively little general consensus. The Court decisions on which it is based have significant implications for the familial institution far beyond the issue of abortion. In several areas, the implementation of this policy has resulted in consequences quite different from those intended by its advocates. A consideration of the policy's impact on public health suggests that there may be more adverse effects than originally anticipated. For all these reasons, then, it is time to reassess our abortion policy to attempt to determine if it should be changed so that our goals of optimum maternal and child health, strong families, and enhanced personal freedom might be achieved by more efficacious means which have the wholehearted support of a large majority of our citizens.

REFERENCES

Adamek, R. 1974. Abortion, personal freedom, and public policy. *The Family Coordinator* 23:411–19. Several excerpts from that article have been incorporated into the present chapter, by kind permission of the editor.

Akron Beacon Journal. 1977. Adoption program pushed by Califano. 1 July: A-10.

———. 1978. Abortion payment policy is clarified. 28 January:B-7.

Belsey, M. A. 1977. The association of induced abortion with adverse outcome in the subsequent pregnancy. Unpublished paper. Geneva, Switzerland: Human Reproduction Unit, World Health Organization.

Blake, J. 1977. The Supreme Court's abortion decisions and public opinion in the United States. *Population and Development Review* 3:45–62.

Cates, W., Jr., and Rochat, R. W. 1976. Illegal abortions in the United States: 1972–1974. *Family Planning Perspectives* 8:86–92.

Center for Disease Control. 1978. *Abortion surveillance 1976.* Atlanta: U.S. Department of Health, Education, and Welfare.

Davis, J. A. 1978. *General social surveys, 1972–1978: cumulative codebook.* Chicago: National Opinion Research Center.

Denes, M. 1976. *In necessity and sorrow.* New York: Basic Books.

Family Planning Perspectives. 1976. Most abortions by suction in 10th week or less; typical patient is young, unmarried, white, never-before pregnant. 8:70–72.

————. 1978a. Five studies: no apparent harmful effect from legal abortion on subsequent pregnancies; D&C is possible exception. 10:34–38.

————. 1978b. Seven-nation WHO study finds future pregnancies not endangered by 1st trimester legal abortion. 10:238–39.

————. 1979a. Repeated abortions increase risk of miscarriage, premature births and low-birth-weight babies. 11:39–40.

————. 1979b. Deaths from legal and illegal abortion drop after 1973 decisions. 11:318.

Forrest, J. D., Tietze, C., and Sullivan, E. 1978 and 1979. Abortion in the United States, 1976–78. *Family Planning Perspectives* 10:271–79 and 11:329–41.

Francke, L. B. 1978. *The ambivalence of abortion.* New York: Random House.

Frederiksen, H., and Brackett, J. W. 1968. Demographic effects of abortion. *Public Health Reports* 83:999–1010.

Fulton, G. B. 1973. The mortality of induced abortion: lies, damned lies, and statistics. Unpublished paper. Toledo: University of Toledo.

Gallup, G. 1978. Huge majority would grant right to abortion but circumstances and stage of pregnancy are determinants. *Gallup Opinion Index* 153:25–29.

Geis, G. 1972. *Not the law's business?* Washington, D.C.: National Institutes of Health.

Health Research, Inc. 1978. A prospective study of the effects of induced abortion on subsequent reproductive function. Unpublished progress reports submitted to the National Institute of Child Health and Human Development, Bethesda, Maryland.

Hilgers, T. W. 1972. The medical hazards of legally induced abortion. In T. W. Hilgers and D.J. Horan, eds., *Abortion and social justice.* New York: Sheed & Ward.

Hilgers, T. W., and Shearin, R. 1971. *Induced abortion: a documented report.* Rochester, Minnesota: Mayo Clinic.

Hogue, C. 1977. Review of postulated fertility complications subsequent to pregnancy termination. Unpublished paper. Chapel Hill: University of North Carolina.

Jain, A. K. 1977. *Single service organizations: a comparative study of twelve abortion clinics in Ohio.* Ph.D. dissertation. Cleveland: School of Applied Social Services, Case Western Reserve University.

Kahn, J. B., Bourne, J. P., Asher, J. D., and Tyler, C.W., Jr. 1971. Surveillance of hospital abortions in the United States, 1970. Reviewed in *Family Planning Perspectives* 3:59.

Kansas City Star. 1978. Planned Parenthood to counterattack. 29 January:4-A.

Maine, D. 1979. Does abortion affect later pregnancies? *Family Planning Perspectives* 11:98–101.

Miller, E. R., Fortney, J. A., and Kessel, E. 1976. Early vacuum aspiration: minimizing procedures to nonpregnant women. *Family Planning Perspectives* 8:33–38.

Pakter, J., and Nelson, F. 1971. Abortion in New York City: the first nine months. *Family Planning Perspectives* 3:5–12.

Planned Parenthood Federation of America. 1975. *A five year plan: 1976–1980.* Seattle.

Richardson, J., and Dixon, G. 1976. Effects of legal termination on subsequent pregnancy. *British Medical Journal* 29 May:1303–1304.

Rosen, R. H. 1977. The patient's view of the role of the primary care physician in abortion. *American Journal of Public Health* 67:863–65.

Tietze, C. 1973. Two years' experience with a liberal abortion law: its impact on fertility trends in New York City. *Family Planning Perspectives* 5:36–41.

———. 1975. The effect of legalization of abortion on population growth and public health. *Family Planning Perspectives* 7:123–127.

———. 1978. Repeat abortions—why more? *Family Planning Perspectives* 10:286–88.

Tietze, C., and Lewit, S. 1971. Legal abortions: early medical complications. *Family Planning Perspectives* 3:6–14.

Tietze, C., Jaffe, F. S., Weinstock, E., and Dryfoos, J. G. 1975. *Provisional estimates of abortion need and services in the year following the 1973 Supreme Court decisions.* New York: Alan Guttmacher Institute.

Tietze, C., Bongaarts, J., and Schearer, B. 1976. Mortality associated with the control of fertility. *Family Planning Perspectives* 8:6–14.

Time. 1978. Risky abortions. 27 November:52.

Trussell, J. 1973. Third thoughts on abortion. *British Journal of Hospital Medicine* May: 601–604.

U.S. Bureau of the Census. 1977. *Statistical Abstract of the United States: 1977.* 98th ed. Washington, D.C.: Government Printing Office.

U.S. Department of Health, Education, and Welfare. 1971. *The effects of changes in state abortion laws.* Washington, D.C.: Government Printing Office.

U.S. Supreme Court. 1965. *Griswold v. Connecticut. United States Supreme Court Reports* 14 L Ed 2d, 7 June:349–73.

———. 1972. *Eisenstadt v. Baird. United States Supreme Court Reports* 31 L Ed 2d, 22 March:510–42.

———. 1973. *Roe v. Wade* and *Doe v. Bolton. United States Supreme Court Reports* 35 L Ed 2d, 22 January:147–222.

———. 1976. *Planned Parenthood v. Danforth. United States Supreme Court Reports* 49 L Ed 2d, 20 August:788–825.

———. 1977a. *Beal v. Doe* and *Maher v. Roe. United States Supreme Court Reports* 53 L Ed 2d, 20 June:464–505.

———. 1977b. *Poelker v. Doe. United States Supreme Court Reporte* 53 L Ed 2d, 20 June:528–33.

Willke, J. C., and Willke, B. 1972. *Handbook on abortion.* Cincinnati: Hiltz.

World Health Organization. 1978. Long-term complications of induced abortion. Unpublished paper. Geneva, Switzerland.

Wynn, M., and Wynn, A. 1972. *Some consequences of induced abortion to children born subsequently.* London: Foundation for Education and Research in Child-Bearing.

2

PREDICTING POLAR ATTITUDES TOWARD ABORTION IN THE UNITED STATES

JUDITH BLAKE AND JORGE H. DEL PINAL

THE LATE 1970S have witnessed the rise of increasingly powerful antiabortion interest groups in the United States. Ideologically, these groups are against the legalization of abortion for any and all reasons, or they would allow it only in the special case where the mother's physical health or life was seriously endangered by pregnancy and / or childbirth. At the other extreme are those who would allow a woman complete freedom legally to have an abortion "if she wants one." Within this group, individual views may range from moral approval of abortion to moral tolerance of it as a lesser evil.

What influences people to entertain sharply negative or positive views of the legitimacy of legal access to abortion? Are these views primarily a religious issue? If so, do they pit Roman Catholics against the remainder of the population? Is approval or disapproval of legal abortion in any important measure a racial issue? Is it a topic of division between old and young, or between the sexes? Is there an educational or social-class component of abortion attitudes? And, finally, in considering predictors of abortion attitudes, are people for or against legalized pregnancy termination because of their attitudes toward other issues to which abortion is relevant—attitudes toward nonmarital sexual relations, toward family size, or toward individual volition in the matter of taking life?

In this paper we examine predictors of the positive and negative extremes in attitudes toward legalized abortion. We develop a set of explanatory variables that explain an unusually high proportion of the variation in such attitudes. We then proceed to two additional analytical issues. The first is what we call "the short-circuiting of constituency" for abortion support, and the second is the trend in consensus and disagreement about legalized abortion during the 1970s.

Our empirical work is based on a nationwide sample of approximately fifteen hundred American adults interviewed annually (between February and April) by the National Opinion Research Center of the University of Chicago. With regard to the legalization of abortion, our research rests on the results of the following questions:

Please tell me whether or not *you* think it should be possible for a pregnant woman to obtain a *legal* abortion . . .
   a. If there is a strong chance of serious defect in the baby?
   b. If she is married and does not want any more children?
   c. If the woman's health is seriously endangered by pregnancy?
   d. If the family has a very low income and cannot afford any more children?

In this paper, we consider primarily the survey taken in 1978. However, our trend analysis includes the entire set of seven surveys since 1972. The reader should note as well that we will concentrate on only those respondents who answered negatively to all of the questions listed above (or who favored only the justification given in question *c*), and those respondents who favored all of the justifications found in questions *a* through *d*. For the 1978 survey, these individuals comprise a subsample of 761 respondents.

A word or two is in order about our method of analysis. Throughout this work we have used a form of multivariate analysis called Multiple Classification Analysis. Technically, this is a form of multiple regression that allows independent, or predictor, variables to be categories rather than interval scales. We are, therefore, able to use such predictors as religious affiliation and community size in our calculations. It is, moreover, not necessary in Multiple Classification Analysis that relationships be linear.

There are three major summary statistics in our analysis that require a brief explanation. One is the amount of variance explained, R^2; another is the beta coefficient; and a third is the "adjusted percentage." Very briefly, the R^2 is a measure of the percentage of the variability in the dependent variable that can be explained by the predictors, or independent variables. How well can you predict the value of the dependent variable, given your knowledge of the independent variable? R^2 is the square of the multiple correlation coefficient R which tells you how closely the values you would predict from your independent variables coincide with the actual values. An R of unity says that you can predict perfectly—100 percent of the time. An R of .75 says that you can predict 75 percent of the time with the given independent variables. By convention, the square of R is used most frequently, as in this paper. We should note at this time that an R of .75, or an R^2 of .56, is highly unusual in the social sciences outside of laboratory conditions. On mass observation data, it is more usual to obtain R^2s between .20 and .30, or even below.

A second important statistic is the beta coefficient. The beta is a summary measure, for each independent variable, of the amount of difference in the dependent variable for each category of the independent, holding other independent variables constant. If Catholics differ greatly in abortion attitudes from Protestants, and so on for each category of religious affiliation, then the beta for religious affiliation will be high. The beta varies between zero and one. The values of the betas for one survey cannot be compared in absolute terms with the values from another survey (even when the same questions have been asked on both), since the level of the beta for an independent variable in any given survey is affected by that variable's correlation with other predictors (independent variables). However, the *rank order* of betas can be compared among surveys.

Finally, throughout this paper we use "adjusted percentages." For example, we look at the percentage who are negative toward abortion among Catholics *after* having adjusted for the fact that Catholics have very few blacks and rural residents in their flock. In general, in the real world, variables are correlated. Young people, for example, are more likely to have lower incomes and higher educations that older people. Multiple Classification Analysis "adjusts" for these differences in distribution by estimating what the mean for a group would be if it had the distribution of the total sample on all other variables.

PREDICTING POLAR VIEWS ABOUT THE LEGALIZATION OF ABORTION

What influences people to entertain sharply negative or positive views of the legalization of abortion? In answering this question, we will consider respondents in 1978 who were against all justifications for abortion (or who tolerated it only in the event of threats to the mother's health), in contrast to those respondents who favored all reasons for pregnancy termination. Turning first to social and demo-

graphic attributes of respondents (such as religious affiliation, church attendance, educational level, age, sex, race and
so on), it is clear from table 1 that religious affiliation, combined with a measure of church attendance, is the key variable. Among background variables, nothing else comes close
in relative importance, although the other variables obviously do contribute somewhat. The combined effect of the
background predictors (including religion and attendance)
explains 33 percent of the variance in abortion attitudes.[1]

TABLE 1

POLAR VIEWS OF ABORTION ACCORDING TO SELECTED
BACKGROUND CHARACTERISTICS[a]

Predictors	Beta Coef-ficients	Number	Percent		Adjusted Percent[b]	
			Pos.	Neg.	Pos.	Neg.
Religion and Church Attendance	.50					
Frequent Attenders						
Catholics		109	31	69	29	71
Baptists and Fundamen-talist Protestants		127	36	64	42	58
Infrequent Attenders						
Catholics		75	88	12	89	11
Baptists and Fundamen-talist Protestants		131	73	27	77	23
Methodists, Lutherans, and Presbyterians		172	88	12	86	14
Episcopalians, Jews, None		136	93	7	88	12
Education	.18					
Grade School		87	40	60	51	49
High School 1–3		104	68	32	63	37
High School Complete		268	67	33	70	30
College 1–3		152	74	26	73	27
College 4+		150	86	14	80	20
Community Size	.11					
Under 3,500		137	55	45	59	41
3,500 to 49,999		311	73	27	73	27
50,000 to 249,999		168	73	27	70	30
250,000 to 999,999		104	70	30	71	29
1 million +		41	71	29	69	31

TABLE 1, Continued

Predictors	Beta Coefficients	Number	Percent Pos.	Percent Neg.	Adjusted Percent[b] Pos.	Adjusted Percent[b] Neg.
Family Income	.10					
Under $5,000		100	63	37	72	28
$5,000–$9,999		144	63	37	65	35
$10,000–$14,999		142	74	26	72	28
$15,000–$19,999		99	67	33	65	35
$20,000–$24,999		103	72	28	73	27
$25,000 +		135	81	19	73	27
Race	.09					
White		669	71	29	70	30
Black		82	52	48	59	41
Sex	.07					
Male		332	70	30	66	34
Female		429	69	31	72	28
Age	.06					
Under 25		87	78	22	75	25
25–34		227	76	24	69	31
35–44		152	63	37	66	34
45–54		92	67	33	68	32
55 +		203	64	36	71	29
Total		761				
Grand Mean			69	31		
R^2 (adjusted for degrees of freedom)	.327					

SOURCE: National Opinion Research Center, General Social Survey, 1978.
[a]This regression includes only respondents who are against abortion for all reasons (or who favor it only when the mother's health is in danger) and respondents who favor abortion for all reasons.
[b]Through the use of a dummy variable regression technique (Multiple Classification Analysis), the percentages in any one classification have been adjusted for the effects of the other variables in the table.

Turning to the detailed percentages by religion and church attendance (table 1), it is evident that antiabortion sentiment characterizes not only Roman Catholics but fundamentalist Protestants as well. Moreover, among both of these groupings, the most significant element is behavioral religiousness: church attendance. For Catholics, in particular, extreme negativism toward abortion is characteristic only of frequent church attenders. Infrequently attending Catholics are as positive as Episcopalians, Jews, and those having no affiliation; or as Methodists, Lutherans, and Presbyterians. Although fundamentalist-Protestant frequent attenders are almost as negative as Catholics, it is of interest that infrequently attending fundamentalist Protestants are more negative than infrequently attending Catholics. Since both groups are doctrinally opposed to abortion, infrequent attendance among fundamentalist Protestants apparently is not as indicative of doctrinal disaffection as is the case for Catholics.

It should be remembered that the adjusted percentages for all categories in table 1 control for the effects of the other variables in the table. Hence, fundamentalist Protestants are not more negative simply because they are less educated on the average or because they include more blacks. Controlling for such factors does reduce the degree of negativism somewhat (the difference between unadjusted and adjusted percentages: 64 as compared with 58). However, it does not obliterate it.

Turning to other characteristics, it is apparent that there is a pronounced positive relation between acceptance of the legality of abortion and educational achievement. Moreover, whites are more positive than blacks; there is some tendency for the youngest respondents to be the most positive, but age does not make much difference after that; persons in rural areas and very small towns are substantially less positive than urban residents, and, after controls (but not before), women are more positive than men.

Although background factors explain a high percentage of the variance in the extremes of abortion attitudes, the question arises of what additional attitudinal factors might generate even more explanation. In our research we have tested for a wide variety of attitudes that seemed theoretically relevant. For example, we tried attitudes toward homosexuality, toward pornography, toward government spending on a variety of social welfare programs, toward the role of women in the home and in economic and public life, toward "prolife" issues such as capital punishment and war, and a scale of alienation from the society. These factors by and large showed very low correlation with attitudes toward abortion, and the correlations that did exist "washed out" in the multiple regressions.

The "successful" attitudinal variables were views on euthanasia, premarital sex, divorce laws, and family size. Although being against abortion does not correlate with being "prolife" generally, it does relate to individual discretion over death in the event of unbearable conditions, as in euthanasia (table 2). It is also clear from our analysis that attitudes toward abortion are not simply a function of generalized conservatism on sexual issues (as might be reflected in views on pornography and homosexuality), but that they relate specifically to disapproval of premarital sexual relations (table 2). Finally, people who are against legalized abortion appear to be more family oriented—they oppose easier divorce and prefer larger families than those who favor it.

Four questions, one on each of four topics (premarital sex, euthanasia, divorce laws, and ideal family size), explain 16 percent of the unexplained variance remaining after background factors have been used in the equation (table 2). In effect, the attitudinal variables have been applied to the residual or unexplained variance. The *total* variance explained by the background factors and the four attitudinal variables is 43.5 percent: a multiple correlation coefficient of .66. The reader should note that the use of residuals, although theoretically appropriate, results in a conservative estimate of the total explained variance. For example, when the same background and attitudinal variables are used in one equation, the total explained variance is 48.7 instead of 43.5 percent.

Would our analysis of the determinants of abortion attitudes change greatly were we to include respondents who

TABLE 2

Predictors	Beta Coefficients	Number	Percent		Adjusted Percent[b]	
			Pos.	Neg.	Pos.	Neg.
Divorce Laws	.13					
Easier		240	77	23	72	28
Stay Same		212	77	23	75	25
More difficult		274	58	42	64	36
Don't know		35	62	38	66	34
Premarital Sex	.19					
Always wrong		181	50	50	57	43
Almost always wrong		76	66	34	70	30
Wrong only sometimes		145	78	22	77	23
Not wrong at all		346	77	23	72	28
Don't Know		13	75	25	81	19
Ideal Family Size	.09					
0-1		28	74	26	71	29
2		424	75	25	72	28
3		144	66	34	68	32
4		79	59	41	67	33
5 +		86	55	45	61	39
Euthanasia	.23					
Yes		452	79	21	76	24
No		280	54	46	59	41
Don't Know		29	64	36	68	32
Total Respondents		761				
Grand Mean			69	31		
R^2 (adjusted for degrees of freedom)	.161					

SOURCE: National Opinion Research Center, General Social Survey, 1978.
[a]The wording of the questions was as follows:
Divorce Laws—Should divorce in this country be easier to obtain, more
    difficult to obtain, or stay as it is now?
Premarital Sex—There's been a lot of discussion about the way morals and

had less extreme views on the subject? For example, suppose we wished to contrast those who were against abortion for all reasons, plus those who favored it only for "hard" reasons (such as the mother's health or possible defects in the child), with those who favored it either for all reasons or for reasons of health, defects, and economic stress (1–3 versus 4–5 in table 3). As may be seen, when we include these more moderate positions, we find that people differ less by background variables and by attitudinal ones as well—the amount of variance explained by both background and attitudinal factors declines. However, the R^2 is still creditable: 17.5 percent for background factors, 9.6 percent for attitudinal variables, a total of 25 percent of the overall variance explained by the background and attitudinal variables taken together. In sum, there are major differences between people who cut short their approval at "hard" reasons and those who are willing to include one or more "soft" reasons as well. Moreover, as table 3 shows, the background and attitudinal variables behave in very much the same ways as was the case for those respondents who took the extreme positions we have considered in the bulk of our analysis so far.

What of other combinations of the five possible positions on abortion laid out in the footnote to table 3? Table 3 shows six theoretically relevant combinations in all. We see that variation according to background and attitudinal variables is around 25 percent in all cases except one—people who favor no reasons and those who favor only "hard" reasons. We may thus conclude that the explanatory variables in our

---

attitudes about sex are changing in this country. If a man and a woman have sex relations before marriage, do you think it is always wrong, almost always wrong, wrong only sometimes, or not wrong at all?

Ideal Family Size—What do you think is the ideal number of children for a family to have?

Euthanasia—When a person has a disease that cannot be cured, do you think doctors should be allowed by law to end the patient's life by some painless means if the patient and his family request it?

[b]The percentages in this table are adjusted for the effects of the other variables in the table. The effects of background variables have been removed.

analysis "work" well with persons who have less extreme views on abortion than the ones we initially considered.

To summarize this section, we have seen that in one year (1978) a national subsample of our adult population was deeply divided in its views on the advisability of legalized abortion. This is evident from the fact that a small set of background variables explains 33 percent of the variance in the extremes of abortion attitudes and that four additional attitudinal variables bring the total R^2 up to 43.5 percent.

TABLE 3

BACKGROUND AND ATTITUDINAL PREDICTORS OF SELECTED COMBINATIONS OF ATTITUDES TOWARD ABORTION.

Dependent Variable[a]	Predictors	Background[b] R^2	Beta Coefficients	Attitudes R^2	Beta Coefficients	Total R^2
1 versus 5 (647)		.301		.195		.437
	Religion/Attendance		.50		—	
	Education		.16		—	
	Community Size		.11		—	
	Income		.09		—	
	Race		.07		—	
	Sex		.06		—	
	Age		.04		—	
	Euthanasia		—		.21	
	Premarital Sex		—		.20	
	Ideal Family Size		—		.17	
	Divorce Laws		—		.14	
1–4 versus 5 (1319)		.179		.094		.256
	Religion/Attendance		.33		—	
	Education		.18		—	
	Income		.09		—	
	Community Size		.08		—	
	Race		.06		—	
	Age		.05		—	
	Sex		.03		—	

TABLE 3, Continued

BACKGROUND AND ATTITUDINAL PREDICTORS OF SELECTED COMBINATIONS OF ATTITUDES TOWARD ABORTION.

| Dependent Variable[a] | Predictors | Background[b] | | Attitudes | | Total |
		R^2	Beta Coefficients	R^2	Beta Coefficients	R^2
	Ideal Family Size		—		.15	
	Divorce Laws		—		.13	
	Premarital Sex		—		.13	
	Euthanasia		—		.12	
1–3 versus 4–5 (1319)		.175		.096		.254
	Religion/Attendance		.35		—	
	Education		.15		—	
	Community Size		.10		—	
	Income		.08		—	
	Race		.05		—	
	Age		.04		—	
	Sex		.04		—	
	Euthanasia		—		.15	
	Premarital Sex		—		.13	
	Ideal Family Size		—		.13	
	Divorce Laws		—		.11	
3 versus 5 (956)		.151		.100		.236
	Religion/Attendance		.28		—	
	Education		.18		—	
	Income		.09		—	
	Community Size		.09		—	
	Age		.08		—	
	Race		.06		—	
	Sex		.02		—	
	Ideal Family Size		—		.19	
	Premarital Sex		—		.15	
	Divorce Laws		—		.12	
	Euthanasia		—		.10	

TABLE 3, Continued

BACKGROUND AND ATTITUDINAL PREDICTORS OF SELECTED COMBINATIONS OF ATTITUDES TOWARD ABORTION.

Dependent Variable[a]	Predictors	Background[b] R^2	Beta Coefficients	Attitudes R^2	Beta Coefficients	Total R^2
1 versus 3 (547)		.103		.113		.204
	Religion/Attendance		.31		—	
	Income		.14		—	
	Age		.13		—	
	Race		.09		—	
	Education		.06		—	
	Community Size		.05		—	
	Sex		.05		—	
	Euthanasia		—		.24	
	Ideal Family Size		—		.18	
	Divorce Laws		—		.14	
	Premarital Sex		—		.07	

SOURCE: National Opinion Research Center, General Social Survey, 1978.
[a]With regard to attitudes toward justifications for abortion, respondents were divided into the following categories:
1. Against all justifications for abortion
2. Favors only mother's health, against others
3. Favors mother's health and child deformity, against financial stress and abortion on demand
4. Favors all but abortion on demand
5. Favors all justifications for abortion.
The dependent variables in the table above were derived from combinations of these categories. Thus, in the case of "1 versus 5" the only respondents considered are the 647 who favor no justifications and all justifications.
[b]The R^2 values in this table have all been adjusted for degrees of freedom.

Given the fact that this represents a multiple correlation coefficient of .66, this is an exceptionally high level of association for data based on mass observation. It demonstrates that extreme views on abortion are remarkably structured.

We have also seen that the variable of overriding importance is religious affiliation (coupled with church attendance among Catholics and fundamentalist Protestants). Indeed, in 1978, if religion and attendance are dropped from the regression (but all other background variables are retained), the R^2 for background variables tumbles from 33 to 10 percent! By contrast, dropping education from the equation (but retaining religion, attendance, and other background variables) lowers the R^2 only 2 points—it drops to 31 percent.

It is also true, as we have seen, that within the classification of religious affiliation and attendance, there is enormous polarization. Essentially, extremely antiabortion sentiments are the province of actively observing Catholics and fundamentalist Protestants.

We must conclude, therefore, that the question of whether one is antiabortion for all reasons (or favors it only for reasons of health) or proabortion for all reasons is almost entirely an ideological matter. Educational level provides some help with explanation, but its independent effect is relatively small. Nor is it true, if we run the regression without religious affiliation and attendance, that other variables are helped much in their explanatory power. Other variables get some small payoff when religion and attendance are dropped, but essentially the role of religion is unique.

TRENDS IN THE STRUCTURE OF ABORTION ATTITUDES

Having considered the factors that differentiate abortion attitudes in one year, 1978, let us now turn to trends in the structure of these attitudes over the time period of the 1970s. The question we will ask is: Do the predictors we have been considering differentiate abortion attitudes more in recent years than in the past? In effect, do our predictors explain more or less variance over time? If there has been a change in the amount of variance explained, which predictors account for this change? Our data begin in 1972 and our analysis will include only background variables, since similar attitudinal items are not available for each survey between 1972 and 1978.

As may be seen from table 4, in 1972, background factors explained 29 percent of the variance in the extremes of abortion attitudes. This is a level of difference among respondents that approaches the one for 1978. Beginning with 1973, the proportion of variance explained started to decline, and it reached a low in 1975. After that it started to rise, and it has risen steadily ever since. This means that the country was sharply divided, according to background characteristics, on the extremes of the abortion issue in 1972, that it reached more consensus during the mid-1970s (a period of more positive views on abortion), and that since 1975 people have again polarized on abortion according to their background characteristics.

Are the *kinds* of differences of equal importance in 1978 as in 1972? The answer is both yes and no. During the entire period, the betas show that religion / attendance has been the most important variable (table 4). However, in 1972 the religious variable shared top billing very closely with educa-

TABLE 4

PERCENTAGE OF VARIANCE EXPLAINED, AND BETA COEFFICIENTS FOR
BACKGROUND VARIABLES, AMONG RESPONDENTS WHO HOLD EXTREMELY
NEGATIVE AND POSITIVE VIEWS TOWARD THE LEGALIZATION OF ABORTION

	1972	1973	1974	1975	1976	1977	1978
R^2	.286	.239	.277	.183	.284	.278	.327
Betas							
Religion/							
Attendance[a]	.33	.40	.43	.35	.45	.45	.50
Education	.29	.19	.15	.23	.16	.11	.18
Community Size	.08	.06	.07	.05	.07	.11	.11
Income	.07	.11	.10	.07	.08	.13	.10
Race	.11	.10	.08	.08	.07	.12	.09
Sex	.01	.00	.04	.06	.02	.11	.07
Age	.06	.06	.06	.05	.09	.04	.06
Number	808	821	757	780	800	781	761

SOURCE: National Opinion Research Center, General Social Surveys, 1972–1978.
[a]The beta coefficients are in the order of their importance in 1978.

FIGURE 1. TREND IN THE PERCENT AGAINST ABORTION BY RELIGIOUS GROUP (NORC SURVEYS)

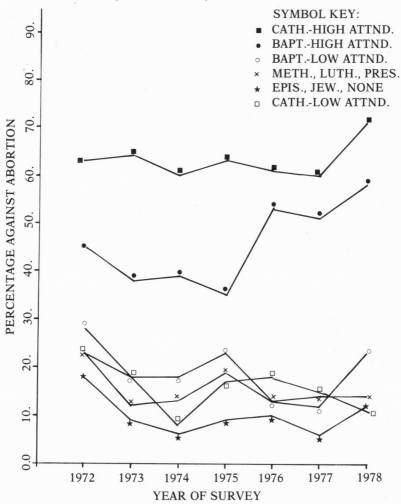

SYMBOL KEY:
■ CATH.-HIGH ATTND.
● BAPT.-HIGH ATTND.
○ BAPT.-LOW ATTND.
× METH., LUTH., PRES.
★ EPIS., JEW., NONE
□ CATH.-LOW ATTND.

tional level. In 1972 the beta coefficients for religion / attendance and educational level were .33 and .29 respectively. Moreover, no other background variable approached these two in importance—not race, sex, age, community size, or family income. Since 1975 there has been a marked rise in the importance of religion / attendance and, in general, a drop in the relative importance of educational level as a variable (see beta coefficients). By 1978 the beta coefficient for religion / attendance was .50 and for educational level it was .18. The betas for the other variables ranged from .06 to .11. In effect, among major background variables, it is clear that the rise in divisiveness on the abortion issue is not a class issue, not a racial issue, not a battle-of-the-sexes issue—it is a religious issue.

Moreover, the situation regarding religion is increasingly polarized. Among the subsample considered in this paper (those who favor either all indications or none for legalized abortion), figure 1 shows that were it not for practicing (high-attending) Catholics, Baptists, and other fundamentalist Protestants this subsample would preponderantly favor all reasons for abortion. Further, it is negative opinion among Baptists and fundamentalist Protestants that has really skyrocketed over the time period since 1975. Negative opinion among practicing Catholics has been high and has remained high. But Baptists and fundamentalist Protestants apparently lessened their negativism during the early and mid-1970s and, since then, have become markedly solidified against abortion.

THE SHORT-CIRCUITING OF CONSTITUENCY

We have isolated powerful predictors of attitudes toward abortion. We may now use this knowledge to attempt to understand a perplexing problem: Why is it that groups of respondents who, a priori, might be expected to be unique supporters of legalized abortion are not disproportionately favorable? For example, many people expect that women generally should be disproportionately positive toward a wide spectrum of choice regarding pregnancy. Abortion options relieve women of a major constraint in the reproductive sphere and hence, on this ground alone, many believe that women should form a proabortion constituency. Yet, compared to men, women do not significantly favor the legalization of abortion.[2] Is this because women are more likely, as a group, to be characterized by attributes that, as we have already seen, predispose people to unfavorable views of legalized abortion? Further, are these attributes more influential on abortion attitudes among women than among men? In this manner, are women "short-circuited" from becoming a proabortion constituency?

The same kind of question might be asked about many groups that are "natural" constituencies for abortion. Why are people who favor social welfare measures not disproportionately supportive of broadening abortion options? Why are blacks, whose reproductive options may be foreclosed by lack of access to abortion if it is illegal and, hence, expensive, not among the principal supporters of choice in this sphere? What short-circuits these groups as proabortion constituencies?

Using our subsample of respondents who have polar views on abortion, we shall concentrate here on the short-circuiting of two potential constituency-forming characteristics: gender and social welfare attitudes.

Women and Abortion

Why are women not a uniquely supportive constituency for abortion choices? One answer, as may be seen in table 5, is that women are more likely than men to have characteristics that predict *anti*abortion attitudes. The predictors shown in table 5 are those on which men and women differ. As for the other predictors in our analysis (race, community size, age, divorce laws, family size ideals, and views of euthanasia), there is little or no difference by sex. In no case do the differences by sex offset the results shown in table 5. In effect, one reason the women in our subsample are not more supportive of abortion than they are—and, in particular, markedly more supportive than men—is that women are more likely to be observing Catholics, less likely to be Episcopalian or Jewish or to have no religion, less educated, and less advantaged economically. Moreover, women are more disapproving of premarital sex.

An additional facet of this story is told by a multivariate analysis by sex. Here (table 6) we see that the background variables that characterize women more than men also are frequently more influential on abortion attitudes among women than among men. For example, the fact that women are overrepresented among the less educated is exacerbated by the fact that education also has relatively more influence on women's than men's attitudes toward abortion.

Obviously, the reasons we have outlined are not the only ones why women do not form a conspicuous proabortion

TABLE 5

PERCENTAGE DISTRIBUTION OF MEN AND WOMEN ACCORDING TO SELECTED
BACKGROUND CHARACTERISTICS AND ATTITUDINAL VARIABLES RELATED TO
OPINIONS CONCERNING ABORTION

Predictors	Women	Men
Religion and Church Attendance		
Frequent Attenders	*Percent*	
Catholics	18	10
Baptists and Fundamentalist Protestants	17	16
Infrequent Attenders		
Catholics	9	11
Baptists and Fundamentalist Protestants	18	16
Methodists, Lutherans, and Presbyterians	22	24
Episcopalians, Jews, None	15	21
Education		
Grade School	13	10
High School 1–3	15	13
High School 4	39	30
College 1–3	20	21
College 4 +	14	27
Family Income		
Under $5,000	17	8
$5,000–$9,999	21	16
$10,000–$14,999	19	18
$15,000–$19,999	12	15
$20,000–$24,999	10	18
$25,000 +	15	21
Premarital Sex		
Always wrong	26	21
Almost always wrong	10	10
Wrong sometimes	20	18
Not wrong at all	42	50
Don't Know	2	1
Total	429	332

SOURCE: National Opinion Research Center, General Social Survey, 1978.

TABLE 6

Predictors	Background		Attitudes		Total
	R^2	Beta Coefficients	R^2	Beta Coefficients	R^2
			Women		
	.351		.184		.470
Religion/Attendance		.49			
Education		.27			
Community Size		.15			
Income		.11			
Race		.10			
Age		.08			
Euthanasia		—		.24	
Ideal Family Size		—		.17	
Divorce Laws		—		.17	
Premarital Sex		—		.13	
			Men		
	.315		.144		.414
Religion/Attendance		.49			
Income		.14			
Age		.14			
Community Size		.13			
Education		.11			
Race		.10			
Premarital Sex		—		.29	
Euthanasia		—		.22	
Ideal Family Size		—		.11	
Divorce Laws		—		.08	

SOURCE: National Opinion Research Center, General Social Survey, 1978.
[a] These regressions were run on those respondents who were against all justifications for abortion (or who favored it only when the mother's health was endangered) and those who favored all reasons for abortion.

constituency. Another major reason, already suggested by Blake some years ago, is that some women may feel that ease of abortion diminishes the cardinal importance of their re-

TABLE 7

PERCENTAGE DISTRIBUTION OF PRO AND ANTIWELFARE RESPONDENTS
ACCORDING TO SELECTED BACKGROUND CHARACTERISTICS AND ATTITUDINAL
VARIABLES RELATED TO OPINIONS CONCERNING ABORTION

Predictors	Prowelfare	Antiwelfare
Religion and Church Attendance		
Frequent Attenders		
Catholics	11	13
Baptists and Fundamentalist Protestants	18	10
Infrequent Attenders		
Catholics	10	11
Baptists and Fundamentalist Protestants	20	14
Methodists, Lutherans, and Presbyterians	22	27
Episcopalians, Jews, None	16	23
Education		
Grade School	14	7
High School 1–3	15	12
High School 4	33	37
College 1–3	16	23
College 4 +	22	21
Family Income		
Under $5,000	23	6
$5,000–$9,999	20	17
$10,000–$14,999	19	19
$15,000–$19,999	10	13
$20,000–$24,999	10	17
$25,000 +	14	25
Sex		
Male	40	47
Female	60	53
Race		
White	81	93
Black	17	4

TABLE 7, Continued

PERCENTAGE DISTRIBUTION OF PRO AND ANTIWELFARE RESPONDENTS
ACCORDING TO SELECTED BACKGROUND CHARACTERISTICS AND ATTITUDINAL
VARIABLES RELATED TO OPINIONS CONCERNING ABORTION

Predictors	Prowelfare	Antiwelfare
Ideal Family Size		
0–1	4	4
2	56	59
3	17	19
4	11	8
5 +	12	10
Euthanasia		
Yes	60	67
No	35	30
Don't Know	5	3

SOURCE: National Opinion Research Center, General Social Survey, 1978.

productive role.[3] To have total discretion over reproduction may, for some women, seem to trivialize what they regard as the cosmic importance of motherhood. Blake suggested as well that, for women who wish to use pregnancy as an instrumentality in their relations with their husbands or lovers, easy access to abortion lessens rather than increases feminine power. A pregnancy that has been embarked upon for the purpose of precipitating a marriage, or holding one together, no longer has the clout that once it did. For these and other reasons, one can understand that legalized abortion will not necessarily seem to "open options" for all women.

Social Welfare and Abortion

The same type of analysis may be applied to understanding why people who are generally in favor of social welfare policies, "liberals," are not disproportionately a constituency for abortion. For example, from responses to the following question: "Are we spending too much, too little, or

about the right amount on welfare?" we divided respondents into two groups, those who thought the government
was spending "too much" on welfare and those who believed
that the amount spent was not enough or was just right.
Counting those who said "too much" as "antiwelfare" and
the remainder as "prowelfare," we find no difference in the
attitudes of these groups toward legalization of abortion.
Why are supporters of social welfare policies not also disproportionate supporters of abortion?

Obviously, measurement problems could be involved
here. People may not consider liberalization of abortion to
be a welfare measure, or as related to social welfare. However, even granting that the entire explanation does not lie
with our model, we shall see that it is suggestive in explaining the short-circuiting of constituency in this instance.

First, we may note that prowelfare respondents (as compared with antiwelfare ones) are disproportionately characterized by attributes that predict antiabortion attitudes (table 7). As for religion, although high-attendance Catholics
are slightly underrepresented among prowelfare respondents, this is more than compensated by an overrepresenta-
tion of Baptists and other fundamentalist Protestants, and
an underrepresentation of Episcopalians, Jews, and those
having no religion. With regard to other attributes, prowelfare respondents are less educated, have substantially lower
incomes, include more women, and contain a higher proportion of blacks. As for attitudinal variables, prowelfare respondents are more negative toward euthanasia, and have
slightly larger family-size ideals.

Pushing the analysis further to the relative influence (beta
coefficients) of these variables on abortion attitudes among
pro- and antiabortion individuals (table 8), we see that a
number of variables like education and race are relatively
more important as predictors of abortion attitudes among
prowelfare than antiwelfare respondents. Moreover, it is
frequently true that the *pattern* of the relationships (table 9)
with abortion attitudes among prowelfare respondents is
more linear than is the case for those who are against welfare. This is clearly the case with education. As well, among
those favoring welfare, poorer respondents are more nega-

TABLE 8

BACKGROUND AND ATTITUDINAL PREDICTORS OF ATTITUDES TOWARD
ABORTION AMONG RESPONDENTS WHO FAVOR AND OPPOSE SOCIAL WELFARE[a]

Predictors	R^2	Background Beta Coefficients	R^2	Attitudes Beta Coefficients	Total R^2
			Prowelfare		
	.308		.151		.412
Religion/Attendance		.42			
Education		.29			
Age		.13			
Race		.12			
Income		.11			
Community Size		.08			
Sex		.01			
Euthanasia		—		.29	
Premarital Sex		—		.18	
Divorce Laws		—		.14	
Ideal Family Size		—		.13	
			Antiwelfare		
	.314		.196		.448
Religion/Attendance		.53			
Community Size		.18			
Income		.17			
Education		.11			
Sex		.10			
Age		.10			
Race		.07			
Premarital Sex		—		.23	
Euthanasia		—		.21	
Ideal Family Size		—		.18	
Divorce Laws		—		.13	

SOURCE: National Opinion Research Center, General Social Survey, 1978.
[a] These regressions were run on those respondents who were against all justifications for abortion (or who favored it only when the mother's health was endangered) and those who favored all reasons for abortion.

TABLE 9

Predictors	Beta Coefficients	Number	Percent Pos.	Neg.	Adjusted Percent[a] Pos.	Neg.
			Prowelfare			
Education	.29					
Grade School		38	45	55	55	45
High School 1–3		40	85	15	89	21
High School 4		88	83	17	83	17
College 1–3		42	88	12	92	08
College 4 +		59	95	05	89	11
Race	.12					
White		216	84	16	83	17
Black		44	68	32	71	29
			Antiwelfare			
Education	.11					
Grade School		25	72	28	80	20
High School 1–3		46	80	20	74	26
High School 4		139	77	23	81	19
College 1–3		89	85	15	81	19
College 4 +		81	90	10	89	11
Race	.07					
White		362	81	19	82	18
Black		15	87	13	94	6

SOURCE: National Opinion Research Center, General Social Survey, 1978.
[a]Education and race have been adjusted for the other background variables used in this analysis so far—religion/attendance, family income, community size, etc.

tive toward abortion than are the well-to-do, whereas among those against welfare, the variability of abortion attitudes by income shows no consistent pattern. A similar situation is evident for race. Among prowelfare respondents, blacks are markedly more negative toward abortion than are whites. Among those against welfare, blacks are less likely to disfavor abortion than are whites. In effect, not only are there more poor, poorly educated people and blacks among those favoring welfare, but being poor, poorly educated and black is more predictive of being against abortion among prowelfare than among antiwelfare respondents.

SUMMARY AND CONCLUSION

The political history of legalized abortion during the 1970s has been guided by those who hold clearly positive or negative views on the subject. Supreme Court decisions on abortion have been, by and large, victories for those favoring the legalization of voluntary pregnancy termination. Yet these decisions have precipitated the rise of highly organized antiabortion action groups. These groups are ideologically committed to outlawing abortion altogether, or to allowing it only when the mother's life would be threatened by a continuation of the pregnancy. Their success in impeding the implementation of the Court's decisions is well known.

The sharp polarization of abortion-related political activity during the 1970s has led us to ask a question that has not been broached previously. What influences people to entertain distinctly negative or positive views of the legitimacy of legal access to abortion? That is, if we consider *only* individuals who are against all reasons for legalizing abortion (or who favor it only in the event the mother's health is endangered), on the one hand, and those who favor it for all reasons, on the other, what are the factors that influence such strongly negative or positive sentiments?

Using national survey data for 1978, we have divided our analysis of determinants into two parts. First, we have considered major "background" variables: religious affiliation and church attendance, education, age, sex, race, family income, and community size. Through multiple regression analysis, we have found that religion / attendance is the preeminently important determinant. Moreover, negativism toward abortion is virtually preempted by frequent church attenders among Catholics, Baptists, and fundamentalist Protestant denominations (such as Mormons and Jehovah's Witnesses). Infrequently attending Catholics do not differ from the remainder of the population, and infrequently attending Baptists and members of other fundamentalist denominations do not differ very greatly. Hence, even among those who count themselves as Catholics or fundamentalist Protestants, extremely negative views of abortion are the province only of frequent participants in religious observances. Our analysis demonstrates that, except for educational level, no other background variables are of unique importance in explaining whether a person will favor or disfavor abortion. Even educational level is a poor second to religion / attendance as a predictor.

A further component of our analysis of the determinants of abortion attitudes was to ask whether, *after* background variables have exerted their influence, there are attitudinal components of extreme views on abortion? There are many theoretical possibilities here. One obvious one is suggested by the self-designation of antiabortion groups as being "pro-life." Others relate to attitudes toward women's roles, toward sexual activity generally, toward the legitimacy and fairness of the body politic, and toward political "liberalism." All of these were tried. The fact is that respondents who are against abortion are not more "prolife" than those favoring abortion, nor are they generally more conservative about sex, more alienated from political and judicial processes or institutions, or less politically "liberal." Four sets of attitudes do, however, provide a high level of prediction of whether one will favor or disfavor abortion—attitudes toward euthanasia, toward premarital sex, toward divorce laws, and toward ideal family size. People who are extremely negative toward abortion are more likely to disapprove euthanasia, premarital sex, ease of divorce. They also favor somewhat larger families. In sum, even if the direct effect of background influences on our population were removed, there would still be attitudinal determinants of views on abortion.

We turned next to the trend in consensus or dissensus concerning abortion. Concentrating on background factors alone, we asked whether, between 1972 and 1978, there has been a change in the amount of agreement or disagreement on abortion. We found a definite trend between 1972 and 1978. In 1972, lack of consensus was almost as high as in 1978. However, the relative importance of two of the most important predicting variables was different. In 1972 religion/attendance was the best predictor, as in 1978. But it was closely seconded by educational level, indicating that, prior to the Supreme Court decisions on abortion, support for legalized abortion was a significant issue among highly educated as against less educated respondents. During the mid-1970s, differences lessened greatly. This was due, in large measure, to the fact that major antiabortion groupings—the least educated respondents and the frequently attending fundamentalist Protestants—became more positive in their views. Why they did so is something of a mystery. It may be that they were particularly influenced by positive media presentations on the issue, an influence that was later dissipated when antiabortion groups began to make effective media presentations and fundamentalist churches became focused on abortion as an issue.

In any event, after 1975 dissensus rose again. Fundamentalist Protestants, in particular, skyrocketed in their negativism, and the less-educated reacted in a similar, if less amplified, fashion. By 1978 there was more disagreement by background characteristics than in 1972. But the predictors of disagreement had changed in relative importance. Although there was still a sharp relation between education level and abortion attitudes, it was clear, by 1978, that antiabortion sentiment was uniquely the province of frequently observing Catholics and fundamentalist Protestants. The remainder of the subsample under consideration here— including infrequent church attenders among Catholics and fundamentalist Protestants—preponderantly favored all justifications for abortion. A clear-cut, crystallized position against all, or almost all, reasons for abortion characterized only a deeply religious subset of Catholics and fundamentalist Protestants.

Having found exceptionally powerful predictors of positive and negative views concerning abortion, we were led to ask why some predictors that seem theoretically important were not actually so. Why have seemingly "natural" proabortion constituencies not proven to be disproportionate supporters of legalized voluntary pregnancy termination? We analyzed two such potential constituencies—women and political "liberals." We found that among both women and supporters of social welfare policies in our subsample, there was a disproportion of characteristics that predict antiabortion attitudes. For example, more women than men are highly religious Catholics, poorly educated, and negative toward premarital sex. Moreover, the relation of a number of these characteristics to antiabortion views is stronger among women and prowelfare respondents than among men and antiwelfare respondents. In effect, these "natural" constituencies for abortion are "short-circuited" by other characteristics and attitudes.

In concluding, we must remind the reader that this analysis has been directed to a subset of national samples of the U.S. population who are clearly proabortion or anti-abortion. The purpose of our work has been to shed light on the views of those most likely to play an active role in the abortion controversy. It is well to remember, however, that the bewildered, the inconsistent, and the apathetic are as politically significant.

NOTES

1. Our data included information on over 100 denominations and religions. The particular combination of religious affiliation and church attendance used in this study was achieved through our theoretical knowledge of the religious groupings and through a form of multivariate analysis called automatic interaction detector.

2. This result is not only apparent from the surveys analyzed here, but shows up consistently in a long series of Gallup surveys on abortion as well. See Judith Blake, "Abortion and Public Opinion: The 1960–1970 Decade," *Science* 171 (February 12, 1971): 540–49; Blake, "Elective Abortion and our Reluctant Citizenry: Research on Public Opinion in the United States," in Howard J. Osofsky and Joy D. Osofsky, eds., *The Abortion Experience: Psychological and Medical Impact* (Hagerstown, Md.: Harper and Row, 1973), pp. 447–67; "The Supreme Court's Abortion Decisions and Public Opinion in the United States," *Population and Development Review* 3 (March / June 1977): 45–62; "The Abortion Decisions: Judicial Review and Public Opinion," in Edward Manier, William Liu, and David Solomon, eds., *Abortion: New Directions for Policy Studies* (Notre Dame, Ind.: University of Notre Dame Press, 1977), pp. 51–82.

3. Blake, "Abortion and Public Opinion," pp. 540–49.

3

THE ABORTION DECISION: NATIONAL AND INTERNATIONAL PERSPECTIVES

HENRY P. DAVID

SOCIOCULTURAL AMBIVALENCE and political sensitivities continue to inhibit abortion-related social science research in the United States and many other lands. For example, during thirty-eight days of testimony, between February and August 1978, the Select Committee on Population of the U.S. House of Representatives heard from 150 specialists from the United States and abroad on subjects ranging from the reliability of demographic data to the safety of modern contraceptives and from the problem of teenage pregnancy to the impact of an aging U.S. population. By the time of its dissolution in March 1979, the committee had issued eleven volumes of hearings and six reports containing 133 recommendations for legislative or administrative action (Tydings 1979). Not one of those 133 recommendations concerned the divisive issue of elective pregnancy termination. In accord with prior agreement, each session chairman had forewarned every witness not to talk about abortion and threatened to cut off promptly anyone who tried to discuss this topic more extensively (Green 1979).

It is the purpose of this chapter to review what is presently known about the complex factors influencing an individual's or couple's decision to terminate an unwanted pregnancy. To place this topic in perspective, the chapter begins with a historical overview of the practice of abortion in nineteenth-century America, followed by a discussion of legislative trends in the United States and other countries from the period between the two world wars to the present. Next will come a discussion of statistical indices of abortion-seeking behavior, beginning with a note on constraints on demographic and psychosocial research in the United States. This discussion is followed by a presentation of the latest reported U.S. statistics on the incidence of abortion and a comparison with experience in other lands.

The topic of decision making in problem pregnancy resolution is introduced with a presentation of conceptual approaches and decision-making phases. Coping styles are considered with examples presented from unusually well-designed research studies conducted in Hawaii and Michigan. The special problem of repeat abortion seeking is then discussed in terms of incidence and public perception as well as the dynamics of decision making, with an example from Yugoslavia, where safe abortions and modern contraceptives are equally available, accessible, and virtually cost free.

The last section of the chapter discusses the importance of societal decision making as reflected in abortion denials and delays. Data are presented from the continuing longitudinal study of children born to women twice denied abortion for the same pregnancy, on initial request and on appeal, in Prague, Czechoslovakia, and a matched control group. A personal commentary concludes the chapter.

HISTORICAL CONTEXT

Nineteenth-Century America

At the beginning of the nineteenth century, when abstinence was widely advocated and withdrawal was the most commonly practiced method of contraception, not a single jurisdiction in the United States had any statute restricting the practice of abortion (Mohr 1978). Adhering to British common law tradition, abortion before "quickening" was not deemed a crime. It was condoned as a means of terminating unwanted pregnancies, particularly among young, unmarried, and economically disadvantaged women (Mohr 1978). It was widely assumed that the fetus was not really alive until the woman felt the first recognizable fetal movement, popularly called "quickening." This generally occurred in the sixteenth to eighteenth week of pregnancy, although it could and still does vary a good deal from woman to woman (Hellman, Pritchard, and Wynn 1971).

Since there were no reliable tests for diagnosing pregnancy, only quickening could confirm with certainty that a woman was really pregnant. Other signs of pregnancy could always be explained on the assumption that something might be "blocking" normal menstrual cycles. Medically, the procedure for restoring menstrual flow was similar to that of inducing early abortion. Moreover, potions designed to remove an obstruction to menstruation were well described in home medical guides and were easily available from physicians, midwives, and pharmacists. "The practice of aborting unwanted pregnancies was, if not common, almost certainly not rare in the United States during the first decades of the 19th century" (Mohr 1978). Indictments for abortion were seldom brought before American courts, which regularly sustained the most lenient interpretations of the quickening doctrine.

In 1803 in England, during the reign of George III, Lord Ellenborough's Act made procurement of an abortion before quickening a felony "to be punished by fine, imprisonment, or exposure in the pillory, or that the criminal may be publicly or privately whipped or transported beyond the sea for any term not exceeding 14 years" (Hodge 1869). Procuring an abortion after quickening was considered murder, punishable by death. The act was modified under George IV, and supplanted, during Queen Victoria's reign, by the Offences Against the Person Act of 1861, which decreed surgical abortion at any stage of pregnancy a criminal offense, punishable by life imprisonment (Williams 1957; Dickens 1966).

The first law dealing specifically with the legal status of abortion in the United States was passed in 1821 by the General Assembly of Connecticut. It restricted the administration of a "noxious or destructive substance . . . to any woman then quick with child" (Connecticut 1821). Surgical abortion before quickening was first prohibited by a section of the New York Revised Statutes of 1829 (enacted in 1828), which also contained an express therapeutic exception, justifying abortion "if necessary to preserve the life of the mother" (Means 1968).

A review of documents contemporary with the passage of the New York State legislation suggests that the primary concern at the time was not with the unquickened fetus but with protecting the life and health of women with unwanted pregnancies from damage by abortion (Means 1970). This was the pre-Lister era of medicine, when every operation entailed the possibility of life-threatening infection. The emphasis of the New York legislators on preventing unnecessary surgery is reflected in their decision to place the abortion statute in the Penal Code instead of the Medical Practices Act, where every previous or subsequent law governing medical and surgical procedures is to be found. The influence of technological development on nineteenth-century abortion legislation is well documented by Della-penna (1979).

Around mid-nineteenth century, abortion was a flourishing practice in the United States. At this time American medical schools were operated as private proprietary businesses, competing for paying pupils and seldom denying admission or failing students. By using thinly disguised mail order and newspaper advertising, it was possible to earn more than one million dollars per year (in 1845 dollars!) in helping women terminate unwanted pregnancies. By 1840, sixteen of the twenty-six states still had no abortion legislation (Mohr 1978).

After the founding of the American Medical Association in 1847, organized drives were gradually launched to professionalize medical training and health services, and to obtain legal and public acknowledgment of the professional status of physicians. An antiabortion campaign, portraying doctors fighting the health risks associated with botched abortions and opposing the brazen advertisements of greedy abortionists, seemed a "perfect" way to further these objectives. For example, in 1864 the AMA offered a prize for the most popular antiabortion tract and allied itself with others in a public policy crusade against abortion (Mohr 1978).

After the end of the Civil War in 1865, the antiabortion drive was strongly supported by upper-class, white, Anglo-Saxon Protestants, anxious about declining birth rates among native-born married women and concerned about the reproductive potential of new immigrants. They were eventually joined by antiobscenity crusaders and by feminists, who counseled abstinence as the only sure protection against unwanted pregnancy and perceived abortion as an undesirable byproduct of the suppression of women (Gordon 1976; Mohr 1978).

The religious press was largely silent on the abortion issue. The Protestant churches did not approve therapeutic abortion before quickening (Noonan 1970). In the Catholic church there had been a theoretical discussion about when human life began, but this was more important in the theoretical than in the practical order. However, in 1869

Pope Pius IX "made a sharp change in church law by eliminating any distinction between a formed and unformed fetus in meting out the penalty of excommunication for abortion," even to save the life of the woman (Callahan 1970). It is of historical interest, however, that while American churchmen did not oppose the AMA's antiabortion crusade, they also did not become conspicuously involved (Mohr 1978). Therapeutic abortion on medical indication was not explicitly and publicly condemned by any Roman Catholic authority before 1895 (Means 1970).

Between 1860 and 1880, more and more American states dropped traditional quickening doctrines, revoked common law immunities for pregnant women, and recognized the American Medical Association as the primary arbiter of medical training and practice. The doctrine that interruption of pregnancy at any point was a crime was accepted and remained in force with little change for nearly a century. By 1900 abortion was illegal in all American jurisdictions. In most states, a threat to the life of the pregnant woman was the sole legal ground on which abortion could be performed; in a few, a threat to the woman's health sufficed (Mohr 1978). Women deciding to terminate unwanted pregnancies for social or economic reasons were forced to seek more dangerous illegal abortions.

Twentieth-Century Legislation

In 1920 the Soviet Union became the first country to legalize in-hospital abortion on request of the woman in the first trimester of gestation. The liberalization had been intended to be temporary, designed to recognize the equal status of women and protect their health from the ravages of illegal procedures. The theory was that as social conditions improved and the state assumed more of the burdens of child rearing, the problem of unwanted pregnancies and abortions would gradually decline (David 1970). Stimulated by a desire to increase births and concerned about the rise of Hitler Germany, Soviet legislation enacted in 1936 again made abortion a criminal offense except when performed for compelling medical and eugenic reasons. The accompanying commentary justified the 1920 decree as a "regrettable necessity" of the Civil War period of social chaos (Field 1956).

A modified abortion law was passed in Iceland in 1935, introducing the concept of medicosocial indications (World Health Organization 1971). Legal history was made in 1938 in London when Aleck Bourne, a gynecologist at St. Mary's Hospital, was acquitted at a trial under the 1861 Offences Against the Person Act. Mr. Justice MacNaughton in *Rex* v. *Bourne* established the precedent that a physician may perform an abortion if he believes that continuation of the pregnancy would endanger the woman's life or make her "a physical and mental wreck" (Dickens 1966; Potts 1971). The late 1930s also saw modifications of the Danish and Swedish abortion statutes, introducing the concept of socioeconomic indications (WHO 1971).

In Nazi Germany abortion was strictly prohibited, punishable by the death penalty after 1943 (Harmsen 1950). In France abortion laws were made extremely stringent during 1940–41. The Penal Code was extended by court decrees so that even a nonpregnant woman or one who was unsuccessful in her abortion attempt could be deemed guilty of a criminal offense. Trials were convened before a special state court whose judgment was final and could not be appealed. In 1942 the death penalty was invoked when, following the example of Nazi Germany, abortion was declared an act against the state. The last person to be executed under the harsh conditions of Occupied France was a laundress, Mme. Giraud, convicted on the charge of having performed twenty-six illegal abortions. Following the liberation of France in 1944, the death penalty was rescinded and the special state court abolished (Gebhard et al. 1958). No one has been executed for performing abortions in the subsequent thirty-five years anywhere in the world.

The next wave of liberalization occurred after World War II. In 1948 occupied Japan adopted its Eugenic Protection Act, making abortion widely available for a broad range of indications, in part to reduce the steeply rising incidence of illegal abortion (Muramatsu 1974; WHO 1971). On 25 November 1955, two years after the death of Stalin, the Supreme Soviet repealed the 1936 restrictions. The reasons presented were to reduce "the harm caused to the health of women by abortions performed outside of hospitals," and "to give women the possibility of deciding for themselves the question of motherhood" (Field 1956). All of the socialist countries of Central and Eastern Europe except Albania eventually passed similar legislation. The People's Republic of China adopted a policy of elective abortion in 1957 (Chen 1970; Faundes and Luukkainen 1972).

In 1965 Tunisia became the first Moslem nation to permit abortion on request, initially only for women with five living children and subsequently for all women in the first trimester of gestation (Nazer 1972). In 1966 Romania suddenly restricted its previously liberal abortion legislation (David and Wright 1971; Berelson 1979). Legal and administrative restrictions were gradually reimposed in Bulgaria, Czechoslovakia, and Hungary, but few women in social need were denied termination of an unwanted pregnancy on initial request or subsequent appeal (David and McIntyre 1980). New Zealand (1977) became the first (and thus far only) parliamentary democracy ever to rerestrict abortion following liberalization.

In the United States, until about 1960, the vast majority of physicians interpreted the then-existing abortion legislation very narrowly and terminated few unwanted pregnancies (Tietze 1970). Indeed, legal abortion rates and ratios had been declining at least since the 1940s as the incidence of various diseases believed to justify interruption of pregnancy decreased and obstetricians learned how to help even very ill women cope with the risks of pregnancy and childbirth (Erhardt, Tietze, and Nelson 1970).

After 1960 the attitude of the medical profession gradually changed, with mental health gaining increasing acceptance as a valid reason for terminating unwanted pregnancies. This was in accord with the recommendations of the American Law Institute, published in 1962. Between 1963 and 1967 the number of legal abortions performed in the United States was estimated to range between 5,000 and 9,000 per year (Tietze 1970). Beginning with Colorado in 1967, about a dozen states liberalized their statutes in conformity with the American Law Institute (1962) recommendations. Approval was granted when a psychiatrist found a "substantial risk" that continuation of the pregnancy would gravely impair the mental health of the woman. It was soon recognized that medicolegal standards of "substantial risk," "gravely impair," and even "mental health" defied objective and consistent assessment, leaving wide scope for subjective interpretation and raising serious doubts about the reliability of psychiatric determinations and clinical case reports (Group for the Advancement of Psychiatry 1969).

In 1970 Alaska, Hawaii, and New York enacted legislation (and the state of Washington passed a popular referendum) which did not specify conditions for performing an abortion, thus in effect authorizing its performance on demand. For example, the New York State statute stipulated that abortion was a matter entirely between the woman and her physician without requirement for state residency, mental health or other consultation, or performance of the abortion in hospital. As the result of a Federal Court decision abortion also became an elective procedure in the District of Columbia. With the increasing availability of legal abortion in major metropolitan centers, the total number of abortions increased from an estimated 18,000 in 1968 and 50,000 in 1969 to around 200,000 in 1970 (Tietze 1979a). Total abortions reported by health authorities to the Center for Disease Control rose to around 500,000 in 1971 and nearly 600,000 in 1972 (Smith, Kahan, and Burr 1974). On 22 January 1973 the U.S. Supreme Court ruled that in the first trimester the question of terminating an unwanted pregnancy is to be resolved solely by the pregnant woman and her physician. Subsequently, the number of abortions more than doubled, to 1.4 million in 1978, the latest year for which data are available (Forrest, Sullivan, and Tietze 1979).

As of mid-1979, the worldwide legal status of abortion ranges from complete prohibition to elective abortion at the request of the pregnant woman (David 1979a; Tietze 1979a). About two-thirds of the world's population live under conditions of liberal abortion legislation, mostly in Asia, North America, and Europe. In some countries, however (e.g., India and Zambia), abortion resources are very limited and many women are unaware of their existence or legality. In others, such as France and Italy, conservative attitudes among physicians and hospital administrators have effectively curtailed full implementation of existing legislation, especially for economically disadvantaged women. In the United States, translating a constitutional right into free choice and equal accessibility to services, regardless of economic circumstances, has become part of the continuing abortion controversy (Alan Guttmacher Institute 1979).

The other third of the world's population live in countries, mostly in Central and South America, Africa, and a few in Europe, where abortion is either completely illegal or permitted only on strictly defined grounds to protect the woman's life or health (Cook and Dickens 1978; Tietze and Lewit 1978; Tietze 1979a; David 1979a). For example, in the Caribbean and Latin America, Cuba is the only country where abortion is widely available without cost during the first trimester (David 1979b). In many other countries where abortion is technically illegal, statutes are not always strictly enforced. Terminations are often tolerated when performed by skilled physicians and/or paramedics without adverse consequences.

In retrospect, it is apparent that during the last quarter-century a social revolution occurred in the realm of abortion legislation. In 1954 abortion was illegal in all countries of the world with the exception of Iceland, Denmark, Sweden, and Japan. In subsequent years more than thirty countries changed their formerly restrictive laws or policies to permit abortion on request or on a broad range of social indications. The relaxation of abortion laws in diverse countries with different sociocultural heritages can generally be traced to three interrelated components: (a) recognition of the threat of illegal abortion to public health; (b) support for women's rights to terminate an unwanted pregnancy under safe conditions at an early stage of gestation; and (c) provision of equal access to abortion for rich and poor women alike. Sweeping technological changes in world culture, coupled with the increasingly vocal demands of well-organized women and their male supporters, could no longer be resisted by reluctant legislatures (Dellapenna 1979). In only two countries, Singapore and Tunisia, was abortion legalized expressly to limit the population growth and enhance economic development (Tietze and Lewit 1978).

STATISTICAL INDICES OF ABORTION-SEEKING BEHAVIOR

Constraints on Abortion Research and Data Interpretation

While more statistics are available on abortion than on any other surgical procedure, difficulties in interpretation persist. For example, in the United States statistics are gathered by two major organizations, the Center for Disease Control (CDC), an arm of the Department of Health and Human Services, and the private Alan Guttmacher Institute (AGI). CDC obtains most of its data from state health departments (Smith 1977; CDC 1979). However, most states did not establish central abortion reporting systems until late 1973 or subsequent years; six have yet to do so. The AGI survey gathers information from questionnaires sent directly to all health centers and private practitioners known to be providing abortion services (Forrest, Sullivan, and Tietze 1979). Not surprisingly, the total number of abortions reported by AGI has consistently exceeded the total number reported to the CDC. For example, AGI reported just over 1 million abortions performed in 1975, a figure not reached by CDC until 1977 (Sullivan, Tietze, and Dryfoos 1977; CDC 1979). AGI estimated an incidence of 1.2 million abortions for 1976, 1.3 million for 1977, and 1.4 million for 1978, reflecting a continued but slowing upward trend in the use of abortion services (Forrest, Tietze, and Sullivan 1979). Whereas the total number of abortions increased by 21 percent between 1974 and 1975, the year-to-year increase slowed to 15 percent between 1974 and 1975 and 11 percent between 1975 and 1976 (Tietze 1979a). It rose again to 12 percent between 1976 and 1977 before declining to 4 percent between 1977 and 1978 (Forrest, Sullivan, and Tietze 1979).

Sociodemographic and psychosocial research have long been handicapped by the absence of a uniform national reporting system, which has made it difficult to obtain nationally representative population samples from the range of public and private service providers (Smith 1977). The situation is further compounded by the lack of comparability between local and regional studies, the complexities of obtaining adequate follow-up access to the woman and her partner, and the absence of standardized instruments for the assessment of psychosocial determinants (David 1978). CDC data on adolescents are limited because abortion figures for single age-year cohorts between ages thirteen through nineteen are reported only by thirty-two states. Other states pool adolescent data by age ranges as under fifteen years and between fifteen and nineteen years of age. Ethnic information is divided into two segments: white and black plus other minorities. Separate data are not available on Hispanics and American Indians. Sociodemographic information is usually limited to marital status and parity. Such constraints constitute a caveat to much of the published research on psychosocial characteristics of abortion and the abortion decision in the United States (e.g., Adler 1976).

Abortion / USA

The latest Abortion Surveillance Report released by the Family Planning Evaluation Division of the Center for Disease Control (CDC 1979) provides data for the year 1977. Of the women whose legal abortions were reported to CDC from the fifty states and the District of Columbia, 30.8 percent were under age twenty, 34.5 percent between twenty and twenty-four years, and 34.7 percent over twenty-five years old. Among the abortors 53.4 percent had no living children, 19.1 had one child, 14.5 percent had two children, and 13.1 percent had three or more children. About 91.5 percent had the procedure within twelve weeks of pregnancy. Less than 1 percent of all abortions were performed after the twenty-first week of gestation. Of the teenage abortions reported by thirty-two states, 4 percent were under age fifteen, 40 percent between fifteen and seventeen years, and 57 percent were over age eighteen. The number of unmarried women among all abortors exceeded that of married women by about 3:1 (75.7 percent to 24.3 percent). While 66 percent of all women were white, the proportion of abortions obtained by black and other minority women increased from 23 percent in 1972 to 34 percent in 1977. The legal abortion ratio per 1,000 live births among blacks and other minority groups was about double that of white women.

As in every year since CDC began issuing its abortion findings, women obtaining abortions were largely young, white, and unmarried, often terminating their first pregnancy. About one-third had consistently been under age twenty. The proportion of married women declined from 27 percent in 1973 to 24 percent in 1977, paralleling the decline of married women aged fifteen to forty-four in the U.S. population from 60 percent to 57 percent during the same time span. The proportion of black and other minority women reported to CDC increased from 28 percent in 1973 to 34 percent in 1977. Particularly noteworthy is the steady increase in the performance of abortion earlier in gestation, when the procedure is safer and less costly. The proportion of first trimester abortions rose from 83.7 percent in 1973 to 91.5 percent in 1977, when 51.2 percent of all abortions were performed under eight weeks and less than 1 percent over twenty-one weeks of gestation (CDC 1979). Unwed adolescents continue to predominate among second trimester aborting women (David 1979c).

A review of the AGI survey shows that between 1967 and September 1979 about 7 million women, or almost 14 percent of all women of reproductive age (15–44), obtained about 9 million abortions (Tietze 1979d). By 1978 the U.S. abortion rate had risen to (an estimated) 27.5 abortions per 1,000 women aged fifteen to forty-four years, an increase of 62 percent from the 1973 rate of less than 17 per 1,000. The abortion ratio per 1,000 live births delivered six months later increased from 239 in 1973 to 406 in 1978, meaning that 29 percent of pregnancies were voluntarily terminated, not counting those ended by miscarriages or stillbirths. This represents an increase of 52 percent from 1973, when 19 percent of pregnancies were terminated by abortion (Forrest, Sullivan, and Tietze 1979; Tietze 1979a).

The increase in the total number of abortions following the Supreme Court decision needs to be considered within the context of the number of unintended pregnancies. For example, Tietze (1979c) recently calculated that unintended pregnancies occurred at a rate of about 2.0 million to 2.3

million per year during the early 1970s. Assuming that the number of unintended pregnancies has not changed dramatically in subsequent years, Tietze deemed the rapid rise in the number of legal abortions since 1973 "quite predictable." After legal abortion had become available, many women decided to use it to resolve unintended and unwanted pregnancies. However, even in 1977 not all such pregnancies were terminated, either because the woman chose to carry to term or because the option of abortion was not readily available (Tietze 1979c).

The number of abortion providers grew by 67 percent, from 1,627 in 1973 to 2,716 in 1977. In that year, the proportion of abortions performed in nonhospital clinics rose to 66 percent, while the proportion reported by hospitals declined to 30 percent; the remaining 4 percent were provided in private physicians' offices. Although the number of service providers increased, only 37 percent of all private non-Catholic hospitals and 20 percent of public hospitals provided any abortion services in 1977. Women residing in 77 percent of U.S. counties had to travel to metropolitan centers in the other 23 percent of U.S. counties if they wished to obtain pregnancy termination services. In seven of the fifty states no public hospital offered any abortion facility in 1977. Approximately 28 percent of women estimated to want abortion services in 1977, and 26 percent in 1978, were unable to obtain them, primarily because services were unavailable in their home or nearby communities. Poor, rural, young, and black women were disproportionately represented among those not served (Forrest, Sullivan, and Tietze 1979; Tietze 1979a). Whereas the need for abortion services was met for 74 percent of women seeking them, it is likely that the availability of abortion services is the single most powerful determinant of variations in abortion rates among U.S. metropolitan areas and in explaining the increase in abortion rates following the U.S. Supreme Court decision (Borders and Cutright 1979).

Incidence Worldwide

The total number of pregnancies terminated each year by induced abortion throughout the world is not known and perhaps never will be. According to available estimates and surveys conducted by the International Planned Parenthood Federation (1974, 1978) in 180 countries, about one pregnancy is deliberately terminated for every three live births, totaling approximately 55 million abortions per year, or 34 million not counting the People's Republic of China. These estimates must be regarded with considerable caution since they combine information from countries where abortion is legal and reliably reported with estimates from countries which do not report abortion data (e.g., China and the U.S.S.R.) or where induced abortion remains illegal, as in many developing countries of Africa and Latin America. No reliable method has yet been developed to estimate the incidence of illegal abortions (Tietze 1979a). While there is little doubt that desperate women will resort to abortion no matter what the legal circumstances or risks to well-being, the frequently quoted statement that induced abortion is the world's leading method of fertility regulation has no basis in verifiable fact and is almost surely wrong (Berelson, Mauldin, and Segal 1979).

The 1977 U.S. rate of 26.9 abortions per 1,000 women of reproductive age (fifteen to forty-four years) is slightly above that for Denmark (24.3), German Democratic Republic (22.0), Norway (19.7), and Sweden (19.3), but somewhat below that of Czechoslovakia (28.0) and Singapore (28.4). It is considerably below the latest figures reported from Bulgaria (64.5), Cuba (61.0), and Hungary (39.2), but substantially above those for England and Wales (10.6) and Scotland (7.8), all countries where abortions are legal and well reported (CDC 1979; Forrest, Sullivan, and Tietze 1979; Tietze 1979a). The U.S. reported the highest proportion of teenagers and lowest proportion of currently married women among all abortors in countries recently publishing such data (CDC 1979; Tietze 1979a).

THE DECISION-MAKING PROCESS
Conceptualization

Although the desire for conception control has been virtually universal in all forms of society throughout recorded history (Himes 1936), the availability of reliable methods is of historically far more recent origin. Discovery of the physiology and timing of ovulation in humans in the late 1930s (Dickinson & Bryant 1938) provided the basis for the development of clinically effective and safe hormonal and mechanical contraceptives, such as the oral pill and intrauterine devices. Similarly, safe abortion procedures were greatly simplified by the development of electric vacuum aspiration curettage in the People's Republic of China (Wu and Wu 1958), which permitted the establishment of free-standing abortion centers (Branch 1972; Hern 1979).

Technical advances in fertility regulation have been followed by a gradual awareness of the psychological complexity of contraceptive risk taking (e.g., Luker 1975, 1977), the planning and wanting of a child (e.g., Pohlman 1969), and the interaction of individual, partner, and societal influences at recurrent hazard points in a woman's fertility career (e.g., Miller 1972, 1973, 1976, 1978). Efforts to understand fertility behavior were often initiated by demographers who, in the absence of interested psychologists, developed psychological concepts to meet the needs of their demographic theories (e.g., Vincent 1961; Rains 1971; Sklar and Berkov 1974). A certain amount of semantic confusion was perhaps inevitable. For example, demographers often assume a decision-making model that focuses on "desired family size" without ever establishing whether or not desired family size is an actual consideration in couple decision making (Miller 1978). Also, there is an occasional failure to differentiate between intendedness and wantedness of conception and pregnancy. Unintended conceptions can become wanted pregnancies and intended conceptions can become unwanted pregnancies as a couple's life circumstances change.

The psychoanalytic approach was an early favorite among attempts to assess psychological determinants or antecedents of fertility-regulating behavior and pregnancy resolution. However, its scope was largely limited to impressionistic clinical case studies and proved resistant to systematic larger-scale empirical investigations (Wyatt 1967). A subsequent approach endeavored to assess motivation on the basis of attitudinal inquiries. A frequent critique of

questionnaire-based studies is that they often rely on super-
ficial conceptualizations of attitudes and inadequately designed psychological assessment instruments (e.g., Fawcett
1970, 1973; Smith 1973). When attitudes are measured in a
simplistic fashion, they are rarely predictive of actual behavior and have little relevance for recommending alternative policies (Simmons 1977).

In recent years research findings have become increasingly available on demographic and social characteristics of
women who chose to deliver or terminate their pregnancy
(e.g., Diamond et al. 1973; Hass 1974; Fischman 1975;
Hatcher 1975; Bracken, Klerman, and Bracken 1977, 1978;
Zelnick and Kantner 1974, 1977). Psychological perspectives
on the decision-making process have emerged far more
slowly. This may be, in part, because researchers, like most
people, often find decision making painful or stress-
inducing, preferring to avoid the subject along with other
unpleasant matters.

Strategies in decision making can be considered in terms
of available options or branches on a decision tree. In decisions regarding pregnancy resolution the simplest progression would be from intended conception through wanted
pregnancy to term delivery. Complications arise when the
conception is unintended or the pregnancy unwanted. The
woman, alone or with her partner, must then decide how to
resolve what to her is a problem pregnancy. Her options
usually are to carry to term and keep the child, or carry to
term and give the baby up for adoption, or seek an abortion.
While the options available are evident, the process of reaching a decision is more complicated. Consideration is usually
given to such variables as socioeconomic and cultural-
environmental factors, personal characteristics and current
life-stage circumstances, and partner relationships and perceptions of each other's attitudes (David and Friedman
1973; Friedman, Johnson, and David 1976).

Decision-Making Phases

Of particular importance in studies of decision making is
the process, or "coping patterns" (Janis and Mann 1977;
Goethals 1979), that people experience when a decision is

required. Janis and Mann (1977) have described conditions under which each of several coping patterns is used, and whether a given pattern results in effective or ineffective decision making. One of the most important concepts is "defensive avoidance," the coping pattern employed when it is realized that there are serious risks both in continuing on the present course and in switching to an alternative option, and when there seems to be little chance of finding a better solution. The three major varieties of defensive avoidance are procrastination, shifting responsibility for decisions onto others, and bolstering an eventual decision by avoiding and/or denying challenging information. Effective decision making involves the concept of "vigilance," which occurs when people retain hope of finding a satisfactory solution and believe they have time to search and deliberate. It is also suggested that the more thoroughly a person has considered the consequences of a decision, the better he or she will be able to cope with eventual subsequent stress.

In studies of the abortion decision making process there is a particular need to determine empirically to what extent women and/or couples are deciding which options are available and what the eventual consequences of each are likely to be (Smith 1978). Building on the stages-of-the-decision-making model proposed by Janis and Mann (1977), as modified by Bracken and Kasl (1975, 1976) and in discussion with colleagues (David 1979e), seven phases will be described that a woman may experience on discovering that she is pregnant. This will be followed by a discussion of coping stages.

Phase 1 is the acknowledgment of the pregnancy. It begins with the last menstrual period when chances of pregnancy are zero. When the next menstrual period is missed, awareness of pregnancy depends upon regularity of menstrual cycles and early recognition of the implications of a missed period. For some women the discovery of unwanted pregnancy may be more stressful than any subsequent decision on pregnancy resolution. Other pregnancy symptoms may or may not be recognized if denial is used to postpone awareness of reality. Eventually, pregnancy is obvious and consciously acknowledged.

Phase 2 is the formulation of alternative forms of pregnancy resolution. Women who unequivocally want to carry the pregnancy to term seldom consider abortion or giving the baby up for adoption. When conception is unintended and pregnancy unwanted, decision making is more complex, leading to a review of available options and their ramifications in Phase 3.

Phase 3 involves more extensive consideration of abortion, adoption, and motherhood as perceived within the woman's present life circumstances. Either alone or in consultation with her partner and/or significant others, socioeconomic consequences and cultural-environmental factors are weighed, usually within a context of future planning, often depending on the woman's perceived sense of personal efficacy and control in decision making. There may also be, at least for a time, considerable indecision and ambivalence, depending on her perception of social-environmental support for her decision and her susceptibility to potentially conflicting pressures from others. The more factors that are resolved (e.g., anxiety, guilt), the more satisfactory the eventual outcome is likely to be (e.g., Osofsky and Osofsky 1972; Bracken, Hachamovitch, and Grossman 1974; Bracken 1978; Bracken, Klerman, and Bracken 1978; David 1978).

Phase 4 occurs when a commitment has been made to one option over another. In the case of pregnancy termination, the woman may or may not inform others of her plans before actively seeking an abortion facility. An attitude set in favor of her choice is developed and reinforced by selective reading of supportive materials and rejection of new information about alternative options. A small proportion of women will continue in a state of considerable ambivalence that may result in postponing an abortion decision until well into the second trimester or until it is too late to implement the decision. Some women may actually telephone an abortion clinic to make an appointment but change their minds and decide to carry to term.

Phase 5 is reached when the woman keeps her appointment at the abortion clinic. At that point the vast majority will go through with the procedure. Those experiencing considerable ambivalence or reporting that they are coming to the clinic under pressure from others are often referred to more appropriate counseling centers. Well-trained staff at enlightened abortion centers recognize that they are not mental health specialists and that additional consultation is required to help seriously ambivalent women resolve their conflicts.

Phase 6 is a special category for those women who delay decisions beyond twelve weeks of gestation. Although fewer than 9 percent of all abortions are presently terminated in the second trimester of pregnancy, the total number was about 118,000 in 1977 (Forrest, Sullivan, and Tietze 1979). As just noted, delayed decision making is of particular social relevance because abortion after the twelfth week of gestation is associated with higher mortality and complication rates, is more expensive, and often requires greater technical skill (e.g., Cates, et al. 1977; Cates 1979; CDC/MMWR 1979; Tietze 1979a). A review of available literature (David 1979c) suggests that women who delay are most frequently unmarried teenagers experiencing their first pregnancy, along with women with lower levels of completed education and socioeconomic status. Economically disadvantaged women and rural black women are usually overrepresented among women obtaining second trimester abortions. They appear to be handicapped by lack of information on availability or location of services, financial difficulties, bureaucratic delays, parental notification requirements, and inaccurate medical diagnoses, each of which can influence the abortion decision. Additional reasons for delay are ambivalence, fear or hesitation to confide in partner or parents, and late recognition or denial of pregnancy until signs and symptoms become obvious. By the time some teens finally confront the reality of pregnancy, it may be too late for medically low-risk termination (Hiatt 1976).

Phase 7 includes women who fail to keep their appointments at abortion clinics after having made an initial contact. Insofar as can be ascertained, there has been only one U.S. follow-up study of abortion applicant dropouts (Swigar et al. 1976, 1977). A checklist of reasons for remaining pregnant did not elicit any statistically significant demographic differences between women who changed their minds after requesting abortion and decided to carry to term and a control group of women who implemented their plans for abortion during the same time period. Public controversies about the morality of obtaining abortion influenced several couples' decision; the second most important deciding factor was the partner's desire for a baby. Fear of the procedure and possible complications ranked third.

Coping Styles

In experiencing varied phases of the decision-making model a woman employs a range of coping styles to deal with her dilemma. It may well be a truism that there is no psychologically painless way to cope with an unwanted pregnancy. Although an abortion may elicit feelings of guilt, remorse, or loss, alternative solutions such as forced marriage, bearing an out-of-wedlock child, giving a child up for adoption, or adding an unwanted child to an already strained marital relationship are also likely to be accompanied by psychological problems for the woman, the child, the family, and society (David 1972a,b, 1973). In viewing the range of available options it is likely that major differences in decision making are reflected in differences in personal coping styles of which the woman concerned may or may not be always totally aware.

No woman becomes pregnant entirely by herself. The decision to practice or not to practice contraception is strongly influenced by the partner relationship and the accuracy of partners' perceptions of each other's views. The partners' attitudes and degree of control in the couple relationship are likely to determine the contraceptive method used (McCormick et al. 1977). As noted several decades ago, the quality of couple communication has a "clear and consistent relationship" with the effectiveness of fertility regulation and decisions about eventual pregnancy resolution (Stycos, Back, and Hill 1956; Misra 1966). For some couples, it is much harder to talk about sex than to do it.

Psychosocial research of the late 1960s identified as a key variable in coping style a perceived sense of personal efficacy, control, or competence (e.g., Rotter 1966; DeCharms 1968). Far more attention has been devoted, however, to "dysfunction" than to healthy coping. For example, impressionistic clinic case material has been used to illustrate that teenage pregnancy may be a product of pathological relationships within the family (e.g., Ooms and Maciocha 1979) or that abortion can be a symptom traceable to strained early parental relationships (e.g., Abernethy 1973; Tunnadine and Green 1978). Much less attention has been focused on indicators of effective family functioning and successful coping behavior in pregnancy resolution (e.g., David and Johnson 1977; David 1979d; Rosen and Martindale 1978). The importance of perceived competence and coping in the abortion decision making process is well illustrated in research findings reported from Hawaii and Michigan.

Hawaii

Following liberalization of Hawaii's restrictive abortion law in 1970, data were collected for specified periods during 1970–71 from virtually all women, regardless of age or marital status, who had a legal abortion or term delivery in every hospital in the state (e.g., Steinhoff 1973; Steinhoff et al. 1972, 1975; Diamond et al. 1973; Pion, Smith, and Hale 1973). Among the many analyses was one focusing specifically on the decision-making process (Steinhoff 1978).

Examination of the options premaritally pregnant women considered revealed no uniform hierarchy of preferred choices. Every option was actively rejected by some women and deliberately selected by others. Marriage was both the most widely considered and the most widely rejected option. Adoption was seldom considered and even more rarely chosen. Among the women who considered abortion, most decided on it as the best solution for them. It was further noted that not every premaritally pregnant woman made a conscious decision or deliberately selected among alternatives. Most of the women who married had not considered any other option, even if they were ambivalent about either getting married or having the baby. Similarly, some women never considered any solution other than induced abortion. Very few women indicated that they had thought about the full range of options; all those who did decided on abortion. Typically, a woman considered two or perhaps three options but found herself gravitating naturally toward one (Steinhoff 1978).

The crisis of premarital pregnancy elicited each woman's basic coping capabilities. Those who carried to term more often had lower aspirations, were more passive about their lives, and had little orientation to future planning. Aborting women were more future-planning oriented, had higher personal aspirations, and were more idealistic about marriage and eventual motherhood. The link between the demographic distribution of different forms of pregnancy resolution and the psychological experience of decision making seemed to reside in the effect of social class and age on the woman's perceptions of her pregnancy, the range of options available to her, and her capacity to make an independent decision (Steinhoff 1978).

Michigan

Further support for the importance of perceived competence in coping with unplanned problem pregnancies is derived from a 1974–75 questionnaire study conducted throughout the state of Michigan, including 921 aborting women in twenty-six clinics and hospitals and 360 women coming to counseling centers who decided to deliver and keep their child (Rosen and Martindale 1978). A two-stage, stratified sampling design was used. The mean age of women seeking abortion was somewhat older (twenty-two years) than those carrying to term (eighteen years). Over 80 percent of both groups were unmarried. Religious affiliation was reasonably matched, but black women constituted 55 percent of the deliverers compared to 35 percent among the abortors. The results indicate that most women in both groups were actively involved in their eventual decision. Regardless of age or race, the aborting women were significantly higher in perceived competence than those who chose to carry to term. Also, regardless of age, black women who decided to terminate had less traditional perceptions of the female role than did those who decided to deliver and keep the child.

REPEAT ABORTIONS

One of the most sensitive subtopics within the emotion-laden issue of abortion is the perceived rise in the incidence of repeat abortions. Some abortion counselors are disappointed when a counselee returns for another abortion, certain social scientists worry about "neurotic recidivism," and policy-makers are concerned about public opinion. Misperceptions abound. For example, the president of the United States stated in a 21 July 1977 press conference in Yazoo City, Mississippi, that "it is very disturbing how many of the recipients of federal payments for abortion in the past have been repeaters." He cited the "encouragement to depend on abortions to prevent pregnancy," rather than using contraception, as one of his major reasons for opposing federal funding of abortions for economically disadvantaged women (Carter 1977). Responding in a letter to the *Washington Post*, the late Fred Jaffe (1977) observed that no studies of repeat abortion among Medicaid recipients had ever been conducted and that federally funded research had demonstrated a significant increase in contraceptive practice following the legalization of abortion among married couples (e.g., Westoff and Jones 1977) and among sexually active unmarried teenagers (e.g., Zelnick and Kantner 1977).

The proportion of repeat abortions, experienced as a percentage of all abortions, has increased most rapidly in countries, such as the United States, where restrictive abortion laws and practices have only recently been replaced by relatively easier access to pregnancy termination. For example, in the United States the proportion of repeat abortions rose from about 12 percent of all reported abortions in 1973 to 24 percent in 1977 and probably continued to rise somewhat in 1978 (Tietze 1978; CDC 1979; Forrest, Sullivan, and Tietze 1979). In New York City 38 percent of all reported 1977 abortions were repeat abortions (Tietze 1979b). In Washington, D.C., the proportion of repeat abortions was about one-third of all abortions (Feinberg 1978). In Denmark, which liberalized its abortion legislation in the same year as the United States, a gradual increase in the repeat abortion ratio has also been observed (Denmark 1978). In

Hungary, however, which legalized abortion in 1956, the proportion of repeat abortions reached a plateau by the late 1960s (Hungary 1969; Tietze 1979a). The U.S. rate of repeat abortions per 1,000 women aged fifteen to forty-four was 70.3 in 1976 compared with a first abortion rate of 20.5 per 1,000 women without prior abortions (Tietze and Jain 1978). These data must be considered cautiously since responses to questions about repeat abortion are notoriously subject to error, selective forgetting, and deliberate denial regardless of the legal status of abortion (Hogue 1975; Tietze 1979a). Moreover, the District of Columbia and New York City provide second trimester abortions to nonresidents unable to obtain them in their home areas.

As noted by Tietze (1978), at least five factors combine to place women who had at least one abortion at greater risk for a repeat abortion compared to women who have not had a prior termination. First is the factor of age. Among women who have had at least one abortion there are greater proportions in the sexually most active prime reproductive ages (20–29 years) and lower percentages of teenagers and older women compared to the pool of women without prior abortion experience. Second, it can be assumed that nearly all women who had abortions were sexually active and probably resumed sexual activity after their abortions. Third, all women with abortion experience were able to conceive compared to the 40 percent of all women aged fifteen to forty-four without abortion experience who were unable to conceive, had undergone surgical sterilization, were married to vasectomized men, or were not sexually active. Fourth, women who have had one abortion are likely to resort to another to avoid a future birth, whereas women at risk of having a first abortion probably include a substantial number who would not choose to terminate an unintended conception. Finally, there is a very small group of women who consciously prefer to rely on abortion rather than on contraception, plus a larger number who find it difficult to practice contraceptive vigilance consistently and effectively. These women are at high risk for both first and repeated abortions.

In sum, an increasing proportion of repeat abortions

among all legal abortions and a repeat abortion rate substantially higher than a first abortion rate can be expected for a number of years after abortion has been legalized as the pool of women at risk for repeat abortion continues to rise to an eventual plateau. This phenomenon should not be interpreted as a decrease in the practice of contraception. Indeed, after considering all the factors already mentioned, plus a certain amount of unavoidable contraceptive failure, Tietze (1978) concludes that, after experiencing their first abortion, "a substantial majority" of women "did in fact practice contraception with a high degree of consistency and success."

The research literature suggests that most repeaters are more likely to have used contraception at time of conception than are first abortors but were less vigilant in their contraceptive practice than sexually active nonpregnant women (e.g., Bracken, Hahamovitch, and Grossman 1972; Schneider and Thompson 1976). While there is little evidence of a distinguishable subset of demographic characteristics, age, education, and parity have been associated with specific method choices among teenage repeaters, who more frequently stopped using one method of contraception without adopting another (Cahn 1976). Studies of adult women with multiple abortions suggest a relatively lower frustration tolerance for continued contraceptive vigilance (e.g., Cobliner, Schulman, and Smith 1976). There have been some suggestions from the United States and from England that women of Catholic background may be overrepresented among repeat abortion seekers. This is attributed to reluctance to practice contraception while resorting to abortion to resolve a problem pregnancy (Francome and Francome 1979).

A study of fifty women who had three or more legal abortions has been reported from England (Brewer 1977). At the time of their latest abortion, twenty-three women were pregnant because of contraceptive method failure, twenty-four reported erratic contraceptive practice, and three had changed their mind about an initially welcomed pregnancy. There was a significant relationship between erratic contraceptive practice and a history of psychiatric consultations, with further indications that unsettled relationships and low educational status also led to less effective contraceptive behavior. Inappropriate contraceptive advice was an important factor in several cases. There was no evidence, however, that repeat abortion was deliberately used as a preferred method of birth control.

It is quite likely that for some women motivation to practice contraceptive vigilance will require something more than the reward of a nonoccurring event—the absence of an unwanted pregnancy. Of particular interest in this regard is a cooperative research study conducted during 1973–74 in Yugoslavia, a country where legal abortion and modern contraceptives are equally available, accessible, and virtually cost free (Kapor-Stanulovic and Friedman 1978). Interviews were conducted simultaneously but separately by male and female interviewers with both marital partners shortly after the wife had had an abortion but before onset of her next ovulation. While both partners had thought about plans for preventing future pregnancies and each tended to believe that agreement had been reached jointly, there was actually very little concordance on the extent to which a decision had been made or the specific method of contraception to be used. In most cases the woman was at considerable risk for another abortion (Kapor-Stanulovic and Friedman 1978).

A second study, conducted in Novi Sad, attempted to understand why a majority of women continued to choose abortion over modern contraception and what might be done to alter the behavior pattern of aborting women to one more similar to that of women successfully relying on contraception. The extensive findings reflect a pattern of differences between the two groups suggesting a greater degree of personal control, future planning, and husband-wife agreement in the group of successful contraceptors as compared to the abortors. Having a low sense of efficacy or personal control threatens the effectiveness of a fertility-regulating method which requires a woman's initiative and consistent contraceptive discipline. For such women it may be more appropriate to suggest a long-lasting contraceptive requiring a single decision and entailing a second decision only when a child is wanted (Kapor-Stanulovic and Friedman 1978).

SOCIETAL DECISION-MAKING

Abortion Denied

Although the dynamics of intended and unintended conceptions and wanted and unwanted pregnancies and childbearing have long been debated (e.g., Pohlman 1969; David 1972a; Haas 1974; Miller 1978), it has never been possible in the United States systematically to follow women denied abortion or the children they were compelled to bear (Institute of Medicine 1975). The only longitudinal study with matched controls ever reported is still in progress in Prague, Czechoslovakia (Dytrych et al. 1975; David et al. 1977). Unique circumstances combined to make available for detailed medical, psychological, and social assessment 110 boys and 110 girls born in 1961–63 to Prague women twice denied abortion for the same pregnancy and a matched control group of children whose mothers had not applied for pregnancy termination. "Unwantedness" was operationally defined in terms of requesting or not requesting termination of an unwanted pregnancy. The study children were born to women whose original request for abortion had been denied by the District Abortion Committee and again on appeal by the Regional Abortion Committee, usually for reasons of health, or because the pregnancy was of more than twelve weeks duration, or because the applicant had had another abortion during the previous twelve months. The control group was formed on the basis of pair-matching. Criteria included: age, sex, number of siblings, birth order, and school class. The mothers were matched for age, marital status, and socioeconomic status as determined by the husband's occupation and his presence in the family. The research staff was not involved in the matching process and did not know which child belonged to what subgroup.

The children were about nine years old at original assessment and have been followed ever since (Matejcek, Dytrych, and Schüller 1978, 1979a). Initial findings demonstrated that compulsory childbearing has varied and sometimes unfavorable consequences for the subsequent life of the

85

child. While the aggregate differences between study and control children were not statistically significant, these differences were consistent to a high degree, pointing in the same direction, and cumulatively impressive, especially for boys. Some examples are: a higher incidence of morbidity and hospitalizations under identical biological conditions; worse school marks and performance despite the same level of intelligence; poorer social ranking in the peer group despite similar family socioeconomic levels; and greater maladaptation and increased irritability and proneness to anger.

Subsequent follow-up at age fourteen showed that more study than control children had come to the attention of child psychiatric and/or school counseling centers in Prague for reasons entirely independent of this research and without any awareness of their identity among the professional staff. The study children were seen significantly more often because of serious behavior disorders, whereas the control children came to attention because of comparatively less serious developmental deficits requiring administrative rather than therapeutic intervention.

A more extensive follow-up study, now in progress, while the children are sixteen years old, is based on questionnaire data collected from the families, the schools, and the children themselves. It was possible to locate 216 of the original 220 study children and 215 of the 220 controls; only 9 (or 2 percent) of the original 440 children were lost to follow-up. Initial findings show that school performance of the study children continues to worsen in comparison to the controls, reaching the 1 percent level of statistical significance for those graduated from the nine-year elementary to secondary schools. The study children again received lower ratings from their teachers and mothers; the differences with the controls reached statistical significance for those still in primary school. In comparison to the controls, the study children report that they experience less positive reinforcement and warmth from their parents, feeling either neglected or oppressed by parental authority. There is also a more marked discordance between parental attitudes toward the study children (Matejcek, Dytrych, and Schüller 1979b).

In reviewing all of the data from the continuing longitudinal study of the Prague children, it becomes apparent that a woman's originally rejecting attitude toward her pregnancy does not inevitably lead to behavioral difficulties in the child. The belief that every child unwanted during pregnancy remains unwanted is not necessarily true. It is equally untrue that the birth of an originally unwanted child causes a complete change in maternal attitude. Not every woman who becomes a mother will love her child. The Prague study confirms the risk of potentially unfavorable developmental consequences of compulsory pregnancy for the unwanted child. Perhaps of greatest significance is that the differences between study and control children have persisted and become even more significant after fifteen years of family life. It can still be concluded in 1979, as it was in 1975, that the child of a woman denied abortion is born into a potentially handicapping social situation that seems more stressful for boys than for girls. The children and their controls will continue to be followed.

Service Provider Influences

As previously noted, the attitudes of medical and allied health personnel are central to the equitable provision of abortion services. As "gatekeepers" they often control access to abortion and effective implementation of a woman's decision.

For many physicians and nursing staff, performing abortions represents an ethical and moral dilemma, posing conflicts between a personal commitment to save lives and the woman's decision to terminate her unwanted pregnancy (e.g., Char and McDermott 1972; Bourne 1972; Kessler and Weiss 1974; Rosen et al. 1974; Nathanson and Becker 1977). Conditions of practice, perceptions of professional roles, and the woman's economic status seem to be interrelated. Women with greater economic resources historically have had far fewer difficulties in obtaining abortions from qualified physicians than have economically disadvantaged women, whether the abortion sought was legal or illegal (Gordon 1976). Non-university-affiliated physicians practicing primarily among low-income groups often tend to express more conservative attitudes (LoSciuto, Balin, and Zahn 1972). Inequity is increased in those areas where private judgment is permitted to become public policy because physicians and hospital administrators refuse to perform, or to permit, legal abortions (Stewart 1978).

The medical staff dilemma is particularly apparent in the choice of procedure for a second trimester abortion. If a woman requests termination during the fourteenth week, should the physician wait until week sixteen or seventeen, relying on intra-amniotic instillation of either saline or prostaglandin, or proceed immediately with the newer dilatation and evacuation (D and E) procedure? Recent experience with the D and E method suggests that it is significantly safer than saline or prostaglandin, far less time-consuming, more economical, can be administered in the "grey" zone of the 13–16 week gestational interval, and greatly reduces pain and risk of psychological trauma for the woman (e.g., CDC 1976; Cates 1979).

In some respects the process of obtaining an abortion differs markedly from traditional medical practice. Women wishing to terminate an unwanted pregnancy are usually "healthy" and seldom in need of medical diagnosis or medical treatment of a medically identified disease. Some physicians are prepared to perform abortions to save a woman's physical health, but not to preserve the economic well-being of her family (Potts 1979). Women requesting implementation of their abortion decision do so because their pregnant condition is personally aversive or perceived to be socially stigmatizing (Adler 1979a,b). The role conflict between serving as a medical implementor of a woman's decision and the more traditional orientation of medical decision-maker is perhaps a greater divisive influence in the abortion debate than the more widely discussed moral and ethical issues.

The recent rash of contested local and state abortion legislation (e.g., *Akron* 1978; Nebraska 1979) has endeavored to impose an administrative time delay in implementing the woman's decision and/or to confront her with new information on alleged potential consequences of abortion that must be communicated on presentation of required consent forms. Within such a context more emphasis is likely to be placed on negative rather than positive consequences, although the health risks of carrying to term are actually greater than those associated with pregnancy termination (Tietze, Bongaarts, and Schearer 1976; Tietze 1979a).

Thus far, it has not been possible to assess the effects of administratively imposed abortion delays or consent requirements. It is very likely that women who are firm in their abortion decision will not be swayed by additional implementation obstacles. More suggestible women, those less certain of their decision, may be exposed to additional stress and anxiety when confronted with authority figures perceived to be less supportive. Some of the women coming to the clinic late in the first trimester may delay further and then be forced to resort to second trimester procedures which can be more hazardous to physical and mental health as well as being far more expensive (Cates et al. 1977; David 1979c). The social cost of such legislation is likely to be reflected more in an increase of second trimester abortions among young, economically disadvantaged, and black women than it is in a significant gain in the birth rate.

CONCLUDING NOTE

A discussion of abortion often evokes more heat than light. That is why I would like to conclude this presentation with a personal note. I appreciate the privilege accorded me to discuss freely my interpretation of psychosocial research findings in the area of abortion-seeking behavior. I am aware that there may be other interpretations and am prepared to discuss them on the basis of scientific research evidence.

It seems to me that the topic of abortion creates more social dissent than any other elective surgical procedure. Indeed, it appears at times that policy makers and legislators are more concerned about the act of abortion and its possible consequences than is the woman seeking help to terminate an unwanted pregnancy.

Abortion raises dilemmas for all concerned. Clinic

facilities are seldom sufficiently staffed to provide for the special needs of truly ambivalent women, concerned male partners, or distraught mothers of teenagers. Congressional hearings and legislative acts rarely offer clear solutions to human predicaments. The problem will not disappear. Its scope will increase as sexual debut occurs at ever earlier ages and moral barriers to premarital and extramarital sexuality decline in perceived importance.

Recent research conducted with peer counselors in the Washington, D.C., public high schools suggests that meaningful reductions in the abortion rate are unlikely to occur until the community accepts and is willing to cope with the phenomenon of adolescent sexuality (David and Johnson 1979). This implies a readiness to make available and accessible to sexually active adolescent men and women nonprescription contraceptives marketed to meet their specific needs. Other community solutions suggested by peer counselors include greater parental initiative in discussing sex and pregnancy with their children; revision of present public school sex education programs to place more emphasis on women's needs and effective communication with males; and encouragement of women's rights in asserting equality with men in sexual and contraceptive decision making. Such a context may free men from the perceived need of having to play a dominant role while also reducing barriers to open discussion of responsible sexuality, pregnancy, and pregnancy resolution.

The personal decision to terminate an unwanted pregnancy or to carry to term is seldom easy. It is one of the many difficult decisions that must be made by women and men who are increasingly confronted with complicated choices in planning their future lives, together or alone. Perhaps the time has come to shift the focus of debate from dysfunction, negative sequelae, and compulsory childbearing to successful coping, healthy functioning, and growing maturity in the face of stress and anxiety. Unintended conception and unwanted pregnancy create a conflict which each couple, or woman, should be free to resolve within a reasonable period of time and with a minimum of interference.

(The author is pleased to acknowledge the contributions to the

compilation of data on the incidence of abortion in the United States of Willard Cates, Jr. [Center for Disease Control], Jacqueline Darroch Forrest [Alan Guttmacher Institute], and Christopher Tietze [Population Council].)

REFERENCES

Abernethy, V. 1973. The abortion constellation: early history and present relationships. *Archives of General Psychiatry* 29:346–50.

Adler, N. E. 1976. Sample attrition in studies of psychosocial sequelae of abortion: how great a problem? *Journal of Applied Social Psychology* 6:240–59.

———. 1979a. Abortion: a social-psychological perspective. *Journal of Social Issues* 35:100–19.

———. 1979b. Psychosocial issues of therapeutic abortion. In D. Youngs and A. Ehrhardt, eds., *Psychosomatic obstetrics and gynecology*, pp. 159–77. New York: Appleton-Century-Crofts.

Akron Center for Reproductive Health v. City of Akron. 1978. C78-155A, N.D. Ohio.

Alan Guttmacher Institute. 1979. Abortions and the poor: private morality, public responsibility. New York.

American Law Institute. 1962. *Model penal code.* Philadelphia.

Berelson, B. 1979. Romania's 1966 anti-abortion decree: the demographic experience of the first decade. *Population Studies* 33:209–22.

Berelson, B., Mauldin, P., and Segal, S. 1979. *Population: current status and policy options.* Working paper no. 44. New York: Population Council, Center for Policy Studies.

Borders, J. A., and Cutright, P. 1979. Community determinants of U.S. legal abortion rates. *Family Planning Perspectives* 11:117–33.

Bourne, J. P. 1972. Abortion: influences on health professionals' attitudes. *Hospitals* 46:80–83.

Bracken, M. B. 1978. A causal model of psychosomatic reactions to vacuum aspiration abortion. *Social Psychiatry* 13:135–46.

Bracken, M. B., Hachamovitch, M., and Grossman, G. 1972. Correlates of repeat abortion. *Obstetrics and Gynecology* 40:816–825.

———. 1972b. The decision to abort and psychological sequelae. *Journal of Nervous and Mental Disease* 158:154–62.

Bracken, M. B., and Kasl, S. V. 1975. Delay in seeking induced abortion: a review and theoretical analysis. *American Journal of Obstetrics and Gynecology* 121:1008–19.

———. 1976. Psychosocial correlates of delayed decisions to abort. *Health Education Monographs* 4:6–44.

Bracken, M.B., Klerman, L.V., and Bracken, M. 1977. Abortion, adoption, or motherhood: an empirical study of decision–making during pregnancy. *American Journal of Orthopsychiatry* 130:251–62.

———. 1978. Coping with pregnancy resolution among never-married women. *American Journal of Orthopsychiatry* 48:320–33.

Branch, B. 1972. Outpatient termination of pregnancy. 1972. In M. Potts and C. Wood, eds., *New concepts in contraception: a guide to developments in family planning*, pp. 175–99. Baltimore: University Park Press.

Brewer, C. 1977. Third time unlucky: a study of women who have three or more legal abortions. *Journal of Biosocial Science* 9:99–105.

Cahn, J. 1976. Correlates of repeat abortions. Paper presented at the Annual Meeting of the Planned Parenthood Federation of America, October 1976.

Callahan, D. 1970. *Abortion: law, choice, and morality*. New York: Macmillan.

Carter, J. 1977. Remarks at Press Conference, Yazoo City, Mississippi, 21 July 1977, cited in *Washington Memo*, 3 August 1977.

Cates, W., Jr. 1979. D&E after 12 weeks: safe or hazardous? *Contemporary Ob/Gyn* 13:23–29.

Cates, W., Jr., Schulz, K. F., Grimes, D. A., and Tyler, C. W., Jr. 1977. The effect of delay and method choice on the risk of abortion morbidity. *Family Planning Perspectives* 9:266–72.

Center for Disease Control. 1976. Comparative risks of three methods of midtrimester abortion. *Morbidity and Mortality Weekly Report* 25, no. 46.

———. 1979. *Abortion surveillance, 1977*. Atlanta: 1979 and earlier years.

———. 1979. *Morbidity and Mortality Weekly Report*, 28, no. 4.

Char, W. G., and McDermott, J. F. 1972. Abortions and acute identity crisis in nurses. *American Journal of Psychiatry* 128:66–71.

Chen, P. C. 1970. China's birth control action programme, 1956–1964. *Population Studies* 24:141–58.

Cobliner, W. G., Schulman, H., and Smith, V. 1976. Dynamics of contraceptive failures. *The Journal of Psychology* 94:153–62.

Connecticut. 1821. *The public statute laws of the State of Connecticut, 1821*. Pp. 152–53. Hartford.

Cook, R. J., and Dickens, B. M. 1978. A decade of international change in abortion law, 1967–1977. *American Journal of Public Health* 68:637–44.

David, H. P. 1970. *Family planning and abortion in the socialist countries of Central and Eastern Europe*. New York: Population Council.

———. 1972a. Unwanted pregnancies: costs and alternatives. In C. F. Westoff and P. Parke, Jr., eds., *Demographic and social aspects of population growth*. Vol. 1 of the Commission on Population Growth and the American Future Research Reports, pp. 439–66. Washington, D.C.: Government Printing Office.

———. 1972b. Abortion in psychological perspective. *American Journal of Orthopsychiatry* 42:61–68.

———. 1973. Psychological studies in abortion. In J. T. Fawcett, ed., *Psychological perspectives on population*, pp. 241–73. New York: Basic Books.

———. 1978. Psychosocial studies of abortion in the United States. In H. P. David, H. L. Friedman, J. v. d. Tak, and M. Sevilla, eds., *Abortion in psychosocial perspective: trends in transnational research*, pp. 77–115. New York: Springer.

———. 1979a. International abortion legislation and practices in historical perspective. Unpublished paper.

———. 1979b. Notes from Cuba. *Abortion Research Notes* 8, nos. 1 and 2.

———. 1979c. Second trimester abortion: social issues. Paper presented at the Conference on Second Trimester Abortions: Perspectives after a decade of Experience, Chapel Hill, 1979. (To be published).

———. 1979d. Healthy family functioning: cross-cultural perspectives. In P. Ahmed and G. Coelho, eds., *Toward a new definition of health*. New York: Plenum, forthcoming.

———. 1979e. Informal discussions with Lawrence Balt, Michael Levy, and Judith Levin, Omaha, Nebraska, August 1979.

David, H. P., and Friedman, H. L. 1973. Psychosocial research in abortion: a transnational perspective. In H. J. Osofsky and J. D. Osofsky, eds., *The abortion experience: psychological and medical impact*, pp. 310–37. Hagerstown: Harper and Row.

David, H. P., and Johnson, R. L. 1977. Fertility regulation in the early childbearing years: psychosocial and psychoeconomic aspects. *Preventive Medicine* 6:52–64.

———. 1979. Teen problem pregnancies: peer counselors' perceptions about community concerns and solutions. Unpublished paper, 1979.

David, H. P., Matejcek, Z., Dytrych, Z., Schüller, V., and Friedman, H. L. 1977. Developmental consequences of unwanted pregnancies: studies from Sweden and Czechoslovakia. In Y. H. Poortinga, ed., *Basic problems in cross-cultural psychology*, pp. 184–89. Amsterdam: Swets and Zeitlinger.

David, H. P., and McIntyre, R. J. Forthcoming. *Reproductive behavior: Central and Eastern European experience.* New York: Springer.

David, H. P., and Wright, N. H. 1971. Abortion legislation: the Romanian experience. *Studies in Family Planning* 2:205–10.

DeCharms, R. 1968. *Personal causation: the internal affective determinants of behavior.* New York: Academic Press.

Dellapenna, J. W. 1979. The history of abortion: technology, morality and the law. *University of Pittsburgh Law Review* 40:359–428.

Denmark/National Health Service. 1978. *Statistics on legal abortion*, 1977 (and earlier years). Copenhagen.

Diamond, M., Steinhoff, P. G., Palmore, J. A., and Smith, R. G. 1973. Sexuality, birth control, and abortion: a decision-making sequence. *Journal of Biosocial Science* 5:347–62.

Dickens, B. M. 1966. *Abortion and the law.* Bristol: Macgibbon and Kee.

Dickinson, R. L., and Bryant, L. F. S. 1938. *Control of conception: a clinical medical manual.* 2nd ed. Baltimore: Williams and Wilkens.

Dytrych, Z., Matejcek, Z., Schüller, V., David, H. P., and Friedman, H. L. 1975. Children born to women denied abortion. *Family Planning Perspectives* 7:165–71.

Erhardt, C. L., Tietze, C., and Nelson, F. G. 1970. United States: therapeutic abortions in New York City. *Studies in Family Planning* 1, no. 51, pp. 8–9.

Faundes, A., and Luukkainen, T. 1972. Health and family planning services in the Chinese People's Republic. *Studies in Family Planning* 3:165–76.

Fawcett, J. T. 1970. *Psychology and population.* New York: Population Council.

———. 1973. *Psychological perspectives on population.* New York: Basic Books.

Feinberg, L. *Washington Post*, 11 September 1978.

Field, M. G. 1956. The re-legalization of abortion in Soviet Russia. *New England Journal of Medicine* 255:421–27.

Fischman, S. H. 1975. The pregnancy resolution decisions of unwed adolescents. *Nursing Clinics of North America* 10:217–27.

Forrest, J. D., Sullivan, E. and Tietze, C., 1979. Abortion in the United States, 1977–1978. *Family Planning Perspectives* 11:329–41.

Francome, C., and Francome, C. 1979. Towards an understanding of the American abortion rate. *Journal of Biosocial Science* 11:303–13.

Friedman, H. L., Johnson, R. L., and David, H. P. 1976. Dynamics of fertility choice behavior: a pattern for research. In S. H. Newman and V. D. Thompson, eds., *Population psychology: research and educational issues*. HEW Publication no. (NIH) 76-574, pp. 171–98. Washington, D.C.: Center for Population Research.

Gebhard, P. H., Pomeroy, W. B., Martin, C. E., and Christenson, C. V. 1958. *Pregnancy, birth and abortion*. New York: Harper.

Goethals, G. R. 1979. The decision-making balance sheet. *Contemporary Psychology* 24:611–13.

Gordon, L. 1976. *Woman's body: woman's right*. New York: Grossman/Viking.

Green, C. 1979. Personal communication.

Group for the Advancement of Psychiatry. 1969. *The right to abortion: a psychiatric view*. Report no. 75. New York.

Haas, P. H. 1974. Wanted and unwanted pregnancies: a fertility decision-making model. *Journal of Social Issues* 30:125–65.

Harmsen, H. 1950. Notes on abortion and birth control in Germany. *Population Studies* 3:402–5.

Hatcher, S. L. 1975. The adolescent experience of pregnancy and abortion. In D. G. McGuigan, ed., *New research on women at the University of Michigan*, pp. 120–25. Ann Arbor: University of Michigan Center for Continuing Education.

Hellman, L. M., and Pritchard, J. A. with Wynn, R. M. 1971. *Williams Obstetrics*. 14th ed. New York: Appleton-Century-Crofts.

Hern, W. M. 1979. *Abortion services handbook*. Chicago: Interfacia.

Hiatt, F. 1976. Mother was surprised. *The Washingtonian*, December 1976.

Himes, N. E. 1936. *Medical history of contraception*. Baltimore: Williams and Wilkins.

Hodge, H. L. 1869. *Foeticide or criminal abortion*. Philadelphia: Lindsay and Blakiston.

Hogue, C. 1975. Low birth weight subsequent to induced abortion: a historical prospective study of 948 women in Skopje, Yugoslavia. *American Journal of Obstetrics and Gynecology* 123:675–81.

Hungary/Central Statistical Office. 1969. *Survey techniques in fertility and family research: experience in Hungary*. Budapest.

Institute of Medicine. 1975. *Legalized abortion and the public health*. Washington: National Academy of Sciences.

International Planned Parenthood Federation. 1974. *Survey of world needs in population*. London.

———. 1978. Unmet needs. *People*, 5, (3), pp. 25–32.

Jaffe, F. 1977. Letter to the *Washington Post*. *Washington Memo*, 3 August 1977.

Janis, I. C., and Mann, L. 1977. *Decision making: a psychological analysis of conflict, choice, and commitment*. New York: Free Press.

Kapor-Stanulovic, N., and Friedman, H. L. 1978. Studies in choice behavior in Yugoslavia. In H. P. David, H. L. Friedman, J. v. d. Tak, and M. Sevilla, eds., *Abortion in psychosocial perspective: trends in transnational research*, pp. 119–44. New York: Springer.

Kessler, J., and Weiss, T. 1974. Ward staff problems with abortion. *International Journal of Psychiatry in Medicine* 5:97–103.

LoSciuto, L. A., Balin, H., and Zahn, M. A. 1972. Physicians' attitudes toward abortion. *Journal of Reproductive Medicine* 9:70–74.

Luker, K. 1975. *Taking chances: abortion and the decision not to contracept.* Berkeley: University of California Press.

———. 1977. Contraceptive risk taking and abortion: results and implications of a San Francisco Bay area study. *Studies in Family Planning* 8:190–96.

McCormick, E. P., Johnson, R. L., Friedman, H. L., and David, H. P. 1977. Psychosocial aspects of fertility regulation. In J. Money and H. Musaph, eds., *Handbook of sexology*, pp. 621–53. Amsterdam: Excerpta Medica.

Matejcek, Z., Dytrych, Z., and Schüller, V. 1978. Children from unwanted pregnancies. *Acta Psychiatrica Scandinavica* 57:67–90.

———. 1979a. The Prague study of children born from unwanted pregnancies. *International Journal of Mental Health* 7:63–77.

———. 1979b. Follow-up study of children born from unwanted pregnancies. Unpublished paper, 1979.

Means, C. C. 1968. The law of New York concerning abortion and the status of the foetus, 1664–1968: a case of cessation of constitutionality. *New York Law Forum* 14:411–515.

———. 1970. A historian's view. In R. Hall, ed., *Abortion in a changing world*, vol. 1, 16–24; vol. 2, 137–42. New York: Columbia University Press.

Miller, W. B. 1972. Personality and ego factors relative to family planning and population control. Conference proceedings: *Psychological measurement in the study of population problems.* Berkeley: University of California, Institute of Personality Assessment and Research.

———. 1973. Psychological vulnerability to unwanted pregnancy. *Family Planning Perspectives* 5:199–201.

———. 1976. Sexual and contraceptive behavior in young women. *Primary Care* 3:427–53.

———. 1978. The intendedness and wantedness of the first child. In W. B. Miller and C. F. Newman, eds., *The first child and family formation*, pp. 209–43. Chapel Hill: Carolina Population Center.

Misra, B. 1966. Correlates of male attitude toward family planning. In D. Bogue, ed., *Sociological contributions to family planning research.* Chicago: University of Chicago Press.

Mohr, J. C. 1978. *Abortion in America: the origins and evolution of national policy, 1800–1900.* New York: Oxford University Press.

Muramatsu, M. 1974. The Japanese experience. In H. P. David, ed., *Abortion research: international experience*, pp. 135–36. Lexington: Lexington Books.

Nathanson, C. A., and Becker, M. H. 1977. The influence of physicians' attitudes on abortion performance, patient management and professional fees. *Family Planning Perspectives* 9:158–63.

Nazer, I. R. 1972. *Induced abortion: A hazard to public health?* Beirut: International Planned Parenthood Federation.

Nebraska, State of. 1979. Nebraska Criminal Code, sections 28–101 to 28–1335 of 1977, operative as of 1 January 1979 and as amended by Legislative Bill 316 of 1979.

New Zealand. 1977. Act of 1977, no. 112.

Noonan, J. 1970. *The morality of abortion: legal and historical perspectives.* Cambridge: Harvard University Press.

Ooms, T., and Maciocha, T. 1979. *Teenage pregnancy and family impact.* Washington: George Washington University Family Impact Seminar.

Osofsky, J., and Osofsky, H. 1972. The psychological reactions of patients to legalized abortion. *American Journal of Orthopsychiatry* 42:48–60.

Pion, R. J., Smith, R. G., and Hale, R. W. 1973. The Hawaii experience. In H. J. Osofsky and J. D. Osofsky, eds., *The abortion experience*, pp. 177–87. Hagerstown: Harper and Row.

Pohlman, E. W. 1973. *The psychology of birth planning.* Cambridge, Mass.: Schenkman.

Population Crisis Committee. 1979. World population trends. *Population*, no. 9.

Potts, M. 1971. Impact of English abortion laws on the practice of medicine. In A. J. Sobrero and R. M. Harvey, eds., *Advances in planned parenthood*, 6, pp. 145–57. Amsterdam: Excerpta Medica.

———. 1979. Perspectives on fertility control. *International Journal of Gynaecology and Obstetrics* 16:449–55.

Rains, P. M. 1971. *Becoming an unwed mother: a sociological account.* Chicago: Aldine-Atherton.

Rosen, R. A., Werley, H. A., Ager, J. W., and Shea, F. P. 1974. Health professionals: attitudes toward abortion. *Public Opinion Quarterly* 38:158–73.

Rosen, R. A., and Martindale, J. J. 1978. Sex role perceptions and the abortion decision. *Journal of Sex Research* 14:231–45.

Rosoff, J. I., ed. 1979. *Washington Memo*, 6 July: W-10.

Rotter, J. B. 1966. Generalized expectancies for internal versus external control of reinforcement. *Psychological Monographs* 80(1):1–28.

Schneider, S. M., and Thompson, D. S. 1976. Repeat aborters. *American Journal of Obstetrics and Gynecology* 126:316–20.

Simmons, A. B. 1977. The VOC approach in population policies: new hope or false promise? Paper presented at the IUSSP International Population Conference, Mexico City, August 1977.

Sklar, J., and Berkov, B. 1974. Teenage family formations in postwar America. *Family Planning Perspectives* 6:80–90.

Smith, J. C. 1977. Development of national abortion statistics in the United States. Paper presented at the IUSSP International Population Conference, Mexico City, August 1977.

Smith, M. B. 1973. A social-psychological view of fertility. In J. T. Fawcett, ed., *Psychological perspectives on population*, pp. 3–18. New York: Basic Books. 3–18.

———. 1978. Decision making and psychological antecedents: a discussion. In W. B. Miller and C. F. Newman, eds., *The first child and family formation*, pp. 266–72. Chapel Hill: Carolina Population Center.

Smith, M. S., Kahan, R. S., and Burr, W. A. 1974. Legal induced abortions in the United States, 1969–1972. Paper presented to the World Population Society, February 1974.

Steinhoff, P. G. 1973. Background characteristics of abortion patients. In H. J. Osofsky and J. D. Osofsky, eds., *The abortion experience*, pp. 206–31. Hagerstown: Harper and Row.

———. 1978. Premarital pregnancy and first birth. In W. B. Miller and C. F. Newman, eds., *The first child and family formation*, pp. 180–208. Chapel Hill: Carolina Population Center.

Steinhoff, P. G., Palmore, J. A., Smith, R. G., Morsky, D. E., and Pion, R. J.

1975. Pregnancy planning in Hawaii. *Family Planning Perspectives* 7:138–42.

Steinhoff, P. G., Smith, R. G., and Diamond, M. 1972. The Hawaii pregnancy birth control and abortion study: social-psychological aspects. Conference proceedings: *Psychological measurement in the study of population problems*, pp. 33–40. Berkleley: Institute of Personality Assessment and Research, University of California.

Stewart, P. L. 1978. A survey of obstetrician-gynecologists' abortion attitudes and performances. *Medical Care* 16:1036–44.

Stycos, J. M., Back, K. W., and Hill, R. 1956. Problems of communication between husband and wife on matters relating to family limitation. *Human Relations* 9:207–15.

Sullivan, E., Tietze, C., and Dryfoos, J. G. 1977. Legal abortion in the United States, 1975–1976. *Family Planning Perspectives* 9:116–29.

Swigar, M. E., Breslin, R., Pouzzner, M. G., Quinlan, D., and Blum, M. 1976. Interview followup of abortion applicant dropouts. *Social Psychiatry* 11:135–43.

Swigar, M. E., Quinlan, D. M., and Wexler, S. D. 1977. Abortion applicants: characteristics distinguishing dropouts remaining pregnant and those having abortions. *American Journal of Public Health* 67:142–46.

Tietze, C. 1970. United States: therapeutic abortions, 1963–1968. *Studies in Family Planning* 1, no. 59, pp. 5–7.

———. 1978. Repeat abortions—why more? *Family Planning Perspectives* 10:286–88.

———. 1979a. *Induced abortion: 1979*. 3rd ed. New York: Population Council.

———. 1979b. Induced abortion: worldwide trends. Paper presented to the American Psychological Association, New York, September 1979.

———. 1979c. Unintended pregnancies in the United States, 1970–1972. *Family Planning Perspectives* 11:186–88.

———. 1979d. Personal communication, October 1979.

Tietz, C., Bongaarts, J., and Schearer, B. 1976. Mortality associated with the control of fertility. *Family Planning Perspectives* 8:6–14.

Tietze, C., and Jain, A. K. 1978. The mathematics of repeat abortion: explaining the increase. *Studies in Family Planning* 9:294–99.

Tietze, C., and Lewit, S. 1978. The universal practice. *People* 5(2):4–7.

Tunnadine, D., and Green, R. 1978. *Unwanted pregnancy: accident or illness?* New York: Oxford University Press.

Tydings, J. D. 1979. Congress leads the way in U.S. population policies. *Draper Fund Report*, no. 7, pp. 3–5.

United States Supreme Court. 1973. *Roe* v. *Wade* and *Doe* v. *Bolton*. 22 January 1973.

Vincent, C. 1961. *Unmarried mothers*. New York: Free Press.

Washington Post. 8 March 1979.

Westoff, C. F., and Jones, E. F. 1977. Contraception and sterilization in the United States, 1965–1975. *Family Planning Perspectives* 9:153–57.

Williams, G. 1957. *The sanctity of life and the criminal law*. New York: Knopf.

World Health Organization. 1971. *Abortion laws: a survey of current world legislation*. Geneva.

Wu, Y. T., and Wu, H. C. 1958. Suction in artificial abortion: three hundred cases. *Chinese Journal of Obstetrics and Gynecology* 6:447.

Wyatt, F. 1967. Clinical notes on the motives of reproduction. *Journal of Social Issues* 23:29–56.

Zelnik, M., and Kantner, J. F. 1974. The resolution of teenage first pregnancies. *Family Planning Perspectives* 6:74–90.

————. 1977. Sexual and contraceptive experience of young unmarried women in the United States, 1976 and 1971. *Family Planning Perspectives* 9:55–71.

4

SCIENCE AND ITS USES: THE ABORTION DEBATE AND SOCIAL SCIENCE RESEARCH

MARY ANN LAMANNA

I T SEEMED CLEAR to both Auguste Comte, a nineteenth-century sociologist, and myself, at the time a sophomore French major, that social science has the wonderful purpose of illuminating important social issues, solving social problems, and shaping public policy. Comte, founding father of sociology, saw "the rational coordination of the fundamental sequence of the various events of human history" (Comte 1839) to be an outcome of the positive science of sociology.

Convinced, I abandoned Proust for probability, thinking by such education to become involved in research leading to international cooperation and domestic social reform. It has proved not quite that simple, for reasons that go beyond my own inevitably limited abilities. For one thing, as I learned more about the woodsy lore of random samples and response rates, of interval scales and linear models, of tests of significance and nonrecursive systems, I found it easy enough to raise questions about the validity of social science research. Such an impediment to the marriage of social science and public policy is easy enough to understand. However, my faith remains that social science can have something valid to say.

What was and remains somewhat astonishing to a *naïf* such as myself was the discovery that social science research is often neither used nor useful in the consideration of public issues. Opinion formation on many problems often proceeds as though relevant social science research neither exists nor could exist. The abortion debate has been a striking example of the failure of the public discussion of an important social issue to be informed by the knowledge which social science has to offer.

In this study I will summarize research on the social aspects of abortion, noting the gap between this research and arguments for and against abortion (and by "abortion" I mean legalized, unrestricted abortion). Many assumptions about abortion are called into question by social science research, yet the debate goes on, on its own terms.

THE ABORTION ISSUE

Abortion is an issue which won't go away. Long a controversial matter, it appeared resolved by the Supreme Court decisions of 1973. But there is continuing litigation and legislation—Nebraska, my home state, has passed abortion laws implementing the Supreme Court decisions, only to have them partially struck down in federal district court through lawsuits filed by both abortion providers and right-to-life groups seeking to act as guardians ad litem for the abortees. This is not untypical.

Abortion continues to be a major political issue, with debatable effects on election outcomes (e.g., Rosoff 1975). The effort to amend the Constitution to forbid abortion gains momentum, while a concern by proponents of legalized abortion about tacit refusal of many public and private hospitals to perform abortions (only one-fifth of public hospitals performed *any* abortions in 1975 and abortion services were unavailable in 78 percent of the U.S. counties—Forrest, Tietze, and Sullivan 1978) is accentuated by the cutoff of federal funds, restricting access to abortion on the basis of economic resources (Alan Guttmacher Institute 1979). Pictures of women dead from illegal abortions and maps of firebombed abortion clinics (*Newsweek* 1978a) are exchanged for pictures of dead fetuses.

And so the abortion debate continues. It grows more raucous and strident and seems to be settling in as a permanent feature of the American political scene, like the gold standard in its time, though with perhaps less oratorical style.

THE ABORTION DEBATE AND SOCIAL SCIENCE

Public debate and private discussion on abortion are necessary preliminary steps toward the resolution of controversial issues. Debate and discussion could clarify and could lead to convergence on a middle ground of common concerns, but this is not happening in the abortion debate. The two sides seem to be shouting past each other. The abortion debate has the character of a shadow play, with stereotyped arguments and images that are flattened and without detail.

The abortion debate can be reduced to two slogans: "right to life" and "a woman's control over her own body." To term these phrases "slogans" is not to discount the validity of the principles they represent. It is to point out that these principles for decision making about abortion are absolutes; by their claims they foreclose dialogue. (One can hardly argue against a right to life or a right of a woman to control her own body.)

Social science has little to offer those who have taken their position on abortion or made decisions about abortion on the sole basis of either of these principles. If the fetus has an absolute right to life, there is nothing further to be said. If the woman has an absolute right to control the reproductive use of her body, there is nothing further to be said. But these valid principles are in conflict. Furthermore, each obscures by its arbitrary resolution of the issues that some of the terms can be questioned.

We have cultural systems for resolving conflicting principles, as life in society rarely presents us with easy cases. Ethics can be viewed as not the arbitrary application of a single principle, but the process of resolving tragic conflicts between two goods or two evils in particular cases. The legal system deals with rights in conflicts. Politics offers a pragmatic compromise of varying interests and values in a pluralistic society.

Part of such resolution of conflicting principles or values involves a consideration of the anticipated effects of questionable acts. Here social science can be of some use. It can tell us about the effects of an act, here abortion, on the individuals who make up a society and on the society as a whole. Individual and societal decisions about abortion can hardly be made without knowledge of the social effects of abortion. Yet debate focuses on two simple, polar phrases, without serious and detailed consideration of the effects of the act of abortion.

Social science can inform the debate on abortion by providing us with knowledge about its social effects. This will do several things for the abortion debate, which I term: (1) "fleshing out"; (2) "facing reality"; and (3) "meeting in the middle."

1. Social science research can flesh out the abortion debate. For the most part, rhetoric on abortion does not tell us much about the human detail of abortion or the outcomes:

Who gets abortions and why? How do they feel about it? What are their lives like? What would their lives have been like? What happens to the women and their families in the future? What happens to children who are unwanted, if they are born, etc.? These are questions about abortion which have been or could be answered by social science research.

2. Social science research can help both sides face reality. One of the striking features for a social scientist of the public debate on abortion is the extent to which each side is able to ignore important facts which would threaten the simplism of its position. "Right-to-lifers" find it easy to ignore the plight of the pregnant teenagers and the illegal abortion death rate. Proponents of abortion find it easy to ignore the tenuous nature of unwantedness and the negative emotional effects of abortion. One task falling to the social scientist is to cry out the realities ignored in absolutist positions. These represent factors which must be taken into account if a workable solution to the abortion problem is to be found.

3. Perhaps social science, by bringing the abortion debate into the realm of empirical reality, can effect some meeting in the middle. By focusing on realistic detail, the social scientist can draw energy from rhetorical stances into realistic problem solving which might spark some commonality of concern. While there has heretofore been no middle ground in the abortion debate, there is nowhere else to meet but the middle.

In essence, social science research can contribute the details about social effects necessary for weighing alternatives in a nonabsolutist political, legal, or ethical resolution of this tragic dilemma of abortion. Can do so, but doesn't necessarily, for there is a gap between the rhetorical portrayal of abortion and the research evidence. In the middle sections of this paper, I will discuss the social science research relevant to some aspects of the abortion debate. In the last section, I will discuss some reasons for the gap between the abortion debate and social science research, a gap which will be demonstrated in the course of this review.

CHALLENGING ASSUMPTIONS

One reason that the abortion debate has been reduced to

the simplistic juxtaposition of two principles is that each position is supported by a number of unstated assumptions—unstated, that is, as essential to the position, but nevertheless functioning to make a focus on one or another slogan more palatable. Social science research can challenge some of these assumptions, of both sides of the debate, though it may also support some. In any event, it can bring the abortion debate into the realm of empirical reality, where any viable solution must be found.

Some Proabortion Assumptions

Assumptions sometimes expressed in support of the proabortion position are the following:

1. Abortion is health care (Sullivan et al. 1977; Institute of Medicine 1975).
2. Abortion is needed to resolve the problem of rape / incest pregnancies (Rothstein n.d.; Yeo 1977).
3. Abortion is needed to resolve the problem of genetically defective children (Rothstein n.d.; Yeo 1977).
4. Abortion is needed to resolve a threat to the mother's life or to her physical health (Furlong-Cahill 1974; National Association for the Repeal of Abortion Laws n.d.; American Lutheran Church 1970).
5. Abortion is needed by mothers of large families, who would not have the economic or emotional resources to take care of their existing children if they had the responsibility of a new pregnancy (Yeo 1977).
6. Abortion is necessary to eliminate poverty (Rothstein n.d.; David et al. 1978:4).
7. Abortion is necessary to improve the position of blacks (American Lutheran Church 1970).
8. Abortion is necessary for female equality (Furlong-Cahill 1974; Smeal 1974).
9. Abortion can enable a woman to straighten out her life and make it busy, productive, and nondependent (on welfare), eventuating in a stable, happy family life (Rothstein n.d.).
10. Abortion is supported by a clear majority of the American public including Catholics (Mulhauser 1978; Smeal 1974).

11. Abortion is not emotionally upsetting, but is taken in stride by women (Rothstein n.d.). It does not produce "psychological problems" (Rodgers 1979). It is an easy decision, with few regrets (Yeo 1977). Abortion affects only the woman ("a woman's control over her own body").
12. The children who are aborted are unwanted (Rothstein n.d.).
13. These unwanted children would have miserable lives, would be rejected by their parents, perhaps beaten, would live in dire poverty, and would be better off not born (Yeo 1977; American Lutheran Church 1970).
14. Legal abortion is necessary to cut abortion deaths (American Lutheran Church 1970). It is a very safe medical procedure (National Association for the Repeal of Abortion Laws n.d.; Schardt 1973; Mulhauser 1978).
15. Abortion will lower the birth rate; is necessary to lower the birth rate (Religious Coalition for Abortion Rights n.d.).
16. Abortion is an emergency solution, not a regular means of fertility control.

These assumptions, taken together, say that abortion has many good effects and is not really hurting anybody. The child, having little to lose in the way of a good life, is included in this conclusion. If one believes these assumptions, one can indeed permit to the woman the free choice of elective abortion without controls or restrictions.

Some Antiabortion Assumptions

Supporting assumptions to the "right to life" or antiabortion position are as follows:

1. "Babies are always a joy" (observation by a professor at a large university medical school).
2. Women who have abortions do so for frivolous reasons (Rothstein n.d.)
3. Women who have abortions are promiscuous, and any problems arising from the pregnancy are deserved punishment (Rothstein n.d.; comment in a health planning agency meeting).
4. Women who have abortions were irresponsible in hav-

ing intercourse and/or not using contraception, therefore should assume the responsibility of the baby (comment by prolife spokesman).

5. Women who carry to term will love and want the baby (Rothstein n.d.).

6. Women can have the baby and give it up for adoption ("Adoption, not Abortion"—bumper sticker).

7. Women who have abortions will suffer incapacitating guilt and emotional turmoil (American Lutheran Church 1970).

8. If abortion is not legally available, it will die out (Schardt 1973).

9. If abortion is available, people will not use contraception but will come to rely exclusively on abortion for fertility control (Rothstein n.d.; Somers and Gammeltoft 1976).

10. Proabortionists are not concerned about human life or about women, but about population control (The Master's Plan n.d.).

Taken together, these assumptions are saying that pregnancy is not a problem, and if it is, the woman's needs are mitigated by her culpability and/or her responsibility for the pregnancy. Resistance to abortion can be viewed as resistance to a conspiratorial and inhuman regulation of population. If one believes these assumptions, one can assert the right of the infant to life as compatible with the social good and unqualified by competing needs of the mother or others.

Both absolutist positions are more tenable with their supporting assumptions. These serve as techniques of neutralization, which deny a victim or injury, condemn the condemners, and appeal to high loyalties or goods (Brennan 1974, extended). Social science can inform us of the validity of these assumptions; a review of the relevant data will show some of them to be myths.

The above assumptions, on both sides of the debate, may be grouped into several research questions:

1. What categories of women obtain abortions; why, and with what effects on their social and personal circumstances?

2. What is the process of deciding about an abortion and what

is its emotional impact?

3. What might have been the future of an unborn child if not aborted?

4. What are the demographic and public health effects of abortion? More generally—what individual and social problems is abortion solving? At what cost?

ARE ABORTIONS HEALTH CARE?

Before going any farther, it is necessary to deal with the common assumption that abortion is health care, i.e., that it is exclusively within the decision-making province of medical professionals. For example, Forrest, Tietze, and Sullivan (1978) refer to "the reluctance of the established medical system to provide this necessary medical service" (p. 276). The earlier prevalence of the term "therapeutic abortion" and the current "a woman and her doctor" support the conceptualization of abortion as a medical event. The Institute of Medicine's comprehensive report on abortion (1975) claims that " 'health effects' is a broad concept that could include almost all aspects of personal and social well-being. . . . The health effects of abortion include physical, mental, and social outcomes of the procedure" (p. 9). The Supreme Court did place abortion decisions within the competence of the physician. In an argument for Medicaid support for abortion, which might better have rested on the grounds of social equality, Senator Brooke maintained that "the Senate should not dictate medical decisions which a physician, and a physician alone, is trained to make" (Alan Guttmacher Institute 1979).

If, in fact, abortion is simply health care, then the issue is removed from political, legal, and ethical decision making and becomes the technical implementation of a medical service. But is abortion health care—or only health care?

Very few abortions can be considered health care in the sense of the maintenance of physical health. Data indicate that few abortions are performed for maternal physical health reasons, probably under 2 percent (Illsley and Hall 1978; U.S. Department of Health, Education and Welfare 1971). In the remainder of cases abortion is employed as a solution to individual and social problems—problems of the stigma and burden of a pregnancy out of wedlock, of reduction of family responsibilities for poor or working women; problems of teenage marriage and parenthood, of poverty and discrimination, of population growth, of physically and mentally handicapped children, of child abuse and neglect. Calling abortion a health remedy obfuscates the decisions that are being made and prevents evaluation of abortion as an efficacious solution to the problems named.

Sociologists and socially oriented psychiatrists such as Thomas Szasz have pointed out the tendency in our society toward the medicalization of deviance, by which forms of deviant behavior or "problems in living" are converted to health questions. This transformation of social behavior into illness and therapy permits the avoidance of philosophical and political conflict and of personal responsibility for controversial forms of behavior (Szasz 1960, 1974). The power of the medical incantation relative to abortion can be seen by the degree to which invoking medical authority ("a woman and her physician") elevates the percentage of the public supporting abortion (Blake 1973, 1977a). Calling attention to the limited use of abortion as purely a health remedy forces the issue into the political and social arena and places it within the framework of ethical choice, where it belongs.

WHO OBTAINS ABORTIONS: WHAT PROBLEMS DO THEY SOLVE?

The debate over abortion could be illuminated considerably by simple attention to data on who obtains abortions. The case for abortion is often made in terms of the rape-pregnancy of a young girl (Michael Rappaport, cited in *Omaha World Herald* 1979). More comprehensively, abortion is presented as a solution to problems of rape/incest pregnancy, children who will be genetically defective, "tired mothers," teenage pregnancy and illegitimacy, racial and ethnic discrimination, poverty, and women's liberation. By looking at data on who obtains abortion we can get some sense of the actual social impact of abortion.

1. *Rape/incest victims; genetic defect.* Abortions do not primarily go to victims of rape or incest or to cut short pregnancies likely to result in defective children. As a debate strategy, the rape victim can provide a foothold for an attack

on absolute opposition to abortion. As a legitimation of abortion, however, it falls short, since at most 5 percent of abortions are performed for reasons of rape or incest, genetic defect, and mother's health taken together (DHEW 1971; Luker 1975).*

2. *"Tired mothers."* Abortions do not primarily go to "tired mothers," women exhausted by childbearing and the care of large families. Only 23 percent of the women obtaining abortions in 1977 were married. The number of abortions decreases with parity; over 50 percent of all abortions go to women with no children; 20 percent to women with one child; 15 percent to women with two children; only 3.4 percent to women with five or more children (U.S. DHEW 1979). Abortion, then, is serving very few mothers of large families.

3. *Teen parents.* Does abortion prevent a life of poverty and other disadvantages of teenage parenthood? One-third of all abortions are obtained by teenagers, 3.7 percent of whom are fifteen or under. The group of women under fifteen had the highest abortion ratio (of abortions to live births), with more abortions than births. Abortion ratios for the remaining teen years are also high (U.S. DHEW 1978). Abortions, then, *are* ending the pregnancies of teenagers.

The effects of continued pregnancy and birth on the future of these young parents are open to debate. A host of data suggest that teenage parenthood reduces the life chances of women and their families in the areas of occupational attainment, income, and assets; education and welfare dependency; stable marriage and fertility (Furstenberg 1976a, 1976b; Card and Wise 1978; Alan Guttmacher Institute 1976; Moore 1978; McCarthy and Menken 1979; Freedman and Thornton 1979).

Furstenberg's *Unplanned Parenthood* (1976b), for exam-

---

*These data are old and/or geographically limited, but it seems reasonable that the direction of change since legalization of abortion is toward a smaller percentage of abortions in these categories. Abortions can now be easily obtained for other reasons. The Center for Disease Control's Abortion Surveillance does not collect data on the indications for abortion; formal indications, of course, are no longer required. A national sample survey of abortion patients would be a desirable, though difficult, alternative.

ple, reports a study of 404 mostly low income and predominantly black adolescents who were under eighteen and pregnant. They were interviewed for the first time between 1966 and 1968, and reinterviewed twice, the last time in 1972, when their child was about five. Comparisons with classmates indicate that the study population was likely to marry sooner, but less stably, having a less-than-even chance of the marriage surviving beyond the first four years. The rate of breakup of classmates' marriages was half that. "Ironically, most of the young mothers who managed to avoid single parenthood by marrying either before or shortly after delivery ended up as a single parent several years later" (Furstenberg 1976a:147). While many expressed a desire to finish high school or better and 70 percent returned to school after giving birth, few received as much education as the control group. They were also in less favorable circumstances in terms of jobs, income, and avoidance of welfare.

Note that this is a study comparing early parents with classmates who did not become parents, not a study comparing pregnant women who aborted with those who did not. Such a study was conducted at Johns Hopkins (Cushner et al. 1973), comparing thirty-eight patients who had abortions with a similar number who had babies. It found the former less likely to be on public assistance, more likely to have higher incomes, less likely to have had another baby, more likely to have married—thus, in many respects, better off than the latter.

These data do support the notion that babies in the situation of early parenthood not only present a considerable immediate burden, but deflect the lifetime trajectory downward in terms of the material conditions of life and family stability. One study found that not only first unions, but also remarriages of early parents were more likely to break up (McCarthy and Menken 1979). The high abortion ratio of teenagers suggests that abortion is a frequent solution to the problem of teenage pregnancy. Although teenage contraception is improving, a Planned Parenthood publication maintains that "the availability of legal abortion will remain critically important if adolescents are to be enabled to avoid unwanted births" (Alan Guttmacher Institute 1976).

Only Furstenberg questions the inevitability of the connection between early parenthood and life disadvantage. Furstenberg advocates facing openly the pregnancy risk of teenagers and implementing aggressive contraceptive programs. He supports abortion, but mentions that his sample parents were ambivalent or unfavorable in their attitudes toward abortion and speculates:

> What would happen if service programs made it easy, not difficult, for women to restore order in their lives following an unplanned pregnancy? Let us imagine that there were truly comprehensive and extended services for young parents and their children. Suppose, for example, that family planning programs to prevent unplanned pregnancies and to counsel women who did have unwanted conceptions were established in the schools. Suppose that a woman who elected to bring her pregnancy to term would be granted a child care allowance to purchase daycare services or to pay a relative or friend to care for her child while she completed her education or entered the labor force. And whether or not she remained in school, took a job, or assumed fulltime child care responsibilities, the young mother would receive an income sufficient to meet the needs of her family. Furthermore, suppose the fathers were invited to join special education or job-training programs or were provided with a steady job. Our results indicate that under conditions of economic security, most fathers would contribute to the support of the family and willingly maintain a relationship with their children. (Furstenberg 1976a:167)

Additional research does indicate that some of the detrimental consequences of early parenthood can be mitigated by support from family, friends, the child's father, and public assistance (Furstenberg and Crawford 1978; Presser 1978; Colletta and Gregg 1979). Furstenberg and Crawford in particular stressed the importance of kin and of governmental agencies working through kin:

> Present policies strike us all as ill-conceived and shortsighted because many of the solutions devised for coping with early parenthood run counter to or undermine existing natural support systems. Nothing in the behavior of the young women in our study or their families suggests that they were alienated from one another. Quite the contrary, these predominantly low income families provided support of all types, often at what must have been considerable sacrifice.

> Public programs should build on the strengths inherent in these

families. Financial assistance and other appropriate aid, such as child care, should be extended to families willing to help their young daughters to pick up the threads of their lives and advance their educational and occupational prospects. Assistance should go, as well, to the fathers if they show interest in supporting the young women and their children. Assistance should be given, when needed, to young married couples to try to strengthen their marriages. Present welfare rules often guarantee the breakup of many of these marriages since assistance is usually provided only when there is no male head of household. This is shortsighted, punitive and self-defeating. (Furstenberg and Crawford 1978:333)

The work of Furstenberg and Crawford, Presser, and Colletta and Gregg is based primarily on black subjects, among whom the pattern of early and out-of-wedlock childbearing is common, as is involvement of extended kin. Seventy percent of the whites in Furstenberg's sample (who were older and in more favorable economic circumstances) married, while 84 percent of blacks deferred marriage until after childbirth (Furstenberg and Crawford 1978).

Along these lines one has to consider an earlier and a contemporary study which focused on long-term consequences of early (Cutright 1973) or premarital (Freedman and Thornton 1979) pregnancy. (The preceding studies report short-term consequences; Moore's sample, for example, were all under twenty and Furstenberg's [1976a and b] under twenty-five.) Cutright's data indicated that fifteen to twenty years later, among ever-married women, "long-run effects of timing of the first birth seemed small" (p. 594). Thus, "while a premaritally conceived first birth may still create havoc and depressed circumstances in the early years of life; the lack of long run effects, however, indicates that most premaritally pregnant mothers act in ways which tend to overcome an initial disadvantage for themselves and their children" (p. 594).

Similarly, Freedman and Thornton found in a fifteen-year follow-up of white women giving birth in 1962 that

although couples in which the wife was pregnant at marriage are somewhat worse off economically than others, their disadvantage is less severe than might be expected, given commonly held views about the adverse consequences of extramarital conceptions. . . .

113

The study findings raise some question as to whether the long-run economic consequences for young people of a marriage precipitated by pregnancy may be less disastrous than the fairly severe short-term effects. Possibly, the emphasis in most popular and some scientific articles on the unfavorable consequences of premarital conceptions may reflect a lack of long-range perspective. Few single events are so life-shattering that they cannot be moderated, if not overcome, by at least some of those who experience them. Clearly, our study demonstrates that an early pregnancy-induced marriage has relatively unfavorable long-run economic consequences—consequences which may affect the futures of the children of such marriages. But at the same time, it must be acknowledged that over the long run the differences between the PMP couples and the others are not as dramatic as the early differences might have led us to expect.

Admittedly, the findings of the present study are only suggestive and we cannot ignore the possibility that the economic status of the PMP couples in this study reflects the sample composition and a propitious economic climate. The tentative findings do highlight the need for studies which permit a precise identification of underlying causal mechanisms. (Freedman and Thornton 1979:19 and 20)

One must note, as it limits generalizability to today's young women deciding about abortion, that the women in Freedman and Thornton's study were older, had married the father of the child, were white, and had part of their years of economic activity in good times.

While abortion is seen as one solution to the problem of teenage pregnancy, it nevertheless appears that social science researchers, having documented the negative impact of early or unwed parenthood on short-range life chances, have gone on to observe a less discouraging long-range impact and to study mechanisms for reducing the negative effects of such parenthood, if chosen. Social science research has taken seriously such supportive alternatives to abortion in a way that perhaps the general abortion debate has not.

One of the problems of this solution for teenagers, however, is that of maternal and child health complications for younger teenagers (here abortion can be a legitimate health issue). Teenage pregnancy carries a higher risk of maternal death, toxemia, and anemia. Babies of teenagers are more likely to be premature and of low birth weight; low birth weight is associated with infant mortality as well as with other childhood illness, and with birth injuries, including neurological deficits resulting in retardation (Alan Guttmacher Institute 1976).

While abortion, birth, and adoption are the only solutions to a pregnancy once conceived, social science researchers have taken considerable interest in contraception as a feasible preventive solution (Zelnik and Kantner 1978a) to an otherwise potentially increasing problem of teenage pregnancy (Tietze 1978a). They have documented public support for contraceptive services for teens (*Family Planning Perspectives* 1978a); the willingness of teens to utilize general family planning facilities (Dryfoos and Heisler 1978); the fact that provision of contraceptives does not encourage promiscuity among teenagers (Reichelt 1978); the importance of not requiring parent notification (Torres 1978); and increasing teenage contraceptive effectiveness (Zelnik and Kantner 1977).

4. *The poor and the black.* It is difficult to assess the impact of abortion on the problems of poverty and racial discrimination. Abortions *are* going disproportionately to poor women and to black women. Abortion rates are three times higher among very poor women, i.e., those eligible for Medicaid (Forrest, Tietze, and Sullivan 1978; Alan Guttmacher Institute 1979). In contrast to what might be predicted from traditional negative attitudes of blacks toward abortion (Rainwater 1966), blacks make up an increasing proportion of those receiving abortions—now one-third. The abortion rate is three times higher for blacks than for whites (U.S. DHEW 1978).

A study of abortion rates by area in New York City finds percentage black the single most important correlate of area abortion rates and concludes that, "by enabling blacks to avert what must have been a substantial number of unwanted births, and thereby to reproduce at a rate more compatible with the well-being of the family unit, abortion may rank as one of the great social equalizers of our time" (Kramer 1975). We need, however, more study of the interaction of poverty and abortion. The Kramer study is one of areas, not individuals, and subject to the ecological fallacy. The conclusion that abortion has reduced black poverty goes well beyond her data. We actually know little about the direct effects of abortion on poverty or on the lot of blacks. As noted earlier, studies do indicate that teen parents are economically disadvantaged, using welfare status as an indicator, but only one of the studies reviewed here is a specific comparison of abortion vs. term delivery teen patients (Cushner et al. 1973). We know little about the effects of abortion on the poverty status of older mothers and already formed families.

There is considerable magical thinking in the abortion rhetoric, especially considering that most women undergoing abortion have no or few children. The poverty effect of abortion would seem to have to do with a very young person's start in life, rather than with relieving an established family of the burden of too many mouths. With or without abortion, much remains to be done to wipe out poverty and discrimination, and in my opinion too much efficacy should not be attributed to abortion.

There are two other points which need to be made about the connection between poverty and abortion. In the Kramer study discussed above, it was reported that *within* black and white racial groups in the New York City study, it was the relatively better-off areas, those with higher education and higher income, which had the highest abortion rates (Kramer 1975). A study in Hawaii found middle-class patients more likely to resort to abortion, especially the young and never-married (middle- and working-class women were equally likely to undergo a later abortion; Steinhoff 1973). Luker (1975) found in California that less than one-third of the women obtaining abortions in 1970 could be classified as poor. She points out that many abortion patients are not victims of poverty, but rather women who have relationship-testing, -maintenance, or -enhancement reasons for not using contraception or for letting themselves get pregnant, or women who have miscalculated the risk of pregnancy or the ultimate desirability of an additional child. They are, in other words, women with less pressing economic and family-size circumstances, who are often contraceptively sophisticated. Some abortions, then, are going to disadvantaged classes and mitigate their distressed circumstances; others are going to relatively advantaged groups and do not have much reference to poverty.

One can also question the choices open to poor pregnant women. As Harrison (1978) says in her *Ms.* review of a book on abortion,

> many poor women abort because they are poor; many women "wanted" babies, but couldn't "afford" them. Where should one direct one's anger? Toward the life-isn't-fair people who would deny the women the right to abort, or toward the economic system (perpetuated, of course, by the same life-isn't-fair people) that allows poverty and affluence to coexist and forces women to abort? (p. 98; see also Dyck 1972)

5. *Other.* We have singled out some categories of women presumed to have special need for abortion—the physically ill; bearers of potentially defective children or rape/incest conceptions; mothers of large families; teenagers; poor women; black women. Abortion is usually justified in terms of some or all of these categories. But these categories do not account for all of the women who obtain abortions—who are the others, who are white (two-thirds of all abortions), out of their teens (two-thirds), with one or no children (two-thirds), of non-Medicaid status (over three-fourths*—Medicaid status, of course, is an indicator of only the direst poverty)? We have no way of combining women in the various preceding categories to learn how many abortions go to women who have none of these indications. Nevertheless, it seems likely they are a substantial proportion of all abortions.

The abortion need of this residual category is rarely discussed. Prolifers reject what are considered to be more compelling reasons. Proponents of elective abortion leap from justification of abortion by the claims of rape/incest and other previously mentioned categories to abortion as an unquestioned right, skipping over this residual group. Reasons for abortion of this group of older (than teenage),

---

*Calculated as follows:

$$1 - \frac{\text{Medicaid-paid abortions fiscal year 1977 (AGI 1979)}}{\text{Total abortions, 1977 (estimated, Forrest, Tietze, and Sullivan 1978:272)}}$$

which, if anything, would overstate the percentage of Medicaid abortions, because the total abortion denominator is for 1977, and would be smaller than the total for fiscal year 1977, which would include part of 1978, with an increased rate of abortion.

not desperately poor women with few or no children have not been catalogued quantitatively.*

We can at any rate assume that these abortions are intended as a solution to personal problems related to personal goals and interpersonal relationships of the parents—cases in which a pregnancy might create marital problems because it was conceived in an extramarital relationship; or where another child would generally strain the marriage or increase the tension of an already stressed household; cases where divorce is imminent (Rindfuss and Bumpass 1977 point out the extensiveness of "post-marital" fertility); where promising careers might be derailed; where an effort to convert a relationship into a marriage failed. Inasmuch as three-quarters of abortion recipients are single, one can assume that problems of stigma, or of deteriorated family relationships, and fears of single parenthood (Bracken, Klerman, and Bracken 1978) are part of the decision.

I would not characterize such reasons for abortion as frivolous. Indications for abortion which do not fit into any other category are often summarily dismissed as whimsical and unserious. Of course, there can be such reasons among abortion seekers, and Harrison complains about women who "chose to abort because . . . they didn't want to be cursed with morning sickness while on a Caribbean vacation" (1978:97). At present we have no way of knowing for what reasons and with what degree of seriousness abortions in this residual category are obtained. But certainly many of the reasons are matters that we would consider serious personal problems if presented to friends or counselors.

---

*This could be a good point at which to note the paucity of comprehensive national data on women who abort. The Abortion Surveillance of the Center for Disease Control (U.S. DHEW 1978) confines itself to basic demographics, not including class, religion, or motive for abortion. Other studies are of small, not necessarily representative, samples. We need a more comprehensive registration and reporting system, which is not likely, given court decisions about privacy and our traditional absence of social accounting—the most complete data comes for the socialist regimes of Eastern Europe or from the Scandinavian societies, also accustomed to extensive social controls. We need a national survey which includes depth interviews—again, it would be difficult to contact abortion recipients given closed records, and one could not depend on a general sample survey's capturing a sufficiently large, representative sample of abortion recipients.

We need to give this residual category more attention in the abortion debate. At present, proabortionists tend to legitimate abortion in terms of more acceptable categories of needs, while antiabortionists dismiss such reasons as frivolous and refuse to hear problems. The abortion debate should include discussion of this miscellaneous category, for it is likely to increase as a proportion of all abortions. To the extent that poverty is decreased and teenagers learn to contracept, those categories will account for fewer abortions. Physical health, genetic defect, rape/incest, and tired mother reasons account for few now, so that the residual category will make up an ever-increasing proportion of abortions. Furthermore, among those who are normally effective contraceptors, personal crisis and strained interpersonal relationships are associated with erratic use of contraception (Luker 1975; Rindfuss and Bumpass 1977). Such situations are likely to increase with the stress of social change in contemporary society and in particular with the change that is occurring in male-female premarital and marital relationships (Luker 1975).

Antiabortion rhetoric trivializes such personal crisis reasons—reasons that may involve the breakup of a marriage, family stress, and the poor bargaining position of today's young women in the marital marketplace (Francke 1978; Luker 1975). The public does not view such grounds as sufficient justification for abortion. Only the so-called hard reasons for abortion—mother's life and health in a narrow sense, rape/incest pregnancy, and genetic defect—come anywhere near majority support; unmarried pregnancy, economic reasons, and the simple preference of the family not to have another child are disapproved by a majority as reasons for abortion (Blake 1973, 1977a, 1977b; *Family Planning Perspectives* 1978a). It then becomes tempting to argue the case for abortion in terms that are powerfully appealing to the American public; hence the rape victim. Not only is this sleight-of-hand fraudulent, it is also unlikely to lead to a stable solution to the abortion problem. The case for abortion ought to be argued in terms not of these "hard" indications (on which there is considerable national consensus), but in terms of the reality of abortion—teenagers, poor and black women, *and* the unmarried and others with personal problems of a more or less serious nature. Will one accept these indications for abortion—or not?

In the process, the same problem of magical thinking about the problem-solving efficacy of abortion referred to in the discussion of poverty needs to be considered more generally; that is, will an abortion solve an individual's problems? In some cases a one-time situational problem will be solved by abortion; in others, the abortion and the need for it are part of a real or perceived lack of control over one's life and/or fertility to which one abortion will make little difference (Francke 1978; Kapor-Stanulovic and Friedman 1978; Leach 1977) and a pattern of repeated pregnancies can be expected (Bracken, Klerman, and Bracken 1978). We will discuss the issues of repeat abortions and contraceptive efficacy in a later section; here, it's appropriate to note that the issue of the woman's responsibility for bearing the child—given her contraceptive "failure"—is often raised.

So also is the "moral character" of the woman an issue for some, for whom any problem caused by the pregnancy is viewed as just punishment for sexual activity out of wedlock. While some would condemn any sexual activity, in many cases this is put in terms of the presumed promiscuity of the woman seeking abortion. Such denigration of the victim obviates empathy and any need to respond to the woman's claims for help (Ryan 1971; Walster, Berscheid, and Walster 1973). Contrary to such stereotypes, empirical studies indicate that most women who obtain abortions are not promiscuous, but rather become pregnant in the context of a relationship of some length and emotional depth. In Bracken's study the male partner in almost 75 percent of the cases had the status of regular boyfriend; there was an ongoing sexual involvement of least a year in more than half the cases, and in only 13 percent of the cases was it less than three months (Bracken, Klerman, and Bracken 1978). In Leach's study of repeat and initial abortion patients, nine-tenths of both groups described their partner as a husband or steady and said they cared more about him than about any other man (Leach 1977). Relationships eventuating in aborted pregnancies appear to be serious, involved relationships, but ones for which parenthood and often marriage were deemed unsuitable or in which the woman had unsuccessfully tried to effect commitment (Luker 1975).

We have talked about the most basic questions—who obtains abortions and what problems are they thought to solve? Let us move on to consider: (1) the abortion process and its emotional impact; (2) the potential future of the child; and (3) the public health effects of abortion.

THE EMOTIONAL IMPACT OF ABORTION

David et al. (1978) maintain that "abortion is rarely a psychologically traumatic event. . . . If there are psychological sequelae, the most common one, by far, is relief" (p. 3). Popular articles claim that abortion "produces few psychological problems" (Rodgers 1979).

Words are important. The literature on the emotional effects of abortion was initially conceptualized and reported in terms of "psychiatric sequelae," a term which implies psychosis or serious mental illness, or mental or emotional disorders requiring professional attention. It is literally true that there is little evidence of psychosis or indeed any psychiatrically significant impairment as a common outcome of abortion. For example, Danish data based on the criterion of psychiatric treatment within three to six weeks after abortion finds abortion to have less mental health impact than childbirth (David 1979b). Unfortunately, the failure to find treatable mental illness in short-term follow-up has been transmuted into the assumption that abortion has little emotional impact beyond transient guilt (Illsley and Hall 1978; David 1978): "It seems reasonable to conclude that for the vast majority of women abortion engenders a sense of relief and represents a maturing experience of successful coping and crisis resolution" (David 1978:97).

This conceptualization of the problem—Does abortion engender significant mental illness?—obscures the need to investigate negative emotional impact of abortion falling short of this criterion. Initially, little scientific attention was paid to media reports of such problems. We are going to look at studies of the abortion process to get some indication of the ease or difficulty with which women and their partners come to a decision to get an abortion and pull their emotional lives together in the aftermath.

Early Research

It was early assumed that abortion would be an emotionally traumatic experience. But reviews of the psychiatric literature found little in the way of psychiatric sequelae— even patients who were initially mentally disturbed, hence receiving "therapeutic" abortions, were at least as well off after the abortion, and in many cases stress appeared to be relieved. There is no point in reviewing much of the earlier research as it has been severely criticized on methodological grounds (see summaries by Simon and Senturia 1966; Walter 1970; Osofsky, Osofsky, and Rajan 1973), but certainly it shows little evidence of psychosis as a common outcome of abortion.

More recent studies done in the context of liberalized abortion laws (reviewed by Osofsky, Osofsky, and Rajan 1973 and Smith 1973) find either improvement in the psychological state of abortion patients or no difference between abortion patients and other groups. An exception is Burnell et al. (personal communication to Osofsky, Osofsky, and Rajan 1973), who found that of 300 women undergoing abortion, 300 normal pregnancy, and 300 pregnancy and adoption, the abortion and adoption groups experienced more psychological problems during pregnancy than the normals, although at follow-up the abortion patients were better off than the adoption patients. Almost none of the abortion groups reported worsened adjustment (Osofsky, Osofsky, and Rajan 1973:193–94, based on personal communication). Studies of Niswander, Singer, and Singer (1972) and Brody, Meikle, and Gerritse (1971), relying on the well-established MMPI psychiatric scales, found that abortion patients who demonstrated psychopathology before the abortion improved after the abortion—in the first case compared to women in normal pregnancy experience and in the second compared to women refused abortion.

Athanasiou et al. (1973) at Johns Hopkins report a carefully designed study of some women interviewed during pregnancy between October 1970 and February 1972.

Matched groups of thirty-eight women who had term deliveries, thirty-eight who had early abortions, and thirty-eight who had late abortions were developed from this pool. During the follow-up interview it became possible to administer the MMPI and Symptom Check List. The only significant differences among subgroups on the MMPI were the higher scores on paranoia for term-birth women, interpreted to mean concern about others' knowledge about the baby (a substantial majority of these patients were unmarried). Most scores were within the normal range for all groups, only the means for "psychopathy" and "mania" being more than one standard deviation from the mean for all three groups. Scores on the Symptom Check List were similar for all patients, the only statistically significant difference being that the early abortion patients had fewer complaints. There were no differences on the Srole anomia scale, the Rosenberg self-esteem scale, or in change in relationships or sexual behavior or emotional recovery. As a byproduct of the study, procedures were developed for identifying individuals who might experience problems with abortion. Such persons were characterized by low self-esteem, high alienation, pathological MMPI patterns, large number of body symptoms, high levels of sexual activity, and delay in seeking abortion. The population expected to have difficulties in general adjustment was small, and the authors conclude that "abortion appears to be a benign procedure compared to term birth, psychologically and physically" (p. 231).

Cushner et al. (1973) report additional data from the Johns Hopkins study, particularly attitudes toward and subjective reactions to abortion. Respondents were classified as (1) positive, (2) negative, and (3) conditional, ambivalent, or mixed, in terms of their attitude toward abortion. Total figures are thirty-eight positive, forty conditional, and thirty negative, with the live-birth group most negative and the early abortion group most positive (these were attitudes at the follow-up interview, although attitudes before pregnancy and at the time of pregnancy were ascertained retrospectively). More of the aborted women were more negative before pregnancy and at follow-up than during the actual hospital stay.

Osofsky, Osofsky, and Rajan (1973) report data from Syracuse, interviewing abortion patients shortly after abortion, again within one month at a follow-up exam, and employing six- and twelve-month telephone follow-up where possible (about 40 percent of the sample). Follow-up interviews were conducted by individuals with varying backgrounds and personal convictions on abortion. Data on predominant mood, physical emotionality, feelings about abortion, and attitudes toward self after abortion were very positive, including much verbal and nonverbal demonstration of positive emotionality. Initial decision was characterized as not difficult in 56 percent of the cases. At the one-month follow-up 94 percent reported satisfaction that the right decision was made; 85 percent did so at the six-month follow-up (because of sample attrition, it is difficult to compare these two figures). On the whole, psychological reactions seem not only not negative, but quite positive. Catholics experienced more emotional difficulty and guilt than others.

Smith (1973) followed up a nonsystematic sample, mostly single, white, student or professional, young clients of a pregnancy consultation service. Even though this was a state (Missouri) without legalized abortion, 78 percent of the women denied negative psychological reactions after abortion and 90 percent of the women reported having done well at the time of follow-up. Ninety-four percent were satisfied with their decision. During the follow-up period only 18 percent experienced conscious guilt; 15 percent, feelings of sadness and depression; and 10 percent, decreased sexual interest or pleasure. The few women who did report difficulties were mostly unmarried teenagers, particularly those who felt their decision had been influenced by others. Catholic women appeared to have no greater discomfort than others. Many of the group viewed their abortion as a growth-producing experience during which they learned to cope with adversity and discovered their inner strength. Forty percent felt the abortion had had a positive effect on their lives; 47 percent, no effect.

These studies do seem to indicate that there is no obvious psychological trauma resulting from abortion and that the abortion recipients experienced no personal regrets about the decision. Methodological objections can be made to the telephone follow-up used by Osofsky et al. and Smith (not likely to elicit deep emotional reactions or negative reports); to Osofsky et al.'s sample attrition (Adler 1976 points to sample attrition as a bias which makes outcomes appear more positive); and to Smith's nonsystematic sample; but the results are consistent.

Feminist Critique and Other Reservations

These benign results contrast markedly with some of the literature on reactions to use of oral contraceptives and sterilization. Bardwick (1973) found psychosomatic reactions to the pill which she attributes to fears about control of the body and anxiety in sexual relationships:

> Sexual anxieties and ambivalence are generally characteristic of this population. Participation in sex as well as the assumption of contraceptive responsibility seemed to increase powerful negative emotions. . . . Based on the subjects we have seen, we think that conflict about the sexual use of the body has not diminished in this college generation in spite of safe contraception and an evolving sexual freedom in the culture. The origin of the conflict lies in the girl's ambivalence toward her reproductive system, her vulnerability in interpersonal relationships, her difficulty in experiencing sex as a physical rather than psychic involvement, and the residues of an older morality that are still powerful and that have been internalized as a standard of behavior. (P. 301)

Much of this discussion of vulnerability in relationships and anxiety about sexual self-definition is echoed in Luker's interviews (1975).

Bardwick's work is based on oral contraceptive users, and perhaps the anxieties and fears she found associated with reproductive control and sexual use of the body cannot be generalized to abortion patients. Nevertheless, as she points out, much family planning research does not probe intrapersonal depths. Certainly with regard to the previously reported studies of abortion patients, one can question the validity of telephone follow-ups or simple, one-shot questions such as "do you feel this is the right decision?" The Johns Hopkins study (Athanasiou et al. 1973; Cushner et al.

1973) did achieve psychic depth with use of the MMPI and some control for psychosomatic complaints with the Symptom Checklist.

It is of interest to note that some feminists have recently given abortion the same scrutiny they earlier gave the pill, sterilization, and hormone treatments, with much the same conclusion: that women are being oversold on abortion. In a review of Francke's *The Ambivalence of Abortion* in *Ms.* magazine, Harrison (1978) asks, "Is it really so awful to admit to confusion and unhappiness over the issue of abortion?" She notes that in the book

> women spoke of relief, they also spoke of anger . . . directed toward doctors, clergymen, husbands, lovers, men in general, mothers, fathers, and the Women's Movement, and the fetus; they spoke of anguish, grieving, remorse, physical and emotional estrangement from loved ones. Not a few of the women interviewed felt betrayed by feminists who'd led them to believe that abortion was as easy as pulling a tooth. (P. 9)

Van Gelder (1978), also writing in *Ms.*, comments:

> It is . . . near heresy in some feminist circles to acknowledge that abortion might be any more complicated than having a wisdom tooth pulled. [But] . . . I'm now convinced that public honesty on the emotional ambivalences, while perhaps temporarily "helping the other side," would in the long run help women who need affirmation and support (Pp. 65–67)

More in-depth research by open-minded social scientists on the effects of abortion on feelings of bodily integrity, sexual identity, vulnerability in relationships, and similar concerns is needed.

The Ambivalence of Abortion: Recent Research

Recent research looks at abortion and its consequences, not in terms of "psychiatric sequelae," but in terms of the decision process and general subjective response.

Jacobs et al. (1975) interviewed fifty-seven unmarried women who sought pregnancy termination and were interviewed prior to abortion (as part of an evaluation) and approximately one month after abortion. Abortion patients had scores between normals and neurotics on psychiatric evaluation instruments, but 19 percent of this abortion sample had had previous psychiatric intervention. What is more to the point is that there was a "significant reduction in distress in most outcome measures" (p. 83). The authors stress "the emotional benefits that 'normal' women receive from therapeutic abortion" (p. 87). There are some problems with the study as no control group was used; a substantial minority had psychiatric histories; somatic measures of emotional impact were confounded by the change in the physiological state from pregnant to nonpregnant; and the researchers used a very short-term follow-up. At the time of the follow-up (approximately one month after abortion) no adverse effects were perceived by large portions of the subjects on their attitudes toward sex (81 percent), marriage (98 percent), and having children (95 percent). Seventy-nine percent said it was a learning experience. *Thirty-five percent said they would not have an abortion again.*

Freeman (1978) conducted a study of women obtaining abortion which combined written questionnaires (N = 329) with follow-up questionnaires four months after abortion (N = 106). The majority of women were under thirty, unmarried, and white. Only 15 percent viewed the abortion as an "ordinary" experience. Since most of the women had not previously thought of themselves as candidates for abortion, "for many, the abortion decision contradicted their perception about themselves. The ambivalence about pregnancy termination continued after the procedure. . . . For a majority of the women, abortion was a necessity forced on them by external circumstances" (p. 152). Sixty-five percent of the women "didn't know" if they would choose abortion again in the event of an unwanted pregnancy; 13 percent said they would have an unwanted child; and only 22 percent would definitely have an abortion again.

The women studied by Freeman did perceive a cessation of high levels of anxiety and depression reported to have existed between confirmation and termination of the pregnancy. Fifty-five percent reported relief as the predominant feeling following abortion. Resolution of negative feelings at the four-month follow-up was related, not to the amount of ambivalent or negative feelings, but to the ability to cope with them, e.g., positive self-image, sense of mastery, and other personality characteristics. Fifty-eight percent reported changes in self toward increased self-management associated with the abortion, but 40 percent "continued to be troubled or regarded their abortion as too upsetting to think about" (p. 153). Freeman described abortion as,

> not the idiosyncratic choice of a few typical women, but rather an experience undergone by women who are neither independent and individualistic nor emotionally disturbed. . . . [While] most of them recognized that the alternative to abortion is an unwanted child, with far more complex emotional and social ramifications than the abortion itself, . . . [and] abortion was a difficult solution to what was perceived as an insurmountable problem, . . . abortion was for most an emotionally upsetting experience. (Pp. 154–55)

Freeman advises counseling, maintaining that "ambivalence about abortion is no reason to counsel against it" (p. 154).

Bracken and colleagues have undertaken a series of studies. In a review of abortion counseling, Bracken stresses the seriousness of the abortion decision, maintaining that "it is highly stressful" (Bracken 1977:266). He cites a World Health Organization statement that "although countries with conditional abortion legislation tend to exaggerate risks, those with permissive laws tend to underestimate them" (Working Group . . . 1973, cited in Bracken 1977:265). He reports that in several studies at least one-third of the women changed their minds about the abortion at least once before having it. He counsels support for indecisive clients and accentuates the positive gain—"an experience rich in the possibilities for increased self-awareness" (p. 269)—in his writing, but in an interview (Francke 1978) Bracken expressed concern: "When I first got into the whole area of pregnancy and abortion, clinic personnel were quite rightly . . . trying to convince women that abortion was not such a bad thing after all. . . . I think the public has bought the fact of abortion so well that the clinics have in fact oversold it" (p. 31).

Bracken explores the dynamics of abortion decision making in a study of 249 never-married women aborted in 1975–76, matched with 249 women giving birth—all young, most of them black, two-thirds on welfare. One-third were pregnant for the first time, one-third had been pregnant before but never aborted, and one-third had had a previous abortion.

Both groups were unhappy at the pregnancy, though term-birth patients less so. Term-birth mothers were also more likely to have discussed their decision with significant others and received support. "Women who aborted were significantly more likely to report their decision to be a relatively difficult one, to reject initially that choice, and to regret having made that decision" (Bracken et al. 1978a:257). (With reference to decision making, Bracken notes the surprising finding that only 2 percent even considered adoption as an alternative.)

A thoughtful study of the "passage through abortion" of forty women (Zimmerman 1977) focused not so much on emotional reactions per se as on the social shaping of definitions of abortion. At the time of the interviews, six to ten weeks following abortion, approximately half of the women were untroubled and half troubled by their experience. Prior to abortion 70 percent had disapproved of abortion to some degree, and 80 percent believed that a majority of the community disapproved. Although there was some ambivalence in initial reactions to the pregnancy—30 percent had initially wanted to have the baby—emotional adjustment following abortion was more closely tied to the social integration of the woman ("affiliated" or "disaffiliated") and her perception of abortion as a deviant act than to initial attitudes toward the pregnancy. These women believed abortion to be an immoral act, disapproved of by society and significant others. Coping with the consequences of their abortion decision took the form, not of changed attitudes toward abortion, which remained negative, but of disassociating the self from the deviant act by denial of responsibility—"no other choice."

In her concluding comments, the author expresses considerable concern about the future stability of this adjustment:

By denying full responsibility for their actions, they could protect their identity from stigma to some extent. How successful this will be in the long-run is another question. . . . The act of abortion appears to have put them in a fragile position as far as their worth as persons was concerned. The women were balancing precariously. Even for those with a smooth abortion passage, one wonders if, in the future, they were suddenly challenged about the abortion, they would not find their experience, in retrospect, becoming problematic. (Pp. 195, 203)

Zimmerman, then, reports a problematic adjustment to abortion for a number of women interviewees. However, she sees this, not as intrinsic to abortion, but as arising in a social context in which abortion is socially defined as a deviant act.

To sum up, several recent studies stress the difficulty and ambivalence with which the decision to abort is made and the fact that some women experience lingering emotional reactions. While the emotional impact of abortion has to be measured against the impact of unplanned parenthood or of bearing and giving up a child for adoption (see Baran, Panhor, and Sorosky 1977—we need far more research here, also), these studies show that perhaps the wrong question about the emotional impact of abortion was asked in the past. We need to know, not whether or not women who undergo abortion become mentally ill or emotionally disturbed in a form which comes to psychiatric attention, but rather whether there is a negative emotional impact of abortion which must be counted as one of the costs. As Francke (1978) states: "All persons entering or leaving the abortion experience without recognizing the probability of these emotions are simply fooling themselves" (p. 11).

The Men in Abortion

Concern for the emotional impact of abortion must be extended to the male partner. Again, a journalistic source suggests this need (Francke 1978:113–17), and Luker (1975) concludes from her qualitative data that

> one would tend to suspect that the psychological impact on men who have abortions [sic] may be as significant in some respects, though less visible, than the psychological trauma that women face, particularly since women have social permission and a variety of institutions where they may discuss the effects of abortion and ventilate psychic stress. (P. 137)

Shostak (1979) reviews the three studies available on men and reports his own research. Seventy-two percent of fifty interviewees "disagreed" or "strongly disagreed" with the statement that "males generally have an easy time of it and have few, if any, disturbing thoughts" (p. 571). He concludes:

A sizeable minority of young males find their abortion experience more . . . emotionally costly than public and academic neglect would indicate. Although a clear majority . . . denied any serious emotional consequences, . . . a distinct minority of those men studied have found the abortion experience to be bewildering and painful beyond their coping abilities. Until some of these reforms [optional mental health services] are secured, it is possible that the abortion experience of many American males may cast a long and troubled shadow over their future fatherhood experiences. (P. 574)

The male's attitude has also been found to be significant in the degree of upset experienced by the woman (Freeman 1978; Zimmerman 1977). Some counseling programs for men are being developed (Gordon and Kilpatrick 1977). Insufficient research has been done to date on the men involved in abortion (Shostak 1979).

Francke, summing up her (nonscientific, but nevertheless suggestive) interviews, states that abortion puts extreme stress on male-female relationships and that all relationships involving singles eventually broke up. More careful studies report much smaller, but nevertheless substantial amounts of breakup of relationships among the unmarried. Freeman (1978) found that four months after abortion, two-thirds still had the same partner; one-third had broken up. Approximately 50 percent of the relationships reported by Zimmerman's (1977) respondents were broken up by the man (generally before the abortion) or the woman (generally after abortion). Seventy-five percent of the men in Shostak's sample continued their relationship; one-fourth broke up. Some couples have reported beneficial effects on their relationship of the shared crisis (Zimmerman 1977). The area of couple relationships in abortion needs further research, as does its long-range emotional impact on both parties (most of the studies involve short-term follow-up).

THE FUTURE OF THE UNBORN CHILD

A very important assumption supporting abortion is that the child, if born, would have no worthwhile human future anyway. Such a conclusion centers around notions of the stability of unwantedness and the assumption that an unwanted child would receive very poor care and parenting, perhaps becoming a victim of family violence. The motto "every child a wanted child" and the numerous references in the abortion debate to the quality of life imply that children who are wanted will receive more loving and competent care and presumably a better material environment—a plausible assumption. This assumption is often extended to the conclusion that children would be better off unborn than unwanted. Rather than argue this point of logic, let us turn to a consideration of the life circumstances that are likely, in fact, to greet the unwanted child.

What is Unwanted?

An immediate conceptual problem arises: What is "wanted" and what is "unwanted"? Pohlman (especially 1965b and 1969) has done the most to explicate this concept, which has many dimensions: Wanted at what time? By whom (both husband and wife)? Conscious or unconscious attitudes? Self-report or that of the outside professional observer? The reported tendency of parents to change their minds as pregnancy progresses (Sears, Maccoby, and Levin 1957; Westoff, Potter, and Sagi 1963; Blake 1969; see also Pohlman 1965b and 1969) warrants uneasiness about the assumption that unwantedness at conception precludes a warm or adequate reception for the baby. So do reports about the instability of abortion decisions (Bracken, Klerman, and Bracken 1978), including Freeman's finding that four months after abortion 39 percent declared that the child had been wanted (Freeman 1978). Furstenberg (1976a) found although three-fourths of his young black mothers stated they did not want to be pregnant and three-fifths were unambivalently negative, by the time the child was born, 85 percent were content with motherhood and "few could be classified as rejecting" (p. 161).

Other data (Kruegel 1975) suggest that wantedness / unwantedness can be retrospective, hence unstable. While Pohlman notes the logical appeal of an assumption of consistency, social science research is notorious for its discovery of inconsistencies. Some observers discount self reports of later acceptance of an unwanted baby and assume unconscious hostility remains (Pohlman 1968). Sears, Maccoby, and Levin (1957) did find a correlation between a retrospective report of initial preference not to have a child at that time and behavioral warmth toward the child. Nevertheless, evidence is sorely lacking (Pohlman 1967, 1969) that unwanted children are really unwanted in a sense that would affect their life chances. Reviewing the literature, Pohlman is even reluctant to accept the oft-stated connection between child abuse and premarital pregnancy. The Institute of Medicine's report (1975) concludes that "evidence that planned pregnancies more frequently produce psychologically healthy children is mostly inferential" (p. 96).

Children of Mothers Refused Abortion: The Czech Study

Another approach to estimating the life chances of the "unwanted" child is to bypass attitudes of the parents and their behavior with the child to focus on outcomes for the child—which are easier to assess. One here defines as "unwanted" a child whose mother had sought to have him/her aborted. The oft-cited landmark study of this sort is that of Forssman and Thuwe in Sweden (1966) of children born to mothers whose applications for abortion were refused. This study found 60 percent of unwanted children, as compared with 28 percent of control children, to have an insecure childhood and is often cited as evidence of the poorer life chances of unwanted, i.e., preferably aborted, children. The study is, however, inconclusive, because among the "unwanted" children there were more who were born out of wedlock, a circumstance that would have affected their outcomes independently of being unwanted.

A long-awaited study, the only well-designed prospective study with a control group, was published in 1975 based on data collected from Czech children about age nine who were born after their mothers were twice refused abortion (Dytrych et al. 1975, Dytrych et al. 1978). Two hundred and twenty of these children were matched with control children on grade in school, sex, birth order, number of siblings, mother's marital status, and father's occupation. Both groups of children seemed biologically comparable at birth, so that differences were attributed to wantedness/unwantedness.

With regard to health, acute illness was significantly more common among the study children. There were no significant differences in long-term disease, accidents, surgery, or hospitalization, and there were no significant differences in general somatic development or state of health.

Mothers' reports of children's preschool behavior found mothers denied abortion significantly more apt to describe their children as bad-tempered; differences in the same direction on "naughty" and "stubborn" were not statistically significant.

Few differences in school-relevant traits were reported by mothers and teachers. Study children were significantly lower in diligence. Other trends, not statistically significant, were for study children to show less concentration, initiative, and tidiness, but *more* self-confidence.

Children were rated on eleven personal characteristics by mothers and teachers. Both rated study children significantly more excitable and less conscientious, but there were no significant differences on ambitiousness, obedience, mobility, dominance, sociability, sense of humor, sensitivity, stubbornness, or demandingness.

Comparisons of school achievement suggest that the study children are doing less well, especially in the Czech language, the academic subject most closely tied to family interaction. Differences are all in favor of the control children, though only in Czech are grades significantly different. Since IQ's are similar for both groups, this suggests that the performance of the study groups is below capability.

Teachers' assessment of study children's behavior and performance at school, capacity for work, and intelligence was less favorable than of controls', though not significantly so. Study children seemed less likely to be chosen by peers and more apt to engage in conflict, showing off, or withdrawal. The only significant differences, however, were in being "refused as a friend" and in "sense of humor" (which favored the study children, but was given a negative interpretation as prankishness and clowning).

Generally, there was more of a difference between study and control boys than girls. Study girls, in fact, scored highest in initiative and self-confidence.

On various dimensions of family life, i.e., cultural level, internal family life, care of the child, and cooperation with school, study group children were rated lower. Social workers also found the study mothers significantly less informed about the child and more detached. Perceptions by the children of their family life did not show differences. The most striking difference between the two groups of families would be family change in terms of widowhood, divorce, remarriage, and pregnancy among the study families. Study children significantly more often lived with a stepfather, an important difference between the two groups which is confounded with initial unwantedness. Study group mothers were more apt to have experienced dissatisfaction with the children, although initial differences in wantedness had lessened by the time of the study and were not significant.

This major study lends itself to ambiguous interpretation of the half-full, half-empty sort. If nonsignificant differences are included, the study children emerge as less well adjusted than control children, although there are a few areas in which, especially among girls, the study children excelled the controls. However, if only statistically significant differences are considered, one would have to say the most striking feature of the report on the children at age nine is the failure to find major differences in outcomes between children whose mothers were denied abortion and children who were "wanted." Only seven comparisons out of a total of forty-four presented (Dytrych et al. 1978) are statistically significant ("sense of humor"—table 95, p. 212—was excluded from the comparison because of the ambiguity of its interpretation). Yet the conclusion commonly drawn from the report is that the unwanted children were significantly disadvantaged (e.g., Illsley and Hall 1978:24). Dytrych et al. themselves conclude that "compulsory childbearing has varied and sometimes unfavorable consequences for the subsequent life of the child" (p. 22), although they confess that "the aggregate differences between the children born following unwanted conception and the control children are not dramatic at nine years of age" (p. 221). "This seems to suggest that there are, after all, mechanisms activated during the child's life in the family that act positively to close any gap between unwanted and wanted children" (Matejcek, Dytrych, and Schüller 1979:75).

Since first publication of results, analysis has continued. The researchers developed a Maladjustment Scale by summing selected items for each child. This aggregation of disadvantage does produce mean scores which are significantly different for study and control groups, with the former more "maladjusted," girls as well as boys (Matejcek, Dytrych, and Schüller 1979). One must note, as do the authors, the ad hoc (p. 71), *post factum* nature of this methodology. The authors also caution that "a considerable number of unwanted children are just as well-adjusted as their control counterparts" (p. 73), while 18 percent of the control children achieved a very high MS" (p. 73). In other words, while group means differ, there is noticeable overlap (p. 72, table 3). The authors again summarize their research evenhandedly:

> The idea commonly held among many psychiatrists and clinical psychologists that eventual difficulties in the behavior of an unwanted child are inevitably linked with the originally rejecting attitude of the mother toward his existence is not wholly supported for both boys and girls. On the other hand, the view commonly entertained by the lay public that the birth of the child changes everything and every mother comes to dearly love her child is apparently also invalid. (Matejcek, Dytrych, and Schüller 1979:75)

Finally, David (1979a) in a review paper in this volume (chapter 3) reports very recent results from follow-up at ages fourteen and sixteen which indicate continuing disadvantage, although evaluation of the extent of this disadvantage must await full publication of those data.

It still seems reasonable to conclude that while the Czech case is toward the extreme of unwantedness (children whose mothers were twice refused abortion), outcome differences do not seem to be of the magnitude envisioned when one discusses the miserable life anticipated for an unwanted child. An interpretation of this study to suggest that "unwanted" children will almost surely have a poor future would be misleading; the study children seem to be leading relatively normal lives.

Children of Teen Mothers

A study exploring the effects on children of having very young parents reported comparable outcomes. Such children may not be subjectively "unwanted," but they have clearly come at a bad time in the lives of their mothers—with what result for parenting?

A study done in Baltimore deals with this issue (Oppel and Raysten 1971). It is a study of the social, psychological, and physical development of 172 children of mothers younger than eighteen, with controls matched for socioeconomic status, birth weight, number of previous live births of the mother, and race of mother. Children born to mothers younger than eighteen were less likely to be living with both parents six to eight years after birth; only twenty of eighty-six children in the study group, compared with forty-three of the controls.

Data about adjustment is less than conclusively unfavorable to the children of younger mothers. Both groups of children were rated by the psychologist as normally adjusted. Children in the first group (mothers under eighteen) were more often rated as outgoing, but also as more dependent and distractible; there were no differences on nine (i.e., most) personality traits. Children of the older mothers were taller and had a more advanced reading level. Younger mothers were rated as less anxious and more likely to think the six- to eight-year-old children should be free to act independently, and also to have a less intense emotional and behavioral involvement with the children (these characteristics are often viewed by sociologists as desirable for parents; Rossi 1964). On the whole, it is difficult to conclude that these children of younger mothers are sufficiently disadvantaged as to have been better off not born. Although in some respects their adjustment is less good, the differences seem minor. Yet the investigators state that "the study findings support a contention that the youth of the mothers is a contributing factor to the less adequate nurture of the children." It is difficult to derive this interpretation from the data as reported.

To sum up, the single studies directly investigating the effects on children of being unwanted or being born to a mother under eighteen suggest that such children may be less well adjusted in some respects than other children, but not strikingly so. The fuzziness of the concept of "unwanted" and the degree to which initially unenthusiastic mothers become more favorable over time at the conscious level (perhaps not at the unconscious) make it difficult to conclude that such children are unwanted to the degree that they will not have normal lives. Nor has any association of child abuse with unwanted pregnancy been established.* What is needed here is more research to eliminate some of the uncertainties and ambiguities about the life chances of "unwanted" children. In the meantime, to conclude that there is a clearly specifiable class of children who are "unwanted" and better aborted for their own good is risky.

DEMOGRAPHIC EFFECTS OF ABORTION

A fourth area in which social science research can support or refute assumptions about abortion is in the area of demographic and public health effects of abortion: mortality, morbidity, fertility, and fertility control through contraception or repeat abortion.

Mortality

There can be no denying or overlooking—as antiabortionists may be prone to do—the dramatic drop in the maternal death rate from abortions following legalized abortion. Abortion-related deaths dropped more than 40 percent in 1973 (U.S. DHEW 1975) and have continued to decline (U.S. DHEW 1978). Abortion is now safer than childbirth (Tietze, Bongaarts, and Schearer 1976). Although Berger (1975) states that "in the context of [a] long-term trend [decline in abortion deaths] it is difficult to determine to what extent the decline in the number of abortion-related deaths in the

---

*I have heard of, but not seen published reports of, research which reports 90 percent of abused children to have come from planned pregnancies.

1970's is attributable to the legalization of abortion" (p. 168), he nevertheless claims "a protective effect on the health of women" (p. 168) and suggests that "total elimination of maternal mortality due to abortion is a feasible goal" (p. 168). That was before the elimination of federal support for abortions. Future impact of the Medicaid fund cutoff is uncertain, depending upon the state and private financial alternatives available (Alan Guttmacher Institute 1979; *Omaha World Herald* 1978a). Delegalization of abortion might have considerable impact; in Romania the death rate from abortion increased regularly following restriction, to 315 deaths in 1970 (Berger 1975).

Morbidity

While legalization of abortion is a clear plus in terms of mortality rates, abortion, particularly repeat abortion, does carry some morbidity risk. Data suggest a 10 percent complication rate, with a 1.2 percent rate of major complications (Tietze and Lewit 1971). A recent *Time* (1978) magazine article on Chicago clinics called attention to some problems in maintaining health standards.

There is particular concern about the effects of abortion on future reproduction. A sociologist attributes the recent upturn in the fertility rate to complications of repeat abortions (Broderick 1978). A biostatistician's review of studies on reproduction following first trimester abortion concludes that "the following complications appear to be significantly associated with a history of induced abortion: bleeding during pregnancy; prolonged third stage of labor; premature delivery; and low birth weight" (Hogue 1977:15–16), though ectopic pregnancy and secondary infertility are not established as complications of abortion. Later reports associate abortions with miscarriages (Levin et al. 1978; World Health Organization 1978). However, a recent study claims that interruption of postabortion pregnancies is due to pre-1973 techniques (Harlap et al. 1979). Contradictions are difficult to resolve, but a number of studies do indicate some risk of reproductive complications following abortion, especially repeat abortion.

Fertility

Legalized abortion is sometimes thought of as a solution to the problems of excess fertility and population growth. The reduction of the birth rate in Japan is a dramatic example of fertility decline attributable to abortion (Muramatsu and van der Tak 1978). While few have advocated the use of abortion as a primary means of population control in this country and others have expressed fears about this possibility, it *is* sometimes assumed that one of the beneficial byproducts of abortion is population control.

The effects of abortion on fertility, however, are complex. At first glance, legalization of abortion would seem to decrease fertility to the extent that it goes beyond replacing illegal abortions. Some local studies in Hawaii (Steinhoff 1973); Maryland (Rosenwaite and Melton 1974); and New York City (Tietze and Murstein 1975) find the legalization of abortion accompanied by fertility decline. But it is hard to separate decline due to availability of abortion from decline due to other causes. It is estimated that of the decline of births in New York City following local liberalization of the law, 50 percent was due to abortion, while the other half would have occurred anyway as a result of changing motivations and values about family size (Tietze and Murstein 1975; Tietze 1975).

In general, demographers tend to believe that abortion does not lead directly to fertility decline, but rather that both are a part of a modernization process which includes changes in family-related behavior (Berger 1975; Mazur 1975). In other words, declines in fertility are probably not dependent on any one means such as abortion, but will tend to occur as a result of changing values regardless of access to abortion, as the example of Romania illustrates. In Romania the birthrate was declining; when abortion was delegalized, it turned up momentarily, but then resumed its downward trend (partly due, though, to illegal abortion) (David and Friedman 1973). Klinger and Szabady (1978) comment, with reference to Hungary's precipitous decline in average family size (from 6 at the turn of the century, to 3 in the 1940s and 1950s, to 1.8 in 1962), that "although this sharp decline was facilitated by legalization of abortion in 1956, it was ultimately motivated by rapidly changing social and economic conditions, which depressed family size goals" (p. 177). Tietze continues to maintain, based on simulation models, that "it is unlikely that any population has ever attained a low level of fertility without the use of abortion, legal or illegal, and that abortion is not likely to disappear at the levels of contraceptive effectiveness currently attained and attainable" (Tietze and Bongaarts 1975:119).

One must note that abortion increases the potential number of pregnancies in the absence of contraception, since pregnancy and lactation remove women from the risk of additional pregnancy. For this reason estimates suggest that at least one abortion would be necessary to replace every live birth, even at high rates of contraception. "For young, highly fecund women (those obtaining most abortions at present) using no contraception, abortion is not a very effective birth control method," requiring 1.78 abortions to avert every live birth (Williams and Pullum 1975:31).

Means of Fertility Control: Contraception or Repeat Abortion

With the passage of time, the number of repeat abortions is increasing. While, logically, if one approves abortion, repeat abortion should be acceptable, the repeat abortion rate, now at about 25 percent (Tietze 1978b), has caused concern. The concern is that abortion will be habitual; persons who would find abortion an acceptable emergency solution to a one-time problem may view with alarm and distaste the utilization of abortion as a standard method of fertility control. They are concerned that the availability of abortion will lead to contraceptive casualness, i.e., pregnancies that would otherwise have been prevented will occur and will be aborted.

At a macrosocial level, it appears that rather than abortion driving out contraception, contraception replaces abortion. This has happened in Japan (Muramatsu and van der Tak 1978) and in Hungary (Klinger and Szabady 1978). As countries modernize abortion rates first increase. Motivation to regulate family size develops, but contraceptive skills are weak, hence many become pregnant, then abort. In time contraception improves and replaces abortion as a means of fertility regulation (Requeña 1970). This was the pattern in New York City, where the abortion rate went first up, then down (*Family Planning Perspectives* 1977a). Though abortion was legalized in 1973, contraception among both teenagers (Zelnik and Kantner 1977) and adults (David 1978) in the United States continues to improve.

At the micro level, most studies report that women who have abortions improve their contraceptive skills as a result of counseling (Jacobs et al. 1975; Freeman 1978; Smith 1973; Athanasiou et al. 1973; Osofsky, Osofsky, and Rajan 1973; Steinhoff et al. 1975; Margolis et al. 1974).

But a cautionary note was sounded in Kristin Luker's book, *Taking Chances* (1975). Luker described the contraceptive risk-taking of the California women she interviewed in an abortion clinic. Knowledgeable enough about contraception and often previously successful contraceptors, they at some point preferred not to contracept for reasons of romanticism, self-concept, relationship-testing, method inconvenience, and others, with the knowledge that abortion was available as a backup. (They also made some erroneous calculations about their degree of risk.) One implication of her study is that if abortion had not been available, the women would have contracepted effectively and prevented, rather than aborted, pregnancies.

Several studies report additional data relevant to this issue. Somers and Gammeltoft (1976) conclude from their research that the increase in abortions in Denmark following liberalization of the law can be partly attributed to decreasing contraception—a conclusion supported by data on the decline in pill sales. In contrast, Freeman's U.S. respondents for the most part (all but 28 percent) reported that they did not view abortion as birth control, but rather obtained abortions as an after-the-fact solution (Freeman 1978). Steinhoff's Hawaiian data, in which abortion records were linked with vital statistics data, supports the conclusion that "there is no evidence that availability of abortion has led to the abandonment of contraception or relaxation of contraceptive vigilance" (Steinhoff et al. 1979:30). The repeat abortion rate there of 18.5 percent five years after legalization is "as low as could be expected with currently available contraceptive technology" (Steinhoff et al. 1979:30).

Steinhoff et al. view their study as a test of Tietze's model. Tietze (1974, 1978b) concludes, from models of contraceptive efficacy and abortion, that even with high levels of contraception, a substantial amount of repeat abortion will occur. As more abortions take place, more women are at risk for repeat abortions, which will inevitably occur as contraceptive methods fall short of 100 percent effectiveness. His point is that an increasing proportion of repeat abortions does not necessarily mean contraceptive deterioration. But also this model forces recognition of the fact that with acceptance of legal abortion will come a substantial proportion of repeat abortions, which can be counted as one of the costs of legalization.

Attention turns to the women who obtain repeat abortions, and several studies have been reported (Leach 1977; Steinhoff et al. 1979; Bracken, Klerman, and Bracken 1978). In her research at private and public clinics in Atlanta, Leach found repeat abortion patients to have a high level of education—a mean of twelve–thirteen years. Nine-tenths of the repeaters had received contraceptive information after the previous abortion and begun to use the method of choice, but only one-third were using contraception at the time of the current pregnancy. Most of the repeaters had had the last abortion recently, within the previous year. Leach's study suggests that conventional postabortion contraceptive counseling programs are not so effective in averting further abortions and that contraceptive effectiveness cannot be assumed to be a concomitant of education.

Leach reports some characteristics and attitudes of repeat abortion patients which suggest why they are not more effective contraceptors. Repeaters, as compared with initial patients, were more likely: (1) to want to change themselves; (2) to say they had "bad luck"; and (3) to have a more negative emotional tone. These findings suggest that many repeat abortion patients feel unable to control their lives, especially in the areas of sexuality and reproduction. A

Yugoslav study also found that abortors had a weaker sense of personal efficacy and control over their own lives than successful contraceptors. Both groups thought contraception best and saw abortion as the most costly means of fertility control, but the abortors appeared to find contraception harder to manage than did the contraceptors (Kapor-Stanulovic and Friedman 1978).

Steinhoff et al. (1979) found comparable contrasting fertility planning patterns in their initial and repeat abortion groups. Women with a "long-range planning" orientation to fertility (who were more often middle class, well educated, nulliparous, and in their twenties) postponed the first unwanted birth with abortion, but used contraception effectively afterward. Women with a "short-range retrospective" orientation (more likely to be working class and either very young or already the parent of several children) resolved their current problem pregnancy by abortion, but without a long-range orientation they were likely to find themselves pregnant again. In some cases, then, a single abortion is followed by contraception and a generally goal-oriented and self-sufficient future. In other cases, abortion does not solve underlying problems, which are likely to continue and to include future pregnancies and abortions.

The preceding studies suggest the classification of women into two groups, those who control their lives and fertility and those who don't, the latter needing special help with both fertility control and a general sense of efficacy. This distinction will only be helpful if the categories are not reified and if "blaming the victim" (Ryan 1971) is avoided. Moreover, it is obvious that more study of the interplay between contraception and abortion is needed at both the macro and the micro levels. The latter should include exploration of the difficulties of obtaining and using contraception as perceived by women themselves, a subject discussed in more detail in Luker (1975), Freeman (1978), and elsewhere than it is possible to do here.

ASSESSING THE SOCIAL EFFECTS OF ABORTION

By now one may be getting lost in detail. That is partly the point, however, for one of the functions which social science can perform for the abortion debate is to flesh it out by adding some detail to the sharply simplistic assumptions visible in the spoken and printed word.

Conclusions from research on the social effects of abortion are complex and qualified. Women obtaining abortions do not usually experience psychosis or mental disturbance of the sort registered with psychiatrists—on the other hand, neither do they emerge emotionally untouched. Depressing effects on the life chances of the teen mother are noted; but long-range disadvantage is not as severe as one might have expected. The effects on children of being "unwanted" can be documented but are not "dramatic." Abortion is obtained by teenagers and by poor women—but also by others, with unclear effects on quality of life. For some women, abortion is a one-time emergency solution; for others, problems and failed fertility control continue. Legal abortion has cut the abortion mortality rate, but there can be future reproductive problems for women who have obtained abortions.

Abortion is a mixed bag. In contrast, the abortion debate is stark. But a solution is more likely to be reached in gray than in black and white. By documenting the mixed and middling social impact of abortion, research can channel proponents of each polar position toward the middle ground of social reality. Such research challenges some of the assumptions of either side which serve to obscure complexity, discount arguments, and distance dissenters.

Legitimations Challenged

Social science research challenges some of the assumptions of those arguing the case for abortion in terms of its efficacy as a solution to social problems. Data on the categories of women who receive abortions calls into question the legitimation of abortion on the grounds of physical health, rape/incest pregnancy, genetically defective children, and tired mothers. It suggests that the extent to which abortion contributes to the solution of problems of poverty and discrimination has not been established, and it indicates that abortion is not an efficient means of fertility control. It suggests that for some teen pregnancies there are other viable solutions besides abortion, including parenthood, and that perhaps there ought to be more choices for poor women also.

Since abortion cannot be wholly legitimated in terms of these special categories of need, then the abortion debate must take place in other terms. One may argue the compelling nature of unwed status and other personal problems deriving from unwed pregnancy. One may seek to prove the efficacy of abortion as a solution to the problems of poverty and social justice, or to justify it as one among several valid options for teenagers. One may conclude that there are no compelling social problem–solving justifications for abortion, but that one supports abortion anyway. One may change one's mind about abortion. At any rate, the debate ought to take place around the reality of who is or is not helped by abortion and must include consideration of the costs of abortion. The reality of the negative emotional impact of abortion on all concerned ought to be counted a cost, so also the risk to future reproductive capacity. The fact that legalized abortion means an increasing number of repeat abortions must also be faced.

The hardest reality brought to attention by a careful scrutiny of social science data is that so-called unwanted children are only tenuously so; attitudes toward them change throughout pregnancy, and indeed throughout a lifetime. And such children are likely to be received into normal lives which are only marginally less satisfying than those of children more wholeheartedly desired by their parents.

Problems Which Cannot Be Ignored

Social science research may force those opposed to abortion to face the implications of their position. Opponents of abortion often appear to ignore the personal needs and social problems which lead to abortion. Abortion is not happening because people enjoy getting abortions; it is happening because it solves problems for people or for categories of people. There is some small number of abortions which occur for the publicly acceptable reasons of physical health, rape/incest pregnancy, and genetic defect. But abortion is also a solution to other problems—of teenage pregnancy; of poverty, combined often with racial discrimination; of the stigma of unwed motherhood followed by the burden of single parenthood; of other personal, relationship, and family problems and stresses. Abortion is a costly solution; it is a solution not usually preferred or welcomed by its users. But unless other solutions are available, there will be pressure for its use.

Those opposed to abortion, then, have the obligation to take these problems seriously and to work with some dedication for their solution. This may mean strong support for aggressive contraceptive programs for teenagers.* It means respect and concern for women who are unhappily pregnant, rather than the unsupported assumption that such women are promiscuous and irresponsible. It means an imaginative effort to help women who have repeated problems both with fertility control and life planning. It means backing and helping to pay for support programs for those who choose to have their babies, and acceptance of such families in the community. It means a recognition that to reduce the availability of abortion is to recreate a situation in which there are likely to be deaths from illegal abortions.

Assumptions that if abortion is available it will lead to contraceptive decline and that abortion creates severe psychic damage may, at least for the present, be relinquished. It must also be recognized that adoption is not always a viable solution for an unwanted pregnancy. For one thing, it is culturally alien to many of those for whom it is intended and does not always enter the decision process (of course, this could change). For another, it does not mitigate the health risk and presumed psychological stress of pregnancy, particularly to young teens.

The End of Abortion? Alternative Solutions to Social Problems

Once these realities are faced, it is more difficult to main-

---

*This does not preclude counseling for teenagers which incorporates values about sexuality and presentation of abstinence as a valid choice. It does recognize the upward trend in sexual activity of teenagers that seems unlikely to reverse and the fact that at present a period of sexual activity usually precedes contraceptive efforts, particularly effective ones (Tietze 1978a; Zelnik and Kantner 1977).

tain a polar position. It is easier to meet in the middle and take a problem-solving approach to abortion. One can view individuals and society as having problems for which abortion is one possible solution. It may be the only solution for some problems, but *it is a solution with some serious costs*. In some cases the benefits may outweigh the costs. But in many cases there are less costly alternatives which ought to replace abortion.

A prolife (no abortion) position or a restricted abortion policy would effect this replacement through social control. It would, however, be impossible to administer a limited abortion policy fairly and safely. Then perhaps, with an awareness of the costs versus the benefits of abortion, even under a policy of legally available abortion individuals will choose to replace abortion with alternative solutions and will receive support and assistance for doing so. Perhaps social imagination and effort will reduce the magnitude of the social problems presently being dealt with through abortion or will institutionalize alternative solutions.

At any rate, dialogue ought to take place around a central concern for the problems people are attempting to solve by abortion, for the costs of this solution, and for the development of less socially costly alternative solutions.

SOCIAL SCIENCE AND THE ABORTION DEBATE: THE GAP

A careful examination of research on the social impact of abortion does contribute something to the abortion debate. But for the most part, the abortion debate has taken place on one plane, social science research on another, at least until recently. What are some reasons for this?

One can look first to social science. There are still gaps in the social science research literature vis-à-vis the need-to-know (about abortion). It is shocking to think that there is only one satisfactory study of the effects on children of being born to mothers who had wished to abort them. It is shortsighted that, until recently, research on the emotional aftermath of abortion focused on psychiatric admissions and treatment and, finding that absent, ignored the emotional distress of "normal" women. Basic national demographic information is lacking, as is a systematic, large-scale study of the motives and occasions for abortion.

Social scientists have been handicapped in their study of abortion for reasons additional to the obvious methodological difficulties of studying a normatively and legally private matter. They have been done in by their guiding myth of a value-free sociology, which for a long time caused social scientists self-consciously to remove themselves from public problems and public decisions. But social scientists seem to be gaining renewed zest for public policy; they now are paying more attention to the information needs of policy makers and the public.*

Social scientists have their political and moral biases. Most are "liberal," which would include being proabortion. They may be reluctant, as are the feminists described by Harrison and van Gelder, to raise questions about abortion or even to explore sensitive areas which might produce data to be used by "the other side." (The "other side" may, in turn, be reluctant to trust the work of social scientists.)

Being a social scientist, however, I am more inclined to find the gap developing out of lack of receptivity to what social science has to offer the abortion debate, rather than out of the quality of our offering. I am amazed at the way in which inaccurate statements about abortion seem to go rolling along indefinitely. I attribute this partly to lack of respect among the public, perhaps among public officials, certainly among humanists, for social science. Senator Proxmire's attention has not helped and, I think, is often unfair. In fact, I hope the topic of abortion will be an example of how sociological researchers can inform public debate on social issues.

Structurally, there seems to be an absence of vehicles for transmitting social science knowledge to the general public, in spite of such popular magazines as *Society*, *Human Be-*

---

*For example, a coalition of family organizations composed of the National Council on Family Relations (professional association of family sociologists, educators, and therapists), the American Association of Marriage and Family Counselors, the American Home Economics Association, and the Family Service Association of America (social work) was recently formed to disseminate policy-related information and to provide expert testimony.

havior, and *Psychology Today*. Information and need do not seem to make connection. Lewis Coser commented on the need for middle-level interpreters of social science (Coser 1972), and Boys' Town Center in Omaha has taken the dissemination of social science research as one of its tasks—may its tribe increase!

Finally, I have to speak as a social scientist again in noting the many social-psychological studies of attitude formation and person perception which document the strong need humans have to maintain cognitive consistency and to validate their perceptions of the world (Vander Zanden 1977). But solutions to problems are not found in the rigid maintenance of cognitive consistency, as studies of creativity consistently indicate. They are found in an openness to complexity and to new ways of conceptualizing problems (Aldous 1975). This takes place in the realm of empirical reality and can only be benefited by a rapprochement between the abortion debate and social science research. Judging by comparisons between my initial review of the abortion literature several years ago and this more recent one, such an interplay of research policy is starting to happen. Social science research on abortion will be of little use unless it is absorbed into the public dialogue and helps to mediate between polar positions, for as Auguste Comte (1824) stated, "The true solution will become possible only if it is based on civil cohesion."

REFERENCES

Adler, N. E. 1976. Sample attrition in studies of psychosocial sequelae of abortion: how great a problem? *Journal of Applied Social Psychology* 6:240–59.

Alan Guttmacher Institute. 1976. *Eleven million teenagers: what can be done about the epidemic of adolescent pregnancies in the U.S.* New York.

———. 1979. *Abortions and the poor: private morality, public responsibility.* New York.

Aldous, J. 1975. The search for alternatives: parental behaviors and children's original problem solutions. *Journal of Marriage and Family* 37:711–22.

Ambrose, L. 1978. Misinforming pregnant teenagers. *Family Planning Perspectives* 10:51–57.

American Lutheran Church. Commission on Research and Social Action. 1970. Abortion, Christian counsel, and the law. Minneapolis.

Arney, W. R. and Tresher, W. H. 1976. Trends in attitudes toward abortion, 1972–75. *Family Planning Perspectives* 8:117–24.

Athanasiou, R., et al. 1973. Psychiatric sequelae to term birth and induced early and late abortion: a longitudinal study. *Family Planning Perspectives* 5:227–31.

Baran, A., Panhor, R., and Sorosky, A. D. 1977. The lingering pain of surrendering a child. *Psychology Today* 11 (June):58ff.

Bardwick, J. 1973. Psychological factors in the acceptance and use of oral contraceptives. In J. T. Fawcett, *Psychological perspectives on population*, pp. 274–305. New York: Basic Books.

Bauman, K. D., Udry, J. R., and Noyes, R. W. 1970. The relationship between legal abortions and birth rates in selected U.S. cities. Paper reported in *Family Planning Perspectives* 7:11–12.

Berger, G. S. 1975. Legal abortion: an appraisal of its health impact. *International Journal of Gynecology and Obstetrics* 13:165–70.

Blake, J. 1969. Population policy for Americans: is the government being misled? *Science* 164:522–29; see also 165:1203.

———. 1971. Abortion and public opinion: the 1960–1970 decade. *Science* 171:540–95.

———. 1973. Elective abortion and our reluctant citizenry: research on public opinion in the United States. In H. G. Osofsky, and J. D. Osofsky, eds., *The abortion experience*, pp. 447–67. New York: Harper and Row.

———. 1977a. The abortion decision: judicial review and public opinion. In W. Liu, E. Manier, and D. Solomon, eds., *Abortion*. Notre Dame: University of Notre Dame Press.

———. 1977b. The Supreme Court's abortion decisions and public opinion in the United States. *Population and Development Review* 3:45–62.

Bok, S. 1974. Ethical problems of abortions. *Hastings Center Studies* 2:33–52.

Bracken, M. B. 1978. Coping with pregnancy resolution among never married women. *American Journal of Orthopsychiatry* 48:320–34.

Bracken, M. B., Klerman, L. V., and Bracken, M. 1977. Psychosomatic aspects of abortion: implications for counseling. *Journal of Reproductive Medicine* 19:265–72.

———. 1978. Abortion, adoption, or motherhood: an empirical study of decision-making during pregnancy. *American Journal of Obstetrics and Gynecology* 130:251–62.

Brackett, J. W. 1971. Demographic consequence of legal abortions. In Newman, S. H., Beck, M. B., and Lewit, S., eds., *Abortion obtained and denied*, pp. 97–112. New York: Population Council.

Brennan, W. C. 1974. Abortion and the techniques of neutralization. *Journal of Health and Social Behavior* 15:358–65.

Broderick, C. 1978. Up with marriage. Paper presented at the National Symposium on Building Family Strengths, University of Nebraska, Lincoln, Nebraska, 3–5 May.

Brody, H., Meikle, S., and Gerritse, R. 1971. Therapeutic abortion: a prospective study. *American Journal of Obstetrics and Gynecology* 109:345–53.

Card, J. J., and Wise, L. L. 1978. Teenage mothers and teenage fathers: the impact of early childbearing on the parents' personal and professional lives. *Family Planning Perspectives* 10:199–205.

Cates, W., Jr., and Rochat, R. W. 1976. Illegal abortion in the U.S. *Family Planning Perspectives* 8:86–92.

Colletta, N. D., and Gregg, C. H. 1979. The everyday lives of adolescent mothers: variables related to emotional stress. Paper presented at the annual meeting of the National Council on Family Relations, Boston, August.

Comte, A. 1824. *Système de la politique positive*. Vol. 3, p. 364. Cited in R. Aron, *Main currents in sociological thought*, 1:129. New York: Doubleday, 1968.

————. 1839. *Cours de philosophie positive*. Vol. 4. Cited in R. Aron, *Main currents in sociological thought*, 1:94. New York: Doubleday, 1968.

Coser, L. c. 1972. The celebrity intellectual. Lecture, University of Notre Dame, Notre Dame, Indiana.

Cushner, I.M., et al. 1973. The Johns Hopkins experience. In H. J. Osofsky, and J. D. Osofsky, eds., *The abortion experience*, pp. 135–64. New York: Harper and Row.

Cutright, P. 1973. Timing the first birth: does it matter? *Journal of Marriage and the Family* 35:585–95.

————. 1974. Teenage illegitimacy: an exchange. Letter in *Family Planning Perspectives* 6:132–33.

Daily, E. F., Nicholas, N., Nelson, F., and Pakter, J. 1973. Repeat abortions in New York City: 1970–1972. *Family Planning Perspectives* 5:89–93.

David, H. P. 1978. Psychosocial studies of abortions in the United States. In H. P. David, H. L. Friedman, J. van der Tak, and M. J. Sevilla, eds., *Abortion in psychosocial perspective: trends in transnational research*, pp. 77–115. New York: Springer.

————. 1979a. The abortion decision: national and international perspectives. Paper presented at the National Conference on Abortion, University of Notre Dame, Notre Dame, Indiana, 17 October. (Chapter 3 of this volume.)

————. 1979b. Personal communication to the author.

David, H. P., and Friedman, H. L. 1973. Psychosocial research on abortion: a transnational perspective. In H. G. Osofsky, and J. D. Osofsky, *The abortion experience*, pp. 310–37. New York: Harper and Row.

David, H. P., Friedman, H. L., van der Tak, J., and Sevilla, M. J., eds. 1978. *Abortion in psychosocial perspective: trends in transnational research*. New York: Springer.

Diamond, M., Steinhoff, P. G., Palmore, J. A., and Smith, R. G. 1973. Abortion in Hawaii. *Family Planning Perspectives* 5:54ff.

Dobell, E. R. 1979. Abortion: the controversy we can't seem to solve. *Redbook* (November):42ff.

Drinan, R. F. 1970. The state of the abortion question. *Commonweal* (17 April):1–2.

Dryfoos, J. G., and Heisler, T. 1978. Contraceptive services for adolescents: an overview. *Family Planning Perspectives* 10:223–33.

Dyck, A. J. 1972. Perplexities of the would-be liberal in abortion. *Journal of Reproductive Medicine* 8:351–54.

Dytrych, Z., et al. 1975. Children born to women denied abortion. *Family Planning Perspectives* 7:165–71.

————. 1978. Children born to women denied abortion in Czechoslovakia. In H. P. David, H. L. Friedman, J. van der Tak, and M. J. Sevilla, eds., *Abortion in psychosocial perspective: trends in transnational research*, pp. 201–24. New York: Springer.

Family Planning Perspectives. 1977a. Fall in NYC abortions in '75 is credited to birth control. 9:33.

———. 1977b. More abortion patients are young, unmarried, nonwhite: procedures performed earlier and by sanction; one-fifth repeats. 9:130–31.

———. 1978a. Large majority of Americans favor legal abortion, sex education, and contraceptive services for teens. 10:159–60.

———. 1978b. Available contraception lowers teen birthrates. 10:160–61.

———. 1978c. U.S. cities shortchange pregnant teens. 10:167.

———. 1979. With help from family, friends and welfare, unwed mothers can overcome serious obstacles. 11:43–44.

Forrest, J. D., Tietze, C., and Sullivan, E. 1978. Abortion in the United States, 1976–1977. *Family Planning Perspectives* 10:271–79.

Forssman, H., and Thuwe, I. 1966. One hundred and twenty children born after application for therapeutic abortion refused. *Acta Psychiatrica Scandinavica* 42:71–88.

Francke, L. B. 1978. *The ambivalence of abortion*. New York: Random House.

Frederikson, H., and Brackett, J. W. 1968. Demographic effects of abortion. *Public Health Reports* 83:999–1010.

Freedman, D. S., and Thornton, A. 1979. The long-term impact of pregnancy at marriage on the family's economic circumstances. *Family Planning Perspectives* 11:6–21.

Freeman, E. W. 1978. Abortion: subjective attitudes and feelings. *Family Planning Perspectives* 10:150–55.

Furlong-Cahill, J. 1974. Testimony before the U.S. Senate, Washington, D.C., 12 September 1974. In *Abortion: the double standard*. New York: Catholics for a Free Choice.

Furstenberg, F. F., Jr. 1976a. The social consequences of teenage parenthood. *Family Planning Perspectives* 8:148–64.

———. 1976b. *Unplanned parenthood: the social consequences of teenage childbearing*. New York: Macmillan.

Furstenberg, F. F., Jr., and Crawford, A. G. 1978. Family support: helping teenage mothers to cope. *Family Planning Perspectives* 10:322–33.

Gordon, R. H., and Kilpatrick, C. A. 1977. A program of group counseling for men who accompany women seeking legal abortions. *Community Mental Health Journal* 13:291–95.

Harlap, S., et al. 1979. A prospective study of spontaneous fetal losses after abortions. *New England Journal of Medicine* 301:677–81.

Harmonizer. 1977. Court rulings on abortion prompt activities in state legislatures and court. 17 July, p. 1.

Harrison, B. G. 1978. On reclaiming the moral perspective. *Ms.* 6 (June):40, 97.

Hogue, C. S. 1977. An evaluation of studies concerning reproduction after first trimester induced abortion. *International Journal of Gynecology and Obstetrics* 15:167–71.

Hulka, J. F. 1969. A mathematical study of contraceptive efficiency and unplanned pregnancies. *American Journal of Obstetrics and Gynecology* 104:443–47.

Illsley, R., and Hall, M. 1976. Psychosocial aspects of abortion: a review of issues and needed research. *Bulletin of the World Health Organization* 53:83–106.

———. 1978. Psychosocial research in abortion: selected issues. In H. P. David, H. L. Friedman, J. van der Tak, and M. J. Sevilla, eds., *Abortion in psychosocial perspective: trends in transnational research*, pp. 11–32. New York: Springer.

Institute of Medicine. 1975. *Legalized abortion and the public health*. Washington, D.C.: National Academy of Science.

Jacobs, D., Garcia, C-R., Rickels, K., and Preucel, R. W. 1975. Psychosocial effects of therapeutic abortion. *Contemporary OB/GYN* 5:81–87.

Kapor-Stanulovic, N., and Friedman, H. L. 1978. Studies in choice behavior in Yugoslavia. In H. P. David, H. L. Friedman, J. van der Tak, and M. J. Sevilla, eds., *Abortion in psychosocial perspective: trends in transnational research*, pp. 119–44. New York: Springer.

Kellerhals, J., and Pasini, W., with Wirth, G. 1978. Abortion seeking in Switzerland. In H. P. David, H. L. Friedman, J. van der Tak, and M. J. Sevilla, eds., *Abortion is psychosocial perspective: trends in transnational research*, pp. 35–56. New York: Springer.

Klinger, K., and Szabady, E. Patterns of abortion and contraceptive practice in Hungary. In H. P. David, H. L. Friedman, J. van der Tak, and M. J. Sevilla, eds., *Abortion in psychosocial perspective: trends in transnational research*, pp. 168–98. New York:Springer.

Kramer, M. J. 1975. Legal abortion among New York City residents: an analysis according to socioeconomic and demographic characteristics. *Family Planning Perspectives* 7:128–37.

Kruegel, D. L. 1975. The validity of retrospective reports of unwanted births in the United States: effects of preference for children of a given sex. *Studies in Family Planning* 6:345–48.

Leach, J. 1977. The repeat abortion patient. *Family Planning Perspectives* 9:37–39.

Levin, A., Schoenbaum, S. C., Monson, R. R., and Ryan, K. J. 1978. Induced abortion and the risk of spontaneous abortions. Paper presented at the annual meeting of the American Public Health Association, Los Angeles, 15–19 October 1978. Cited in *Family Planning Perspectives* 11 (1979):39–40.

Luker, K. 1975. *Taking chances: abortion and the decision not to contracept*. Berkeley and Los Angeles: University of California Press.

McCarthy, J., and Menken, J. 1979. Marriage, remarriage, marital disruption and age at first birth. *Family Planning Perspectives* 11:21–30.

Margolis, A., Rindfuss, R., Coghlan, P., and Rochat, R. 1974. Contraception and abortion. *Family Planning Perspectives* 6:56–69.

The Master's Plan. N.d. *Sister* 4(July).

Matejcek Z., Dytrych, A., and Schüller, U. 1978. Children from unwanted pregnancies. *Acta Psychiatrica Scandinavica* 57:67–90.

———. 1979. The Prague study of children born from unwanted pregnancies. *International Journal of Mental Health* 7:63–77.

Mazur, P. D. 1975. Social and demographic determinants of abortion in Poland. *Population Studies* 29:21–35.

Moore, K. A. 1978. Teenage childbirth and welfare dependency. *Family Planning Perspectives* 10:233–35.

Ms. 1977. Abortion alert. November.

Mulhauser, K. c.1978. Membership solicitation letter for the National Abortion Rights Action League.

Muramatsu, M., and van der Tak, J. 1978. From abortion to contraception: the Japanese experience. In H. P. David, H. L. Friedman, J. van der Tak, and M. J. Sevilla, eds., *Abortion in psychosocial perspective: trends in transnational research,* pp. 145–67. New York: Springer.

National Association for Repeal of Abortion Laws. N.d. The evils of criminal abortion. Pamphlet.

Newsweek. 1978a. Getting violent. 13 March.

———. 1978b. Abortion under attack. 5 June.

Niswander, K., Singer, J., and Singer, M. 1972. Psychological reaction to therapeutic abortion. II. Objective response. *American Journal of Obstetrics and Gynecology* 114:29–33.

Omaha World Herald. 1978a. Data collected on impact of abortion funding. 17 February.

———. 1978b. Study finds three abortions per ten births. 11 August.

———. 1979. Federation study indicates 90 percent for abortions sometimes. 15 November.

Oppel, W. C., and Raysten, A. B. 1971. Teen-age births: some social, psychological, and physical sequelae. *American Journal of Public Health* 61:751ff.

Osofsky, J. D., Osofsky, H. J., and Rajan, R. 1973. Psychological effects of abortions: with emphasis upon immediate reactions and follow-up. In H. J. Osofsky, and J. D. Osofsky, eds., *The abortion experience,* pp. 188–205. New York: Harper and Row.

Pakter, J., Nelson, F., and Svigir, M. 1975. Legal abortion: a half-decade of experience. *Family Planning Perspectives* 7:248–53.

Peled, T. 1978. Psychosocial aspects of abortion in Israel. In H. P. David, H. L. Friedman, J. van der Tak, and M. J. Sevilla, eds., *Abortion in psychosocial perspective: trends in transnational research,* pp. 56–76.

Pohlman, E. W. 1965a. Results of unwanted contraceptions: some hypotheses up for adoption. *Eugenics Quarterly* 11:11–18.

———. 1965b. "Wanted" and "unwanted": toward less ambiguous definitions. *Eugenics Quarterly* 12:19–27.

———. 1967. Unwanted contraceptions: research on undesirable consequences. *Eugenics Quarterly* 14:143–54.

———. 1968. Change from rejection to acceptance of pregnancy. *Social Science and Medicine* 2:337–40.

———. 1969. *The psychology of birth planning.* Cambridge, Mass.: Schenkman.

———. 1971a. Abortion dogmas needing research scrutiny. In R. Bruce Sloane, ed., *Abortion: changing views and practice.* New York: Grune and Stratton.

———. 1971b. The children born after denial of abortion request. In S. H. Newman, M. B. Beck, and S. Lewit, eds., *Abortion obtained and denied,* pp. 59–73. New York: Population Council.

Potter, R. G., and Ford, K. 1977. Repeated abortions. *Demography* 13:65–82.

Presser, H. B. 1970. The timing of the first birth, female roles, and black fertility. Paper presented at the annual meeting of the Population Association of America.

Presser, H. G. 1978. Sally's corner: coping with unmarried motherhood. Paper presented at the annual meeting of the American Sociological Association, 4–7 September 1978. Reported in *Family Planning Perspectives* 11 (1979):43–44.

Quick, J. D. 1978. Liberalized abortion in Oregon: effects on fertility, prematurity, fetal death, and infant death. *American Journal of Public*

Health 68:1003–8.
Rainwater, L. 1966. The Negro family: the crucible of identity. *Daedalus* 95:172–216.
Reichelt, P. A. 1978. Changes in sexual behavior among unmarried women utilizing oral contraception. *Journal of Population* 1:57–68.
Religious Coalition for Abortion Rights. N.d. We affirm: excerpts from statements about abortion rights as expressed by national religious organizations. Pamphlet. Washington, D.C.
Requeña, M. 1970. Abortion in Latin America, In R. E. Hall, ed., *Abortion in a changing world*, New York: Columbia University Press, 1:338–52.
Rindfuss, R. R., and Bumpass, L. L. 1977. Fertility during marital disruptions. *Journal of Marriage and Family* 39:517–28.
Rodgers, J. E. 1979. Abortion update. *Mademoiselle*, February.
Rosenwaite, I., and Melton, R. J. 1974. Legal abortion and fertility in Maryland, 1960–71. *Demography* 11:377–95.
Rosoff, J. I. 1975. Is support of abortion political suicide? *Family Planning Perspectives* 7:13–22.
Rossi, A. S. 1964. Equality between the sexes: an immodest proposal. *Daedalus* 93:607–52.
Rothstein, P. N.d. Legal abortion: arguments pro and con. Pamphlet. Westchester Coalition for Legal Abortion, affiliated with New York State National Abortion Rights League.
Russell, K. P., and Jackson, E. W. 1973. Therapeutic abortion: the California experience. In H. J. Osofsky, and J. D. Osofsky, eds., *The abortion experience*, pp. 175–76. New York: Harper and Row.
Ryan, W. 1971. *Blaming the victim*. New York: Knopf.
Sarvis, B., and Rodman, H. 1974. *The abortion controversy*. 2nd ed. New York: Columbia University Press.
Schardt, A. 1973. Savage abortion. *Civil Liberties*, September.
Sears, R. R., Maccoby, E. E., and Levin, H. 1957. *Patterns of child rearing*. Evanston, Ill.: Row, Peterson, and Company.
Shostak, A. 1979. Abortion as fatherhood lost: problems and reforms. *Family Coordinator* 28:569–74.
Simon, N., and Senturia, H. G. 1966. Psychiatric sequelae of abortion: review of the literature. *Archives of General Psychiatry* 15:378–89.
Sklar, J., and Berkov, B. 1974. Teenage family formation in postwar America. *Family Planning Perspectives* 6:80–90.
Smeal, E. c.1974. Membership solicitation letter for the National Organization for Women.
Smith, E. M. 1973. A follow-up study of women who request abortion. *American Journal of Orthopsychiatry* 43:574–85.
Somers, R. L. 1977. Repeat abortion in Denmark: an analysis based on national record linkage. *Studies in Family Planning* 8:142–47.
Somers, R. L., and Gammeltoft, M. 1976. The impact of liberalized abortion legislation on contraceptive practice in Denmark. *Studies in Family Planning* 7:218–23.
Steinhoff, P. G. 1973. Background characteristics of abortion patients. In H. J. Osofsky, and J. D. Osofsky, eds., *The abortion experience*, pp. 206–31. New York: Harper and Row.
Steinhoff, P. G., et al. 1975. Pregnancy planning in Hawaii. *Family Planning Perspectives* 7:138–42.

Steinhoff, P. G., et al. 1979. Women who obtain repeat abortions: a study based on record linkage. *Family Planning Perspectives* 11:30–38.

Sullivan, E., Tietze, C., and Dryfoos, J. G. 1977. Legal abortions in the U.S., 1975–76. *Family Planning Perspectives* 9:116–29.

Szasz, T. 1960. The myth of mental illness. *American Psychologist* 15:113–18.

———. 1974. Our despotic laws destroy the right to self-control. *Psychology Today* 8:(December)19–24ff.

Tietze, C. 1974. The "problem" of repeat abortions. *Family Planning Perspectives* 6:148–50.

———. 1975. The effects of legalization of abortions on population growth and public health. *Family Planning Perspectives* 7:123–27.

———. 1978a. Teenage pregnancies: looking ahead to 1984. *Family Planning Perspectives* 10:205–7.

———. 1978b. Repeat abortions—why more? *Family Planning Perspectives* 10:286–88.

Tietze, C., and Bongaarts, J. 1975. Fertility rates and abortion rates: simulations of family limitation. *Studies in Family Planning* 6:114–20.

Tietze, C., Bongaarts, J., and Schearer, B. 1976. Mortality associated with the control of fertility. *Family Planning Perspectives* 8:6–14.

Tietze, C., and Lewit, S. 1971. Legal abortions: early medical complications. *Family Planning Perspectives* 3:6–14.

Tietze, C., and Lewit, S., 1973. A national medical experience: the joint program for the study of abortion (JPSA). In H. J. Osofsky, and J. D. Osofsky, eds., *The abortion experience*, pp. 1–28. New York: Harper and Row.

Tietze, C., and Murstein, M. C. 1975. Induced abortion: a factbook. *Reports on Population/Family Planning* no. 14 (December), 2nd ed.

Time. 1978. Risky abortions: Chicago clinics are exposed. 27 November, p. 52.

U.S. Department of Health, Education and Welfare. 1971. *The effects of change in state abortion laws*. Washington, D.C.: Government Printing Office.

———. 1975. Surveillances summary: abortion-related mortality 1972 and 1973—United States. *Morbidity and Mortality Weekly Report* 24:22.

———. Center for Disease Control. 1979. *Abortion surveillance, 1977*. Washington, D.C.: Government Printing Office.

van der Tak, J. 1974a. Abortion in selected capitals of Latin America. In H. P. David, ed., *Abortion research: international experience*, pp. 145–53. Lexington, Mass.: D. C. Heath.

———. 1974b. Impact of changing abortion legislation and practice on fertility trends. In H. P. David, ed., *Abortion research: international experience*, pp. 39–53. Lexington, Mass.: D. C. Heath.

Vander Zanden, J. 1977. *Social psychology*. New York: Random House.

van Gelder, L. 1978. Cracking the women's movement protection game. *Ms*. 7 (December):66–68, 101.

Venkatcharya, K. 1972. Reduction in fertility due to induced abortions: a simulation model. *Demography* 9:339–52.

Walster, E., Berscheid, E., and Walster, G. W. 1973. New directions in equity research. *Journal of Personality and Social Psychology* 25:151–76.

Walter, G. S. 1970. Psychological and emotional consequences of elective abortion. *Obstetrics and Gynecology* 36:482–91.

Weinstock, E. W., Tietze, C., Jaffe, F. S., and Dryfoos, J. G. 1976. Abortion needs and services in the United States, 1974–75. *Family Planning Perspectives* 8:58–68.

Westoff, C. F., Potter, R. G., and Sagi, P. C. 1963. *The third child: a study in the prediction of fertility*. Princeton: Princeton University Press.

Williams, S. J., and Pullum, T. W. 1975. Effectiveness of abortion as birth control. *Social Biology* 22:23–33.

Working Group on Induced Abortion as a Public Health Problem. 1973. *WHO Chronicle* 27:525ff.

World Health Organization. 1978. Special Programme of Research, Development, and Research Training in Human Reproduction. Seventh Annual Report, Geneva, November 1978. Reported in *Family Planning Perspectives* 11 (1979):39–40.

Yeo, E. 1977. *Abortion, a painful decision*. Washington, D.C.: Religious Coalition for Abortion Rights.

Zelnik, M., and Kantner, J. F. 1974. The resolution of teenage first pregnancies. *Family Planning Perspectives* 6:74–80.

———. 1977. Sexual and contraceptive experience of young unmarried women in the United States, 1976 and 1971. *Family Planning Perspectives* 9:55–71.

———. 1978a. Contraceptive patterns and premarital pregnancy among women aged 15–19 in 1976. *Family Planning Perspectives* 10:135–42.

———. 1978b. First pregnancies to women aged 15–19: 1976 and 1971. *Family Planning Perspectives* 10:11–20.

Zimmerman, M. K. 1977. *Passage through abortion: the personal and social reality of women's experiences*. New York: Praeger.

5

UNWANTED PREGNANCY: A PSYCHOLOGICAL PROFILE OF WOMEN AT RISK

VIRGINIA ABERNETHY

THE TITLE of this study, "Unwanted Pregnancy: A Psychological Profile of Women at Risk," may be controversial because for some, no pregnancy is unwanted: every pregnancy could eventuate in a wanted baby. However, from my perspective, a pregnancy is unwanted if a woman is distressed to learn that she is pregnant and sees no reasonably feasible way in which she can keep the resulting child. Nonetheless, the title is useful because it allows me to say at the outset that almost every woman is at risk at some time in her life for unwanted pregnancy: unwanted in her terms. For some, the risk is great during a protracted span, for others it is associated primarily with one or more events of life stress or change. The topics covered here address the calculus associated with contracepting or risking pregnancy, the ego mechanisms that promote effective decision making, life-cycle events that increase vulnerability to unwanted pregnancy, and finally, the personality profile associated with a rather more chronic vulnerability.

CONTRACEPTION AS A DECISION

Avoidance of pregnancy typically depends on decisions either (1) to avoid sex or (2) to contracept, because a 4 percent risk of pregnancy is associated with every contraceptively unprotected act of sexual intercourse. An 80 percent probability of pregnancy is associated with unprotected sex of average frequency randomly distributed over a year's time.

A decision-making model assumes that use or nonuse of contraception is the resultant of balancing the positive and negative values attached to contraception against the positive and negative values attached to pregnancy, and then evaluating the risk of pregnancy from unprotected coitus. Thus, values associated with contraception and pregnancy, as well as the probability of pregnancy, must each be examined. This model has been developed in detail by Kristin Luker in her book, *Taking Chances: Abortion and the Decision Not to Contracept* (1975).

Contraception, per se, has one positive value attached to it that is, I would say, overriding: it can prevent unwanted pregnancy. However, a moment's thought will show that essentially all other of its attributes have a negative valence. Briefly, most methods are contrary to pronatalist religious tradition, the more effective methods cost money, many methods have costs in terms of the spontaneity of sexual performance, there are side effects from some contraceptives, obtaining contraception may cause embarrassment with a physician and/or druggist, and all methods require planning ahead to a greater or less degree. The requirement of planning ahead is of particular interest because it entails integration of one's self-image as a sexually active person, that is, anticipation of sexual intercourse within a particular relationship. For many women, particularly young women, acceptance of the self as sexual is problematic because of the strong tradition that nice girls "don't": "don't" have it and "don't" like it. The wrongness of these "don'ts" is somewhat mitigated, however, by not having planned it, by being swept off one's feet, so to speak, and by being in love. This romantic-cum-puritanic tradition makes it difficult for young women to be contraceptively prepared early in any relationship, and particularly in initial premarital relationships. To summarize, contraception is unpleasant in various ways, expensive, and a challenge to a young woman's value system almost exactly to the degree that she accepts traditional stereotypes of the female role.

The second parameter, pregnancy, tends to be valued or not valued as a function of marital status, age, parity, and financial flexibility. Pregnancy for an unmarried teenager has mostly negative values, which need not be enumerated. The surprise is that there are positive values, too. For example, there may be unrealistic fantasies about a baby being something of one's own, something to love that will return love; there may be expectations that pregnancy will be an effective bargaining counter for marriage; in some subcultures motherhood defines adulthood although a girl may continue to live with her parents; and there may be peer pressure to become pregnant when there is a high adolescent pregnancy rate, such as exists in some black communities. Moreover, Aid to Dependent Children may be perceived as a large allowance by a very young teenager, and has an unknown effect. Finally, a number of young women apparently desire the reassurance about their own fecundity that they gain from pregnancy; this motive appears to be exacerbated after some individual in the family has died or, less traumatically, has experienced a gynecologic problem.

Given that there is some balancing of positive and negative values associated with contraception and pregnancy, decision making depends still upon the evaluation of the likelihood of a particular outcome. Even an extremely negative weighing of pregnancy does not promote contraceptive use if the risk of pregnancy is thought to approach zero.

Acquisition of a personal perspective on the statistic that 80 out of 100 women will be pregnant after being sexually active for one year is not automatic or without its difficulties. There is no such thing as 80 percent pregnant. Moreover, a 4 percent probability of pregnancy from one unprotected coital act easily approximates zero risk and is therefore difficult to translate into precautionary behavior. When it does not rain after a weather forecast of a 50 percent probability of rain, it is easy to believe that a weatherman is always wrong with his warnings. Just so with anyone who has ever taken a risk without an untoward outcome; each coital experience that does not result in pregnancy reinforces belief in one's luck or in personal subfecundity.

The difficulty in evaluating risk is particularly severe for young teenagers, who are just beginning to integrate the fact of their own sexuality and who (not surprisingly) encounter their own, less visible, reproductive capacity with disbelief. Moreover, there may be so much misinformation that the very young teenager equates kissing or other sexual intimacy with coitus; when the former behaviors do not lead to pregnancy, skepticism about fecundity or belief in luck are reinforced. With each succeeding experience, denial of real risks is facilitated and can be overcome only with determinedly delivered information. When the psychological defense mechanism of denial is prominent, however, even the most explicit information appears insufficient. This is discussed below.

CAPACITY FOR DECISION MAKING

A number of personality traits impinge upon the capacity

for rational and effective decision making with respect to reproductive behaviors. Decisions tend to have best results when, to coin a phrase, one knows what one wants. Knowing both what one wants and what is within the realm of the possible requires complex integrative functions from the ego; that is, from the executive powers of the mind. Warren Miller has focused on various motives, or wants, that must be reconciled in order to achieve a rational outcome: the ego must integrate (1) motives that arise from within oneself with those that are generated externally in the social field; (2) "motives oriented to the achievement of pleasure and happiness"; (3) "present-oriented and future-oriented motives"; (4) "current motives with previous motives and past behavior" (Miller 1973a). Translated into terms germane to reproductive behavior, motives that should be integrated relate to one's self-image as a sexual, adult person; past and present heterosexual relationships; financial considerations; time constraints on child rearing; and career and personal goals.

The ego's capacity for integrating these factors is impaired by a number of psychological defense mechanisms that may be conceptualized as traits when they are sufficiently pervasive in the personality. Prominent among these are repression, or banishment from conscious thought of unpleasant feelings or realities, and denial, which is closely related to magical thinking, so that what one wishes is perceived as reality or as actually occurring. For example, denial might lead to ignoring the pregnancy risk of contraceptively unprotected coitus, to false expectations about the commitment of one's sexual partner to the relationship, or to the false belief that a relationship was based on a sound friendship rather than on sexuality alone. Repression might foster forgetting of past experiences of abandonment by a sexual partner and, therefore, a failure to learn and modify behavior.

Thus, the capacity for making contraceptive and reproductive decisions with a good probability of a favorable outcome depends upon the executive function of the ego in integrating, or reconciling, (often) conflicting motives. A good appraisal of reality is essential in this process, but such an appraisal is impaired by some psychological defense mechanisms, notably repression and denial.

VULNERABILITY AS A FUNCTION OF LIFE-CYCLE EVENTS

Change, even positive change, is a source of psychological stress. In periods of change, the individual is focused more than usually upon the task of adaptation, while normal attention in other dimensions of living is attenuated. Warren Miller identifies life-cycle changes, eight in all, during which a woman is likely to be more than ordinarily vulnerable to unwanted pregnancy (Miller 1973b). Two likely contexts for contraceptively unprotected sexual relations are early adolescence and the start of a sexual career. At least three social and psychological dimensions are conducive to adolescent, especially premarital, pregnancy at these stages. First, there are the real obstacles that society places in the way of a teenager's acquiring information or assistance with contraception. Second, as noted above, there is the unpreparedness for physical changes: although the reproductive process may be understood on an intellectual level, there is sometimes a quality of fantasy suggesting that some teenagers do not believe in their own fecundity, responding to it with surprise that has the aspect of innocence. Last, there is the matter of exposure to pregnancy. Because of today's permissive mores, there is a wide range in sexual behavior of which some of the more important variables appear to be (1) age at which sexual experimentation begins and (2) the alternatives of promiscuity or premarital monogamy, even if the latter is serial monogamy.

It appears that the younger the girl when she begins to have sexual relations, the longer she is exposed before attempting to obtain contraceptive protection (Settlage, Baroff, and Cooper 1973). Secondly, compared to multiple ongoing contacts, a monogamous relationship, even premaritally, is associated with more effective contraceptive use (Sorenson 1973). This finding is congruent with Miller's identification of further occasions predictive of diminished contraceptive vigilance: either when a sexual relationship is in the early stages of development or when it has become unstable, so that coitus tends to be unexpected except for experimentation, impulsive visits, or reconciliations. The remaining contexts when vigilance may be lax have in common that they also relate to major life change: the inclusive list is geographic mobility, just before or after marriage, after each pregnancy, in relation to the decision to *stop* childbearing, and during menopause (Miller 1973b).

UNCONSCIOUS MOTIVATION AS A FACTOR IN CHRONIC VULNERABILITY

It appears that unconscious motivation, which theoretically is implicated with developmental/experiential factors, also impinges upon contraceptive use. This topic can be initiated by reference to Franklin Wilson and Larry Bumpass's 1973 paper entitled "The Prediction of Fertility Among Catholics: A Longitudinal Analysis."

Wilson and Bumpass report that a four-years-later follow-up of Catholic women originally interviewed for the 1965 National Fertility Study shows that having an additional pregnancy in the study interval is positively correlated with having had a premarital pregnancy. The strength of the association increases when there are statistical controls for "life-cycle" and "social background" items, and other "fertility-planning" variables, including (1) current contraceptive method and (2) fertility intentions. That is, with social class, religion, parity, age, plans to avoid an additional child, and contraceptive method all held constant, premaritally pregnant women had a net difference of .33 higher fertility than those who had not been premaritally pregnant. In effect, at least two unwanted pregnancies are implied when a woman who had been premaritally pregnant tries unsuccessfully to avoid a subsequent birth. Wilson and Bumpass (1973) conclude that this is "clear evidence of the continuing influence [on fertility] of factors other than explicit goals and means."

"Factors other than . . ." are the subject of the remainder of this paper. Congruent with the Wilson and Bumpass findings, it appears that there is an early experiential constellation association with the predisposition to risk unwanted pregnancy, so that for some women the knowledge and availability of modern contraceptive technology is not enough (Abernethy 1973; Abernethy et al. 1975). However, in apparent self-recognition of their vulnerability, many such women do eventually achieve effective birth control by adopting methods for which continuous vigilance by themselves is relatively unnecessary. Compared to matched controls who do not have a history of unwanted pregnancy, these women are significantly more likely to rely on the IUD, a tubal ligation, or condom use by their partner (Abernethy 1973).

The constellation thought to be associated with risking an unwanted pregnancy consists primarily of an early familial experience characterized by a parental marriage which is distant and hostile, the daughter's alienation from and/or denigration of her mother, and the daughter's maintaining an intimate, quasi-consort relationship with the father. Absence of a paternal figure may have a similar effect on a young woman's developing model for male-female relationships; she is free to fantasize a relationship, unfettered by reality-testing, in which she is more successful than the mother had been in focusing the husband/father's affections and commitment. Lacking in opportunities to develop a positive feminine self-image through identification with an esteemed mother, the young girl attempts to define her womanliness and raise her self-esteem through interactions with her father, or in fantasies of a relationship with him.

In evident extension of familial experience to external relationships, a woman with this background appears to feel that friendships with other women are unsatisfactory or worthless, to hold herself and women in low esteem, to measure herself on the standard of male approval and attention, but to be tense in a man's company because of a compulsion to conform to his expectations (Abernethy 1973). A woman may feel that she is required to act innocent, demure, lightheaded, affectionate, tenderhearted, happy, carefree, or even dependent—all postures associated with the female stereotype in our culture (Broverman et al. 1972).

As part of this constellation there appears to be a below-average liking for sex (Abernethy 1973), but this does not much diminish the probability of sexual activity when a woman has renounced control or parity in a relationship. At the same time, passivity allows disclaimers of responsibility, for both coitus and contraception.

There is a second dynamic, in addition to reliance on male approval as the primary basis of self-esteem, that may explain unwanted-pregnancy–risking behavior: the intimate, seductive relationship with the father (especially in the absence of positive feelings for the mother) may produce anxiety in the adolescent girl because of its incestuous overtones. She may respond by using sex with other men to place a barrier between herself and the father. In clinical terms, promiscuity and precocious sex can be seen as counterphobic behavior with displacement from the father to a safer man (Abernethy and Abernethy 1974).

Three lines of evidence from two independent samples form the basis for the foregoing analysis. The hypothesis that there is a causal relationship between experiences in family of origin and the later behavior of risking unwanted pregnancy was first tested using a double-blind design for comparison of sixty-five normal (never hospitalized for mental illness) women who had had an abortion to terminate an unwanted pregnancy and their controls (matched on age, marital status, religion, and education), who had never had an abortion or miscarriage, who had a maximum of two children, and whose last pregnancy (if any) occurred under the condition of "not using a method in order to become pregnant" (Abernethy 1973).

Two findings merit emphasis. First, index subjects suffered from an emotional loss of the maternal figure. This was seen in their significantly greater tendency to favor the mother in early childhood ($F = 8.203, P < .006$), followed by their perception of having had few activities with her during adolescence, also a statistically significant difference between themselves and control subjects ($F = 4.540, P < .036$). Second, index subjects' intimacy with the father was inferred from the greater likelihood of their consulting him about a sex-related problem ($F = 5.108, P < .026$), a statistically significant finding that seems of particular importance because there was no difference between index control subjects when the choice between parents was made in the context of a financial or other social problem (Abernethy 1973).

A second study correlates sexual behavior with the family history of twenty-three adolescents who were inpatients in a psychiatric hospital (Abernethy and Abernethy 1974). On the basis either of their having already had an unwanted pregnancy or of risking such by contraceptively unprotected (and frequently promiscuous) sex, these girls were assigned to Low, Medium, or High risk groups. Independent raters, who did not know the assignments to the behavioral categories, then rated each subject for risk on the basis of self-reported relationship with the mother, grandmother, and father, and the parents' attitudes toward each other. Results showed the predicted association between sexual risk–taking behavior and (1) absence of closeness with a female figure and (2) excessive intimacy with the father (Abernethy and Abernethy 1974).

Contrasting the Low risk group with others again suggests the predisposing role of family history. Girls whose social behavior put them at Low risk for unwanted pregnancy had in no case experienced alienation from a parent or a shift in allegiance between childhood and adolescence (Abernethy and Abernethy 1974).

The two studies described are similar in their methodology: correlating a behavioral measure (risking or having an unwanted pregnancy) with ratings of family role relationships. A third study gives indirect but objective support to the suggested explanation for the underlying dynamic, viz., that anxiety over the sexual content (real or imagined) of the father-daughter relationship propels a woman into other sexual interactions, so that the father and other men are invariably confused. The additional evidence comes from data on fertility and contraceptive histories of sixty young, mentally ill women (including the twenty-three described above) who have an average age of twenty-one years. Forty-one of the sixty have had at least one experience of sexual intercourse, with a resulting seventeen women having been pregnant at least once. Twenty-four or possibly twenty-three pregnancies were unplanned out of the total twenty-six pregnancies. The pregnancy outcomes for the total group were: two terminated by induced abortion, nine reportedly miscarried (a high proportion, it must be admitted), eight children given up for adoption, and seven kept by their mother (Abernethy 1974).

The aborted pregnancies and the adoptions can be safely considered unwanted as well as unplanned conceptions, and it is these ten cases that bear on the family relationship hypothesis. It is of interest that four men (contributing to five of the ten unwanted pregnancies) were more than ten years older than the woman. This seems to be an unusually large number of considerably older sexual partners, and recalls the hypothesized dynamic that in some circumstances coitus is motivated by ambivalent feelings for the father, feelings then generalized to other men.

This paper has been an attempt to summarize the work of several investigations of motivational factors in unwanted pregnancy, and has been especially an effort to illuminate somewhat the black box, "influence of other factors," phenomena discovered by Wilson and Bumpass in their extensively controlled longitudinal study of fertility. Insofar as Wilson and Bumpass compared women who stated in a first interview that they did *not* want another child, the higher interval fertility reported by the subsample who had a premarital pregnancy probably represented (another) unwanted pregnancy.

It has been hypothesized that an experiential and psychological configuration is associated with the predisposition to risk unwanted pregnancy. The research bearing on the issue is consistent in showing differences in family history between women who have had or are risking unwanted pregnancy and others. The critical constellation appears to include (1) the daughter's alienation from her mother, (2) the daughter's taking over elements of her mother's role, which is a corollary to (3) intimacy between the father and daughter that excludes the mother. The etiology, typically, is distance and hostility in the parents' marriage.

Both the demographic and psychological findings reinforce the proposition that, for some women, effective contraception requires more than knowledge and access to birth control technology. It appears that these women, even when using a contraceptive method, are likely to use it in such a way that protection falls short of the potential effectiveness demonstrated by clinically controlled trials. Therefore, in counseling such women it is important both to give assistance in resolving the underlying psychological issues and also to reinforce their decision to use contraception while suggesting, perhaps, a shift to a method that is relatively free from user error.

At the same time it should be recognized that for all women there are periods of life change or stress when contraceptive vigilance is likely to be reduced; and also, that the negative factors associated with contraceptive use, the positive valence associated with pregnancy, and each woman's assessment of risk need to be evaluated and addressed. Particularly when a woman's cognitive style is characterized by emphasis on desired rather than probable outcomes, and by failure to integrate present and future goals, there is a tendency either to achieve less than optimal results in planning a wanted family, or to resort to abortion.

REFERENCES

Abernethy, V. 1973. The abortion constellation: early history and present relationships. *Archives of General Psychiatry* 29:346–50.

———. 1974. Sexual knowledge, attitudes and practices of young female psychiatric patients. *Archives of General Psychiatry* 30:180–82.

Abernethy, V., and Abernethy, G. 1974. Risk for unwanted pregnancy and mentally ill adolescent girls. *American Journal of Orthopsychiatry* 44:442–49.

Abernethy, V., Robins, D. M., Abernethy, G., Grunebaum, H., and Weiss, J. 1975. Identification of women at risk for unwanted pregnancy. *American Journal of Psychiatry* 132:1027–31.

Broverman, I. K., Vogel, S. R., Broverman, D. M., Clarkson, F. E., and Rosenkrantz, P. S. 1972. Sex-Role stereotypes: a current appraisal. *Journal of Social Issues* 28:59–78.

Luker, K. 1975. *Taking chances: abortion and the decision not to contracept*. Berkeley: University of California Press.

Miller, W. B. 1973a. Conception mastery: ego control of the psychological and behavioral antecedents to conception. *Comments on Contemporary Psychiatry* 1:157–77.

Miller, W. B. 1973b. Psychological vulnerability to unwanted pregnancy. *Family Planning Perspectives* 5:199–201.

Settlage, D. S. F., Baroff, S., and Cooper, D. 1973. Sexual experience of young teenage girls seeking contraceptive assistance for the first time. *Perspectives in Family Planning* 5:223–26.

Sorenson, R. C. 1973. *The Sorenson report: adolescent sexuality in contemporary America*. New York: World Publishing Co.

Wilson, F. D., and Bumpass, L. 1973. The prediction of fertility among Catholics: a longitudinal analysis. *Demography* 10:591–97.

6

AN EMOTIONAL HISTORY OF THE ABORTIONS OF THREE WOMEN

ARTHUR KORNHABER

THE RAPID CHANGES that our world is experiencing have profoundly affected the lives of its inhabitants and of the collective society. Margaret Mead has described these rapid changes as "the acceleration of history," remarking upon the profound effect that this "acceleration" has upon human relationships: "for each generation lives in a world markedly different from that of its forebears."

Wilhelm Reich, the psychiatrist, warned of the "emotional plague" that he observed arising in a "technologically polarized" society. In *The Mass Psychology of Fascism* he described the political implications of this phenomenon and described a "plague personality" as "rational in work only, deploring the display of emotions and the spontaneity of children, seeking power, making others conform to his view of the world, decrying the pleasures of the human body."

The rapid acquisition of scientific and technological information is causing our society to become more and more technologically polarized. This event is reflected within the psychic structure of our people. The intellectual, technical segment of our psyche is expanding. Since we seem to have limited conscious power in our minds, this expansion of our intellectual capacity takes over to the detriment of our emotionality and spirituality. The latter, because of educational neglect or biological stasis, has not evolved as quickly as the intellect. This is important, for the intellect has traditionally served as negotiator between the emotions and drives of the person and the world. A condition now exists where, because of the inability of the neglected emotional and spiritual sectors of our psyche to serve as an effective check and balance upon the intellect, the possibility of intellectual anarchy in our society exists. This occurs at the expense of our emotional feelings and spiritual existence and would be socially translated by the indiscriminate application of technology without consideration of the emotional and spiritual consequences.

True learning involves feeling and thinking. We learn, for example, from a teacher we love better than from a television set. What I am observing in my young patients, however, is a withering of their feelings. In children I see a real increase of physical prowess and of their thinking facility. At the same time the emotional and spiritual and creative aspects of their personalities are decreasing. Sitting for hours and weeks and years with the young, I have seen the atrophy of the spirit.

We may view the issue of abortion in this light. The technology of abortion has "accelerated." The procedure is safer, quicker, and less expensive than ever before. In a "plague" society this implies that it should be made more available only because it is "better." The plagued businessman says: "If people will buy it, sell it."

The abortion issue is a battle in a great war that is now taking place in our society and in the minds of all of us who inhabit it. On the one side, there are the forces of "expedience in the service of technology;" on the other, "emotion, humanism, spirituality." Such is the nature of the conflict that is taking place in the society where lived the women that I, their psychiatrist, spoke with.

These complex reactions of thought and feeling appeared in all of the women that we studied, even though they initially appeared to dismiss their abortion in a cursory fashion.

Our experience makes us suspect that we are not paying enough attention to the vast ramifications of a universal human experience.

We further suspect that society would rather that we didn't pay attention to this aspect of things and that is what this paper is all about.

THE WOMEN

The women whom we have chosen to present, from among the many we have worked with over the years, have several things in common. They are white, female, educated, and raised in the same socioeconomic strata. Although they have had varying degrees of religious training, they are not religious participants.

These similarities in their backgrounds limit the variables affecting our observations. Although this is scientifically desirable, it limits our view of the critical role that socioeconomics (and especially social class) plays in the drama of the abortion issue. That dimension of the issue cannot be ignored.

The subject of abortion has been the object of intense scrutiny by many investigators. They have examined the issue in breadth, from the vantage point of their own disciplines.

We speculated that if we examined the depth of the issue through a direct, ongoing dialogue with women as they learned that they were pregnant with an unwanted child, considered having the child (either keeping it or giving it up for adoption) or aborting, made the choice to abort, had the abortion, and experienced the aftereffects, we would be afforded the opportunity to share and to learn about the emotional responses of these women to their abortion experience. In sum, these responses present an emotional history of the women's experience. This is a vital dimension of the abortion issue that is often ignored, because people can't really sit with one another one-to-one long enough to explore it.

Psychiatrists are privileged to be invited into the personal universe of the people who seek their help and are privy to their innermost thoughts and feelings, which are expressed verbally and behaviorally. The psychiatrist observes how the individual uses his biologic birthright, his nature (i.e., temperament, "talent" in social, intellectual, physical, spiritual, and emotional areas of functioning), to assimilate and accommodate to the fashion in which he is nurtured by the world outside of him.

The personality of the individual is in constant flux, constantly "becoming," maintaining a tenuous balance between the forces of nature and nurture. In a woman, an unwanted pregnancy disrupts this balance.

The three women whom we will discuss sought help for reasons unrelated to their abortion, but during the course of therapy they discovered that they were pregnant with an unwanted child. We observed that the undesired conception affected every aspect of their being. We witnessed how they adapted to the experience by unconsciously implementing a series of mental maneuvers to assure their mental integrity.

In order to expand our view, we will also present the experience of another woman: poor, Latin, devoutly religious, and educated, who is contrast to the others, didn't adjust well to her abortion. Her story was told to us by David, a colleague who is an expert in such matters.

We have also chosen women of different ages in the hope of learning how women of different ages cope with the same experience and whether the fact that they were raised in different decades, part of the acceleration history, affected their outlook.

The three women we will discuss are Susie, a sixteen-year-old high school student; Lila, a twenty-six-year-old career woman; Harriet, a thirty-five-year-old homemaker; and, through the eyes of David, Maria, deceased.

SUSIE

Susie is a sixteen-year-old high school student of "good family," who lives with her parents and three sisters and brother in a middle-class suburban community.

By nature, Susie is a "crazy teenager," an impulsive person—a characteristic of her personality that has gotten her in hot water with her family for most of her life. Her sisters say that she does "dumb things." Her peers, loyal to the end, say that she is funny and spontaneous, an "air head." Temperamentally, she is a romantic, compassionate, and emotional person. Easily directed externally, she has relinquished the relatively reasonable direction of her parents for the authority of the consensus of her peers. She is suggestible and easily led. Her compassion is expressed by her wish to be a nurse and by the fact that she is a neighborhood social worker: she nurses many of the wounded youngsters in her environment by "listening to their troubles." Her lack of professional training, however, leads her to "catch" her friends' problems because of her concern for them. This requires the expenditure of a lot of mental energy on her part to the detriment of her academic studies, which disturbs her parents and sets off emotional fireworks at home. As far as her ability to make decisions is concerned, she knows what she is against, but not what she is for. As her father said, "She has got both feet firmly planted in mid-air, but we love her." Her religious training was perfunctory and ended when she was ten. She found it "boring."

She has not achieved a level of maturity where she is able to use her conscience in a preventive way. When she acts impulsively, her conscience asserts itself after the fact, and she "feels guilty." Her mother senses this: "When her room is cleaned up, I know that she has done something wrong." Susie has no compunction, however, about applying the dictates of her conscience to the younger members of her family, who call her "little mother" when they are angry at her. This phrase has become a clarion call to battle in the family.

Her parents have taught her ethics and values. She is just not old enough to apply them to her life all of the time. Her self-control and her judgment are adequate for normal functioning in a "safe" world. When she feels an overwhelmingly strong emotion, or when her conscience is put out of action by alcohol or marijuana, she becomes vulnerable to her own impulses or those of others.

Such were the circumstances on the night of the Junior Prom, when she became pregnant. This initiated a sequence of events in her life whereby, having conceived impulsively, she agonized, then aborted mechanically. Throughout this process she was supported by her boyfriend (who, in her words, "had it all together"), her friends, and society (in the form of Planned Parenthood and the medical profession). Her parents never knew.

It was difficult for her to talk about her experience. She felt it was very private and between her and her boyfriend. It was painful for her to share her experience and relive the emotions that she desperately did not want to feel. Of the three women whom we report on, she was the most conflicted between a need to blurt it all out and a strong desire to put it all out of her mind, thus magically banishing the experience from existence.

After all, she was a kid. She felt better after she talked about it. "I became concerned when my boyfriend told me that he didn't use any protection when we made out on the night of the Junior Prom," she told us. As the days passed and her menstrual period did not arrive, her apprehension about the possibility of being pregnant mounted into terror. In a frenzy of phone calls she talked to her boyfriend, who said he "was nauseous about it," and several close friends, some of whom had "gone through the same thing." She spoke to no adults. When she started getting sick in the morning, her friends told her to go to Planned Parenthood to find out if she was pregnant. She went there with her boyfriend and found out that she was indeed pregnant. She remarked that the people at Planned Parenthood were "kind and understanding" to her. "They didn't make me feel bad," she said. Her boyfriend told her to leave it all to him and made an appointment for her with a local gynecologist. Her boyfriend was seventeen years old at that time. His parents knew nothing about his plight either.

Once the appointment was made, Susie felt "relieved" and "put the whole thing out of my mind." Her emotions kept welling up, however. Since she was attempting to detach herself from the experience and was angry and upset about her situation, she displaced these feelings onto her bewildered parents, who noted that she "was a bitch at home." Susie agreed that "everyone at home is walking on eggs around me."

She was frightened that her parents would discover her situation, which further fueled her anger toward them. She kept her room very clean. She remembers giving her boyfriend a daily report about her "mother's suspicions." She was later able to report that she wished that her mother had found out because she "really needed a mother then." Her boyfriend became a parent to her during this time.

She hesitated to talk about her pregnancy, about "the contents of her womb." When she did she was confused. "Just a bunch of cells in there," she said. "It would be a baby only if I kept it for five months." "If my boyfriend wanted to get married maybe I would have it. . . . The baby: I could never, never give it away for adoption. But it's not a problem, for right now there is only a bunch of mush there, and I hear it's no problem to get it vacuumed out."

Susie went to the doctor with her boyfriend, and the abortion was performed. She was pleased that the doctor told her that it was unusual to see a young man accompany a woman to his office. Her boyfriend took her home and left her to "do errands" for his parents. When she left the office she remembered thinking that she wanted to put the whole thing out of her mind and pretend that it never happened.

In the weeks following the abortion she began to worry if she were damaged by the operation. She felt very angry and weepy. Her anger was vented on her boyfriend, now fallen from grace, whom she called a "dumb jerk for getting me pregnant." Her parents became "awful people who screwed me up." She became "nervous and sweaty" when people mentioned abortion or her friends asked her about it. She would not have told this to anyone else. Had someone done a survey at this point she would have reported that everything was fine. She avoided people, especially children. "I feel weird around children," she said. "I want to stare at them and I don't want to look at them at all." She worried about the future. "I could never tell the person I marry about this. How did this happen to me?"

All during this time she was functioning adequately and no one in her world, according to her, ever knew what was going on inside of her. "I probably wouldn't be in touch with all of this either," she said, "if I wasn't talking about it here. Why me? Why did I have to get pregnant? Was it bad luck?"

It wasn't bad luck in Susie's case. It was a strong, biologically motivated impulse, seeking expression, and powerful enough to override the agents of prohibition, her personal inhibitions (neutralized by alcohol), her conscience (asleep with her parents), and her judgment (relegated to her boyfriend), in an opportune setting, without adult supervision, that contributed significantly to her pregnancy.

Thus, by nature a loving person, she became a naive victim of the biological consequences of loving and of the expression of her passion. She never really linked up lovemaking and the production of children in her mind. She never learned that from her society. The idea that babies came from lovemaking was only an abstract concept to her, even more difficult for her to understand at a time in her life when she is so "into" the present, living in the world of her peers. She went through the experience in a daze, unable to share it with her parents. This is sad. They could have been helpful to her, if their love for her had overcome (which I'm confident it could have) the disturbance that Susie feared her pregnancy would cause them. But she was too frightened to approach them, and she turned to society to help her out.

Eventually, Susie's emotions quieted down within her. She summed it up: "I'm not really a kid anymore, I've lost my childhood. I hope that I can keep the experience out of my mind, to pretend it never happened. I hope so. What a way to grow up."

LILA

Lila is twenty-six years old and devotes her life to her career in the field of television. She is a bright, active, and attractive woman, with an abrupt, yet not rude, manner. She is the picture of "efficiency." You'd like Lila if she walked into the room. She has a terrific personality. She has many friends who call her "Spunky," a name given to her during her grade school years in New England. In her work she travels often and "meets interesting people." She speaks quickly, often flippantly, and her humor tends toward sarcasm. Her only hobby is reading. She is an "atheist."

She feels satisfied with her life and her career, and recognizes the fact that she is "not into raising a family." She "doesn't have much to do with kids" except for "my nieces," and "would rather have been born a man." "Being a woman is definitely second best, like being born in a straitjacket." She likes men and has had several relationships that lasted for some time, but "they all ended up being male chauvinists, couldn't stand to be equal."

She feels that she is a very practical person: "I like to get things done. When I found out that I was pregnant, I had an abortion within a couple of weeks."

She uses scientific terminology whenever possible and avoids emotional communication, although her language became more expressive during the time we worked together. Her abortion was "the abortion procedure." She functions on a level of thought and rationality to the detriment of her emotions. When she became pregnant, the possibility of having the baby never occurred to her. She found some humor in the fact that she became pregnant on, of all days, Labor Day. "Can you imagine?" she exclaimed. "It was a one-nighter in the Hamptons and I was stoned out of my mind." At first, she didn't feel much about being pregnant, although she became annoyed that science had failed her. "The doctor told me that the IUD he inserted was foolproof. Wait until I see him again."

She suspected that she was pregnant when she awoke one morning "sick to my stomach, like my mother described to me." Since she "ignores my damn periods as much as I can," she was caught unaware. "I thought that it was just one of those times when I skipped a period." She described her feelings at the time that she first discovered that she was pregnant:

> I woke up sick to my stomach. It hit me. God! I'm pregnant! Did I get pissed . . . furious . . . I slapped my stomach . . . I suddenly realized why my boobs were getting bigger . . . "That's all I need," I thought.

> In a while, I thought, "Well, at least I know that I'm a woman . . . that's not too bad." I called a girlfriend of mine who had been through the same deal and we chatted about it. We even giggled a bit. She said that she would help me if I needed it, but I told her that I could handle it alone.

Lila went through her abortion alone. She never told her "boyfriend" that she was pregnant. She acted immediately and with dispatch. She was good at "getting things done":

> I called up my GYN and he gave me a date to have a test and the abortion the next day. The test was positive so I went over to his office the next day, hopped up on the table, and he performed the operation. I never missed a day of work [she was very proud of this].

After the abortion, Lila bled for a long while. She started to "feel" anger. She directed it toward the GYN, calling him "the bastard that butchered me." She went to another physician, who hospitalized her for several days in order to "clean out" her uterus. The original doctor had not completely "evacuated the uterine contents," she said. She was furious because she was losing time from work.

During this time her language became peppered with invectives, her expression of anger. When she left the hospital, she threw herself into her work, which aggravated her condition. She had several recurrences of mild bleeding. Lila was experiencing more emotions than her "reason" could handle and was a bit bewildered by it. She was becoming flooded. Her dreams, unavailable to the control of her reason, signaled her unrest:

> I'm having crazy dreams about playing with dolls and losing them, and having to go to work and leaving my toys at home. In another dream all of the other children have toys and I don't.

Although she continued to function, she noticed that she felt a "bit blue." She was concerned about not being as happy to see her niece (she really loved her niece; she was almost another mother for her):

> I just have trouble being with her right now. I get weepy. I don't know what it is . . . rather I do but I don't want to think about it.

She was unable to foreclose the issue of her abortion because she continued to bleed. She couldn't exercise her reason to put the incident out of awareness because her mind could not legislate her bleeding out of existence, and this was her primary coping mechanism for emotional difficulties. This was not to think about it; but she was bleeding, so she couldn't help it:

> I couldn't put it out of my mind because every time I went to the bathroom, there it was, the bleeding . . . to haunt me. I couldn't separate the bleeding from the abortion. I wish that it would have been easier.

She said that she felt changed, that she never knew that "it would be like this":

> I'm not the same person any more . . . I don't know how I've changed, but I have. I feel more . . . I'm thinking more about things that I do. I'm different around children. I look at them differently. The abortion itself was so simple. I never thought about it. It's this time now, after the abortion. If I was religious I would say that I was being punished or something but I know that is bullshit. I guess that one can't fool around with mother nature for free.

When her bleeding stopped, Lila was able to repress the experience more easily. Her reason quickly sought to supersede the emotions that occupied her awareness during the incident. The bleeding, indicative of a wound, facilitated the ascent of her emotions into awareness. She couldn't just brush off her abortion as she would have preferred to do.

Her experience put her in touch with the emotional dimension of her life. She reflected on the experience later: "In some ways I grew from that abortion. It made me stop and take stock of things. I never contemplated myself as a mother before. I guess that I could have had a child. I really am, in a way, a childless mother. I don't like to think about that, it scares me. That's a new feeling for me."

In parting, she said: "Well, there is another way of looking at it. I've joined the club: abortions are becoming an 'in' thing, nowadays."

HARRIET

Harriet, a thirty-five-year-old homemaker, married for fifteen years, had a "great marriage" until the day that she learned that she was pregnant again. Until that time she was content with her role in the home. Her husband "worked hard to support his family and was very successful at it." Her pregnancy caused a crisis in her life resulting from the fact that her pregnancy was not planned. Instinctively, she wanted another child, especially after having enjoyed her other children. Intellectually, she felt another child would be impractical. Her husband, however, was clear on the issue. He didn't want another child:

> No more kids. We've done our share. I love kids but its our turn to have some fun. I've worked hard for a long time and now I want to enjoy myself.

Harriet, however, didn't feel the same way:

> It wouldn't be bad for me. My life is centered around my home and I think that we could absorb another child. In fact, I think that some of my friends are ridiculous the way that they leave their kids to go out and work, as if that's something special.

Harriet eventually had the abortion. Several weeks afterward, she found it difficult to get out of bed in the morning and to function in her normal manner. She lost her healthy appetite ("the best thing about the depression," she said after she recovered), felt sad ("as if someone had died"), and guilty and angry. With therapy she made a rapid recovery; she learned that she was angry about the events that had led to her abortion and was psychologically turning her anger inward. This, in concert with the physical aspects of the experience, led her to mental exhaustion.

As she recovered she became aware of the degree of anger and resentment that she felt:

> How could such a crazy thing happen to me? If I would have thought ten years ago, only ten years ago, to do such a thing, I would have been crazy. Why did I do it?

She directed a great deal of anger toward her husband, who was bewildered by it. "I didn't think that it was such a big deal," he said. Harriet became more and more animated as she talked about her husband's reaction to her pregnancy:

> He was so cold, so distant when I told him that I thought I was pregnant. "Get rid of it," he said. He wouldn't be involved with it. I wasn't strong enough to handle that. What a dummy I was. But what else could I do if my husband didn't want the baby? He made all of the arrangements and I went in to the doctor like some kind of cow to the slaughter. I was numb, couldn't think for myself. My husband is a good person, deep down. When he saw how I reacted afterward, he was truly sorry, but it was too late. The baby was gone. He even said that if it meant so much to me we could have another. He said that he never realized what it meant until he saw how it affected me.

Harriet's decision to terminate her pregnancy was also advocated by many of her friends, who told her it was "impractical" to have a child at this time in her life. Because of her lack of self-confidence, she leans heavily on the advice of other people concerning her actions, "which ends up driving me whacky." She rarely looked inside of herself for answers, preferring to "follow the crowd."

She is different from the other women that we discussed. First, she already has children of her own and has pleasant memories of past pregnancies. Second, because of her age she had lived in a time when abortion was anathema, a shame, and illegal—remember, the acceleration of history. Third, she was exposed, in her youth, to a society that valued human life and family life more than does present-day society. We are not idealizing the past when we say that she had lived in a world where human connections were more celebrated and narcissism was less prevalent. She had received some religious training.

These factors made it difficult for her to accept abortion in an automatic fashion. Her emotional nature served as a counterforce to reason, the intellectual learning experience that was taught to her by society. Before her abortion she found herself caught between these two forces: her experience and her feelings, on the one hand, and the "teachings of society," on the other (operating within her by the mechanism of reason).

Differing temperaments make some people more gifted in thinking; others have stronger instincts or talents for feeling. Neither is superior to the other, but our society places little value on the latter. Feeling people suffer in this society. Harriet's husband was a thinker.

Her husband had the same emotional exposure that she did, but because of his personality, he paid much more attention to the "form and reason" of events than to his feelings about them. This made it easy for society to mold his behavior. He wanted to "enjoy himself." Having numbed his own feelings, he nevertheless was disturbed by the expression of feelings in his wife. He could "feel for" his wife:

> I want to live now, to buy a new car, to travel and see the world, to have all of the things that I didn't have as a child. A new baby would interfere with all this.

Harriet did not agree with her husband's rationale:

> Of course a new baby would interfere with our lives, but what is more important? Is a vacation a reason to get rid of the baby inside of me? We can't control all of our lives, all of the time. That's not the way things are.

He read a lot of magazines and saw pictures of vacations and so on. She delineated the battle lines in her intrapsychic conflict:

> On one side, the world, the media, my husband, some of my friends, against the baby, and a part of me is there too. On the other side, a larger part of me and my children, they are always asking for another brother or sister. There are memories here too, I felt good when I was pregnant, that I was doing something important. I can't enjoy the way I am pregnant now because I will probably end it.

Her attitude toward the contents of her womb depended on whether she would decide to abort or would allow the pregnancy to go to term. She searched for a rationale that would explain her eventual decision:

> I feel that I have a baby in me. I can think what I want to think about it. I can't fool myself. It can be a baby when I want it to be. I mean it really is a baby. Now, if I'm going to have an abortion, well then I'll say it's a bunch of cells. If I'm going to keep it, then I'll have a little baby to get all excited about. This excitement, that's what I'm sitting on. Do you understand? If I didn't listen to others I would have it, but they make sense sometimes. [which is "reason," "thought"]

Every time she looked at her children she became upset:

> If I end the pregnancy, well, it could be a baby like them. I look at my kids and feel that I'm stopping another kid from coming into the world. It would be so much easier to abort if I didn't have kids, for then I wouldn't know what I was doing. I would only think about it after I had a kid.

She terminated the pregnancy and felt angry soon afterward:

> It was so ugly, embarrassing, humiliating. A friend called me afterward and said, "Now, don't you feel like a woman?" "What a sick thing to say," I thought. Crazy; but she's a real women's libber and feels that the fact that a woman can now have control over her body is a wonderful thing. I understand how they would feel that way, but to abort children! They've got their priorities mixed up. I wouldn't do what I did over again. Screw everybody. Now I've earned the right to make my own decisions. I should have followed my feelings. They were all wrong about this. I'm the one who had to go through it.

Her resentment grew. She became angry at herself, her husband, and the world. As her anger waned, her feelings of guilt became more intense. She became afraid that she would be punished:

> I hope that nothing bad happens to me or my family. I'm afraid that God will punish me for what I have done. Who am I to say to God: "O.K., God, I'll keep this baby and not that one," like picking a head of cabbage.

She attempted to reason away her feelings of guilt:

> I can't continue feeling guilty like this. I have to think that it wasn't a life. I heard this Right to Life person saying that using a coil for birth control is murder and that is the stupidest thing that I ever heard. She's way out. I'm trying to make myself think that there is nothing there.

She attempted to detach herself from the situation, to anesthetize the wound within her:

> I've got to stop dwelling on this . . . I can't get my anger toward my husband out of my mind. I'm even having thoughts of divorcing him. I love him, but he's a selfish son of a bitch. He has no idea of how I feel or what I went through. He came with me on the day of the abortion and he was very kind, but the next day he was happy. To him it was like, well, "O.K., dear. It's all over now, you just had a hangnail removed—now that you are fine it's all forgotten." Well, it's not fine and it doesn't go away that easily and he knows I'm mad about it. I can't even have sex with him now and he is complaining about it. At least he's starting to feel something now.

As Harriet assimilated her experience, the intensity of her anger and guilt subsided. She became more detached from the emotional component of her experience and filled this empty space with intellectual rationalizations, thereby bringing a sense of mental order where there was emotional chaos. This psychological process allowed her to accept her abortion and carry on her life. Her period of mourning was coming to a close:

> What would I say to people who contemplated an abortion? It's a lot harder if you have kids. I would say go off in a corner and talk to yourself. It's your baby, don't listen to anyone else. I had a friend of mine who became pregnant and went to the doctor and the first thing that the doctor asked is if she wanted the baby. Can you imagine, she was all happy and excited and the doctor said that. I would say that maybe people don't want babies as much as they used to and maybe we have to fight to have them a little more. I would say that if the baby can't be brought up in a loving home, with plenty of people who care for it, don't get pregnant. Don't listen to other people about abortion. They don't know what it is like. The answer is in yourself, on an individual basis.

She became philosophical as she struggled to impart a sense of order and meaning to her experience:

> It isn't simple and nothing is perfect. It boils down to a choice between two evils. When you have an unwanted pregnancy either way the woman will suffer. Whether she will allow herself to feel it or not, is another matter. Her life is changed, her outlook different. I'm more bitter. No woman should have to be put in such a position.

MARIA

Lila, Susie, and Harriet coped with their abortion experience. They endured. Others are not so fortunate. We will meet such a woman through David, a social worker who works in Spanish Harlem, in New York City. Her name is Maria. To learn about Maria, we must first know a bit about David and the world that he lives in.

David lives in Spanish Harlem and works in a group home for delinquent youngsters. He is a man gifted with extraordinary compassion for and patience with the youngsters he helps. He lives in the world of "what's happening," a melodramatic and emotional society that is a million light-years from where we are today, but exists in almost every city in our land. David, himself, has strong views on the issue of abortion, but the practicality of applying his views to life around him is:

Absurd, it's absurd, I am totally against the idea of abortion but resigned to the deed. What else are you gonna do? If these kids don't have access to a safe and quick abortion they'll get butchered by some bag lady. Their babies are damned from the moment that they are conceived. Don't think that the kids don't know that. I hate to hear myself talk like this. Abortion is murder, no bones about that. It's a crock of baloney to say that it's not murder, but what else are you gonna do? It's the least of two evils. The babies are a mess when they are born, with the mothers in poor health and on drugs. So the mothers kill their kids before they are born. I could never do it. I wouldn't have to. My wife and I would raise a kid if it came along. Kids are important to us because we are important to ourselves, that's the bottom line.

He felt very strongly about abortion's being legalized, and to illustrate his point, he told us about Maria:

Maria was a lovely and devoutly religious Puerto Rican girl who worked with me in the home and the community center for many years. This is a crazy story, but if abortion was legal at the time and Maria went through her abortion legally, maybe she would be alive today. It could have had a different ending if her baby could have been killed by a doctor and not the local abortionist.

It happened when she was twenty-seven. She became separated from her husband after they had a big fight. After a while she took up with another man. One day her husband appeared and said that he wanted a reconciliation and Maria was happy. Soon after, unfortunately, she learned that she was pregnant by her boyfriend. She became quite upset and, knowing that she could never tell her husband, she decided to have an abortion, even though it was against all of her religious beliefs. She was raised to be a strict Catholic by her mother, but in the past five years her mother had become a crazy drug addict and was in the business of dealing drugs. Her mother began to love drugs more than she loved her daughter. In addition, her mother was becoming more and more decrepit and needed Maria to pick up drugs for her, which Maria refused to do.

Maria had the abortion at home. Her mother hid the fetus in a glass jar and told Maria that she would show it to her husband if Maria didn't get drugs for her. Over a period of time, Maria, overcome with guilt about the abortion, started to spend her time in church and when she came home would talk to the baby in the bottle. Her husband left eventually, not knowing about the baby in the bottle, but because Maria was *"loca."* Finally her priest and I told her to close her eyes and flush the fetus down the toilet, so she wouldn't have to see it any more. She was afraid to touch it but eventually mustered enough courage to dispose of it. After it was gone, she became abjectly depressed, and went around the neighborhood saying, "I'm a murderer. I've killed my baby." She soon disappeared from the neighborhood. I heard years later that she became a prostitute, had been in mental hospitals, and died of a heroin overdose. I wonder where she would be if she could have gone to a hospital.

Maria's values did not protect her from the world she lived in. In his parting words, David told us about his inability to teach the youngsters he worked with to avoid unwanted pregnancies. His story illustrates the degree of sexual anarchy that exists at the wellspring of the abortion issue and gives us a view into the life of the poor and underprivileged classes:

It is impossible to teach the girls here to avoid becoming pregnant. They're screwing up a storm. It came to the point that every time we get a new resident the nurse runs down to the vegetable store and buys a cucumber in order to teach the youngster how to put a rubber on an erect penis. When the kids leave the house we always check to see if they have rubbers with them, and even that doesn't work. They really don't care.

COMMENTARY

When a child is conceived, a sequence of reactions is initiated within the mother as a result of a biological event: the fertilization of the egg within her womb. This is a universal, organic, and vital occurrence, linked to the survival of any species.

The nature of these reactions is complex. They involve not only the mother but the people around her, affecting many areas of her life experience (emotional, spiritual, physical, social, and intellectual).

If the mother's pregnancy is interrupted (whether by nature or design), the biological link between herself and her child is ended, but the emotional effects of her having been pregnant linger. They linger in thought and feeling, indicative of a subtle state of mourning, a reaction to the loss of the pregnancy.

Whether one "wants" a child or not, once it happens, pregnancy assumes a biological imperative and takes on a life of its own, a schedule of its own, an inexorable destiny that transcends culture, attitudes, social fads, and presumptions of human beings. From a biological viewpoint, there is little difference between the mother who eagerly awaits a child, only to have it born dead, and the mother who chose to abort her child. As Lisa said, they are both childless mothers, women who were biologically, hormonally "primed" to mother and who are left with this behavior unexpressed within them. When a child begins to nurse at its mother's breast, the mother produces prolactin, which initiates maternal behavior in her. Some scientists are now studying prolactin levels in fathers after birth, to see if there are any hormonal clues to their becoming more fatherly. The point of this is not that mothering and fathering are going to be chemically measurable, but that they surge up powerfully within the body.

The fashion in which this event is experienced by different individuals is affected by several factors: the nature of the society in which they were reared, the degree to which they are in contact with their feeling lives, and the place of spirituality and philosophy in their lives.

The women that we presented, although sharing a similar biologic event, experienced their pregnancies and abortions differently.

192

When they first learned that they were pregnant, they were faced with a basic question that they would eventually answer for themselves, according to the destiny that they chose for their pregnancy. The question was, What, after they became pregnant, was occupying their womb? "What was inside of me?" Was it a bunch of cells, easy to be rid of, or a baby, an early life, whose destruction would raise very complex and emotional issues? For Susie and Lila, the womb contained "mush," easier to "vacuum out." Harriet's viewpoint oscillated. Sometimes she would be carrying a baby that she intended to birth; but when she considered the abortion, she would only have "cells" within her. Maria, who in her own mind murdered her baby, never carried anything but a child within her. This was her only emotional and religious option.

Thus, babies are kept and mush is aborted—the act justified by an adjustment in personal philosophy. A woman instinctively wants a baby and cherishes it. These women had to set aside their wants and accept those thought patterns approved by their society. *—social*

Reason and expedience, applied through thought patterns, conditioned and perpetuated by our contemporary society, were the primary mental processes that favored a "reasonable decision," the decision to abort. Abortion was not an option for women whose feelings and religious considerations were paramount in their life views. Philosophical and spiritual life priorities militated against abortion. In order to abort, the women we spoke with had to quell the voices of biology, feelings, and spirituality. Their spiritual experience was natural and universal or, as demonstrated by Maria, formalized by religious training and church affiliation. Harriet's vacillation was due to her conflict about feeling the universality of the birth experience in the face of the "expedient" position espoused by the society and her husband and friends. Susie and Lila heard only the voice of expedience. "Who needs a baby now?" was for them an unquestioned call to action. No other voices were heard. Maria was overwhelmed by her feelings, aborting in order to stay married, and destroying herself because of the guilt that she suffered as a result of her act. There was little "reason" in what she experienced. She heard no voice of expedience. She didn't think. She was flooded by emotion. She had committed a "sin." Only Harriet would have had an inkling of what Maria had felt.

After the abortion the women tried to put the experience out of their minds as quickly as possible. This was difficult, because memories of the event were stimulated when they saw children or heard the word "abortion." A considerable amount of mental energy was used to suppress the memory of the event, which often made the women irritable or depressed. My impression, from speaking with women who had undergone abortions themselves and now work in abortion clinics, is that they have a high palliative motivation for working there. A woman who had aborted when she was a teenager and subsequently had several children told us that she started to think about her abortion again after she became a mother. "I have more of an idea of what the child I aborted could have been like after I had my own. I think about it a lot and feel bad about it, more than when I was a kid."

The women perceived the emotional dimensions of their experience differently. Harriet, being older, had been exposed to a culture where abortion was a "shame" and illegal. Growing up, she was exposed less to media and more to family. She had religious training. Technology was less advanced. Her education included spiritual and emotional parameters.

The two younger women live in a culture of advancing technology which hails intellectual achievement and celebrates the primacy of work and business. Spiritual and emotional aspects of their education were neglected in Lila's early years and ignored in Susie's rearing. Narcissism, as a social philosophy, was growing with them: the "me" business. Their life decisions were measured in terms of material gains and "progress." Accustomed to making judgments only in material and technological terms, they spent little time pondering matters of feeling, spirituality, and values. Thus, when they became pregnant, it was easy for them to abort. Their feelings had been deadened by their culture. For them, motherhood was not a romantic ideal, it was a "condition," limited to "reproduction." This view is shared by others of their generation.

This portends ominously for the future of children in our society, who are exposed to the societal teachings of materialism, expedience, and the business ethic. Similarly to Lila and Susie, it is possible that children may (and this is deadly) numb their feelings to the point of behaving automatically and inhumanly, judging their actions not by humane measures, but by "efficiency." Thus they are more easily "programmed" by society. Our society has so suppressed motherhood and removed children from parents and grandparents from families, that I shudder to think of being at the mercy of these children, programmed in these ways, when we are old. They could shut us in an old folks' home and not blink an eye.

Once the women made the decision to abort, society offered them a speedy, safe operation, with a minimum of fuss. This efficient process allowed them no time for reflection or even comfort. The women received social approval for their choice to abort. They were lauded for "keeping the population down," "being sensible," or "controlling their destiny."

They did not experience a "social stigma" or have to leave home to obtain an abortion, factors that caused great pain to many women who aborted in the past, when it was illegal to do so.

If legal abortion had not been easily available, Susie said she probably would have got up the courage to tell her parents. "In fact," she said, "the fact that it's so easy to get an abortion now probably had something to do with me being not so scared to make out in the first place." Lila said that she would have gotten an abortion no matter what, even if she had to go to a foreign country to do it. Harriet said that she probably would have had the baby.

When asked how the pregnancies could have been prevented, Susie said that her parents should have locked her up. Lila said that it wasn't her fault and that she should sue her GYN. "Lousy luck," she said. Harriet said, "That's life: if it happens, it happens."

All of the women agreed that the men got off too easily (except for Harriet's husband, who was being punished in the bedroom). Susie expected little from her boyfriend, hastily dispatching him from her life, all the better to forget about her experience. Lila's friend was no more than a "roll in the hay," someone to fill her basic needs for companionship and sex while she devoted her life to her work. A couple of the men offered token financial assistance, but the women bore the brunt of the whole affair. They accepted their destiny with resignation. "That's the way it is," said Harriet. The men we spoke with said they became concerned and frightened when they learned they had conceived a child that they didn't want and hastened to foreclose the issue as soon as possible. Most were insensitive to the woman's needs for nurturing and her ultimate "aloneness" in this experience. This is worthy of further exploration.

Although the premise that "anatomy is destiny" is biologically irrefutable, there is no reason why one destiny has to be better than another. Our society has trained men to be emotionally ignorant of the feeling dimensions of life. We had always hoped that perhaps men would learn about emotion from women, for in the past our society has kept women as its emotional guardians. Unfortunately, the contrary has occurred, for more and more women are abandoning the emotional bastions of their homes to pursue the work ethic that is wreaking havoc upon the emotional lives of men, thus relinquishing their own "motherhood" and their children. As a social force, the depreciation of motherhood continues unbridled today in our society.

Men should be made aware of women's experience. All the more so because so many men in medicine and government run the services that directly affect the lives of women.

Responsible parents, and especially men, must teach their sons to get rid of this double standard, to rid themselves of stereotypes that deride women, and to learn to be more aware of the consequences of their sexual behavior.

CONCLUSION

Unwanted pregnancies have always been part of the human condition. Their fate depends on the philosophy of the society in which they occur, the nature of the people in which they nest, and the interaction between the two.

In a society such as ours, which deadens our senses and devalues the importance of the individual, unwanted pregnancies occur more frequently and are more easily aborted. Indeed, abortion could become a prosperous business, making the service more efficient, thus expanding the market. This could easily happen.

We have permitted worse. We have stood silent witness to the disintegration of the family, which is the bedrock of our emotional life. We have permitted the proliferation of forces within our society that poison our land and our children and isolate our elders. We have allowed ourselves to become a mass of passive consumers, a people afraid to speak out. We have forged a culture of narcissism for our children to inherit—we teach it to them by exposing them to a narrow social curriculum of materials.

Fortunately, we get an opportunity to change things for the better every time a baby is born. We can start all over again. Children embody the emotional dimensions of our existence, dimensions that transcend socioeconomic class, materialism, and technology.

It is ominously symbolic, therefore, that in a society such as ours the issue of abortion has become paramount, for it is about children, and clearly reflects our true attitude toward them.

We do not celebrate our children. Not only do we create them with impunity, we take abominable care of them. Mothers are leaving them in droves. We have relinquished our role as their protectors. We placate them with "things" instead of with the time and attention with which our emotional connections flourish. We have placed them in the hands of the image-makers of the media and of "child care" institutions. We allow business to sell them poisons and make token hypocritical laws to placate our impotent consciences. We stimulate them sexually, so why shouldn't they get pregnant? They don't have a chance.

The kids don't have much of a choice. Their control over their impulses is tenuous, to say the least, and certainly no match for the incessant stimulation that they endure from the media. It's good business. They are exposed to adults who do not want to assume an adult role because they are too damned involved in themselves. They lose on the other end of the scale also, because the natural pathways of sublimation of the sexual and creative drives—imagination, creativ- ity, spirituality, and altruism—are not mentioned on TV or taught to our young in our institutions. It's not good for business.

Children have embodied hope through all of the ages. Children offer a new beginning. Strong families offer a "living" alternative to the negative influence on our young of an unconscionable society.

Only people, one-to-one, directly communicating with a child, can teach the child the necessary emotional and spiritual "skills" to assure him an internal sanctuary against the onslaught of the business-technology culture. Individuals teach the young, by example, how to be an individual. Kids don't listen to what you say. They watch what you do and how you are with them. Children learn to love people by being with them.

What has this got to do with the issue of abortion? A fourteen-year-old youngster explains:

> A person that loves himself is unable to have an abortion. In fact, they wouldn't get pregnant unless they wanted a baby, the child is part of them. The mother loves it and never, never would let anything happen to it.

It frightens kids to think about abortion. It scares them to think "My god, they get rid of babies—what about me? I'm next."

Another youngster, adopted as an infant, agrees: "You gotta be nuts to have an abortion. If my mother had one I wouldn't be here."

We teach our children to value themselves by demonstrating to them that they are valued. A fifteen-year-old youngster that we know has a view of life that is representative of the devastation that we, as a society, have inflicted on many of our young. She lives in a detention home and has been a prostitute, drug addict, and drug dealer:

> I'm a wasted person; any child that came out of me would be a waste. I wouldn't do that to anyone. I'd have a hundred abortions if I had to. If they are like me they are better off dead anyway. I'm numb. I have no feelings. In fact, my mother should have had an abortion. She probably did, except that I lived.

If we bequeath to our children a world where life is celebrated, they, in their turn, will learn how to celebrate life. In such a world there would be few unwanted pregnancies and little abuse of abortions.

From a practical standpoint there are no quick or simple answers to the problem under discussion. Only a long-term plan, clearly formulated, implemented over a long period of time, could allow for the containment and subsequent management of the problem of the use of abortion as birth control.

At the present time, the groups of people involved in the controversial aspects of the problem would do better to join forces to contain it now and to decrease it in future generations.

This is not impossible, for people who are theoretical adversaries in this issue have common ground on which they may unite. There is a common emotional meeting ground: compassion and concern for the mother who faces the abortion choice. There is an intellectual meeting ground: all are opposed to unwanted pregnancies. There is a social meeting ground: all are opposed to the conditions of social and sexual anarchy which breed doomed pregnancies. There is a philosophical meeting ground: all reasonable people are opposed to the banalizing of abortion as a method of birth control and the teaching of this principle to our young.

United, the adversaries in the abortion issue are an awesome force for positive change.

We can allow ourselves to be optimistic about the future if a union between the factions of people involved in the abortion issue can be forged: a union between the passion and love for humanity of some and the practical intelligence and dedication to self-determination of others. It would be a union dedicated to the principles of humanism, to the enhancement of the vital emotional and spiritual dimensions of life, to the renaissance of family life, and to the celebration of our young, and their parents.

7

BETA: REPORT ON A PROGRAM FOR PREGNANT WOMEN IN DISTRESS

KATHLEEN ASSINI PERRY AND
JUDITH YOUNG PETERSON, WITH
DIANE WILSON

THIS PAPER WILL OUTLINE the development of a nonprofit corporation in Orlando, Florida, which operates a comprehensive range of services to women, men, and their families who are involved in a distressful pregnancy.

KATHLEEN PERRY

Our whole approach is different from every other agency handling pregnancy problems. There are many maternity homes, and many of the other services we developed can be found separately as parts of existing community agencies. However, BETA—Birth, Education, Training, Acceptance—has put together a comprehensive program of services that attempts to meet the whole continuum of needs of any woman faced with a distressful pregnancy.

Our services include BETA Center, an emergency pregnancy center; BETA House, a residential facility; BETA School; BETA Industries, a self-help work enterprise; the BETA Women's Free Clinic; a postnatal facility called BETA II to care for the woman and her infant after birth; and a Single Parenting Laboratory to help the single parent develop parenting skills and learn what her child's needs are. In addition, we offer a preventive program, called Life Planning Seminars.

Unlike most human service organizations, BETA's programs, procedures, and guiding philosophy did not precede the organization's existence, but instead were defined by the pregnant women themselves as their needs became apparent. There has been a corresponding difference in services provided and in how they are delivered. We believe our unorthodox approach has resulted in definite benefits. BETA's belief in an individual's ability to take charge of her own life also has significantly shaped the way services are provided.

We started five years ago with an existing volunteer service that provided free pregnancy testing and crisis counseling. We found very quickly that we were not meeting the pregnant women's needs. They were coming to us with very specific needs; some, with basic survival needs of food, clothing, shelter. Some of the women were unable to cope with anything, let alone the financial or emotional ramifications of a pregnancy. Some were not from a supportive, intact family. Some were not ready to plan even very tiny events in their lives. They lived life a day at a time and never thought to set goals.

We realized that this program—giving a free pregnancy test, then offering a pat on the back, an old maternity dress, and a diaper—was not working. We were not meeting the needs of these women. We also knew that if we believed there is a life in the womb, if we believed that these women need a choice, then we had to help them. Otherwise, we had no business making them feel guilty.

We decided we needed a house. We had $87 in the bank. Now, most people would be a little concerned buying a house with only $87 in the bank, but we bought one for $36,900 and we had no way to pay for it. But we figured the Lord would provide, and he did. Judy [Judith Young Peterson] and I had gone to the diocese of Orlando the year before, because we knew the Catholics were very much in favor of women continuing their pregnancies, and the diocese had given us $200. We went again, this time with a budget for $28,000. We were given ten minutes at a financial meeting on Easter Monday and we got $1,700, which we decided to use for the down payment. We also found a realtor who gave us her share of the split commission on the house we bought, which gave us the rest of the down payment we needed.

We didn't even know what closing costs were, let alone how much ours would be, but that came next. Two days before closing, we still didn't have the money. One of our volunteers called to ask how things were going, and I said, "Horrible. We'll never make it." She went to a prayer meeting and passed around a Tupperware container. At 11:30 that night she came to Judy's house with $620; we needed $600. We decided never to doubt again—until we rememberd mortgage payments, electricity, and other expenses. We began calling everyone we knew, people we didn't know, anyone whose telephone number we could find. We told them what we were doing and asked them to pledge $5, $10, whatever they could, each month. Many people said, "Sorry, honey. Gave at the office. Great job you're doing." Finally, after a long day, one man asked, "How much is your mortgage?" Three hundred and seventy-five dollars a month. He said, "Well, bill me for $400 a month." From then on, we just decided that this is the Lord's work, it's not our work. He will find the money. And he has. Now that sounds very naive, and my husband, who happens to be a CPA, gets extremely nervous, but it has been working.

BETA continues to exist independent of federal, state, or local government funding because we believe it is essential to retain control over the direction of programs and to have the flexibility to alter than as client needs dictate. To be truly effective, BETA must respond first to the needs of our clients and not to the requirements of a single or principal funding source. Financial support comes solely from the donations of individuals, community and religious organizations, and local charitable foundations, and this reliance on community involvement may be the most significant aspect of BETA's continuing success and vitality. And our real strength may come from the church sewing circle that makes quilts and layettes for BETA babies, from the electrician who donates services, from the young people who give their time to do yardwork, from the more than 100 dedicated volunteers who staff BETA's many programs because they believe in the cause.

The BETA name also has an interesting history. We had no name for this organization. On a democratic impulse, we asked the volunteers to choose a name, and they had marvelous suggestions, like "Natal Manor." Judy wanted to call it "Umbilical Discord." In the end, my husband thought of the name in church one Sunday. He handed me a piece of paper with the words, "BETA—Birth, Education, Training, Acceptance." I was excited—it sounded really uptown. It would help build self-esteem. It really was a great name. We later found out that the beta symbol is the Greek initial for life, and that was a nice extra. We started with BETA House, and BETA became the name for the whole operation. Judy will describe how the program evolved.

JUDITH PETERSON

We carry the common title of a prolife group, but at the beginning, each of us came to BETA with a little something different in our heart for what we wanted to see happen. We came from many types of concern: concern for the young person, concern for society, concern for the young person's inability to deal with a society inherited from us. My concern did not originate entirely from an inability to accept abortion as a solution to an unplanned pregnancy.

I had some concerns for pregnant women and the solutions they were being offered for their problems. I had a very deep concern for what was happening with teenagers. BETA helps any woman, without qualification. Yet, what it really comes down to is that most women who need long-term services are teenage, unmarried women experiencing an unplanned pregnancy. As we talked with these young women, it became more and more evident that pregnancy was only the symptom, not the real problem, and that if we persisted in dealing only with the symptom and providing technological solutions for these young people, we would not be providing the service they truly needed.

The longer I have been with BETA, the more convinced I have become that our solution must go beyond the great American instant solution—I've got a problem, take an aspirin; I've got an upset stomach, take an antacid; I've got a baby, get rid of it. As we listened to the young women, I became convinced in my own heart that there is no way you can justify taking a life to solve a problem. Under no circumstances can you justify that decision.

Technology is bringing us an easier life, and it's also bringing us much more difficult moral decisions. I have grown into concern for how we are teaching young people to solve problems. We have seen young people needing to face their problems and grow through them rather than simply removing the problem.

Ninety-seven percent of the women who walk through our door know how to prevent pregnancy. They come in with birth control pills in their purses. They do not have the ability or the feeling about themselves to use that knowledge correctly or positively. Our women are fulfilling a psychological need with their pregnancy; it's not through ignorance that they are pregnant. It is through an inability to bring good things into their life on purpose. That is a very simplistic statement, but when you talk with them, it's not all that complicated. They sat across from us day after day and told us, "I know how to prevent the pregnancy." They will sit there and tell you—if you take the time to listen— that the baby is meeting a need in their life. It's a desperate attempt to go beyond a stagnating life, to bring love into their life. But it is not realistic, and it is not what children are about. And again we see a frustrated woman.

As soon as you make the statement that one cannot solve a problem by taking a life, then you bear a great responsibility for providing other solutions. I think that was the hook I bit on, and I think the same thing is true throughout BETA. People have accepted responsibility.

We have really listened to these young women during the past few years. And that's how BETA grew: we listened. It became evident that the first thing the women needed was a place to live. They literally were being thrown out of their houses. We're in the Pepsi generation of disposable women: boyfriends are throwing girlfriends out when they get pregnant; fathers throw daughters out; husbands put their wives out. One husband told me, "Lady, it ain't cool to be married to a pregnant chick. She looks bad on the disco floor." And I admit, I couldn't see her on the disco floor; she was pretty hefty.

Women were under a lot of pressure either to get an abortion or to get out. Making a decision based on an ultimatum, on a threat, is not healthy. There was no assistance in Orange County for the woman who wanted to continue her pregnancy. At that time, the woman in Orange County had lost her right not to abort her child, she had lost her right to continue her pregnancy. The situation was that she really could not choose; there was no choice. To survive, she had to abort her child.

We had a seventeen-year-old woman whose family had left her and gone back North; she had found a boyfriend and was living with him and his mother. The mother was not bothered by the woman's living there, sleeping with her son. The mother was bothered that the girl was pregnant. They told her she could stay if she had an abortion. Brenda called us for help because she was distressed by the idea of abortion. At that point, we didn't have a BETA House. I had inherited a red, five-by-seven-inch box with names of people who could help written on scraps of paper. I started calling people, but they were busy with their own lives and they couldn't help. Every night, I would call her and say, "Brenda, hang on. I'm finding you a home, Brenda. I'm really not kidding you." And she would say, "I'm getting scared. These are the only people I know in this town and they're telling me I have to get out." Finally, on the tenth day, I called Brenda to tell her I had found a home, so proud that I had been such a good volunteer. And she said, "I got so scared, I had the abortion."

We found that it was not a case of women aborting because they wanted to abort. In all the years that we have done this work, I have never had a woman tell me that it's neat to have an abortion. They're aborting because it is the only way they see to solve their problems.

When pregnant women were placed with foster families, the results were not always satisfactory. One problem was that many women lacked interpersonal relationship skills. They couldn't adjust to a seemingly ideal situation. For some, their own family experiences had warped their capacity to respond positively, even when treated well. Others were not comfortable with a family social level very different from their own. And because BETA did not have access to the women on a continuing basis, we were unable to help them face the problems that caused the pregnancy. When we acquired BETA House, our group housing facility, we were able to initiate programs that included counseling, problem solving, communication techniques, life-planning skills, and prenatal and nutritional instruction.

Every woman coming to live at BETA House signs a contract stating what she will do academically and vocationally, negotiating the contract to meet goals she has set for herself—not to meet my goals or BETA's goals. She agrees to attend two group sessions and one individual counseling session a week. She takes responsibility for keeping herself going. We will not get anyone up; we will not remind; we will not encourage. That's her end of the agreement, and we don't take her off the hook. At the same time, we provide a very supportive environment while she succeeds at doing these things.

In counseling sessions, every woman must explore both keeping her baby and placing it for adoption. (BETA is not an adoption agency. All potential adoptions are referred to licensed community agencies.) We will not allow her to close the door on either option without looking at all the information. We work with her over a long period of time (God wasn't dumb when he made it take nine months), and we have a captive audience. A large percentage of our women decide to place their babies for adoption. That is an individual decision and I caution people who think everything is all right if a woman puts her child up for adoption. It is not settled. The counselor helps the woman face her problem, look at the facts in an open environment, and make a decision. We help her look at what will be involved when she places her child for adoption. She must go through a kind of grief therapy, and we encourage her to come back to BETA after her child is born so we can help her face what has happened. She may not be happy that she doesn't have her child with her, but she should be happy with the decision she made. She should feel that it was a positive decision and, most importantly, that she is a good person. If we do not work through this progression with her, if she does not get the experience of sorting through information and making a decision, we will have another pregnancy in a few months. I promise you: she will go out and replace the baby that she lost.

One of BETA's roles is to help a woman grow through her problems and come out on the other side in better shape. We have two lives involved at BETA, and we make an equal commitment to the woman and to the unborn child. If we are concerned only about the unborn child, we have done only half of our job.

We have two house rules that are unbreakable. One is a curfew; the women must be in at a certain time every evening. And while they are with us, there can be no drug use—including marijuana, because legally it still is considered a controlled substance. We also discourage alcohol use; coming into the house high will get them a fast trip out of BETA House.

Everything else is our job to handle. Our women come from juvenile detention facilities and mental institutions;

from broken families and disintegrating marriages; from experiences of physical and emotional abuse; from the street. We know their problems come with them. Our job is not to put them out because of inappropriate behavior—if they are difficult to deal with, or hostile, if they don't bathe, or if they do any of the many things people can do to cause problems in a group setting. Our job is to figure out how to reach them, how to touch them and bring them forward.

Our residents attend two weekly sessions that are both therapeutic and educational in nature. One is a peer group where house problems are discussed and interpersonal conflicts examined. The other deals with life planning, emphasizing coping, decision-making, communication, and consumer skills.

The women living at BETA House defined other needs for us. It became apparent very quickly that simply giving them a place to live was not enough. We started BETA School mainly because the girls had nothing to do, and I promise you, nothing is meaner than a house full of pregnant women with nothing to do. They just sit there all day long watching their bellies grow and thinking about all the problems they have, the least of which is the pregnancy. Their real problem is their inability to plan their lives and to feel that they deserve to have good things happen to them. When we started BETA School, we didn't realize it would become the key to what happens at BETA.

First we approached the school system. "Hello, we would like a pregnant school." "No, you can't have a pregnant school," they said. We decided if they wouldn't give us one, we would start our own school for pregnant women. It began as a volunteer-staffed tutorial program to help the women prepare for the high school diploma equivalency test. The school system heard about our program and approached us six months later about starting a school as part of the Orange County system.

The catch was that to open a class we needed fifteen women and our original house has only ten residents. It became mandatory for every BETA volunteer to attend school one day a week, and we got the school open. As of September 1979, fifty-four women were enrolled in BETA

School. It happened, and it grew.

Something else happened that we did not expect. We saw that when a woman got to school and started learning that she really did have some capabilities, while at the same time she was going through counseling where her own ego grew and healed, we would see almost planned success with her in school. She would begin to experience success at her own level. Now, the level varies among our women, ranging from a seventeen-year-old nonreader to a fourteen-year-old girl who was tutored in college calculus.

The seventeen-year-old wanted to be an auto mechanic, and because she could not read, we asked the Society for the Blind to record her auto maintenance books. She insisted on fixing the BETA van, and it never ran the whole time she lived there. (I won't be the one to tell her she can't do it!) The van lay in parts all over the back yard as she practiced on it, but she succeeded on her level. It was fascinating for this child to discover for the first time, "I am truly a person with capabilities. I am unique. I can do something that no one else in this whole group can do." Then she decided she was worth making good things happen to herself. Once we reach that point with a young woman, we're on our way.

The federal government has confirmed statistically what we thought we saw happening. Nationally, the recidivism rate is 75 percent; most of the repeaters will have not one but three unplanned pregnancies by the time they leave their teen years. The government has said that if the women are counseled and return to school, the recidivism rate drops to 10 percent. BETA's recidivism rate—which is less accurate because we are so young—swings between 4 and 6 percent. Most of the time, the girl who comes back with another pregnancy has come to us from a mental health facility or has a long history of mental illness and has a great deal of trouble relearning how to meet her own needs. Very often, she again tries to bring the things she wants into her life through pregnancy.

As with all BETA programs, BETA School is open to anyone in the community, and to encourage any woman of any age to return to school—pregnant or not—BETA provides free child care while the mother attends classes.

We went on next to start BETA Industries, originally planned as an employment center for pregnant women— probably the worst idea anyone could ever have. The pregnant women in central Florida were unemployable. As with BETA School, we decided that if we couldn't get them employed in the community, we would employ them ourselves. We donate the raw materials to the women, and volunteers instruct them in making quality, handcrafted items that are readily salable. They make macramé purses and plant hangers, silk and dried flower arrangements, and holiday decorations.

Each woman is an independent contractor; she makes an item, we purchase it back from her, and we take responsibility for marketing it. She has no initial investment, and she does not have to wait until the item sells to get her money. The need for positive motivation and immediate success is especially important to the BETA client.

Several things have happened as a result. Number one, the women develop good job skills. They must be at work on time. They must produce, they must make quality items. They have money, which is important to their own feelings or self-worth—the bottom line for everything that happens at BETA.

An unexpected benefit has been the pride they gain by contributing to BETA's financial support—because something else happened we didn't anticipate: we made a profit. We market items through BETA parties sponsored by private individuals, church or civic groups, and every day, volunteers staff a retail outlet, the BETA Boutique. This year, we have sold $31,000 worth of merchandise.

We went on after BETA Industries to start a postnatal facility, which we called BETA II, to provide a support system for the women who choose to keep their babies. Our women do not have a natural support system. They are with BETA because there is no one else. We saw that their ability to cope positively was directly related to the support system around them.

BETA II is a low-rent group residence where mother and baby may live immediately after delivery on a short-term basis. The environment is less controlled than at BETA

House; each woman has a private bedroom and is free to come and go, without supervision. She shares common living areas with the other residents and shares in the responsibility for maintaining the residence, participating in a weekly peer group session to discuss house problems.

While at BETA II, the young mother again signs a contract, continuing her counseling, schooling, and child care training programs. Remember that if we get her back into school, she's less likely to become pregnant again. She also must attend the single parent laboratory with her infant. We are working with a high-risk parent, a mother who has had poor parenting herself, who has little or no support beyond what we provide. She is parenting in a high-anxiety situation and it is dynamite. She needs help in understanding her fears, difficulties, and feelings about her baby.

We cannot care only about the unborn baby. I think it is imperative that we accept responsibility for the quality of life of the mother and of the baby after it is born. Because we are concerned about the kind of parenting a child receives, we looked for a way to solve the problem. There is no infant day care in Orlando, so, to get her back into school, we provide free day care—but we extract a small price: we insist that she and her infant attend the Single Parenting Lab.

Our parenting education emphasizes infant-mother bonding techniques, child development instruction, and in-depth personal and group counseling. As soon as the baby is born, a volunteer BETA nurse helps to initiate the bonding process. She brings the baby to the mother from the hospital nursery and encourages her to hold the baby close and to talk to the baby. Our women are crying out for love themselves; they want to get close and at the same time they have an extraordinarily damaged ability to bring that love to themselves. When I had a baby, it felt good—warm and soft. But it's very difficult for our women. They can't hold the baby close, they hold it away from themselves. We role-play for them, holding the baby, talking to it, showing them how the baby responds.

The lab program includes classroom instruction on infant development, nutrition, child psychology, behavioral principles, and the importance of bonding through close physical contact. The need for verbal stimulation and the importance of play in child development is stressed. Trained volunteers observe while the parent practices her skills with her own child and children of other participants.

By becoming more skilled and secure in parenting, the single parent is less likely to neglect or abuse her child. She is more likely to build a safe, happy, and supportive environment that will give her child a healthy start in life, physically and mentally. The Single Parenting Lab also provides the cooperative day care facility for children of mothers who return to work or school.

We opened a Women's Free Clinic which operates in conjunction with the American Cancer Society and is staffed entirely by volunteer doctors and nurses. BETA offers free Pap smears, breast examinations, gynecological examinations, and pregnancy confirmations to any woman in the community. I think for us the bottom line was that we wanted the woman whose pregnancy we confirmed to be exposed early to a physician who was equally dedicated to the woman's life and the life in utero. We thought it was imperative for her to have at least one contact with a warm, caring, concerned physician who could offer her solutions other than removing the life of her child.

BETA's volunteer doctors also provide interim and emergency medical care for clients awaiting the lengthy qualifying time for county medical care, especially important for very young women and for those with well-advanced pregnancies who have not sought medical assistance.

About a year and half ago, we reached the point of wanting to do something to prevent these unplanned pregnancies from happening at all. We started with a very classic, sex-education approach, going to schools with two physicians and doing an "organ recital," complete with an eight-foot ovary. I told the kids not to let the egg and the sperm meet under any conditions, and to call this telephone number if they got VD. They were bored to death. When you bore somebody with sex, you know you are really boring. Something had to change.

First, we decided what we would not do. We would no longer talk only to girls' classes; the young men would have to be involved, too. We would no longer use a teaching format. And, finally, we would not just deliver the message of protected intercourse and try to scare kids into not getting pregnant. That's really copping out. "I don't care what you do: take your pill, get your abortion, but for God's sake don't make any demands on my time." We decided we do care. So what do we do instead? Help the children develop their ability to deal with their sexuality in a positive manner by using a group discussion setting which involves them in seeking their own solutions.

We developed five discussion programs, called "Life Planning Seminars," which are available to schools, churchs, clubs, parents, or other interested groups. The first one is on rebonding of the family, opening the communication doors so the child can return home to reinforce the values chosen and being considered. At the same time, we have seminars with the parents so they don't close the doors. Fifteen is one of our peak ages for pregnancy, and children in the seminars talk about the pressure they feel when they enter junior high school. I saw one parent respond that he would throw his daughter out of the house if she got pregnant. We tell the parents how to respond. Acknowledge that the child is under a lot of pressure, encourage the child to talk about the feeling, help the child explore what is appropriate in his or her life. How do you raise a responsible child, and what do you do when parental power runs out? Don't interpret responsibility as using contraceptives, but as being a thinking, caring, aware young person seeking solutions beyond immediate gratification.

We help kids understand parenting. What does it mean when parents yell? What does it mean when they get angry? We teach them how to deal with physical changes of adolescence and the accompanying pressures, new feelings and new decisions.

The program on role definitions helps the children sort out the various messages they get about what is appropriate sexuality. How do you deal with media messages? Do you want to be the mother on "Happy Days" or one of "Charlie's Angels"? An eleven-year-old girl trying to be Farrah Fawcett can get into trouble.

We go on to decision making, and how we make choices all the time, even when we avoid making a decision. We talk about the nondecision, the "backseat decision"—never deciding that you want to have a child, but allowing things to happen to you without having the skills, knowledge, and belief in yourself to handle a situation.

We had an eighteen-year-old girl from an extremely religious family whose only message to her was "don't do it"—total denial of very real feelings, which nature intended her to feel, and of societal pressures. She had much difficulty handling dating situations, and when she first had intercourse, she thought the whole world had come to an end. She called BETA, and when we talked, it came down to the fact that she had not made a choice ahead of time to have intercourse with the young man. He had pressured her by threatening to be angry with her, by blaming her for his arousal, and no one had talked to her about how to deal with those pressures.

Young people need help in deciding whether they want to be sexually active. It's a decision they may want to make—help them think it through. Why do you want to be sexually active? Is it the right thing in your life now or are you afraid not to be? Parents can help them grow beyond this fear to really deciding that not being sexually active at this point in their lives can be a very positive thing. The final program is on sex, love, marriage, and commitment.

Our work made us so aware of the difficulties young women experience that at first we discounted the feelings of the young men. An experience with one young man about six months ago triggered our counseling for the unwed father. This boy, the stereotypical eighteen-year-old football player, asked to talk to us after class. He had had a urinary tract infection, but when he told his mother, she accused him of really having VD. The tears started spilling down his cheeks as he said he couldn't tell her he had never had intercourse with a woman because she would have discounted him as a man. He had decided to save the physical experience until he was married because it was very important to him, but he felt he couldn't tell the people around him. Another young man told me, "I am now eighteen years old, I lost my first child, I had no active part in making the decision, and I realize I will never have another first child. He's gone."

Our free counseling now includes the man involved in the unplanned pregnancy as well as the pregnant woman and her family.

BETA is proof that the average citizen can and does have an impact upon serious social and moral problems that we as a nation are facing. It is proof, also, that a community can handle its own problems without reliance on the government to do it for them. But most of all, BETA is proof that the Judeo-Christian ethic of people helping and caring about other people is alive and well and living in Orlando, and can be elsewhere when people are willing.

8

ADOPTION IN AMERICA: THE REALITY VERSUS THE MYTHOLOGY

ELIZABETH S. COLE

T HE ABORTION DEBATE is about choices, and the choices made by men and women about whether or not they want to parent are shaped by their moral convictions, psychology, and the alternatives available to them. Abortion debate centers on the choice to give birth or not.

This paper discusses one alternative open to parents who choose to give birth but do not choose to parent: adoption. As someone who has worked in adoption for the last ten years, I believe that it is a service to children which is widely known and yet poorly understood. Many of the misunderstandings stem from its history and from the fact that the values that underpinned the practice have changed while the public at large has remained unaware of the changes. Perhaps some better understanding may come about by a review of these issues:

(1) How did we come to have adoption in the United States, and what is the legacy of that history?
(2) Who is adopted?
(3) What kinds of children can benefit from adoption services?
(4) How do adoptions actually fare versus how people think they do?

THE HISTORY OF ADOPTION

The first step in understanding adoption is to recognize that it is like all of our social institutions. Its use reflects the predominant needs, values, and conflicts of the times.

The word derives from the Latin *adoptare*, which means to choose. The term refers to the action of the parents. The biological parents choose to transfer their child and their parental rights and obligations to someone who has not given birth to the child but chooses to make it their own. When children were orphaned the government or tribal leader effected the transfer. All societies, whether simple or complex, have had some form of adoption, either formal or informal or both. It is a legal entitlement process.[1]

Adoption as we know it in the United States did not exist until the middle of the nineteenth century. Before that time, children who were orphaned or whose parents were unable or unwilling to care for them were provided for in a variety of ways. The earliest methods were indenture and apprenticeship. In the beginning of the seventeenth century, England shipped hundreds of children to the Virginia colonies. A letter of 28 January 1620 from Sir Edwin Sandys to Sir Robert Naunton, principal secretary to James I, states that the City of London has appointed "one hundred children out of their superfluous multitude to be transported to Virginia; there to be bound apprentices for certain years, and afterwards with very beneficial conditions for the children."[2] Later, when it was found that a number of children would not come to the colonies, the Virginia company was given authority in a warrant which said:

> And if any of them [children] shall be found obstinate to resist or otherwise to disobey such directions as shall be given in this behalf, we do likewise authorize such as shall have the charge of this service to imprison, punish, and dispose of those children, upon any disorder by them or any of them committed, as cause shall require, and so to ship them out for Virginia with as much expedition as may stand with conveniency.[3]

Indenture served as the most common form of providing substitute families for children in colonial America. A reading of colonial history of the care of children yields rich evidence of the belief that children of the poor or bastards were "tainted," would inherit their parents' bad characteristics, and would need to be ruled with a heavy hand to avoid repetition of their parents' flaws.

"Binding out" or apprenticeship continued to be the primary way the late eighteenth- and early nineteenth-century community cared for its orphans and unwanted children. During the last part of the eighteenth century, children in larger cities were often placed in almshouses, where they mingled with older paupers, the diseased, the retarded, and the insane. Orphan homes were then built after the 1830s. Robert Bremner states: "Whether maintained at home, in almshouses, or orphan homes, poor children, upon reaching 'suitable age,' were bound out to serve farmers, tradesmen, sea captains, or housewives during the rest of their minority."[4]

Massive immigration to the United States in the mid-nineteenth century resulted in large numbers of dependent or neglected children. The system of apprenticeship and almshouses and orphanages could not cope with the great numbers. In 1854 the first annual report of the New York Children's Aid Society states that "the pauperism of England and Ireland has been drained into New York."[5] The report talks of hundreds of children without parents living on the streets. "The children are liable to the most bitter want and are exposed to every temptation. They are growing up to be citizens, or women, under the vilest influences."[6]

Foster family care was considered a better solution than street living or overcrowded institutions. Trainloads of East Coast children were shipped to Western farms, this time without the formality of indenture. Children were often placed because of prejudice. It was thought these families could provide the "moral disinfection" which the children needed from their immigrant family influences. As one bigoted agency board member said after a visit to an immigrant family:

> It is a fact worth noticing, that of all of the many children who come under our operations, very seldom indeed, is ever one an American or a Protestant. The Irish emigrants are generally more degraded, even, than the German. They rise more slowly and are cursed with that scourge of their race—Intemperance.

The board member goes on to conclude:

> The whole was very depressing. It seemed like the worst part of Old Europe transplanted. There was not even intelligence about their sensuality. You felt helpless of ever reforming such natures—and, under the common probabilities, the children must be beggars, and prostitutes, and thieves.[7]

The first adoption law in the United States was written in 1850 in Texas. It provided for adoption by deed. While it was a step up from indenture, it still signified that the child was property to be exchanged. Adoption had to be created by statute because there was no tradition for it in English common law, on which our American legal system is based. There are two theories to account for the silence of the common law on this point. One holds that it did not recognize children's rights, only parents' rights. The other holds that adoption was repugnant to the English tradition that inheritance should be based only on a *blood* relationship.[8] Certainly the Texas statute would seem to bear out the reluctance to give adoptees the right to inheritance, for it provided that "if the party adopting such person have, at the time of such adopting, or shall thereafter have a child or children, begotten in lawful wedlock, such adopted child or children will in no case inherit more than the one-fourth of the estate of the party adopting him or her."[9]

In 1851 the State of Massachusetts passed an adoption statute establishing court procedures and guidelines which were to be a model for other states. This law expressed the novel notion that the child's welfare was to be the primary consideration in adoption. It established that the state, through its court officers, had an obligation to protect biological parents from an uninformed and coerced decision to relinquish the child and the adoptive parents from a hasty, uninformed decision to take the child. These principles are still cornerstones of current adoption laws.

Twentieth-century adoption practice grew to serve, fairly exclusively, children born out of marriage. The number of true orphans without extended family was never large. Foster care was to be temporary and was not intended to be used for children who needed a new set of legal parents. As Mary Benet concludes:

> There are many options society can explore in caring for its unwanted children, and Western countries have used several of them. But institutions have, by and large, not met the emotional needs of children, and fostering provides neither the permanence required by the children nor the legal security desired by their substitute parents. Western law and practice has been gradually moving in the direction of ever more secure and complete transfer of parental roles—and this means that adoption has an increasing edge over other methods.[10]

These principles are expressed in a variety of ways in the professional adoption literature but are best encapsulated in the Child Welfare League of America *Standards*:

(1) All children regardless of age, sex, race, physical, intellectual or emotional status are entitled to a continuous nurturant environment.

(2) For most children the biological family in its broadest definition provides the best environment for this nurturance.

(3) When a child's birth family is not willing or able to nurture him or her, he or she is entitled to timely placement with a family who will.

(4) For most children, adoption provides this family better than any other type of substitute parenting.
(5) Adoption is and will continue to be the most cost effective method of substitute parenting which can be used as a child welfare service.
(6) Adoption is a means of finding homes for children and not of finding children for families. The emphasis is on the child's needs.[11]

In the first sixty years of the twentieth century, adoption was seen as the neat solution to the dual problems of illegitimacy and infertility. Pregnant, unmarried women were expected to marry the father of the child. Abortion was not a legally or widely available solution. Children raised by their never-married mothers were considered stigmatized. Their birth certificates were often a different color and the lack of married parents was in some way prominently displayed. Adoption was an effective way to prevent the child and mother from the severe stigmatizing and to free each of them to go on and lead a less problematic life.

On the other hand, there were any number of infertile couples who were willing and able to raise children. Adoption was a means of supplying them with the baby they could not otherwise have.

Children and parents were selected by agencies as suitable for adoption if they were physically and emotionally healthy, intellectually average or above, and free from gross pathology in their backgrounds. Minority children were considered unplaceable because of a belief that minority couples did not wish to adopt or were not financially able to.

Over the last twenty years there have been rapid and radical changes in adoption practice.

The first major realization was that the number of children available for adoption was declining. The myth established to account for that decline was that abortion and widespread use of contraception were reducing the number of children being born to mothers who in the past would have placed the child. In fact, the birth rate to unmarried adolescents has been *increasing*. In 1979, HEW reported: "Each year more than one million girls from 15 to 19 years of age become pregnant. In addition, over 300,000 girls under 15 become pregnant."[12] One analysis states:

As a result of the slow decline in fertility rates among teenagers relative to older women, and large teenage cohorts, the proportion of all babies born to teenage mothers has risen. In 1950, women under the age of 20 bore 12% of all the children born that year, and 20% of all first children. In 1977 they bore 17% of all children and 32% of all first children.

In addition, the proportion of all births that occur outside of marriage has been rising. In 1977, 15.5% of all babies were born to unmarried women, compared to only 4% in 1950. Early and out-of-wedlock childbearing tend to be intertwined: 48% of all out-of-wedlock births occurred to teenagers in 1977, and 39% of teenage births occurred outside of marriage.[13]

Paradoxically, research shows that adolescent motherhood is risky for both child and parent. Consider the following finding:

The deathrate from complications of pregnancy and childbirth is 13% greater for 15-19 year olds than it is for women in their twenties. It is 60% greater for those under 15. Babies born to teenagers are 2 or 3 times more likely to die in their first year than those born to mothers in their twenties. Prematurity and low birth weights make teens' babies face a higher risk of epilepsy, cerebral palsy and mental retardation. Teenage parents will have less education, fewer job options, lower income expectations and have a harder time finding marital stability.[14]

This then is the very group one might surmise would or could be most unwilling or unable to keep or raise a child. But that is also untrue. Four out of every five young mothers coming to an agency for adoption counseling choose to keep their babies after they are born.

There are several reasons for this increase in mothers keeping babies. There has, first of all, been a lessening of the stigma attached to having and raising a child outside of marriage. Until the past several years, most unmarried women who found themselves pregnant had few choices outside marriage. For them the alternative society most accepted was adoption. There is growing evidence that a number of women have always wished to keep the baby they were bearing. They felt pressured by relatives, friends, and society in general to place the baby. They felt frightened and embarrassed and sure they would be somehow "punished," "ruined," and "shunned" as promiscuous if anyone found out. It was believed with some evidence that an unmarried mother had poor chances for finding jobs, a profession, and a husband who would be willing to accept her and another man's child. All of the pressures were towards placing. As one woman says:

> To meet me, you wouldn't think anything was wrong. Blond lady in her 30's. Career woman. You would not assume that I had taken time out of my busy life to have a child. But you would be wrong. I do have a child, a daughter. I've never seen her; I put her up for adoption. It was 1966, and I was young and unmarried: *What else was I to do?* But now I wish more than anything that I'd never given her away.[15]

The increase in women of all classes who are keeping and raising their children is evidence of the changing mores of our society. We are now much more open about sexuality and accepting of men and women living together without marriage. The increased divorce rate has made single parenting acceptable.

Young women may now be receiving pressure not to place their child for adoption. Bearing a "love child" is popularized in modern music and movies. In some circles having a baby is viewed as "cool" and a sign of one's virility or femininity. Sometimes the pressure can be extreme. I remember interviewing a youngster in a youth facility who told me she would be "given the silent treatment" if the others thought she was planning to place her child for adoption.

It seems there is a need for us to begin to recognize and dispel a major American myth—that birth confers on everyone the willingness and ability to raise and nurture the child. This is not true. People should be *equally free to keep or to transfer* the rights and responsibility to nurture a child. There should be no stigma attached to either choice.

Young women become pregnant for several and complex reasons. One theme that appears frequently in the conversation of adolescents is that a baby is a remedy for the isolation and loneliness the parents feel. The baby will be something that is theirs. Not only having the baby, but keeping it, is important.

Another reason unmarried mothers are keeping their babies is that not everyone values or is aware of adoption. Some unmarried women are not aware that they may give their baby to someone else. Some are unaware that there are agencies which will help them make choices.[16]

A recent national survey of social science curricula indicated that school children are taught very little about how families are formed. Where the topic is covered it is handled incompletely. There is almost universally no mention of the fact that children may enter a family through adoption.[17]

To some who understand what adoption means it may have negative connotations. The quality of adoptive families' caring is sometimes suspect. To some an adopted child conjures up visions of Cinderella treated meanly by her stepmother and stepsisters. An adoptive mother who is a teacher told about bringing some of her ninth-grade home economics class home one day. Her daughter, who the class knew was adopted, was in the kitchen making herself a sandwich. Later several students exclaimed that they never knew that an adopted child would have "free run of the house like any other child."

A well-regarded research study found that 94 percent of the adoptive parents contacted had had someone express to them discriminatory opinions about their adoption. These statements made a sharp distinction between biological and adoptive parents. Here are some examples of some of the statements:

"Isn't it wonderful of you to have taken this child."
"He *is* a darling baby and, after all, you never know for sure how even your own will turn out."
"But who are her *true* parents?"
"How well you care for the child, just like a *real* parent."
"Isn't it wonderful he can be such a good father to a little boy who isn't his own son."[18]

Note the fact that many used the terms "own," "real," and "true" in reference only to the biological parent. One also senses the implication that there is little real love for an adopted child, only a sort of "benign fondness." The sense of "role handicap and alienation" are expressed in excerpts from a letter received by the researchers:

We have a teen-age son of our own who has been denied the pleasure of brothers or sisters. Nature seemed to work against us and I was told by the doctor to adopt a child. I've often wondered when a doctor makes this statement if he has ever tried to adopt?

Good fortune came our way, though, when our minister asked us if we were still interested in adopting. Johnny was already in school when "little Richard" came to us, through independent adoption, and one of my first thoughts was "Will I learn to love him?"

Richard came to us when he was a few days old, a loveable little one with the most beautiful round blue eyes, which they remained. I cared for him and nature did the rest. After his death (at less than a year), I often thought, one doesn't love their husband or wife upon first meeting but one grows to love as each shares. To me, the same is true of an adopted child, for if it had been Johnny that was taken, the pain could not have been more severe.

But my interest in adoption is not so much the parents as the attitude of people outside the family. Yes, one hears the statement by others, "I think it is wonderful to adopt," etc. Yet do they really mean it? Sometimes I think they lack interest, understanding or just plain don't care.

The cruelest thing ever said to me was when Richard died. The mortician knew we had legally adopted him. Yet he called one day to fill out Richard's death certificate; this is the statement he made: "For parents, should I put 'unknown'?"

For me, he had not accepted Richard as one of us. Whether it was lack of heart, interest or what, I don't know. Yet he was considered an educated man.[19]

The myth that "blood is thicker than water" is difficult to overcome and may be a real deterrent to adoption.

WHO IS ADOPTED?

The fact that the United States has more sophisticated data collection systems for its agricultural products than for the nation's children was not lost on adoption advocates. Public Law 95–266, passed in 1978, provides for a nationwide collection of information on adoption and foster care in the United States. This system has not yet been put into operation. Its first reports are a few years away.

What facts and figures are we using in the meantime? I can report on what *is* known. With all their statistical limitations, the current reports seem to support the wisdom of conventional practice.

The most recent figures, gathered from forty-two states and jurisdictions, are reported in *Adoption in 1975* (DHEW

Publication no. (SRS) 77–03259). Alaska, Arizona, Colorado, Guam, Idaho, Illinois, Mississippi, Montana, North Carolina, Oregon, Rhode Island, and the Virgin Islands did not report. Figures for Nebraska and South Carolina were incomplete and considered not usable. With these limitations, the report goes on to show:

In 1975, adoption petitions were granted for 104,188 children.

62% (or 64,000) of the children were *related* to the petitioner. (Stepparent adoptions therefore account for the largest single group of adoptions in the U.S.)

36% (or 37,000) of the children were unrelated to their adopters. In 2% of the cases the relationship was unknown.

77% of all nonrelative adoptions were arranged by agencies. (This contradicts the notion that the majority of nonrelated adoptions are arranged by private intermediaries.)

63% of all nonrelative adoptions involved children *under 1 year old*; 25% of the youngsters were between 1 and 6, 10% between 6–12, 2% were 12 and over (adoption still is a service for babies and very young children).

72% of all nonrelative adoptions involved white children, 11% were of black children, 17% of other races.

Only 563 handicapped children are reported to have been placed in nonrelative adoptions.[20]

WHO NEEDS ADOPTION?

Although we know a good deal about the children who were placed in 1975, there is no usable information about the larger population of children for whom families were needed at the time. Such information does exist for 1978, enabling a better assessment of the current situation. In an unpublished background paper prepared for the Model Adoption Legislation and Procedures Advisory Panel, Dr. William Meezan comments:

Projections from the *National Survey of Public Social Services for Children and Their Families* estimate that there are currently 102,000 children legally free for adoption services. Of the 97,000 on whom data is available, 62% are white, 28% are black, 3% are Hispanic and 7% belong to other ethnic groups including Native American and Asian. The median age of these children is over 7 years. Nine percent are under 1 year old, while 31% are between 1 and 6 years old. Fully 40% are over the age of 11.[21]

Both reports point to the kind of children who need to be placed. Twenty-eight percent of all children needing adoptive families are black. In 1975, only 11 percent of the children placed by agencies were black. Strides may have been made in the intervening three years, but the gap between what black children need and what they receive is still large.

Over 40 percent of all children needing families are over eleven. Only 2 percent of all children placed in 1975 in unrelated families were over twelve. Special efforts must be undertaken to find families for this group of youngsters.

One can see from the statistical picture drawn of adoption practice that infants and preschool-aged children are readily placed by most adoption agencies. This includes children of all races. There are at least ten to fifteen couples waiting to adopt for every available baby. The average waiting period is from two to five years.[22]

The older a child becomes, the more difficult it is to find a family. Note that the phrase is "more difficult"—not "impossible." This contradicts a major myth—that older or handicapped children are unadoptable. The hallmark of today's adoption practice is the fact that no child should be considered unadoptable by virtue of age, race, handicap, or the fact that he or she needs to be placed with a large group of brothers and sisters. The social work field now possesses the technology to place all manner of children. The problem is that the knowledge is not possessed by all adoption practitioners.

Recent data from the Family Builders Network, a nationwide group of agencies specializing in making the most difficult placements, bears this out. The majority of children placed by these agencies were ten or over. Over 80 percent had some serious handicap or emotional disturbance. Several of the placements included two or more siblings.[23]

This statistical data is lifeless. The stories of some of the children placed will help us to see what is possible.

David's mother was thirteen when she became pregnant, and two weeks short of her fourteenth birthday when he was born. She was slow to realize that she was pregnant and then fearful to let anyone know. She thought she might be punished by being sent to a foster home or to reform school. As a consequence, she was in her sixth month before she received any prenatal care. David was born one month before he was due. He had spina bifida, a serious birth defect involving the nervous system. A spinal cord lesion resulted in paraplegia. There was every likelihood he was severely retarded. His child mother was advised to place him in a medical group facility. She and her parents quickly realized that they would be unable to give him the care he needed and consented to this placement. David's social worker noted that despite his physical disability he seemed to respond positively to any attention given him. She believed that this medical setting was not meeting his emotional needs and became concerned that adoption should be considered for him. A couple from Minnesota heard of him through an adoption exchange. Through adoption, David has now joined their two daughters as a permanent part of the family.

The high costs of David's medical care are being met by an adoption subsidy given by the state to his family on his behalf. Forty-seven states and the District of Columbia now have programs to provide financial assistance to parents who adopt children with special needs.

Children like Joseph, 12, Ramon, 9, and Robin, 8, are also eligible for subsidy. Their mother and father separated shortly after Robin's birth. The mother, unable to cope, became an alcoholic and then committed suicide. There were no family members or friends willing or able to take these boys in. An adoption agency in California found them a family. They have now acquired four new brothers and sisters.

Pat, aged sixteen, had been in foster care for twelve years. Through no fault of his own or the agency's, he had been in three different foster homes. He had seen in his local paper the pictures and stories of children available for adoption through local agencies. He called the reporter in charge of the series of articles and asked that he be featured. Pat wrote the description of himself that he wanted in the paper and picked the photograph he felt looked most like him. He also helped his social worker select the families he wanted to meet from the number who responded to the story.

One of the first things the reporter had asked Pat was why he wanted to be adopted at his age. It was clear to her that he was "nearly raised" and at an age when most teenagers are thinking of leaving home. Pat replied, "Everyone needs a family, no matter how old you are." One year later his legal adoption was announced by his parents in the local adoptive parents newsletter.

In that same issue was a poem by a ten-year-old boy, John, who had also recently been adopted. He had not been placed sooner because he was considered "unadoptable." The diagnosis: "Emotional retardation and perceptual difficulties." John wrote:

> Once I was a stranger
> And now I know I'm me
> Once I floated everywhere
> And now I am a tree.

There are nearly 100,000 other youngsters like David, Joseph, Ramon, Robin, and Pat awaiting placement today.

The belief that all children are adoptable and the development of a technology to place them are relatively recent occurrences. The most rapid advances in consciousness raising and in the development of professional skills and knowledge have occurred over the past ten years. Today's foster homes and institutions contain thousands of children who were once considered "unadoptable." It is now the challenge of this next decade to identify those children for whom a new adoptive placement is appropriate.

ADOPTION OUTCOMES

The history of adoption has yielded myths and beliefs which have not yet been undone. The notion that the child may be "tainted" and the notion that blood is thicker than water speak to the fear that adoptive parenting may be a second-class way to raise a child. Some foresee only failure for a process built on the "failure" of the birth parents to be able to keep and the "failure" of the adoptive parents to produce a child.

Social scientists have conducted any number of adoption outcome studies. The first evaluation of adoption outcomes was done in 1924 in New York State. Two hundred thirty-five adoptees were contacted twelve to eighteen years after they had been placed. Eighty-eight percent of them were found to be doing well.[24]

Several small studies were conducted in the 1950s. Most families were adjudged to be "getting along satisfactorily." During this decade agencies experimented with placing older children (toddlers). Follow-up studies showed that these children had "good outcomes."[25]

Researchers have found that 2 to 3 percent of infant placements terminate before the family goes to court. The percentage for the older, the handicapped, or the disturbed child is about 15 percent. The more important figure to remember is that 90 percent of those children who were not adopted by their first family go on to be adopted by their second family.[26]

Since the 1950s, a variety of research studies on special types of children continue to add to the evidence that adoptive families fare well.

In the 1960s and 1970s particular attention was focused on specialized groups of children. For example, there have been studies of the adoption of American Indian children, older children, abused children, the handicapped, and those placed in families of different races. Again, all the results point to satisfactory outcomes in the majority of cases.[27]

It is interesting to note that there are no similar outcome studies in the United States on how children fare in the family they were born into. No comparisons are possible.

What these studies do provide is a pattern of "satisfaction" with the adoption process. Most do very well. We know that those which do well seem to be marked by a strong sense of bonding, belonging, entitlement between parent and child—"I could not love her more had she been born to me."

The successful placement of older children is teaching us that adoption is different. It is more like a marriage than giving birth. It can be and is a really rewarding and meaningful experience.

CONCLUSION

This paper has been a message of the do-able. It is good that we know now how to help children who were once considered unadoptable. This is not an argument that all children born to young or unmarried parents should be placed or that this is the preferable choice. The central message is that adoption should not be overlooked as an alternative for a child, simply because of the child's problem or the fact that the adoptive family may encounter some discrimination. The central message is that children who enter this world are entitled to be raised and nurtured and loved by parents who are willing and able to perform those functions.

Our society has an obligation to provide good, honest information, help, support, and guidance to people about parenting choices. Special attention must be given high-risk families, particularly child parents, to enhance their ability to make good choices. We must also find better ways to support those choices once made.

When one looks at the nature of the problems that cut across this topic, one central one appears: ignorance. We as professionals do not know all that our service has to offer. Parents do not know what options are available to them. The community does not allocate the necessary resources to provide service and information. People do not understand adoption, and myths and misunderstandings abound.

We have, then, a primary obligation to educate ourselves and others on these issues. Thomas Paine once said: "Ignorance is of a peculiar nature; once dispelled, it is impossible to re-establish. It is not originally a thing of itself, but is only the absence of knowledge; and though man may be kept ignorant, he cannot be made ignorant."

NOTES

1. Mary Benet, *The Politics of Adoption* (New York: Free Press, 1976), pp. 11–21.
2. Robert H. Bremner, *Children and Youth in America: A Documentary History*, (Cambridge: Harvard University Press, 1970) 1:7.
3. Ibid., p. 8.
4. Ibid., p. 263.
5. New York Children's Aid Society First Annual *Report* (New York, 1854), pp. 3–4.
6. Ibid.
7. Bremner, *Children and Youth*, p. 417.
8. S. B. Presser, "The Historical Background of the American Law of Adoption," *Journal of Family Law* 2 (1972): 448.
9. Bremner, *Children and Youth*, p. 369.
10. Benet, *Politics* p. 15.
11. *Child Welfare League of America Standards for Adoption Services*, rev. ed. (New York: Child Welfare League of America, 1973).

12. Eddie B. Johnson, "Children Giving Birth to Children," *HEW News*, April 1979, p. 3.

13. Kristin A. Moore, Sandra L. Hofferth, Richard Wertheimer, "Teenage Motherhood: Its Social and Economic Costs," *Children Today* 8 (Sept.–Oct. 1979): 12.

14. Johnson, "Children Giving Birth."

15. Lorraine Dusky, "I Gave Away My Baby," *Family Circle* 92, no. 14 (December 1979).

16. William Meezan et al., *Adoptions Without Agencies: A Study of Independent Adoptions* (New York: Child Welfare League of America, 1978).

17. Anthony Codianni, "Report on 'Adoption Builds Families' " (Report, Children's Home Society of Minnesota, 1978).

18. H. David Kirk, *Shared Fate: A Theory of Adoption and Mental Health* (New York: Free Press of Glencoe, 1964), pp. 28–29.

19. Ibid., pp. 33–34.

20. Elizabeth S. Cole, "What We Can Learn from Statistics," *Adoption Report* 4, no. 3 (1979).

21. William Meezan, "Issues in Adoption" (Paper, Dept. of Health, Education, and Welfare, 1978).

22. Elizabeth Cole, "Adoption Services Today and Tomorrow," in A. Kadushin, ed., *Child Welfare Strategies in the Coming Years* (Washington, D.C.: Dept. of Health, Education, and Welfare, 1978), pp. 130–68.

23. John Boyne, "Adoption and the Family Builders Network Agencies" (Unpublished Statistical Report, New York, North American Center on Adoption, 1979).

24. Benson Jaffee, "Adoption Outcome: A Two Generation View," *Child Welfare* 53, no. 4 (April 1974): 211–24.

25. E. Mech, "Trends in Adoption Research," in H. Mass, ed., *Perspectives on Adoption Research* (New York: Child Welfare League of America, 1965).

26. See Cole, "Adoption Services," and Benson Jaffee and David Fanshel, *How They Fared in Adoption: A Follow-Up Study* (New York: Columbia University Press, 1970).

27. See Elizabeth Lawder et al., *A Follow-Up Study of Adoptions: Post-Placement Functioning of Adoption Families* (New York: Child Welfare League of America, 1969), vol. 1; Janet Hoopes et al., *A Follow-Up Study of Adoptions* (New York: Child Welfare League of America, 1969), vol. 2; David Fanshel, *Far from the Reservation: The Transracial Adoption of American Indian Children* (Metuchen, New Jersey: Scarecrow Press, 1972); and L. Grow and D. Shapiro, *Black Children—White Parents: A Study of Transracial Adoption*. (New York: Child Welfare League of America, 1974).

9

ON THE PUBLIC FUNDING
OF ABORTIONS

HADLEY ARKES

ANDREW JOHNSON, who succeeded Lincoln in the presidency, found his own opposition to slavery, not in any wrong done to black people, but in the invidious distinctions that slavery fostered among whites. Slavery was the mark of a caste system, which brought an aristocracy as well as slaves; it created privileges of luxury and leisure that were available mainly to the rich. The decisive moral problem, then, with the existence of slaves was that not every household could have one. In a rather paradoxical prayer Johnson once "wish[ed] to God [that] every head of a family in the United States had one slave to take the drudgery and menial service off his family."[1]

This innocent man was apparently far from recognizing that the problem of slavery, as he conceived it, could have been solved with measures well short of a political crisis and a civil war: the inequities he found among whites could have been remedied in a stroke if the government had merely committed funds from the general revenue and undertaken to provide every family in the country with a slave. With a further touch of inventiveness, he might have considered extending this support through a federal program of "medicaid": a physician might have certified, for example, that the mental health of a mother could be strained if she found it necessary to supply, through her own efforts, the work that would otherwise be done by a slave.

In his neglect of these possibilities Andrew Johnson showed rather notably his distance from the political imagination of our own day. But in the essential form of his argument he showed himself to be the true ancestor of those people who count, as the main test for the morality of a policy, that it not create disparities of any kind between the rich and the poor. I need hardly add, of course, that Johnson would also be a forerunner of those people who would put aside the substantive moral question of abortion—as Johnson put aside the substantive moral question of slavery—and establish the public funding of abortions simply by invoking the "equal protection of the laws." When that formula is applied in a mechanistic way, it produces the kind of high comedy in the law that has been associated over the years with Justice Douglas. And so, when the legislature of

Oklahoma once presumed to set forth the crimes of moral turpitude that were genetically transmissible; when it confidently placed chicken-thieving in that class and went on to fix the number of moving violations that would make the practitioners eligible for sterilization; Justice Douglas sought to strike at the heart of the problem by deploying the Equal Protection Clause: the statute was infirm, he said, because it inflicted a severe penalty on the chicken thieves while it left unsterilized the embezzlers, who might be engaged in far more serious thefts than the snatching of a few chickens. It fell to Chief Justice Stone to point out to Douglas that the statute would hardly be cleansed of its moral defects if the legislature had gone on, with a proper sense of symmetry, to provide for the sterilization of the embezzlers as well.[2]

The tests that come into play with the Equal Protection Clause have the same function that is served in ethics by the "universalizability" test or the Categorical Imperative: they force the question upon us of whether we are indeed operating on the basis of a principle in the strictest sense, which we are willing to apply to all similar cases, even when its application in any single case may cut against our interests. In that manner the need to "universalize" our judgments may bring home to us the fuller consequences of acting on the maxim we have embraced. But nothing in these formal tests can possibly spare us the need to address the substantive question of whether the policy we are dealing with is in fact justified in point of principle. We may be faced, after all, with the classic case of the fanatic Nazi who is quite willing to abide by the formal application of the Categorical Imperative and go to the gas chamber himself as soon as it is discovered that he had a Jewish ancestor. And a judge with a greater passion for consistency than afflicted Justice Douglas might have been willing to satisfy the "equal protection of the laws" by having the embezzlers sterilized along with the chicken thieves.

In a similar way we will find that nothing in the formal tests of "equal protection"—nothing in the differences that may separate the rich and the poor in their access to abortion—can possibly settle the substantive moral question that arises on the public funding of abortions. In the first place, the disparities that may exist between the rich and the poor cannot have any relevance for the question of whether abortion itself is in principle justified. Neither could they have any bearing then on the question of whether it would be justified to extract, through the compulsion of law, the funds that are needed for the support of abortions.

Of course, the argument has been made that, even if abortions were accepted as legitimate operations, that in itself would not make it necessary or justified to support abortions through public funds. This argument has depended in part on a stringent view of the difference between private goods and "social goods." Or, from another angle, it has depended on the difference between private liberties and public obligations—between the things we have a right to do in our private lives without the interference of the government, and the things that the government has a duty to render unto us. But as I will try to show, these kinds of considerations are condemned to fall short of carrying the argument as they, too, become detached from any substantive argument about the justification for abortion. An argument that is cast in the language of private preferences and social goods runs the risk of succeeding only by confirming the main contention of the proabortion movement—namely, that abortion must be, in its essence, a morally neutral act and a matter of the most "private" judgment. But by the same token, the arguments that are offered for the public funding of abortion would encounter vulnerabilities that may prove even more crippling: in order to make the case for the public funding of abortion, it becomes necessary to move beyond the line of defense that abortions involve matters of the most personal, subjective belief—that they are literally beyond the possibilities of moral judgment. It becomes imperative to argue now that abortions partake of some *principle* that makes them a positive "good" and a fit object of public support.

But with a shift of that kind the partisans of abortion implicitly concede that the question is in fact subject to the full discipline and requirements of moral discourse. The argument may not be ended merely with the assertion that "I simply approve abortion, as a matter of my own, personal beliefs"—as though reasons may not be expected, as though the canons of principled argument need not be engaged, and as though the argument itself may not be judged, finally, as valid or invalid. And yet once that threshold of discourse is crossed, the case for abortion exposes itself to requirements of justification that it will be incapable, in my judgment, of meeting.

IS ABORTION A PUBLIC OR A PRIVATE GOOD?

On the surface, at least, the literature on "public and private goods" would not seem to offer much encouragement for those people who would seek the public funding of abortions. The purchase of an abortion is not at all like the purchase of a national defense, where no individual would have either the resources or the interest to purchase the equipment or services on his own. Even in these times of inflation, abortions have been available in licensed clinics for about $150 and often less. In many clinics the cost of an abortion for poor women has been reduced to $60 or even $25. The reductions have been made possible by raising the fees of the "paying" customers and preserving a ratio of 3:1 between the patients who can pay the full charges and the women who are on welfare.[3] In certain instances abortions have even been offered free of charge as a result of private grants to the clinic or *pro bono* work on the part of professionals.

But even when charges remain, they have been well within the reach even of people on welfare. Families on public assistance have shown no hesitation in borrowing money to cover the cost of furniture and appliances that are far more expensive than the cost of an abortion; and if abortions are really as necessary as some people think in saving a family from deepening poverty, these families should have no trouble in recognizing their own material interest here, as they are able to recognize that interest in a variety of other matters. At the same time, there should be no want of people who would find an interest in lending the money. In fact, some abortion clinics have even offered plans for paying an abortion out over time.[4] Despite the alarms we have heard, then, about the withdrawal of public funding, the evidence suggests that almost no one need go without an abortion because of an inability to pay. The costs have been borne without strain by the "private sector"—by families, clinics, and private foundations—and so it is clearly untenable to argue that these services can be sustained only with public funds.

From the standpoint of "public and private goods," it is also worth keeping in mind that an abortion is, after all, a discrete, isolable event. It is not an indivisible commodity, like the air, which is accessible at once to many people, and which cannot be spoiled without creating "externalities"— or extended consequences—which adversely affect the public. Neither doctors nor their patients have much trouble in telling, in abortions, just whose body is being operated upon. Unless they suffer from an overdose of literary symbolism or Russian novels, they know that the abortion they are experiencing is not being performed on the general public. In fact, it has been the persistent claim of the proabortion movement that it is the pregnant woman and *only* that woman who undergoes the experience of the abortion: it is her body alone that is affected; it is she alone who feels the pain and the risk. And so we have been told countless times that the decision on abortion is the most "private" decision, which must be reserved exclusively to the woman. For that reason it may not be shared even with the father of the offspring who may be aborted; if the woman happens to be a minor, her authority to decide may not be shared even with her parents. These judgments have already been raised by the courts to the level of constitutional doctrine, and yet there has been remarkably little awareness of the way in which they may undercut the case for public funding. If the interest in an abortion is the exclusive and "private" concern of the pregnant woman, if there is no legitimate interest in the abortion even on the part of the father of the child or the parents of the pregnant minor: on what possible ground could it be urged that the public at large has an "interest" in this operation? In what way, then, could it be said that this "interest" forms the ground of a public obligation to support the abortion through the use of public funds?

All of this gently passes over for the moment the one "externality" that is unmistakable in abortion—and that is the cost incurred by the fetus. The woman is not, as it turns out, the only party who "experiences" the abortion, and hers is not the only body that is affected. If it is plausible to speak of an interest on the part of the public in supporting abortions, it would seem rather hard to deny the most compelling interest on the part of that one member of the public apart from the mother who *is* being affected in the most direct and fatal way. Of course it was precisely this "externality" in abortions that accounted for the traditional interest of the law in protecting the fetus, as it sought to protect any other human being from destruction at the hands of another. It goes without saying, however, that if this one particular "externality" were not beneath notice—if there were a willingness to recognize the fetus as a being whose suffering is not beyond the concern of the law—then the question of public funding would be moot, since there would be no legal tolerance of abortion itself.

In the most exacting terms, then, the proponents of abortion have persistently refused to recognize any serious "externalities" resulting from abortion—and certainly they have acknowledged no extended effects that may confer rights or duties on third parties to take an interest in these private decisions. But now we have been offered, without embarrassment, a virtual inventory of arguments about the extended consequences and the social ills that may be avoided through the public funding of abortions. There is the contention, for example, that the birth of more children among the poor would simply enlarge the burdens of these people and prevent them from rising from poverty. In addition, the Department of Health, Education and Welfare has been willing to provide very precise estimates of the dollars that would be saved for the federal treasury if poor people were encouraged to have abortions rather than children. Dr. Louis Hellman, the Deputy Assistant Secretary for Population Affairs, calculated that an abortion would cost $350 at the most, while the expenses of a child from prenatal care to the end of its first year would be about $2,200. On the assumption that many of these children would remain on welfare until they were young adults, Hellman estimated that it would cost over $35,000 (at current prices) to raise a child to the age of eighteen.[5] But apart from these calculations, so distracting in their precision, there have also been presentiments of a more ineffable nature about the enlargements that might take place in the national quotient of unhappiness—the unhappiness presumably felt by parents and children alike—as a result of augmenting the national stock of unwanted children.

As far as I can see, there is nothing in the body of theory concerning "public and private goods" that would expose what is in principle spurious and inadmissible in these claims. Despite the mechanistic cast of this theory and the precision of many of its measures, it cannot always mark off unambiguously the class of "private" acts that generates no externalities. It may be taken for granted that a hamburger consumed will not be available to other consumers, but the consumption may take place at a new branch of McDonald's in the neighborhood, which in turn generates traffic that ties up the main thoroughfare and creates a host of ancillary costs. The problem was illustrated well in the commentaries of Adam Smith, for there were few people who took a more restrictive view of what are now called "externalities." He found it hard to see, for example, how other parts of Britain possibly benefited from paving and lighting the streets of London, and so he saw no reason to draw on the general revenues of the nation to support these projects.[6] He was also doubtful that an education supported by public funds could really excite the same effort and responsibility on the part of teachers as a schooling that depended on private patronage. And yet even he was finally willing to provide education through public funds out of a national interest in rendering the people less gullible, less suggestible to the appeals of "faction and sedition," and more competent to judge the measures of its own government.[7] As he advanced in this spirit, Smith was willing to allow, further, that a serious public interest justified a charge on the general revenues to support something as resistant to precise measurement—but as important, nevertheless, to the preservation of the laws—as the "Dignity of the Sovereign."[8]

A theory of public goods that may incorporate the "dignity of the sovereign" and the urbanity of citizens is a theory that must be open everlastingly to the claim that many private benefits may have extended, public consequences. But beyond that, scholars in this field will readily concede that the theory functions in a cast that is inescapably utilitarian: its contributions, such as they are, come through the assessment of material outcomes and consequences. At its most ambitious, it rises to a concern for "optimal distributions" in which no one may be made "worse off" while other people prosper. That is not exactly the same as a concern with "justice," and the assessment of "optimal distributions" still depends ultimately on the "utilities" of individuals who are affected by these distributions. That is to say, whether any distribution leaves individuals worse off depends on the judgment of the individuals themselves on the kinds of outcomes they regard as satisfactory. A serious defect then in this theory is that it provides no grounds for calling into question arrangements or distributions that are manifestly unjust, but which leave all the participants reasonably contented.

The noted economist Frank Knight once pointed out that, for certain people, it might be quite rational to exchange their personal freedom for a long-term contract for indentured labor and personal security. We have the classic case, in other words, of the men who would willingly contract themselves into slavery—and Lincoln had been faced, after all, with the example of slaves who willingly fought for the Confederacy. But our courts of law will not enforce contracts in which men essentially bargain themselves into peonage or slavery,[9] and when we refuse to honor those contracts—those voluntary efforts at an "optimal distribution"—we draw on the recognition of what used to be called "unalienable rights": rights that individuals were incompetent to waive. We would be reminded then, in this instance, that the case against slavery was grounded in nature, in the things that separated human beings from other animals. As the traditional understanding ran, creatures that had the capacity to give and understand reasons over matters of right and wrong did not deserve to be ruled in the way that one ruled creatures which did not have the capacity to understand reasons—in the way that one ruled dogs, horses, and monkeys. With that understanding the wrongness of slavery was established on an independent ground of principle, which had nothing to do with the feelings of any single person. Nor did it have anything to do, therefore, with the question of whether any particular person happened to find pleasure in being a slave. In fact, it was entirely possible, as Knight recognized, that slavery could be a material advantage for some people; it could make them better off than they were likely to be under conditions of personal freedom. And yet, even though the material consequences here might have satisfied the theories of "optimal distribution"; even though they might have succeeded in rendering the slaves more prosperous and even happier; they still would have been, in point of principle, unacceptable.

But it is a cardinal defect in our theories of public goods and social choice that they have not incorporated this understanding of the independent force of principles. They have not yet absorbed the recognition that the authority of principles can take precedence over material outcomes. Some theorists acknowledge what they call "merit goods": goods that are considered "meritorious" in themselves, and which are not allowed to depend for their selection on the vagaries of the marketplace.[10] One such merit good may be "personal freedom," and the supersession of the marketplace may be found in the refusal of the law to permit people to choose slavery for themselves in the market of exchange. But many economists still tend to look suspiciously on any such suspensions in the processes of the market (unless they are carried out in the name of economic "planning" or a "redistribution" of income). As one notable textbook puts it, this overriding of the marketplace by the law "seems in outright contradiction to free consumer choice."[11]

Of course that is exactly what it is, but that is a state of affairs which cannot be avoided, because it reflects the necessary connection between morals and law. That connection was understood by economists in an earlier day, as it was understood by men like Adam Smith and Edmund

Burke, who offered the most literate defense of free econ-
omies. But that understanding was probably given its most
powerful expression by Lincoln, in his classic debate with
Stephen Douglas. Douglas argued in that encounter that the
problem of slavery ought to be solved simply by leaving it to
the sovereign majority in each state or territory to decide
whether slavery will be voted up or down. He would have left
the question, in other words, to the market of consumer
choice. Lincoln pointed out, however, that the matter could
be left to local option in this way only if one could profess,
with Douglas, that one did not "care" whether slavery was
voted up or down in any place—as though one decision were
no better or worse in principle than another. As Lincoln
remarked, Douglas could take that position only if he did not
see anything *wrong* in slavery; "but he cannot say so logically if he admits that slavery is wrong. He cannot say that
he would as soon see a wrong voted up as voted down."
Lincoln continued:

> When Judge Douglas says that whoever, or whatever commun-
> ity, wants slaves, they have a right to have them, he is perfectly
> logical if there is nothing wrong in the institution; but if you
> admit that it is wrong, he cannot logically say that anybody has
> a right to do wrong.[12]

What Lincoln conveyed here in a way rarely expressed
elsewhere is the connection between the logic of morals and
the logic of law. There was a recognition that matters of
moral right and wrong do not refer to questions of subjective
taste or personal belief. It was understood that moral propositions are about the things that are universally right or
wrong, just or unjust—which is to say, right or wrong, just or
unjust, for others as well as oneself. It would be inconsistent,
then, with the logic of a moral proposition if one were to say,
for example, that "it is wrong to kill without justification"—and if one went on from there to conclude: "Therefore, let each person be free to kill or not kill as it suits his
own pleasure." To recognize that a certain act stands in the
class of a moral "wrong" is to say that it is universally
undesirable; that no one ought to do it; that it should be
forbidden to people generally. In short, it might be forbidden

with the binding force of law. And that, in brief, was the connection that Lincoln understood between morals and law.

At the same time, that connection makes us aware of the stern requirements that legislation must satisfy before it may properly claim the standing of "law." We are reminded that it is an awesome, presumptuous thing when some people claim the office of legislating for others, when they are willing to impose their own policy on people who may profoundly disagree. At that moment we would be compelled to ask whether the legislators were presuming to make laws for others on the basis of anything more than their own personal tastes or self-interest. If we applied the traditional understanding in the most rigorous way, we would have to insist that, before some people would be justified in legislating for others, they would be obliged to bring forward, as the ground of their legislation, a principle that defines what is good or just for others as well as themselves. A moral principle in the strictest sense would hold true universally and *categorically*—which is to say, that it will hold true as a matter of necessity; it will not be contingent upon circumstances that are open to change; and its validity will not be dependent on the consequences that it may bring from one case to another.

If we had the space, it could be shown here that the case against slavery was grounded in categorical propositions of this kind. That probably accounts for why we never hear the question, "How has the abolition of slavery worked?": it seems to be understood that the rightness or wrongness of slavery stands on its own terms, quite apart from the consequences of abolishing the institution. Our judgment about the rightness or wrongness of emancipation would not hinge at all on the question of whether the former slaves used their freedom well or badly, whether they became richer or poorer, happier or unhappier. For that reason the law which forbade slavery was established on the firmest ground— indeed, on the only proper ground—that is acceptable for the compulsion of law. As Kant put it, "Laws must ... be categorical"—they must be founded in categorical propositions—"otherwise they would not be laws."[13]

EQUALITY AS A FUNDING GOAL

Let me recall that I was compelled to trace matters back here to the root for the sake of supplying what the literature on "public and private goods" has not managed to incorporate—namely, the connection that must exist, of necessity, between moral principles and law, and the radical irrelevance of material outcomes in determining the validity of categorical moral truths. If we return now to the arguments that have been offered for the public funding of abortions, we would discover that nothing in the inventory of arguments I reviewed earlier bore the properties of a principle. In each instance the case for public funding rested on the prediction of a future state of affairs that was either problematic in itself or *contingent* upon circumstances that were highly mutable.

None of these arguments, in other words, had the force of a categorical truth; none of them arose from a proposition that held true as a matter of necessity. HEW was quite correct, for example, in asserting that the cost of an abortion is much less than the cost of supporting another person enduringly on public welfare. But there is no Law of Nature which guarantees that everyone who is now on public welfare will remain on welfare. There is no requirement that our welfare system be preserved in its current shape, and no certainty that everyone who is on welfare now would be on welfare under a different system. If the advent of more children in welfare families serves to elicit more support from the government, then it should be as apparent to our public commentators as it is to people on welfare that additional children may be a source of further income. And the notion should be as accessible to administrators in Washington as it is to peasants in backward countries that additional children may be sources of production, earnings, and perhaps even financial support in old age. (All of this says nothing, of course, for the poor boy who turns out to be Joe DiMaggio, Elvis Presley, or a major figure in the garment industry—and who not only provides his parents with security, but possibly also with free alterations.) Many of these children may seem unwanted when they are abstract possibilities, but they often have a remarkable capacity to foster senti-

250

mental attachments when they appear on the scene. Besides, it has never been thought in other instances that people lose their claim to live when they become unwanted or unpopular. By that measure we would have lost Harold Stassen in his leaner years, to say nothing of Bella Abzug and Billy Martin.

But all of this is to point up, again, that there is no ground of principle, in this inventory at least, which could create an obligation on the part of the government to tax the public for the support of "nontherapeutic" abortions.[14] The requirements of a principled argument are indeed very demanding, but the redeeming feature of this strictness is that it places a proper burden of argument on the government when it would presume to restrict personal freedom and commit people through the law: if there is no ground or principle on which to say that a wrong has been done, then the law must recede and the individual must be free to pursue his own preferences. If there is nothing of moral significance, for example, in the preference for spaghetti over coq au vin, we would of course assume that it must be legitimate for anyone to choose spaghetti. We could not imagine the possibility of a law that would actually forbid one to choose spaghetti. But it should be equally clear, in that case, that if there is no principled ground on which to enjoin the eating of spaghetti, there could not be any principled ground on which the law could extract money from taxpayers for the purpose of encouraging the consumption of spaghetti.

As I have already suggested, the critical dilemma here for the proponents of abortion and public funding is that they have strained for years to establish, in legal briefs and the public discourse, that the choice over abortion was closer in logic to the choice over spaghetti and coq au vin—that it was a matter of the most private taste or the most personal, subjective belief. When the argument has been picked up by political men and turned to their own purposes, it has become familiar to us in this mode: "I am personally, morally opposed to abortion, but I would not use the law to impose my views on others." That proposition is quickly becoming the most portable cliché in American politics, and it bears all of the same contradictions that Lincoln managed to expose in Douglas's argument on slavery. The same absurdities would of course appear as the "logic" of this position is extended to the matter of public funding, where the argument may take this form: "I am personally opposed to abortions, but while the Supreme Court has established the legality of abortion, it would be wrong to permit an arrangement in which the poor are prevented, in effect, from exercising rights that are freely enjoyed by the wealthy."

But if the exponents of this argument are taken at their word—if it is true that they regard abortion as a "wrong"—then nothing in the nature of that wrong in principle could possibly be nullified by the disparities between the rich and the poor. If comparisons are needed, we might imagine a situation in which it somehow became legitimate in this country to shoot Armenians, provided that it were done from a helicopter. We can suppose further that this state of affairs brings a vigorous protest from those people who have had a deep concern over the years for the question of "equality": they insist that they are strongly opposed to the shooting of Armenians, but while the hunting of Armenians is a legitimate sport in the law, the government ought to make the same facilities available to those who cannot afford helicopters.

If the poor in this country suffer far more impediments than the rich in taking the lives of fetuses, that disparity between the rich and the poor can have moral relevance only if we could somehow put aside the moral question of whether it would be justified to take these lives in the first place. For those people who have no trouble in putting that question aside, the disparities between the rich and the poor take on the quality of a moral question because they suggest a willingness to accept different strata of privilege in the exercise of "constitutional rights." If those disparities come about as a result of restrictions in the law, then presumably the restrictions ought to be removed or the government ought to provide, through public funds, the services that the poor cannot command themselves in the marketplace. But even when the main question in principle is put aside, the implications of this position quickly become untenable. For example, it was a convention for many years among the wealthy in New York to fly to Reno for the sake of obtaining easier divorces. Would we gather then that the federal government should have provided the cost of air fare and hotels to those people who could not have afforded an extended visit to Nevada? Or would we infer that New York simply should not have been permitted to have legislation on divorce that was more restrictive than the laws in Nevada? After all, it was the difference in legislation between the two states that created liberties for the wealthy in New York that were not available to the poor. If we were to respect the argument we have been offered here for the "equal protection of the laws," we would be compelled to deny to the remaining states in the Union the right to have laws on divorce that were any more restrictive than the laws of Nevada. The argument would have the consequence, in other words, of mandating an end to the federal system and replacing it with one uniform code, enforced by one government only, over the territory of the United States.

But the consequences extend even further. As soon as Japan and Sweden had legalized abortion, there were American women who were flying abroad for the purpose of having abortions. At that moment, was it the obligation of the government to furnish the cost of sending poor women to Japan and Sweden? Or would it have been the obligation of the Supreme Court, under the "equal protection of the laws," to have swept away all statutes and ordinances in this country that made abortion any more restrictive than it was in Japan and Sweden?

When its logic is carried through, this argument for "equality" would not merely end the federal system: it would also deny the right of government in the United States to legislate on any subject with more restrictiveness than exists in legislation anywhere abroad—if these differences in legislation created advantages that were more likely to be exploited by the rich.

For its own part, the Supreme Court took care to point out a few years ago that it had not really created "an unqualified 'constitutional right to an abortion.' . . . Rather, the right [established in *Roe* v. *Wade*] protects the woman from unduly burdensome interference with her freedom to decide whether to terminate her pregnancy."[15] In drawing an analogy, the Court went on to observe that it had long recognized the right to establish private schools with a religious character, but that that did not compel the state to furnish support to those parents who wished to send their children to parochial schools.[16] In a similar way, we may have the liberty to speak in public, but that would not entail an obligation on the part of the state to hire a hall for those who cannot afford it. The understanding, then, of the Court is that the matter of abortion involves a private liberty, which the state requires a compelling interest to restrict, but which it need not be obliged to support.

Justice Marshall has complained, however, in dissent, that if the government withholds the cost of abortions in legitimate clinics, "a poor woman may feel that she is forced to obtain an illegal abortion that poses a serious threat to her health and even her life."[17] This argument has been picked up widely in the public debate on the funding of abortions, but it suffers from a number of defects, not the least of which is that it happens not to be true. The Hyde Amendment, which restricted the federal funding of abortions, went into effect in the summer of 1977, and it was predicted at the time by physicians at the Center for Disease Control that there would be about forty-four to ninety deaths within the year as a result of illegal abortions. But by February 1978 it had become clear that the estimates were not being borne out. Dr. Willard Cates, the head of the Abortion Surveillance unit at the Center, conceded that "the 'bloodbath' many predicted simply is not happening. . . . [O]ur numbers don't show that there has been a mass migration to illegal procedures."[18]

In this respect the experience in the United States was foretold in the experience of other countries that have restricted abortions again after a regimen of permissive regulations. In Denmark and Sweden, for example, surveys were taken of women who were turned down in their applications for abortion, and it was discovered that about 85 percent of them had decided to give birth. Only about 11 to 16 percent of these women had obtained illegal abortions.[19] From the reports that have been coming now out of abortion clinics in this country, fewer women on Medicaid have been requesting abortions (in some instances the declines have been as sharp as 55 to 75 percent).[20] In the judgment of experts, the drop-off has not indicated a shift to illegal operations, but a trend toward carrying the pregnancies to term.[21] That assessment was probably supported by the recognition that most illegal abortions had not been carried out by midwives in those legendary backrooms, but had been performed in the same clinics that were now reporting the decline of customers. It is conceivable then that the Hyde Amendment was simply having the effects that its proponents had in mind. The framers of that amendment understood that people were very much affected in their moral judgments by the lessons that were taught through the law; and what they conveyed now, in a dramatic, public way, was that opinion in the country was firming up in moral opposition to abortion on demand.[22] They made clear their intention that the government should not be permitted to use the weight of its patronage for the sake of schooling the public to the acceptance of abortion. And in a large number of cases, where pregnant women were undecided or ambivalent, this teaching apparently had its effect.

It was evidently understood, even by some of the professionals who had raised the gravest alarms, that the withdrawal of public funding was not likely to raise the number of deaths due to illegal abortions. But these same people have been remarkably reticent over the mounting casualties that have arisen from *legal* abortions. A recent survey of hospital records by the Commission on Professional and Hospital Activities found that in 1969, before abortions had been legalized, there were about 9,000 women admitted to hospitals with complications resulting from abortions. In 1977—four years after abortions had been legalized—that figure had jumped to 17,000.[23] Between 1942 and 1952 the number of annual deaths resulting from abortions had fallen from 1,231 to 320. By 1972 the figure had dropped to 83. *Roe v. Wade*,[24] which legalized abortions, was decided in January 1973, and by the end of that year the number of recorded deaths from abortion had fallen a bit further, to 51. During the next year the number declined only slightly, to

47, and by the end of 1975 it dropped to 27 in the official count.[25] In other words, there had been a long-term decline in the deaths resulting from abortion. This decline was brought about mainly by improvements in the quality of medical care, and there is a section of opinion in the medical community which holds that the decline would have proceeded along its course had it not been for the advent of legalized abortions and the casualties they have been generating. The new regimen of legalization has, of course, enlarged the total volume of abortions in the country (at the last count, the annual figure reached 1.4 million), and there have been suspicions that the deaths from botched *legal* abortions have simply been concealed in hospitals under different labels.

There was some confirmation for these suspicions in the fall of 1978, when the *Chicago Sun-Times* brought to light the casualties that were being created by reckless abortion clinics in Chicago, which had turned themselves into the legal equivalent of abortion mills. The investigators brought in reports of about twelve deaths that were attributable to abortions in these establishments.[26] That is to say, the deaths that were produced only in this *sample* of abortion clinics in Chicago accounted for nearly half of the deaths that were reported for abortion in the nation as a whole. And if, as we suspect, the experience in Chicago can find even modest replication in New York, Detroit, Los Angeles, and other cities across the country, then the conclusion may be too melancholy for Mr. Justice Marshall to absorb. It is entirely possible that the total number of deaths resulting from abortion in legal abortions alone will be far higher than the number of deaths that resulted from abortions of all kinds—legal and illegal—in that period when abortions were restrained by the law.

I have tried here to show that the arguments for the public funding of abortion would be notably short of compelling, even when we put aside the question of whether abortions are in principle justified. And yet, so long as the law continues to regard abortions as legitimate medical procedures, the resistance to public funding will be vulnerable to persistent challenges in the courts. The problem was reflected rather well in *Maher* v. *Roe*, when the State of Connecticut refused to make funds available through its own program of Medicaid to support "nontherapeutic" abortions— abortions that were not certified by physicians to be "medically or psychiatrically necessary." The Federal District Court struck down these restrictions, even though Judge Newman conceded, for the court, that there was no constitutional right to a free abortion or to medical services furnished by the State. But a constitutional problem arose, in the view of the court, when the State chose to pay for other medical expenses associated with pregnancy. As Judge Newman put it, "Abortion and childbirth, when stripped of the sensitive moral arguments surrounding the abortion controversy, are simply two alternative medical methods of dealing with pregnancy."[27] The Supreme Court, in *Roe* v. *Wade* and *Doe* v. *Bolton*, had already decided that the right to an abortion was a "constitutional right," and so when the State lends its support to one kind of medical care associated with pregnancy, but withholds it from another, it would discriminate "against those seeking to exercise a constitutional right on the basis that the state simply does not approve of the exercise of that right."[28]

The state argued, in response, that it did not provide support for cosmetic surgery or orthodonture, even though it supported other forms of medical care—and yet no one urged that the state was obliged to cover these medical services because it happened to support others. The court was rather feeble in its rejoinder that abortion somehow represented more a constitutional right than the right to have cosmetic surgery, and the Supreme Court eventually refused to credit that argument. Still, the state did not establish its case on the firmest ground when it likened its aversion to abortions to its aversion toward paying for the straightening of noses. If the argument of the state is that these choices are merely matters of preference or taste—like the choice of spaghetti over coq au vin—then they are choices, also, that do not lend themselves to *justification*. In that event, the state would be in a difficult position to explain why it is justified in providing any of these medical services at all.

The same problem was posed recently in Massachusetts, when the legislature passed a measure that was closer in form to the original Hyde Amendment before that federal act was affected with compromises. The law in Massachusetts allowed payment for those abortions which were necessary to save the life of the mother and for those procedures which were "necessary for the proper treatment of the victims of forced rape or incest" if the incident were properly reported within thirty days. But the legislature refused to accept the provision that was added to the Hyde Amendment for the support of abortions in those instances in which "severe and long-lasting physical health damage to the mother would result if the pregnancy were carried to term when so determined by two physicians." A Federal Court of Appeals, however, refused to let the legislation stand. In the judgment of the court, the restrictiveness of the law was achieved by making an unwarranted discrimination between two kinds of medical need. As the court complained, "The Massachusetts plan reserves abortion services to those in the greatest need—women who will die without an abortion—and denies it to those who need it less—women who will suffer damage to their health, no matter how grievous, but who will survive without the abortion."[29] The court could not believe that it was consistent with the Medicaid Act to deny services to anyone with a serious health problem, and on that ground it regarded the distinction as unjustified.[30]

But the distinction between death and physical disability short of death would be an unjustified distinction only if the difference were not relevant to the ground on which lethal actions of any kind must be justified. The distinction ceases to be unreasonable as soon as one takes seriously the fact that abortion involves the taking of life; for then the interests which are brought forward to justify an abortion must be at least as grave as the interests we demand on other occasions to justify the taking of a life. But it is the irony of our current situation—and the special burden facing governments at all levels in this country now—that this point cannot be made explicit. If it were, it could only be part of an argument in principle against abortion itself; and no legislature can affirm an understanding of that kind as the foundation of its policy without raising a direct challenge to the ruling of the Supreme Court in *Roe* v. *Wade*. As we have already seen, the federal courts will have none of that.[31]

And yet it is precisely this opposition to abortion in principle which explains what the legislatures have been doing when they have refused to lend their sanction to abortion through the commitment of public funds. It also forms, in my judgment, the only ground on which the withholding of public funds can ultimately be defended. But in that event, the withholding of funds will be open to persistent challenge so long as the notion is preserved that it is *unconstitutional* for Congress or the states to hold a different view on abortion from the view that has been put forth by the courts. The case for Congress could be made more strongly than the case for the states, and it would draw on an older understanding, which was shared by Lincoln and the Founders: namely, that Congress and the president have quite as much standing as the courts to act, in their own spheres, as interpreters of the Constitution.

As far as I can tell, it is mainly men in positions of judicial authority who have established the assumption that the Supreme Court must be the final and unchallengeable authority on what the Constitution means (apart, of course, from the authority of the people themselves in amending the Constitution). Hence the surety of Judge Newman in Connecticut that there is, beyond question now, a constitutional right to an abortion, and that any attempt on the part of a legislature to call that right into question must itself be unconstitutional. An earlier generation of American statesmen would have seen that kind of judgment as an enormous act of presumption, and they would have understood our current situation more precisely in this way: they would have understood that the Supreme Court alone has propounded a constitutional right to an abortion, but that the Congress has not been persuaded by the Court and thinks in fact that the Court has made a profound mistake. Under those conditions it could not have been assumed just yet that any legislation which restricted abortion had to be unconstitutional on its face.

It has not been regarded as unthinkable, in other words, that Congress may take a different view on a matter of constitutional interpretation from the view taken by the Court, and that the Congress need not be obliged to recede in favor of the Court. Even in recent years there have been occasions when this understanding has been applied, by liberals as well as conservatives. In the case of the liberals, there was a willingness, in 1965, to have the Congress set aside, in a casual way, the literacy requirement for voting in New York State, even though the Supreme Court had not found that requirement to be unconstitutional.[32] In the case of the conservatives, there has been a continuing attempt throughout the 1970s to restrain the disposition of the courts to order busing and "racial balancing" in the public schools. In either case critics have seen an attempt by the Congress to alter, through ordinary legislation, what the Court has established as constitutional doctrine. The alarm raised over this prospect has been quite exaggerated, in my judgment, and it manages to overlook the most dramatic precedent to support this power of Congress: in June 1862, Congress abolished slavery in all of the existing territories of the United States, and it barred slavery from all of those territories which might be formed or acquired in the future. As Prof. James Randall later wrote of this legislation, "Congress passed and Lincoln signed a bill which, by ruling law according to the Supreme Court interpretation, was unconstitutional." What the president and Congress had done, in the most explicit and direct way, was to counter the decision of the Supreme Court in the infamous Dred Scott case.

But even before this legislation was passed, the Executive was compelled to face the implications of the Dred Scott case—and the question of constitutional authority—in a number of administrative decisions. During the first year of the Lincoln administration, a black man who was an inventor applied for a patent in Boston, and he was refused a patent by the federal office on the grounds that, according to the decision in the Dred Scott case, he was not a citizen of the United States. During the same year (1861) a young black man from Boston applied for a passport to study in France, but the State Department refused to issue the kind of passport that it extended to citizens of the United States. Once again it was assumed that the case would be governed by the Dred Scott decision. The Lincoln administration managed to finesse the matter in both cases and to issue the patent and the passport. And in 1862 the administration firmed up the legal ground for its acts when the attorney general published his legal opinion that free blacks born in the United States were to be regarded as citizens of the United States.[33]

And yet, if we hold to the view of constitutional authority that has become dominant in our own time, these decisions of the Lincoln administration would have to be regarded as unconstitutional. They can be regarded as plausible and constitutional only on the basis of that understanding held by Lincoln about the authority to interpret the Constitution: namely, that the separate branches were warranted in applying, in their own spheres, in the decisions that came before them, their own understandings of the Constitution. If the acts of the Lincoln administration may be regarded as justified in these cases, it must follow in turn that it would be quite as proper today for the Executive and the Congress to apply, in their own spheres, their own judgment about the constitutional authority to restrict abortions.

It is true, of course, that the executive and legislative acts of 1862 would later be supported by the Thirteenth Amendment—much in the way that the restrictive legislation today on abortion may one day have the additional support of a "human life" amendment. But in the absence of such an amendment, the legislation that restricts the funding of abortions would stand on the same plane as the legislation signed by Lincoln before the advent of the Thirteenth Amendment. It would represent an attempt by the administration and Congress to engage the Supreme Court in a continuing dialogue on the question of what the Constitution precisely commands. If the Court finds this legislation unacceptable, it may strike it down and force the matter to be settled through a constitutional amendment. On the other hand, the Court may accept—as it already has—the propriety of what the Congress has established on the public funding of abortions. But then Congress may continue to put the question to the Court in a sequence of cases, moving step by step. Would it be permissible to remove the tax-exempt status of foundations that offer grants to support abortion? Would it not be consistent with *Roe* v. *Wade* to insist that the woman who chooses abortion ought to satisfy a more rigorous understanding of "informed consent"—that she show an awareness of the nature of the operation and the condition of the fetus, or that she consider some rudimentary questions about the grounds on which nascent life may be taken? Would it be possible, also, for the Congress to establish, through a careful statute, a definition of "viability" for the fetus which the Court would finally oblige itself to respect?

It is within the power of Congress to compel the Court to keep moving through a series of questions of this kind. As the Court moved through these questions, it would be forced, however gently, to keep turning the problem around and to view its original decision from a variety of different angles. At some point it might find it necessary to consider, in a more demanding way, the questions it managed to avoid in *Roe* v. *Wade*, viz., on what ground of principle may the human fetus be reckoned as anything less than a human being, and what grounds do we typically require in the way of justification in other cases before human lives may be taken? The Court may also be induced to consider just why it is being forced to keep addressing these questions—just why, in the years since *Roe* v. *Wade*, larger and larger majorities in the country have come to find the reasons of the Court unpersuasive. In this spirit—the spirit of a government of shared powers and reasoned exchange—the Court may be encouraged to take a sober second look at what it has done, and to consider the possibility that it might have been mistaken.

NOTES

1. Quoted in Kenneth M. Stampp, *The Era of Reconstruction* (New York: Alfred A. Knopf, 1965), p. 65.
2. *Skinner* v. *Oklahoma*, 316 U.S. 535 (1942), at 543–45.
3. See the *New York Times*, 11 October 1977.
4. See the *Washington Star*, 16 February 1978.
5. *Washington Post*, 2 June 1977.
6. Adam Smith, *The Wealth of Nations* (New York: Modern Library, 1937), p. 689.

7. Ibid., p. 740.
8. Ibid., p. 766.
9. See *Bailey* v. *Alabama*, 219 U.S. 219 (1911).
10. Richard A. Musgrave and Penny B. Musgrave, *Public Finance in Theory and Practice* (New York: McGraw Hill, 1973), pp. 80–81.
11. Ibid., p. 81.
12. Speech at Quincy, Illinois (13 October 1858), in Roy P. Basler, ed., *The Works of Abraham Lincoln #3* (New Brunswick: Rutgers University Press, 1953) 257.
13. Immanuel Kant, *The Critique of Practical Reason*, 20, trans. Lewis White Beck (Indianapolis: Bobbs Merrill, 1956), p. 18.
14. I leave aside here the abortions that are necessary to save the life of the mother, which would be a wholly different matter.
15. *Maher* v. *Roe*, 53 L. Ed. 2d 484, at 494 (1977). As Chief Justice Burger remarked in his concurring opinion, the Court had simply required in its earlier cases "that a State not create an absolute barrier to a woman's decision to have an abortion. These precedents do not suggest that the State is constitutionally required to assist her in procuring it" (ibid., at 499).
16. See ibid., 496–97.
17. *Beal* v. *Doe*, 53 L. Ed 2d 464 (1977), at 480.
18. *Washington Post*, 16 February 1978.
19. Robert Hall, *Commentary*, in David T. Smith, ed., *Abortion and the Law* (Cleveland: Western Reserve University Press, 1967), pp. 232–33; 39 *Acta Psychiatrica Scandinavica*, Supplementum, 168 (1963): 17, cited in Daniel Callahan, *Abortion: Law, Choice and Morality* (New York: Macmillan, 1970), p. 85.
20. *New York Times*, 4 October 1977.
21. See, for example, *Newsweek*, 6 February 1978, and the *Baltimore Sun*, 4 September 1977.
22. The survey evidence on this point has been collected by Judith Blake in "Abortion and Public Opinion," *The Human Life Review* 4 (Winter 1978):64–81. This article was published originally in *Population and Development Review* 3, nos. 1 and 2 (March and June 1977):45–62.
23. *Hospital Record Study, 1969–77*, Joint Publication of the Commission on Professional Hospital Activities (Ann Arbor, Michigan) and IMS, Limited (Ambler, Pennsylvania).
24. 410 U.S. 113 (1973).
25. The figures from 1942 and 1973 were reported by André Hellegers in "Abortion: A Help or Hindrance to Public Health?" in his testimony before the Subcommittee on Constitutional Amendments of the Senate Judiciary Committee, 25 April 1974. The more recent figures are taken from *Vital Statistics of the United States 1975* (Washington: Government Printing Office, 1977), vol. 2—Mortality, Part A, p. 1–73.
26. See the *Chicago Sun-Times*, 12 November 1978: 6 December 1978; and the special edition in summary, "Abortion Profiteers" (December 1978).
27. 408 F. Supp. 660 (1975), at 663, note 3.
28. Ibid., at 664.
29. *Preterm, Inc.* v. *Dukakis*, 59 F. 2d 121 (1979), at 126.
30. The court also went on from there to question the constitutionality of the Hyde Amendment itself, because the federal act provided support

for abortions that were thought necessary to the physical health of the mother, while it withheld support from abortions that were claimed to be necessary for the "mental health" of the mother. Apparently invoking their best medical judgment, the two judges in the majority found the distinction between these two kinds of "health" to be "nothing less than absurd" (ibid., at 132).

31. The federal appeals court was quite alert, in fact, to this aspect of the movement to restrict the funding of abortions, and it formed part of the disposition of the court to question the constitutionality of the Hyde Amendment. See ibid., 127–31.

32. See *Katzenbach* v. *Morgan*, 384 U.S. 641 (1966). The Court acquiesced in this move, but Justice Harlan pointed out the implications of the decision in his dissenting opinion. See 659–71, especially 666–68.

33. These cases are recorded in *The Works of Charles Sumner* (Boston: Lee and Shepard, 1880), 5:497–98; 6:144.

10

POLITICAL DISCOURSE AND PUBLIC POLICY ON FUNDING ABORTION: AN ANALYSIS

MARY C. SEGERS

D ISCUSSIONS OF PUBLIC POLICY on abortion funding are characterized by a variety of inconsistencies, antinomies, and paradoxes. There seems to be a glaring inconsistency between the original arguments for decriminalizing abortion vindicated in *Roe* v. *Wade* (1973) and later arguments for public funding of what the Supreme Court held in *Wade* to be essentially a private choice. If privacy is a rationale for the right to abortion, then privacy is lost when the state funds abortions through Medicaid.[1]

This antinomy or inconsistency between abortion as an exercise of privacy rights and abortion as a social service to be publicly funded is merely the first of many inconsistencies which characterize public debate about abortion. It seems obvious that the controversy about abortion represents a conflict of basic values between the prochoice emphasis on reproductive freedom and the prolife stress on the equal value of human life at every stage of development. What is not always obvious is that each side in this controversy does not adhere consistently to the prime value it chooses to emphasize.

Prochoice advocates stress the freedom of a woman to terminate a pregnancy she does not desire. Yet they do not emphasize liberty when abortion opponents conscientiously object to positive law or refuse to pay through taxation for Medicaid abortions. While prochoice forces resort to the courts to protect individual or minority rights and to make policy on what they define as a civil liberties issue, they also defend the legalization of abortion by insisting that, because the Court has spoken in *Wade*, the law is therefore binding and compels obedience. For libertarian individualists they reveal a surprising degree of positivist fidelity to law.

Prolife advocates are hardly more consistent. They stress equality, that is, the equal worth of human life, but then neglect equal protection and equal opportunity on the issue of funding the medically necessary expenses of poor women. They speak eloquently of the principle of popular sovereignty, yet their arguments for fidelity to individual conscience or to higher moral law seem to contradict their emphasis on the right of the majority to legislate for a minority.[2]

These inconsistencies reflect, of course, a fundamental

tension, inherent in American politics, between democracy and constitutionalism. Thus, while prolife groups rely upon popular majorities in federal and state legislatures to restrict public funding of abortions, prochoice groups use the courts to challenge every state-legislated restriction on the newly minted constitutional right to reproductive freedom. The determination to pursue these general political strategies is illustrated by the tactics currently employed. Prolife forces such as the Life Political Action Committee have singled out for defeat in the 1980 elections six senators whose positions on abortion are too liberal.[3] On the opposite side, in *Harris* v. *McRae*, prochoice advocates have challenged (without success) congressional restrictions on abortion funding as an unconstitutional establishment of religion and an unconstitutional violation of the First Amendment's free exercise clause.[4]

Daniel Callahan has remarked that one of the difficulties about the abortion controversy in a pluralistic society such as the United States is that opposing groups share common values and a common language which mask important differences between the two positions.

> Each side claims that it represents the true embodiment of basic principles presumably accepted by all. Each side feels that it is the true defender of the common tradition. In the West, that common tradition is a respect for life and for the right of individual choice. One major task for the analyst of the abortion controversy is to attempt to discern, below the level of common discourse, the actual differences in value systems at stake, value systems which *are* different but whose divergences are often masked by the use of very similar language.[5]

In political terms, Callahan's observation is reflected in the commonplace maxim that American political discourse is conducted largely within the parameters of liberal political theory. Advocates and opponents of abortion employ the common language of liberalism concerning rights and duties, liberty and equality. Yet this common language conceals important divergences in underlying value systems. I believe these central divergences may be traced to different assumptions underlying political liberalism. Premises concerning the individual, the nature of society, and the optimum or ideal economic arrangement of society shape and influence the ways in which liberal ideals of freedom and equality are realized. In the case of abortion, each side's rationale for opposing or defending abortion is inconsistent with its argument for opposing or advocating public funding of the abortions of poor women. Prochoice advocates resort to a libertarian, individualistic ethic to justify the legalization of abortion, yet appeal to a cooperative, communitarian ethos to justify Medicaid funding. Right-to-life advocates stress equality and equal rights in their approach to abortion, but give priority to individualistic libertarian rather than egalitarian concerns on the funding issue.

This paper analyzes the prochoice perspective on Medicaid funding and seeks to examine more thoroughly the values and assumptions underlying the arguments of its proponents. (A discussion of the prolife perspective must await another occasion). This analysis should help to clarify why the prochoice case for Medicaid funding is encountering such stiff opposition.

THE POLITICAL CONTROVERSY OVER MEDICAID FUNDING OF ABORTIONS

The Supreme Court's 1973 landmark decisions legalizing abortion left unresolved the question of whether federal and state Medicaid funds could be used to pay for the abortions of poor women. Under Title XIX of the Social Security Act (Medicaid) enacted in 1965, state and federal governments are linked in a financial partnership to provide medical assistance to the needy.[6] Opponents of abortion have therefore directed their efforts to restrict Medicaid funding of abortions at state as well as federal governments.

Before 1976 the federal government reimbursed states for all abortions covered under their Medicaid programs. However, since 1976 three successive riders limiting federal matching funds to the states have been enacted. These riders are popularly known as the Hyde Amendment, after Representative Henry J. Hyde (R., Ill.), who introduced to the Departments of Labor and HEW appropriations bills his amendments restricting federal funding of abortions for the poor in 1976, 1977, 1978, and again in 1979.[7]

Each year the introduction of the Hyde Amendment on the

floors of both houses of Congress has precipitated prolonged congressional debate and necessitated resolution in conference of differing House and Senate bills.[8] The first Hyde Amendment, passed in the fall of 1976, barred the use of federal funds to pay for abortions "except where the life of the mother would be endangered if the fetus were carried to term." Additionally, the 1977 and 1978 amendments allowed funding when two doctors certified that "severe and longlasting physical health damage" would result if the pregnancy were continued to term. These two riders also permitted funding when the woman was pregnant as a result of rape or incest—provided it was reported within sixty days of the incident to a law enforcement agency or public health service.[9]

On 1 October 1976, the effective date of the first Hyde Amendment, a federal injunction resulting from a legal challenge, *McRae* v. *Richardson*, was initiated in the Federal District Court for the Eastern District of New York. Judge John F. Dooling, Jr., immediately issued an order that imposed a nationwide ban on enforcement of the federal funding cutoff until its validity could be examined. In June 1977 this injunction was vacated by the Supreme Court, with directions to the district court to reconsider in light of *Beal* v. *Doe* and *Maher* v. *Roe*.[10]

In *Maher* and *Beal*, the Supreme Court upheld two state statutes which limited Medicaid benefits to those abortions which were "medically necessary" and denied Medicaid for purely elective abortions. In *Beal* v. *Doe*, where a Pennsylvania statute was at issue, the Court held that while states may fund nontherapeutic abortions if they choose, the 1965 provision of the Social Security Act establishing Medicaid (Title XIX) does not require them to do so. In *Maher* v. *Roe*, in which a Connecticut law was under consideration, the Court ruled that the Constitution does not require a state participating in the Medicaid Program to pay for nontherapeutic or elective abortions though it pays for childbirth and for medically necessary abortions. In a classic exercise of judicial restraint, Justice Lewis Powell noted that the Court's decisions in *Beal* and *Maher* did not proscribe government funding of nontherapeutic (elective) abortions, but "left entirely free both the Federal Government and the States, through the normal processes of democracy, to provide the desired funding."[11]

While *Maher* and *Beal* appeared initially to be conclusive on the matter of Medicaid reimbursement of abortion, prochoice advocates soon realized that the Court's decisions left several important matters unresolved. The state laws upheld in *Maher* and *Beal* allowed funds for "medically necessary" abortions but disallowed funds for nontherapeutic or elective abortions.[12] The federal Hyde Amendment, by contrast, did not permit funding of most "medically necessary" abortions and appeared to be far more restrictive. Also, in *Maher* and *Beal* the Court did not consider whether a state or federal government could legally single out and restrict funds for media medically necessary procedures in the Medicaid program. Indeed, in *Beal*, Justice Powell specifically noted that although a state is free to refuse to fund medically "unnecessary" services, "serious statutory questions might be presented if a state Medicaid plan excluded necessary medical treatment from its coverage."[13] The reason is that the Social Security Act requires that all medically necessary physician and hospital services be included in Medicaid programs established under the act.

Prochoice advocates have therefore challenged anew the Hyde Amendment restrictions on federal Medicaid funding of abortions. The legal challenge in *McRae* is novel, formidable, broad, and comprehensive; it attacks the Hyde Amendment on statutory and constitutional grounds. First, plaintiffs argue that the Social Security Act requires the states to continue to fund medically necessary abortions, even if the federal government does not.[14]

Second, they maintain that the federal cutoff violates Fifth Amendment guarantees of due process. Under the Fifth and Fourteenth Amendments, laws affecting a person's right to liberty or property must be precise and give clear notice of the requirements of those laws. Where the existence of rights of liberty or property turns on a legal standard so vague and indefinite that reasonable minds cannot know its meaning, the law denies due process. Plaintiffs contend that the present Hyde Amendment is vague and that the standards set by the government are unknown and/or unworkable in current medical practice, yet, despite vagueness, both doctors and women may be subject to civil and criminal penalties if they violate these standards and regulations. Moreover, plaintiffs present evidence showing that because the law is vague, women are not seeking and doctors are not providing even those abortions to which women are entitled under the Hyde Amendment.

Third, plaintiffs argue that the Hyde Amendment is discriminatory and does not accord poor women the equal protection of the laws implicit in and guaranteed by the Fifth Amendment. The Hyde Amendment, they contend, singles out abortion as the only procedure to receive a different standard for reimbursement under the Medicaid program, which funds all other medically necessary procedures. Applying equal protection analysis, they argue that the discriminatory classification created "does not rationally further any legitimate state interest since the Supreme Court made clear in *Roe* v. *Wade* that any state interest in the potential life of the fetus cannot override a woman's interest in her life or health."[15] Plaintiffs adduce evidence to show that the Hyde Amendment is functioning exactly like the old criminal abortion laws, under which poor women's health needs and life risks are arbitrarily and discriminatorily ignored.

Finally, in the most novel aspect of the *McRae* challenge, plaintiffs argue that the Hyde Amendment violates the First Amendment requirement of separation of church and state because: (1) it enacts into civil law a particular religious view of abortion, namely, the view that the fetus is a human being from the moment of conception; and (2) it violates the free exercise clause by funding childbirth for those women whose religious views are antiabortionist while denying funds to those women whose religious or conscience views lead them to choose to terminate pregnancies. They maintain that the state must remain neutral on the abortion issue and not intrude upon the domain of individual liberty and conscience. Predictably, it is this aspect of the challenge in *McRae* which has provoked the most controversy.[16] The Supreme Court eventually heard the appeal, ruling against the obligation of the government to fund medically necessary abortions.

THE IMPACT OF THE HYDE AMENDMENT

A brief history of this controversy over Medicaid funding of abortions must include some account of the impact of the Hyde Amendment on the availability of abortions for poor women. By all accounts, the Hyde Amendment has resulted in a substantial reduction in the number of free abortions for the poor. Approximately 300,000 of the 1.1 million abortions performed in 1976 were paid for by Medicaid. In 1977 the federal and state governments paid out $87 million for 295,000 Medicaid abortions performed before the Hyde Amendment went into effect in August.[17] By contrast, in the third quarter of 1978, fewer than 900 federally funded abortions were performed.[18]

Of the 295,000 Medicaid abortions performed in 1977, 70 percent were done in states that have since discontinued paying for them.[19] This statistic highlights another aspect of the impact of the Hyde Amendment. Although the amendment concerned federal funding and never stipulated that states stop reimbursing their half of the Medicaid payments for abortion, thirty-nine states have, in fact, done so. To date only nine states, including New York, and one jurisdiction, the District of Columbia, have continued to pay the bills for Medicaid abortion patients. Connecticut and New Jersey allow Medicaid abortions with restrictions.[20] The remaining thirty-nine states have either eliminated or severely restricted Medicaid reimbursement; some have adopted the federal standards,[21] while others are more restrictive, limiting funding to those abortions which are necessary to "prevent death."[22] Thus, approximately 80 percent of the states have discontinued or severely restricted Medicaid payments of abortion.

Staff members of the Reproductive Freedom Project of the American Civil Liberties Union assess the impact of the Hyde Amendment as follows:

> Before implementation of the Hyde Amendment, some 300,000 poor women obtained Medicaid annually. The numbers have

gone down about 99% in those states which have not used state monies to fund abortion.[23]

There is some empirical evidence relating to the claim of proabortionists that cutbacks in federal funding would result in an increase in illegal abortions with an accompanying rise in female mortality. According to a hospital surveillance study conducted by the Center for Disease Control in Atlanta, abortion-related complications, one measure of illegal abortions, have not appeared among women Medicaid recipients.[24] However, in its regular epidemiologic survey of abortion mortality, the CDC did detect three abortion-related deaths of Medicaid recipients living in states that do not provide public funds for abortion. The CDC attributed one death directly and two indirectly to the absence of public funds. The first involved a Texas woman, Rosie Jimenez, who died from septic complications of abortion on October 3, 1977. The two deaths indirectly attributed to the funding cutoff appear to have involved medical complications and late abortions.

In its report, the CDC set this figure in the context of thirty-nine deaths resulting from illegal abortions in 1972 and three deaths from illegal abortions occurring in 1976 after *Roe* v. *Wade*. From this data the CDC concluded that "Medicaid-eligible women are not choosing self-induced or non–physician-induced abortions to any large extent."[25]

If Medicaid recipients are not resorting to illegal abortionists, what are they doing? Although precise statistics are unavailable, there are some indications as to the consequences of Medicaid cutoffs for pregnant women. Some indigent women are able to secure abortions at reduced charges from doctors, clinics, and some hospitals. Others are deciding to continue their pregnancies; Medicaid will pay childbirth expenses and welfare will pay child-rearing expenses. Still other women attempt to raise funds for abortions, with varying results. Some of these women spend so much time trying to gather the funds that by the time they have the desired abortion, they are in the second trimester of pregnancy and the abortion is much more complicated and expensive. In its hospital surveillance study, the CDC compared cases of women who suffered abortion-related complications and found that indigent women living in states with Medicaid cutoffs had obtained their abortions an average of two weeks later than two other groups of women—the nonindigent and the indigent who lived in states where Medicaid was available.[26]

It should be noted that it is difficult to ascertain the full extent of the impact of funding cuts, partly because there is no way of knowing some things, such as how many women who are having babies would have had abortions if the surgery had been free. But the limited statistics that are available, and the comments of doctors and other health-care workers around the country, suggest that the effects of the Hyde Amendment are substantial.[27]

Needless to say, how one evaluates this drastic cutback in Medicaid reimbursement depends on one's perspective: prochoice laments the restrictions upon the exercise of poor women's constitutionally protected rights while prolife applauds the increased numbers of unborn children spared thereby.

ARGUMENTS FOR AND AGAINST PUBLIC FUNDING OF ABORTIONS

Those who oppose public funding of abortion have secured passage of the Hyde Amendment to protect fetal life, a legislative purpose they see as perfectly legitimate. While many abortion opponents believe the fetus to be a human being from the moment of conception, this assumption is not necessary to their argument. If Congress can legislate to protect the snail darter, Congress can enact legislation to protect fetal life. In *Roe* v. *Wade*, Justice Blackmun, writing for the Court, acknowledged the legitimacy of the state's interest in protecting prenatal life and stated:

> Logically, of course, a legitimate state interest in this area need not stand or fall on acceptance of the belief that life begins at conception or at some other point prior to live birth. In assessing the state's interest, recognition may be given to the less rigid claim that as long as at least *potential* life is involved, the state may assert interests beyond the protection of the pregnant woman alone.[28]

Of course, opponents of abortion who do believe in the

humanity of the fetus think they are duty-bound to restrict abortion in any way possible and view funding cutbacks as saving the lives of unborn children rather than as depriving women of constitutional rights. What prochoice advocates view as wrong prolife activists think right. Thus, even in the matter of funding one very quickly comes up against the abortion question itself.

Those who oppose abortion as a grave moral wrong do not think they should be required to subsidize abortion through taxation. They echo here a familiar argument of the 1960s. During the Vietnam War, many in the peace movement argued that they were morally obliged to withhold taxes in protest against an immoral war. This argument holds whether opponents of funding for abortion-on-demand are a minority or a majority. According to recent polls, a majority of Americans do not think government money should be spent for elective abortions.[29] However, even if a minority of Americans held this view, the person morally opposed to abortion might still believe himself or herself bound in conscience to withhold tax monies or to vote against state funding of abortions. Such an individual would be acting according to a libertarian tradition as old as the American nation.

Prolife opponents of funding also question why the public must pay for abortions when the public is so deeply divided on this issue. They argue that if an abortion decision is a private matter, then perhaps private, nongovernmental organizations should engage in fund raising to pay for the abortions of the indigent. Why, they ask, cannot Planned Parenthood, NARAL, various churches, and voluntary associations privately fund this private right to choose to terminate pregnancy? In contemporary American politics, this view accords nicely with conservative trends symbolized by tax revolts and the Proposition 13 movement; in logical terms, however, abortion opponents are simply asking prochoice advocates to adhere consistently to the same individualistic ethic which sustains the right to abortion on privacy grounds.

In response to these arguments against Medicaid funding of abortions, prochoice activists appeal to principles of liberty, equality, utility, and tolerance which have long occupied a prominent place in the tradition of modern Western political thought. The concern with liberty—freedom from dependence upon nature, including one's own biology or human nature—is a powerful impulse in Western thought and a premise of liberalism and Marxism as well as a working assumption of modern science and modern medicine. In this view privacy is a condition of reproductive freedom, and serves to erect a buffer against governmental and societal interference with individual choice. Prochoice advocates also stress equal liberty and the equal worth of liberty. One might be opposed to abortion as morally wrong and socially destructive; however, the fact that abortion has been declared a legal right and is easily available to the middle and upper classes seems to support the idea that, in an ostensibly egalitarian society, it also should be available to the poor. Since equal rights are illusory if one lacks the financial means to exercise such rights, a society committed to liberal principles of equal opportunity and constitutional principles of equal protection must, in fairness, publicly assist the poor in exercising the right to choose whether or not to terminate pregnancy.

Those who favor Medicaid abortions also stress the utility of abortion for the poor. It is said to be less costly than childbirth expenses and welfare payments for child-rearing (an argument which should appeal to fiscal conservatives); in the first trimester, at least, abortion also carries less risk of damage to the woman's health.[30] On practical grounds, prochoice advocates point out that federal funding cutbacks resulting from the Hyde Amendment have the effect of encouraging late abortions, which pose greater risks to maternal health. This is because indigent women in non-Medicaid states are having abortions an average of two weeks later than other women with access to public funding. It is due also to the very nature of the Hyde Amendment, which funds abortions only in life-endangering pregnancies or in pregnancies which threaten "severe and longlasting physical health damage" if carried to term. According to plaintiffs in *McRae*:

The primary direct causes of maternal mortality are hemorrhage, infection and the hypertensive states of pregnancy—preeclampsia, eclampsia and toxemia. All of these are conditions which occur and cause maternal death late in pregnancy.[31]

By the time such a life-endangering situation had developed late in pregnancy, the risks to maternal health of the abortion then permissible would be much greater than if the abortion had been performed in the first trimester. From a practical standpoint, then, the Hyde Amendment works to encourage high-risk abortions. Since it also encourages more costly reproductive behaviors, it does not, from the standpoint of utility and efficiency, appear to be sound public policy.

Finally, as indicated earlier in the discussion of *McRae*, an important prochoice argument against the Hyde Amendment emphasizes the importance of tolerance in a pluralistic society. Those who oppose public funding of abortions are said to be imposing their own religious beliefs upon others who do not subscribe to such views. The enacting of the Hyde Amendment therefore violates the separation of church and state required by the First Amendment. Speaking of the Hyde Amendment, ACLU lawyers state:

> The statute has no secular purpose or effect. The only purpose ... is to eliminate abortions for poor women and therefore aid those religious groups that consider abortions wrong and sinful because of their theological position that human personhood begins at the moment of conception. At the trial of the *McRae* case, the evidence proved that the primary opposition to abortion is by religious not secular groups. It was also argued that the question of when life begins has not been, and may never be, scientifically determined. The question truly rests on religious dogma. Religions are clearly divided on this issue.

> Catholics and Orthodox Jewish groups support an anti-abortion position while many Protestant and the majority of Jewish groups advocate the religious necessity of choice over the abortion question. Plaintiffs, who include the Women's Division of the Methodist Church, asked the Court to find that the government can have no role in enacting into law an abortion statute which clearly elevates one religious belief over another and aids those religions which forbid abortion while inhibiting those persons who hold opposite religious beliefs or no religious beliefs at all. The state must remain neutral on the abortion issue.[32]

The perception of abortion as an issue involving liberty, privacy, equality, and tolerance helps to explain how the issue is defined by proabortionists as well as what political strategy is adopted. Abortion is conceived to be a civil liberties issue involving a constitutionally protected right to limit childbearing; the political strategy adopted is essentially a legal one since, in the American political system, at least since the 1930s, it is the judiciary which has been most active in protecting individual civil liberties. In the continuing struggle between constitutionalism and democracy in American politics, the prochoice forces come down heavily on the side of constitutionalism, seeking vindication in the courts and distrusting democratic majorities in state and federal legislatures.[33]

Prochoice activists are fond of citing *Brown v. Board of Education of Topeka* as precedent and model for this legal strategy. Fearing majoritarian tyranny, they have chosen the courts as the more congenial arena for their political struggle. This reliance upon the courts to make public policy on abortion, together with the positivism evident in prochoice arguments about compliance with the Court's ruling in *Wade*, poses a dilemma for proabortionists when court rulings on Medicaid funding go against them. Nevertheless, the inability of proabortion arguments to command legislative majorities in Congress and in most state legislatures dictates continuation of their legal strategy. It is no accident that the response of Planned Parenthood and the American Civil Liberties Union to *Maher v. Roe* and *Beal v. Doe* was to continue the legal challenge in *Harris v. McRae*.

PROABORTION ARGUMENTS FOR MEDICAID FUNDING: AN EVALUATION

Let us now analyze and evaluate these prochoice arguments for Medicaid funding in terms of philosophical and political cogency. How persuasive are proabortion arguments for public funding of a woman's exercise of her "right of personal privacy" (to cite the characterization of abortion in *Roe v. Wade*)? How compelling is the conception of individual freedom underlying the proabortion case? How politically effective are the utilitarian cost-benefit and health-risk analyses offered by proabortionists? How plausible is the argument for tolerance of competing views in a pluralistic society, the argument which underlies plaintiffs' First Amendment challenge in *McRae*? Finally, how compelling is the appeal to egalitarian principles which underlies arguments for Medicaid funding?

Answering these questions involves analyzing the values implicit in the prochoice position, a task which is properly and preeminently the work of the political theorist. It should be understood that whenever Supreme Court decisions are cited here to illustrate prochoice arguments, my approach is that of the political theorist seeking to elucidate values underlying political discourse and public policy. The perspective adopted here is not that of the constitutional lawyer interested in the role of the Court, the use of precedent, or the internal consistency of judicial doctrine over time.

The Supreme Court's 1973 abortion rulings were based on a constitutional right of privacy held implicit in the concept of personal liberty protected by the due process clause of the Fourteenth Amendment.[34] While admitting that the Constitution does not explicitly mention the right of privacy, the Court cited a series of past cases to indicate its growing recognition of such a fundamental right.[35] The Court then concluded that the right of privacy "is broad enough to encompass a woman's decision whether or not to terminate her pregnancy."[36]

Many who might applaud the outcome of the Court's ruling in *Wade* find rather odd the Court's appeal to personal privacy rights to justify the legalization of abortion. They echo Justice Rehnquist's dissent:

> I have difficulty in concluding, as the Court does, that the right of "privacy" is involved in this case. Texas by the statute here challenged bars the performance of a medical abortion by a licensed physician on a plaintiff such as Roe. A transaction resulting in an operation such as this is not "private" in the ordinary usage of that word. Nor is the "privacy" which the Court finds here even a distant relative of the freedom from searches and seizures protected by the Fourth Amendment to the Constitution which the Court has referred to as embodying a right to privacy.[37]

Although a majority of the justices also recognized the difficulty of applying privacy notions to abortion,[38] the Court seemed to think that its gradualist, three-stage approach to abortion was a satisfactory response to those who doubted the applicability of privacy. And of course the Court rejected the notion that the fundamental right of privacy is absolute and unlimited.[39]

In any case, on the question of Medicaid funding of abortions, which is of direct concern here, the notion of privacy does not seem to serve women well. In her analysis of *Maher v. Roe*, Sidney Callahan observed:

> Privacy is a double-edged sword with its negative as well as positive dimensions. As this last Court decision seems to indicate: to be private is also to be deprived of support. If an abortion decision is a private matter and the developing fetus nothing more than an appendage of a woman's body, then there is logic in leaving a woman to solve the problem herself, no matter how poor she may be. In private enterprise, power and privilege always operate, and unequal outcomes are the norm.[40]

As a justification for abortion, privacy is very closely related to liberty; this is apparent both in the legal reasoning of *Wade*[41] and in moral philosophizing about reproductive freedom. Here privacy and liberty mean independence of and freedom from the control of others—government and society—who might impose restrictive abortion laws; to use the categorization of liberty made famous by Isaiah Berlin, the conception of freedom here involved is negative.[42] Pro-choice advocates stress freedom from biological control as well as freedom from social control. They emphasize autonomy and self-determination in sex- and pregnancy-related medical care.

Again, however, an examination of the values underlying this liberal commitment to reproductive freedom reveals some deficiencies in the conception. The laudable ideal of individual or personal autonomy may be unrealizable so long as society is conceived of as an aggregate of isolated, separate, independent individuals—each having a Lockean natural right to property based on proprietorship of his or her own person. The admittedly extreme proabortion argument that a woman's body is her own to do with as she pleases[43] is reminiscent of Locke's conception of human beings in a state of nature. For Locke, the individual in the state of nature is "free, . . . absolute lord of his own person and possessions, equal to the greatest and subject to nobody."[44]

As Macpherson has stated, "The core of Locke's individualism is the assertion that every man is naturally the sole proprietor of his own person and capacities—the absolute proprietor in that he owes nothing to society for them—and especially the absolute proprietor of his capacity to labor."[45] To the extent that prochoice advocates argue that a woman's body (including fetal tissue) is her own private property for which she is not, in the final analysis, accountable to others—and individualist arguments such as these are implicit in both the case for abortion-on-demand and the case for not requiring spousal consent to abortion made in *Planned Parenthood* v. *Danforth* (1976)—to that extent prochoice activists are making what might be called Lockean liberal arguments for legalized abortion.

The only difficulty with such arguments is that they do very little to advance one's cause when the issue is public funding of abortions for those who are poor, dependent, powerless, and vulnerable. The intensely individualistic perspective of prochoice advocates seems to offer little in the way of social solidarity and support; moreover, such a perspective runs counter to feminist arguments for public assistance to women in their childbearing and child-rearing activities—whether they need public funding of abortions (should they choose to terminate pregnancy) or publicly funded child-care centers (should they choose to bear and rear the children they have conceived). As Sidney Callahan has observed:

> An individualistic ethic which rests the right to an abortion on privacy grounds does not serve women well, and it is unfortunate that most feminists have not addressed the problem. Pregnancy disability payments, family allowances, and public day-care have all been attacked because they are said to infringe on the privacy of the family. Public protection of the fetus and public support for and protection of women's rights are related in principle.[46]

With respect to the values of privacy and liberty, then, I am suggesting that prochoice arguments for the legality of abortion are inconsistent with their arguments for Medicaid funding of abortions. Further, I suggest that this weakness or inconsistency reflects a more general tension between nineteenth-century, individualistic, laissez-faire liberalism and twentieth-century, post–New Deal, welfare-state liberalism.[47] The former conceives society as an aggregate of isolated individuals who seek freedom from the intervention and intrusion of others, while the latter envisions society as an organic community of interdependent, interrelated persons whose freedom is made possible through mutual assistance and cooperation.

In their arguments for Medicaid funding of abortions, prochoice advocates rightly appeal to the egalitarian principles implicit in welfare-state liberalism. Liberalism in contemporary America has stressed the necessity of equality of opportunity if the promise of liberty for all is to be fulfilled.[48] If reproductive freedom includes a right to safe, legal abortions, then equal opportunity to exercise that right and equal access to the abortion option seems appropriate. And equal opportunity in this context requires public funding of abortions for the poor—or so the argument runs. I believe proabortionists are persuasive here when they emphasize the injustice of unequal access to abortions. In fact, appeals to principles of equality and distributive justice were strong planks in the pre-*Wade* movement to legalize abortion as well as in the post-*Wade* movement to subsidize abortion. One of the most effective arguments for legalizing abortion concerned the problem of discriminatory enforcement of antiabortion laws. Mohr has stated this argument forcefully. Noting that in the twentieth century a substantial number of American women continued to seek and to have abortions despite nineteenth-century statutes designed to make them unavailable, he wrote:

By itself, of course, the violation of a law is not an especially persuasive argument for its repeal; few people would advocate the legalization of homicide, for example, simply because a certain number of Americans continue to kill one another each year in spite of the criminal sanctions against doing so. But the evidence about the continued practice of abortion in the United States throughout the twentieth century raised some rather more difficult problems. Wealthy women, it was alleged, could arrange for safe and "legal" abortions by persuading their physicians to interpret the therapeutic clauses of various antiabortion laws very loosely, while poor women could not. Wealthy women could afford to travel to those jurisdictions where the antiabortion laws were not rigidly enforced; poor women could not. The nation's antiabortion laws were thus perceived as discriminating against poor, frequently non-white women in an era of heightened sensitivity to egalitarianism. It was also the poor who were more likely to die at the hands of the gross incompetents who preyed upon the desperation of those without sufficient funds either to terminate their pregnancy safely and discreetly or to make socially acceptable arrangements both for the period of confinement and for the subsequent care and upbringing of the child, through adoption or other means. Unenforceability, in other words, might be one thing, but discriminatory enforcement was quite another.[49]

Prochoice advocates argue that the same inequality is occurring with respect to post-1973 restrictive legislation in general and the Hyde Amendment in particular. To restrict public funding of poor women's abortions merely perpetuates the selective, discriminatory pattern of earlier days.

Of course, prolife advocates have seized upon the well-known deficiencies of the liberal doctrine of equality of opportunity in arguing against the prochoice side.[50] Chief among such deficiencies is the largely formal character of the doctrine. The equal opportunity principle does not specify the nature or value of the opportunities one is to have. In the case of equal access to abortion, it is precisely the value of abortion which is questioned. Thus, from a socialist perspective, even this crucial and otherwise strong egalitarian argument of proabortionists for Medicaid funding seems tinged with the deficiencies of liberalism.

In addition to the values of privacy, liberty, and equality which underlie proabortion arguments, prochoice advocates often appeal to the liberal virtue of tolerance to support the case for public funding of abortions. The most recent example of this, of course, was the First Amendment brief in *McRae*. There plaintiffs argue that the Hyde Amendment violates the constitutional separation of church and state because it enacts into civil law a religious view of abortion—the view that the fetus is a human being from the moment of conception. Abortion is held to be a religious issue, best left to the private conscience rather than to public legislation. In its public policy, the state must remain neutral on the abortion issue and not intrude upon the domains of individual liberty and conscience. Government neutrality is best achieved through the removal of restrictive abortion laws from the books (as in *Wade*). Finally, repeal of anti-abortion statutes is said to pass no judgment on the substantive ethical issues, but merely to allow individuals to make up their own minds.

There are several objections to this train of argument. First, it is hard to know what is meant by the statement that abortion is a religious issue. If it means that for some churches and some religious believers their positions are the direct result of religious teachings, this hardly entails the conclusion that the issue is thus intrinsically religious. One might as well say that racial equality is a religious issue and not subject to legislation, because there are some churches which declare racism immoral on religious grounds. That religious groups take religious positions on many issues (e.g., war, racial equality, poverty, capital punishment, and ecology) does not exempt those problems from public legislation nor turn them into theology.[51]

Abortion seems to be a philosophical and ethical issue, not a religious question. This does not mean the issue is therefore best left to the domain of private conscience. Every serious social issue is philosophical. Questions about the meaning of justice, liberty, or equality arise all the time, and such questions are philosophical and legal in nature. The answers to them shape public policy in a decisive fashion. As one philosopher has remarked:

> It is inconsistent to argue that the right of the fetus is exclusively a philosophical problem, to be left to individual conscience, while the right of women is a matter to be protected or implemented legislatively. If it is legitimate to legislate on the latter (which it is), then it should be equally legitimate to legislate on the former.[52]

One would have to conclude that protection of fetal life, which is the object of the Hyde Amendment, is a legitimate, valid, secular legislative purpose.

Still another objection to arguments for tolerance of abortion in a pluralistic society questions whether it is possible for government to remain neutral on the abortion issue. A governmental decision to remove restrictive antiabortion laws from the books and to leave the question up to individuals hardly seems neutral. Such a policy begs the question of the status of the fetus, or, at the least, assumes that there are no normative standards whatever for determining the rights of fetuses, except the standard that individuals are free to use or to create any standard they see fit. This libertarian policy is not only not neutral; it exhibits a major flaw in liberal political thought—namely, the inability of contemporary liberalism to offer a rationally persuasive conception of universal norms.

The view that it is possible for government to remain neutral on the abortion issue also betrays a certain naïveté about the role of law in society. The Greeks recognized the educative role of the laws[53] and were aware that changes in the law not only often reflect significant shifts in public moral attitudes but also affect individual moral judgments. Mohr has shown the impact in the United States of the nineteenth-century antiabortion statutes upon public attitudes regarding abortion: whereas the great majority of Americans in 1850 did not regard abortion as morally wrong, public opinion in 1950 was invariably opposed to abortion.[54] In the face of such evidence concerning the role of law as a socializing agent—at least with respect to attitudes—it seems naive and disingenuous to pretend that government, law, and public policy are or can be neutral on the question of abortion.

Rather, arguments that America is a pluralistic society in which government must tolerate competing views about the morality or immorality of abortion should be changed to read: America is a liberal, secular society which accords highest importance to individual choice and to worldly values, which cannot achieve public consensus on the abortion question, and which, as a result, must reluctantly leave resolution of the matter to private individual judgment. This clarification of the prochoice argument does not exalt abortion as a civil right grounded in fundamental constitutional privacy rights, but recognizes that abortion is a desperate option, a last resort reluctantly undertaken "in necessity and in sorrow." This may be the best that we can arrive at on the controversial issue; but the point is that such a view offers little justification for coercing others through taxation to fund what they regard as seriously immoral.

CONCLUDING REFLECTIONS

In this chapter, I have attempted to discern value-positions beneath the level of common discourse in public debate about funding abortions. Prochoice arguments have been analyzed; the analysis of the prolife case must await another occasion. My analysis has shown that the prochoice case for Medicaid funding is weak primarily because the individualistic ethic used to justify abortion as a legal right is inconsistent with the cooperative, communitarian ethic presupposed by public funding of the abortions of poor women. I believe this inconsistency reflects a larger tension or conflict between two types of liberalism in America. Nineteenth-century laissez-faire liberalism (1) conceives the individual to be the primary unit of sociological analysis; (2) conceives society to be an aggregate of isolated, independent, private individuals who occasionally interact; and (3) conceives liberty to be freedom from interference and intrusion by society and government. Laissez-faire liberalism is, of course, compatible with a free-market system of private enterprise which mostly resists governmental interference and regulation. Twentieth-century welfare-state liberalism also subscribes to an irreducible individualism, but, in contrast to laissez-faire liberalism, it conceives society to be a community of organically related individuals who are interdependent; and it defines liberty as freedom from necessity in order to be available for moral action. Welfare-state liberalism is, of course, compatible with positive governmental action to "hinder the hindrances to freedom" by providing assistance (such as Medicaid payments) to those who are needy.

The prochoice case for Medicaid funding is weak because the appeal to privacy to justify abortion, which has strong affinities with a laissez-faire liberal perspective, seems inconsistent with the arguments for public support, arguments which are distinctly welfare-state liberal in tone. To the political observer, this may seem obvious. What is not always clear is how the original prochoice conception of abortion as a private, self-regarding action involving a pregnant woman's conduct with respect to her own body undermines any plea she might make for public assistance. The original definition of abortion as a private action is, of course, the sticking point. As long as one adheres to that definition, it is difficult to expect others, who in principle oppose not only the action but also the definition of the action, to help one carry it out. Abortion, opponents would say, interrupts the process of development in one person's body of another human being—and this does not strike them as a private matter.

How might the argument of proabortionists be improved? I believe prochoice advocates should define abortion as an ethical dilemma rather than as a civil liberties issue; or at least they should recognize that appeals to privacy, liberty, and tolerance are legal arguments tailored to constitutional analysis and designed primarily to win victory in courts of law. Such appeals are not persuasive on the moral issue of reproductive freedom and the public assistance necessary to make such freedom genuine for all parts of the population. And it is the moral, not the legal, issue which seems more salient on the question of Medicaid funding, subject as it is to the votes of state and federal legislators who react to public opinion. According to a Yankelovich survey, public opinion is much more closely divided on the morality of abortion as compared with public opinion on the legality of abortion.[55] I believe then that the proabortion case for public funding might be more persuasive if abortion were seen as an ethical dilemma and a moral decision reluctantly made rather than as a civil right defiantly asserted.[56]

I would be remiss were I not to mention the strong points in the arguments made by prochoice advocates. Briefly, these are the following. First, the appeal to utility, couched in terms of the health risks and financial costs of late, as opposed to early, abortions—which the Hyde Amendment encourages—seems to be a strong argument against the Hyde Amendment. Unfortunately, a utilitarian approach may not work well for prochoice activists for the simple reason that the opposite side's stress on the value of each human (including fetal) life seems to be part of a larger trend in contemporary political philosophy (argued in John Rawls's *A Theory of Justice*) against utilitarianism and against utilitarian cost-benefit calculations with respect to human life.

Second, the prochoice appeal to egalitarian principles of equal opportunity and equal protection is a very strong argument for Medicaid funding—especially in view of the fact that other medically necessary expenses of poor women, including childbirth costs, are funded. Even here, however, prochoice advocates must be prepared to answer the objection that the equal opportunity principle is formal and begs questions about the "opportunity" to which everyone is to have equal access. Inevitably, the appeal to the equal opportunity doctrine directs the argument about Medicaid funding back to the original issue of the morality and legality of abortion—and I have suggested why that direction would not be a wise route for prochoice advocates to take. Also, any liberal appeal to the principle of equality of opportunity must be prepared to ground that principle in some more fundamental, basic conception of human equality. And here prolife forces may be on a stronger ground. As Daniel Callahan has observed:

> The great strength of the movement against abortion is that it seeks to protect one defenseless category of human or potentially human life; furthermore, it strives to resist the introduction into society of forms of value judgments that would discriminate among the worth of individual lives. In almost any other civil rights context, the cogency of this line of reasoning would be quickly respected. Indeed, it has been at the heart of efforts to correct racial injustices, to improve health care, to eradicate poverty, and to provide better care for the aged. The history of mankind has shown too many instances of systematic efforts to exclude certain races or classes of persons from the human community to allow us to view with equanimity the declaration that fetuses are "not human." Historically, the proposition that all human beings are equal, however "inchoate" they may be, is not conservative but radical. It is constantly threatened in theory and subverted in practice.[57]

Perhaps the strongest planks in the prochoice platform have relatively little to do with systems of logic and a great deal to do with "real life" existential situations. An essential element in all discussions of abortion is the need for a feminist perspective, by which I mean continued emphasis on what motherhood and pregnancy mean for women who hold themselves as persons with life plans to realize. The demands on time and energy, and the frustrations—as well as the satisfactions—of maternity (and also paternity) in contemporary society must always be acknowledged. It is sad and unfortunate that a prominent, well-intentioned pro-life spokesman such as John T. Noonan almost entirely ignores this aspect of the abortion issue, referring to the pregnant woman as "the carrier of the child" and as "the gravida." No amount of medical terminology should be permitted to desensitize us to the difficult, sometimes agonizing plight of the poor woman faced with an unwanted pregnancy.

From a feminist perspective, it seems unfortunate that the most effective method of restricting abortion to date has been the Hyde Amendment. It is precisely because indigent women are in poverty and thus dependent upon public assistance that the Hyde Amendment is so effective. Because they are poor and dependent upon public funding, their behavior can be controlled in ways that the behavior of upper- and middle-class women cannot be controlled. The poor and only the poor bear the burden of antiabortion legislation.

A feminist perspective on the practical problem of the involuntarily pregnant woman—rich or poor—will construe her immediate situation as an ethical dilemma, a situation of forced choice. She has certain options, she is under great duress, time is of the essence, and she must decide quickly among her options. Conceiving abortion as an ethical dilemma rather than as an individual civil liberty should focus attention on concrete ways to help women avoid such harrowing dilemmas. It should also provide better arguments and a more favorable atmosphere for public assistance to and support of all women in their professional, vocational, and social roles.

NOTES

1. Since this same argument could be made about Medicaid payment for contraceptives and for childbirth expenses, an important caveat must be made at the outset—namely, the legal right the exercise of which is to be publicly funded must not be the object of deep-rooted fundamental controversy. In a pluralistic society such as ours, consensus or at least the lack of dissensus exists concerning childbirth and contraception; however, there is fundamental disagreement about the morality and legality of abortion, let alone about the propriety of public funding of abortions.

2. Commenting on the incongruity of American Catholics and other abortion opponents stressing majoritarian rights, Callahan notes: "Opponents of abortion reform often fail to admit that in the past highly restrictive laws on abortion were kept in force simply by the overwhelming power of majority religious or political groups. When American Catholics in the nineteenth century protested against a public school system which was *de facto* Protestant, when Jews later complained about Sunday blue laws, and when Catholics and Jews together complained about prohibition and dry laws, they were in effect saying one thing: in a pluralistic society the rights of minorities must be taken into account. The proponents of liberalized abortions laws are only claiming the same rights now." (Daniel Callahan, *Abortion: Law, Choice and Morality* [New York: MacMillan Company, 1970], p. 8).

3. *New York Times*, 24 June 1979, section 1, p. 1.

4. *McRae* v. *Califano*, 76 Civ. 1804 (JFD), in United States District Court, Eastern District of New York. On 4 December 1978, final arguments were made in this suit which was filed on 1 October 1976. On 15 January 1980, Judge John F. Dooling handed down his decision in *McRae* v. *Harris*, declaring the Hyde Amendment unconstitutional. He based his decision primarily on First and Fifth Amendment protections, noting that the Hyde Amendment interferes with a woman's religious beliefs in favor of an abortion by forcing her to forego one, that it violates her right to privacy, which cannot be denied without due process, and that limiting free abortions represented unequal treatment for the poor. While accepting plaintiffs' appeal to the free exercise clause of the First Amendment, Judge Dooling rejected plaintiff's argument that the Hyde Amendment violated the establishment clause of the First Amendment. Judge Dooling's decision was immediately appealed by the government, and on 19 February 1980, the Supreme Court agreed to hear the case. On 30 June 1980, the Supreme Court, by a vote of 5-4, reversed Judge Dooling and upheld the constitutionality of the Hyde Amendment. Writing for the majority, Associate Justice Potter Stewart argued that the constitutional right of a woman to choose whether or not to terminate her pregnancy did not include an entitlement to Medicaid payments for medically necessary abortions. The Court rejected the argument that the Hyde Amendment violated the establishment clause of the First Amendment and declared that the plaintiffs lacked legal standing to claim violation of the free exercise clause because none of the original parties to the suit declared that she sought an abortion in accordance with conscientious beliefs.

5. Callahan, *Abortion*, p. 6 (italics in the original).

6. Title XIX of the Social Security Act was enacted in 1965 to "furnish

medical assistance (to eligible persons) to meet the costs of necessary medical services" (42 U.S.C. Sect. 1936). Medicaid is a program of cooperative federalism. The federal law makes substantial amounts of federal funds, over $5.3 billion in 1974 (according to a staff report of the Subcommittee on Health and the Environment), available to those states which choose to participate in the program. All states except Arizona have chosen to do so. The federal act defines the nature of Medicaid. In some areas, the federal law gives the states discretion to determine the shape of their own Medicaid programs. In other areas the requirements of the federal law are mandatory. See *McRae* v. *Califano*, Plaintiffs' Memorandum of Law on Statutory, Equal Protection and Due Process Claims, pp. 3–4.

7. The 1979 Hyde Amendment (for FY 1980) was passed in two different versions by the House of Representatives on 27 June 1979 and by the Senate on 18 July 1979. An integrated version was worked out in conference on 16 November 1979; *New York Times*, 28 June, 1979, p. B14, and 20 July 1979, p. A8. *Congressional Quarterly Weekly Report* 37, no. 46 (17 November 1979), p. 2624.

8. For a comprehensive account of the congressional politics associated with the 1976 and 1977 amendments, see Joyce Gelb and Marian L. Palley, "Women and Interest-Group Politics: A Comparative Analysis of Federal Decision-making," *Journal of Politics* 41 (May 1979): 375–80.

9. The 1978 Hyde Amendment states: "None of the funds contained in this Act shall be used to perform abortions except where the life of the mother would be endangered if the fetus were carried to term; or except for such medical procedures necessary for the victim of rape or incest, when such . . . has been . . . reported . . .; or except in those instances where severe and longlasting physical health damage to the mother would result if the pregnancy were carried to term when so determined by the physicians." Janet Benshoof and Judith Levin, "Current Legal Issues in Abortion Litigation," paper prepared for discussion at the Biennial Conference of the American Civil Liberties Union, Mount Vernon College, Washington, D.C., June 16-19, 1979, p. 11. In its final version, the 1979 Hyde Amendment is more restrictive, prohibiting the use of federal funds for abortion except when required to save the mother's life or in cases of rape or incest. See Gelb and Palley, "Women and Politics."

10. 432 U.S. 438 and 464 (1977). For an analysis of the Court's decisions, see the articles by George J. Annas, Sidney Callahan, and Mary C. Segers in *The Hastings Center Report* 7 (August 1977): 5–9.

11. 45 U.S.L.W. 4783.

12. Obviously a central question in the controversy over Medicaid funding is the definition of "medically necessary" abortions. Opponents of abortion take issue with the relatively broad definition of "medically necessary" abortions offered by the Court in *Doe* v. *Bolton*: "We agree with the District Court . . . that the medical judgment may be exercised in the light of all factors—physical, emotional, psychological, familial, and the woman's age—relevant to the well-being of the patient. All these factors may relate to health. This allows the attending physician the room he needs to make his best medical judgment. And it is room that operates for the benefit, not the disadvantage, of the pregnant woman" (410 U.S. 179 [1973]). Abortion proponents, on the other hand, stress that "the patient's wishes and consent are critical factors in determining what

services are medically necessary." Plaintiffs' attorneys in *McRae* state: "While not solely determinative of medical necessity, the woman's attitude may significantly increase risks of stress and cause aggravation of physical, psychological, emotional and familial problems if the service is denied. In extreme cases, the physician might believe that if a legal abortion is denied the woman will attempt suicide, self-abortion or obtain treatment from an unskilled lay person. This too must affect the physician's judgment whether abortion is medically necessary." See Plaintiffs' Memorandum of Law on Statutory, Equal Protection and Due Process Claims, pp. 31–32, in *McRae* v. *Califano*.

13. 432 U.S. at 444–445 (1977).

14. Plaintiffs in *McRae* are Cora McRae and four other women who desire Medicaid abortions, doctors who want to be able to provide abortions to their poor patients and be reimbursed by Medicaid, and the Woman's Division of the Board of Global Ministries of the United Methodist Church. They are represented by attorneys for the Center for Constitutional Rights, the American Civil Liberties Union, and Planned Parenthood of New York City. Defendants were Joseph A. Califano, Jr., then Secretary of HEW, and four other Intervenor-Defendants: former Senator James L. Buckley, Senator Jesse A. Helms, Congressman Henry J. Hyde, and Isabella M. Pernicone, Esq. Sources for the following summary of arguments in *McRae* are: Plaintiffs' First Amendment Brief, Plaintiffs' Memorandum of Law on the Vagueness Claim, and Plaintiffs' Memorandum of Law on Statutory, Equal Protection and Due Process Claims. The name of this lawsuit was changed to *McRae* v. *Harris* as a result of President Carter's Cabinet changes in July 1979. Harris later became appellant and McRae et al. the appellees.

15. Benshoof and Levin, "Current Legal Issues," p. 13.

16. See, for example, the editorial, "Do Catholics Have Constitutional Rights?" in *Commonweal* 105 (8 December 1978): 771–73; the editorial, "Abortion, Religion and Political Life," *Commonweal* 106 (2 February 1979): 35–38; the essay by Aryeh Neier in *Nation* 227 (30 December 1978): 721–27; "Does the First Amendment Bar the Hyde Amendment?" a symposium with essays by Beverly Harrison, Mary C. Segers, J. Philip Wogaman, and Robert G. Hoyt, in *Christianity and Crisis* 39 (5 March 1979): 34–43; "Is Abortion a Religious Issue?" a symposium featuring essays by Baruch Brody, Frederick Jaffe, and Liza Newton, in *The Hastings Center Report* 8 (August 1978): 12–17, with an introduction by Margaret O'Brien Steinfels.

17. *New York Times*, 20 July 1979, p. A14.

18. *New York Times*, 26 December 1978, p. A1.

19. *New York Times*, 20 July 1979, p. A14.

20. Since August 1977, Connecticut has paid for abortions for women on welfare only when the life of the woman was in danger. Before the imposition of that restriction, the state paid for about 1,750 abortions annually. That figure has now dropped to about 250 abortions a year. The Connecticut ban is now being challenged in Federal District Court by the newly formed Rosie Jimenez Memorial Alliance of New Haven (made up of approximately twenty-five women's organizations). According to a report in the *New York Times*, 24 July 1979, p. B2, the suit charges that state policy is arbitrary and discriminates against the poor. See *Women's Health Services, Inc.* v. *Mahrer*, Civ. No. 405–479 (D. Conn., 17 July 1979).

21. Under Hyde Amendment standards, for example, Medicaid abortions are denied to women who know for certain—through amniocentesis—that the pregnancy they bear will result in a seriously defective child.

22. Benshoof and Levin, "Current Legal Issues," p. 14.

23. Ibid., p. 11.

24. Center for Disease Control, "Morbidity and Mortality Weekly Report," 2 February 1979, as reported in *The Hastings Center Report* 9 (April 1979): 2–3. Of course, illegal abortions are by their nature secret; they rarely come to light unless the woman is severely injured or dies.

25. Ibid., p. 3.

26. *New York Times*, 26 December 1978, p. B14.

27. Ibid.

28. 410 U.S. 113, 150 (1973). Of course, the Court ruled that states may assert this interest only at and subsequent to the point of fetal viability. Also, even during the third trimester, when this state interest in protecting fetal life may be asserted, it must not, according to the Court's ruling in *Wade*, outweigh "the preservation of the life or health of the mother" (id. at 165).

29. Note the responses to a question included in the 1975 Gallup Survey: "Are you in favor of a law which permits a woman to have an abortion even if it has to be at government expense?" 57 percent of respondents answered negatively in 1975 and 35 percent positively, with virtually no variation by age or sex. This is reported in Judith Blake, "The Supreme Court's Abortion Decisions and Public Opinion in the United States," *Population and Development Review* 3, nos. 1–2 (March and June 1977); 45–62. Blake comments as follows: "American women were somewhat less negative than in 1970, when 66 percent opposed government subsidy, but the five-year period clearly did not greatly change Americans' views. It is possible that a share of negative responses to the question relates to hostility toward government expense generally; however, the political implications are the same. Apparently, publicly financed abortion is, like food stamps, an unpopular government expense." *Commonweal* reports the findings of a poll of 9,000 voters leaving voting places in November 1978. Only 44 percent of Democrats and 37 percent of Republicans favored government funding for abortion; *Commonweal* 106 (2 February 1979):36. Finally, according to a public opinion poll conducted by Yankelovich, Skelly, and White and commissioned by *Time*, 58 percent of those polled believe that government funds should not be used to finance elective abortions for the poor. This was so despite the finding that 64 percent believe that, regardless of morality, a woman should be legally free to have an abortion if she wants one (*Time* 21 November 1977, p. 115).

30. *Roe* v. *Wade*, 410 U.S. 113, 163 (1973); "Constitutional Aspects of the Right to Limit Childbearing," A Report of the United States Commission on Civil Rights, April 1975, Appendix I, paragraph 8, p. 103; see also "The Impact of the Hyde Amendment on Medically Necessary Abortions," a report of the American Civil Liberties Union, October 1978, pp. 25–30.

31. ACLU, "The Impact of the Hyde Amendment," pp. 9–10.

32. Benshoof and Levin, "Current Legal Issues," p. 14.

33. Note that prochoice forces use the constitutionalist doctrines of separation of powers and of checks and balances to their advantage with respect to the branches of the national government; they favor dispersal

rather than concentration of power. The opposite is true, however, with respect to federalism and separation of powers between the national government and the states. Here prochoice advocates prefer centralization to decentralization and favor imposition, through Supreme Court decisions, of a national abortion policy upon the states—despite rights left to the states, in *Roe* v. *Wade*, to regulate abortion in the second and third trimesters. This pattern is especially evident in *Planned Parenthood* v. *Danforth* (1976) and in *Colautti* v. *Franklin* (1979). See also the comments by John T. Noonan in *A Private Choice: Abortion in America in the Seventies* (New York: Free Press, 1979), pp. 2–3.

34. The Court summarized the proabortion case as follows: "The principal thrust of appellant's attack on the Texas statutes is that they improperly invade a right, said to be possessed by the pregnant woman, to choose to terminate her pregnancy. Appellant would discover this right in the concept of personal 'liberty' embodied in the Fourteenth Amendment's Due Process Clause; or in personal, marital, familial, and sexual privacy said to be protected by the Bill of Rights or its penumbras . . . ; or among those rights reserved to the people by the Ninth Amendment" (410 U.S. 113, 129 [1973]).

35. Id. at 152–56.

36. "If the right of privacy means anything, it is the right of the individual, married or single, to be free from unwarranted governmental intrusion into matters so fundamentally affecting a person as the decision whether to bear or beget a child" (*Eisenstadt* v. *Baird* 405 U.S. 453 [1972]); the quote from *Wade* is from 410 U.S. 113, 153 (1973).

37. Rehnquist, J., dissenting, 410 U.S. 113, 172 (1973).

38. The Court states: "The pregnant woman cannot be isolated in her privacy. She carries an embryo and, later, a fetus, if one accepts the medical definitions of the developing young in the human uterus. . . . The situation therefore is inherently different from marital intimacy, or bedroom possession of obscene material, or marriage, or procreation, or education, with which *Eisenstadt, Griswold, Stanley, Loving, Skinner, Pierce*, and *Meyer* were respectively concerned. As we have intimated above, it is reasonable and appropriate for a State to decide that at some point in time another interest, that of health of the mother or that of potential human life, becomes significantly involved. The woman's privacy is no longer sole and any right of privacy she possesses must be measured accordingly" (id. at 159).

39. Id. at 154. I have suggested elsewhere that, although the extension of privacy rights to the abortion issue seems strained, there are at least two definitions or denotations of privacy which are at least partly related to decisions regarding abortion: (1) zonal privacy demarcating a public and private sphere; and (2) informational privacy, which concerns the kinds of information (e.g., details of one's personal life) made public in the course of prosecuting in court a certain action (e.g., abortion) regarded as criminal or illegal. See "Some Legal Aspects of Abortion in the United States," paper prepared for a National Endowment for the Humanities Seminar on Constitutionalism, Princeton University, April 1979, pp. 12–15.

40. Sidney Callahan, "The Court and a Conflict of Principles," *The Hastings Center Report* 7 (August 1977): 7.

41. See section 8 of the Court's opinion in *Roe* v. *Wade*.

42. Isaiah Berlin, "Two Concepts of Liberty," in his *Four Essays on Liberty* (New York: Oxford University Press, 1969).

43. The Court rejected this argument in *Wade*: "Appellant and some *amici* argue that the woman's right is absolute and that she is entitled to terminate her pregnancy at whatever time, in whatever way, and for whatever reason she alone chooses. With this we do not agree. . . . The Court's decisions recognizing a right of privacy . . . acknowledge that some state regulation in areas protected by that right is appropriate. As noted above, a State may properly assert important interests in safeguarding health, in maintaining medical standards, and in protecting potential life. At some point in pregnancy, these respective interests become sufficiently compelling to sustain regulation of the factors that govern the abortion decision. The privacy right involved, therefore, cannot be said to be absolute. In fact, it is not clear to us that the claim asserted by some *amici* that one has an unlimited right to do with one's body as one pleases bears a close relationship to the right of privacy previously articulated in the Court's decisions. The Court has refused to recognize an unlimited right of this kind in the past" (410 U.S. 113, 153–54 [1973]).

44. John Locke, *Second Treatise*, chapt. 9, section 123.

45. C. B. Macpherson, *The Theory of Possessive Individualism* (New York: Oxford University Press, 1962), p. 260.

46. Sidney Callahan, "Conflict of Principles," p. 7.

47. The former might be associated with Herbert Spencer, to some extent with Locke and J. S. Mill, and in this country with the late nineteenth-century ideology of Social Darwinism, while spokesmen for the latter would be T. H. Green and L. T. Hobhouse. For a general discussion of these two strands in liberal political thought in America, see Dorothy James, *Outside, Looking In: A Critique of American Policies and Institutions, Left and Right* (New York: Harper and Row, 1972), pp. 1–14.

48. For a general review of liberal doctrines of equality, see Mary C. Segers, "Equality in Contemporary Political Thought: An Examination and an Assessment," *Administration and Society* 10 (February 1979): 409–36.

49. James C. Mohr, *Abortion in America* (New York: Oxford University Press, 1978), p. 255.

50. For a general critique of the principle of equality of opportunity, see John Schaar, "Equality of Opportunity, and Beyond," in J. R. Pennock and J. W. Chapman, eds., *Nomos IX: Equality* (New York: Atherton, 1967), pp. 228–49. See also Jean Bethke Elshtain, "The Feminist Movement and the Question of Equality," *Polity* 7 (Summer 1975): 452–77, for a discussion of the deficiencies of this principle as it relates to the women's movement.

51. For a more detailed explication of these points, see the contributions of Mary C. Segers and Robert G. Hoyt to the Symposium, "Does the First Amendment Bar the Hyde Amendment?" in *Christianity and Crisis* 39 (5 March 1979), pp. 34–43.

52. Daniel Callahan, "Abortion: Some Ethical Issues," in *Abortion, Society, and the Law*, edited by David F. Walbert and J. Douglas Butler (Cleveland: Case Western Reserve University Press, 1973), p. 92.

53. Recall, for example, Socrates' argument concerning the laws in *The*

Crito (Plato, *The Last Days of Socrates,* trans. Hugh Tredennick [Penguin Classics, 1969]), pp. 28–39.

54. Mohr, *Abortion in America,* pp. 262–63.

55. When asked whether it was morally wrong to have an abortion, 48 percent of those who responded to the Yankelovich survey said it was not morally wrong, while 44 percent said it was; on moral grounds women still oppose abortion, 47 percent to 44 percent. By contrast, a far larger majority of those polled (64 percent, including 58 percent of all Catholics) believed that, regardless of morality, a woman should be legally free to have an abortion if she wants one. Results of a Daniel Yankelovich survey as reported in *Time,* 21 November 1977, p. 115.

56. Daniel Callahan has expressed this well: "Although the contending sides in the abortion debate commonly ignore, or systematically deride, the essentially positive impulses lying behind their opponents' positions, the conflict is nonetheless best seen as the pitting of essentially valuable impulses against one another. The possibility of a society which did allow women the right and the freedom to control their own lives is a lofty goal. No less lofty is that of a society which, with no exceptions, treated all forms of human life as equally valuable. In the best of all possible worlds, it might be possible to reconcile these goals. In the real world, however, the first goal requires the right of abortion, and the second goal excludes that right. This, I believe, is a genuine and deep dilemma. That so few are willing to recognize the dilemma, or even to admit that any choice must be less than perfect, is the most disturbing element in the whole debate" ("Abortion: Some Ethical Issues," p. 101).

57. Ibid., pp. 100–101.

11

FOREIGN AID FOR ABORTION: POLITICS, ETHICS, AND PRACTICE

DONALD P. WARWICK

A ID FOR ABORTION is the single most sensitive subject in the entire field of nonmilitary foreign assistance. No topic will make a foreign aid official blanch more quickly, and none will be greeted with greater wariness in disclosing information. The question is so charged that virtually nothing has been written about it. Data on international abortion activities are typically not reported at all, are reserved for classified documents of restricted circulation, or are buried under such generic names and euphemisms as "surgical methods of family planning" or "menstrual regulation." As a consequence it has not been easy to gather data for this paper, which is the first attempt to survey the field. Officials involved with foreign aid for abortion were generally willing to discuss their work, but were vague about details and chary of public discussion. However, by combining information from interviews with scattered fragments of existing data one can construct a composite picture of the international abortion scene.[1]

THE CURRENT SCENE: AN OVERVIEW

Before considering the activities of specific agencies, it is worth noting the broad features of the terrain in which they operate. It is an environment marked by complexity, ambiguity, human misery, political tension, and bureaucratic trepidations.

First, apart from any outside intervention, induced abortion is a common practice in the developing countries. Not only is abortion frequent, but it is a prominent cause of death and illness among women of childbearing age. In Latin American countries illegal abortions often account for a third of maternal deaths and a half or more of the country's hospital beds. And unlike the situation in the United States, where contraception is generally available to those who want it, many of the poor women who resort to this method are unaware of or do not have ready access to modern means of birth control. While the statistics cited are often used to argue for legalized abortion, they have also been a source of concern to those categorically opposed to abortion. They have led some Catholic bishops to soften their opposition to contraception, which they saw as the lesser of two evils for women faced with unwanted children. Whatever one's moral views on abortion, the figures point to a human tragedy that cannot be ignored.

Second, foreign aid for abortion is but a small proportion of the total aid for population activities. Despite occasional rumors that abortion is a mainstay of population assistance, foreign aid for this purpose adds up to less than a quarter of 1 percent of the total spent for population. On the supply side, foreign donors have been prevented by law or inhibited by politics from pouring vast amounts into this controverted area. On the demand side, despite the widespread practice of abortion by individual women, it remains illegal in many countries and a point of moral and political debate in domestic politics. Hence even if the total volume of funds were increased tenfold, the money would not be quickly or easily spent.

Third, with the exception of agencies in the United Nations system, most organizations supplying funds for abortions operate on a clandestine and usually illegal basis. As one expert commented, "Not even your best friends will tell you what they are doing overseas." In some countries, including the Philippines, aid for abortion is not only against the law but against the country's stated population policies. This is not to deny that there are many ambiguities about what, precisely, is "legal," or that officials who speak publicly against abortion may give tacit support to quiet foreign aid. The gap between rhetoric and reality is greater there than in most spheres of development, for understandable reasons. Nevertheless, severe legal and cultural restrictions on abortion create a climate in which private agencies selling abortion services behave more like intelligence operatives than purveyors of foreign aid. This style of operation raises serious ethical questions that will be discussed shortly.

Fourth, the most common type of foreign aid involves the technique known as uterine aspiration. This goes under various code phrases, especially "menstrual regulation" and "menstrual induction." The essential feature is that the womb is efficiently emptied without forceful dilation of the cervix.[2] An agency to be discussed later manufactures the required equipment and almost all of the organizations active overseas distribute kits for this purpose. In many countries doctors, nurses, paramedics, and midwives are being provided with such kits and trained in their use.

Fifth, abortion in the developing countries can be a paying proposition. Especially in urban areas and where a country has tasted the fruits of development, as in Taiwan and Korea, women are willing to pay for services rendered. Where in the typical family planning clinic client fees meet only a small proportion of total costs, with abortion a small amount of money, even a loan, can go a long way toward expanding services. This point has not been lost on business-minded agencies seeking a maximum return on their dollars. In several countries American donors have provided loans to one abortion clinic which then not only repaid the loan but generated enough profits to open new clinics. All signs suggest that private donors will increasingly rely on the hidden hand of private enterprise rather than on the visible arm of state bureaucracy.

Finally, the politics of abortion in the United States have had an overwhelming impact on foreign aid for abortion. The highly charged atmosphere in this country has led not only to an amendment specifically banning the use of foreign aid monies for abortion, but to a series of indirect effects. Mainline philanthropic organizations will not come within a mile of this issue for fear of jeopardizing their core activities. Federal officials, fearing abuse from Congress or reprimands from their superiors, use their discretion to keep U.S. overseas involvement with abortion to a legal minimum. These repercussions extend to agencies tapping American funds, such as the International Planned Parenthood Federation (IPPF). Faced with demands for tight accounting on abortion and anxious to avoid American backlash for visible initiatives in this field, recipient agencies walk a more narrow path than they would prefer. Hence the United States has become both the prime source of capital and the foremost instigator of contraints on activism.

AGENCY ACTIVITIES

As of 1979 only a handful of international donors were

involved in direct support of abortion activities in the developing countries. Others provided indirect assistance for research, meetings, and information activities, but maintained a low profile on this subject. With most of the giants among the donors shrinking from visibility, much of the action has fallen to more intrepid, flexible, and fleet-footed smaller agencies.

The *Agency for International Development* (AID), the principal foreign aid organization of the U.S. government, was an ardent supporter of abortion until it was brought to a standstill by the Helms Amendment. From its beginnings in the 1960s until the amendment was passed in 1973, AID's Office of Population enthusiastically supported the development of new techniques for abortion, including the uterine aspirator. The office director, Dr. Reimert T. Ravenholt, was an outspoken advocate of all methods of birth control, including abortion, and an international salesman for the aspirator. But even with his keenness for "postconceptive" methods of birth control, AID did not invest great amounts of money in abortion programs overseas. The main reason was that political leaders interested in family planning did not wish to be singed by this issue. The prevailing sentiment was that contraception is sensitive enough without loading on the added complexities of abortion. Hence despite Ravenholt's sometimes rhapsodic claims for improved abortion methods, until 1973 there were not many takers among the recipient nations.

In that year Senator Jesse Helms of North Carolina added an amendment to the Foreign Assistance Act that drastically curtailed AID's activities on abortion. It read:

> Section 114. Limiting use of funds for abortion—None of the funds made available to carry out this part [Part I of the Foreign Assistance Act of 1961] shall be used to pay for the performance of abortions as a method of family planning or to motivate or coerce any person to practice abortions.

As this language was necessarily vague about operational implications, the administrator of AID issued the following "policy determination" on June 10, 1974:

1. No AID funds will be used to "procure or distribute equipment provided for the purpose of inducing abor-

tions as a method of family planning."
2. AID funds will not be used for the direct support of abortion activities in the developing countries.
3. "AID does not and will not fund information, education, training, or communication programs that seek to promote abortion as a method of family planning. AID will finance training of developing country doctors in the latest techniques used in OB-GYN practice. AID will not disqualify such training programs if they include pregnancy termination within the overall curriculum. However, AID funds will not be used to expand the pregnancy termination component of such programs, and AID will pay only the extra costs of financing the participation of developing country doctors in existing programs. Such training is provided only at the election of the participants."
4. "AID will continue to support research programs designed to identify safer, simpler, and more effective means of fertility control. This work includes research on both foresight and hindsight methods of fertility control." (Hindsight methods, of course, are those involving some form of abortion.)
5. "AID funds are not and will not be used to pay women in the developing countries to have abortions as a method of family planning. Likewise, AID funds are not and will not be used to pay persons to perform abortions or to solicit persons to undergo abortions."[3]

In short, AID could provide no funds for the direct support of abortion or motivation for abortion, but it could continue certain kinds of training and research involving abortion. It could also contribute to organizations, such as the Pathfinder Fund, which were involved in providing abortion services, provided that AID's money was not used directly for that purpose.

In practice, this restriction has forced AID to withdraw from most abortion activities. In 1979 less than one-half of 1 percent of its population funds were spent on any aspect of abortion. A good part of these funds go to the International Fertility Research Program in North Carolina, an organization conducting studies on effective methods of birth limitation. Among these are various abortion methods, including different techniques of "menstrual regulation." Research on these methods, which is conducted by collaborators in several countries, does involve abortion, but under the terms of the Helms Amendment, it is permissible so long as there is no active promotion or provision of services. AID also supports training programs in which medical doctors are given instruction in abortion methods under the conditions outlined earlier.

Coupled with the political controversies swirling around abortion, the Helms Amendment has affected AID and its funding recipients in many ways. Most importantly, the overall level of monitoring and control in this field has increased at least fivefold. Sensitive to the political dangers at stake for themselves and the agency, administrators, lawyers, contract officers, and auditors in AID and elsewhere in the government keep a close watch on any activities even close to abortion. Within AID officials must be exceptionally careful of what they do in the first instance and then must clear all proposals through multiple levels of approvals. Needless to say, this process dampens the enthusiasm of even the most committed believers in abortion. Organizations receiving AID funds, most notably the IPPF and the Pathfinder Fund, are also under strong pressure to maintain detailed records showing that AID funds have not been used for abortion. Where there is doubt, the burden of proof is on the receiving organization. This is a classical case of the political context of administration constraining public officials to minimize controversy. Recipient organizations have also been forced to change their entire reporting system and add their own auditors to deal with the demands and questions of monitors from the government. One administrator estimated that 50 percent of his time is now spent dealing with AID and other government monitors on precisely these kinds of questions.

The only two major agencies that do operate openly in this field, though without publicity and on a small scale, are the *World Bank* and the *United Nations Fund for Population Activities* (UNFPA). The UNFPA's policy is to respond to country requests for assistance for all kinds of population programs, provided that they are within the organization's terms of reference and do not violate UN policies on human rights. The UNFPA places no restrictions on methods of fertility control, and is willing to entertain requests for abortion assistance. To date it has provided such assistance to India, Thailand, and Tunisia. It also contributes to the Special Program of the World Health Organization, which includes research on methods of abortion, and to university research programs investigating abortion methods. In 1979 UNFPA assistance for all activities in abortion came to less than one-quarter of 1 percent of its total budget. The World Bank operates under similar policies and spends an even smaller proportion of its funds on abortion. While both organizations receive substantial funding from the United States, their position is that the monies provided must come with no strings attached. They will thus resist any attempt by contributing countries to impose restrictions on expenditures on abortion.

Major philanthropic organizations, including the Ford and Rockefeller foundations, have shied away from abortion projects. While Ford has long been a front-runner in support for population activities, and for a time was the largest single contributor to the field, it has consistently shunned any project involving abortion services. The Rockefeller Foundation has been similarly inclined. Despite some urging from AID and other agencies to fill the gap created by the Helms Amendment, the mainline foundations apparently concluded that abortion projects were not in their interest. Two reasons were cited by persons familiar with these organizations. The first is that association with abortion could touch off a nasty contretemps, impairing work in less volatile areas of higher priority. The second is that the illegal nature of abortion in many countries and the common use of clandestine techniques to promote abortion services would cause considerable squeamishness among professional staff members. Critics accuse these organizations of excessive caution springing from a desire to protect their image in the "establishment," while more sympathetic observers commend them for common sense and adherence to their basic institutional values. Whatever the case, the large foundations have given little more than moral support to international programs for abortion services.

The *Population Council* of New York falls somewhere between the foundations which help to keep it in existence and agencies of a more activist bent. As perhaps the single most respected professional organization in population studies, it has had a notable impact on population policies, programs, and research in many nations. In legal constitution, internal organization, staff composition, and institutional demeanor it is much like a large foundation. The word "professionalism" was cited by many staff members as a keynote of the council's behavior, while the desire for cooperative relationships with governments has generally led to an "aboveboard" approach in technical assistance. One might thus expect that it would have some of the same antipathies to abortion projects as the Ford and Rockefeller foundations, with which it is in close contact. At the same time the council has undertaken advisory assignments in the developing countries, including projects carried out in very delicate political environments. It also did not shrink from controversy when it developed and promoted the Lippes loop and when it became a frank advocate of voluntary family planning programs. But from its inception in 1952 until 1976, its activities on abortion were confined to research and writing. During his presidency the late Bernard Berelson had serious ethical and prudential reservations about foreign aid for abortion, and his board seemed to share those misgivings.

In 1976 the presidency passed to George Zeidenstein, who had other ideas. In a report to the board in June of that year, Zeidenstein made three recommendations related to abortion: (1) that the council's purpose should be, *inter alia*, to "stimulate, encourage, promote, conduct, support . . . abortion;" (2) that its Bio-Medical Center engage in "mission-oriented research" on abortion technology; and (3) that the organization add abortion to the "range of services" it provides.[4] This change drew a strong dissent from trustee John Noonan, Jr., who resigned in protest. Despite this shift in policy, over the past three years the Population Council's involvement with abortion has been minimal, and not strikingly different than in the period before 1976. Christopher Tietze continues to conduct statistical research on various facets of abortion and there are some small research efforts overseas, but on the whole the Population Council remains more like the Ford Foundation than the activists to be mentioned. The reasons are probably the same as in the foundations—a fear that controversy over abortion will cripple the organization in other areas, problems of professional self-image for staff members, and difficulty in acting without breaking the laws of other countries. Professional and social respectability remain important considerations for the council, and seem to outweigh Zeidenstein's stated commitment to work on abortion.

The remaining organizations have all been involved in providing abortion services or equipment, and often in attempts to change national laws or social attitudes hostile to abortion. They differ from the previously mentioned donors mainly in their willingness to violate both laws and national policies on abortion and, related to that, in their use of clandestine methods.

The *International Planned Parenthood Federation* of London (IPPF) has been the most outspoken advocate of legal abortion services in the developing countries, though not the most muscular promoter of such services. The IPPF is the central office for several dozen semiautonomous private national family planning associations. As a central body it receives funds from international donors, including AID, and passes money and supplies along to the local association. It also tries to set policies and standards applicable to all associations, including policies on abortion. The IPPF's stated position is that abortion should be legally available to those who desire it and that local associations, when possible, should assist in providing the necessary services. But while it has considerable leverage from its funding position, the IPPF must also respect the constraints and preferences of its local associations. In practice the central office can recommend, lobby, and cajole, but it cannot force a member association to take action on abortion.

Despite its frequent pronouncements on the need for safe and legal abortion services and its lobbying efforts in many countries, the IPPF spends only about one-third of 1 percent of its total funds on abortion. As of 1978 it had carried out specific projects in ten countries as well as various regional and global efforts, mostly in training. In the Philippines, where abortion is both illegal and explicitly against the national population policy, the IPPF provided 200 "menstrual regulation" kits for demonstration purposes. It also conducted a local seminar which set off sharp controversy. One of its largest projects, totaling about $62,000, was in Bangladesh, where 5,000 vacuum aspiration kits were provided to the local family planning association. These kits have also been supplied to Korea, Singapore, Hong Kong, Thailand, Vietnam, and India. Although most of these projects have been relatively small—usually under $30,000—the IPPF has not detailed its activities in its published reports, even in its main report to donor agencies.[5] One reason, apart from the illegal and controversial nature of these activities, may be that the federation is under constant scrutiny from the U.S. government to ensure that it is not violating the Helms Amendment. One observer remarked that the current executive secretary is "running scared" on the abortion question, largely because of its political explosiveness in the United States.

The style of operation of the IPPF and its member associations is well illustrated in the Philippines.[6] Beginning in 1974 the IPPF affiliate, the Family Planning Organization of the Philippines (FPOP), organized a series of meetings under the title of "Symposia on Advances in Fertility." The topics included medical and legal aspects of abortion, procedures and techniques of abortion, and the dangers and attendant health risks of abortion. The first meeting touched off a storm of protest from religious and civic leaders and led the government to reaffirm its official opposition to abortion. Nevertheless, the FPOP continued its symposia, which were clearly aimed at legitimizing discussion of abortion in the Philippines and which were made possible by funding from IPPF.

Further controversy arose when the FPOP distributed "menstrual regulation" kits to local doctors. Although the government had laws specifically prohibiting the importation of abortive devices, these kits were brought into the country as "medical instruments" to obtain "sample tissue for examination." While aware that the vacuum aspirators had been imported and were being distributed to private doctors, the government's official body in this field, the Commission on Population, chose not to take action. Since the FPOP did not take a public stand favoring abortion, and since it did not use these devices in its own clinics, the commission felt that its regulatory powers were limited. Other observers concluded that POPCOM officials were de facto not opposed to such underground activities so long as they generated no public uproar. These examples show the potential of the IPPF and its collaborating organizations for subverting national laws and policies, and also suggest that officials responsible for enforcing those policies may themselves not be totally opposed to their violation.

Another activist agency, and one that has been more willing to "go public" with its activities, is the *Pathfinder Fund* of Boston. Pathfinder was founded in 1929 by Dr. Clarence Gamble to find new ways of promoting birth control. Its trademarks have been small size, quick action, and "innovation." In recent years innovation has meant activities in abortion, particularly the promotion of uterine aspiration. A Pathfinder flyer issued around 1975 states:

> *Abortion*—safe, legal, and available—is important as a backup for contraceptive failure, and as a way to bring women into programs of contraception at the moment they are most susceptible to persuasion. But because of the Helms amendment to the foreign-aid law, no AID money can be spent to promote abortion. Therefore we do this important work with money raised from the private sector.
>
> Pathfinder is encouraging the establishment of abortion as a woman's right. We are promoting the early-abortion procedure known as "menstrual induction"—through publications, distribution of instruments, and direct grants. And Pathfinder has sponsored a major conference.[7]

In recent years Pathfinder has engaged in two main kinds of abortion activities: helping to establish clinics in countries where abortion services are illegal but tolerated by the government; and distributing vacuum aspiration kits to clinics and private practitioners who wish to use them. Thus it has recently worked with a local doctor to open a private abortion clinic in Colombia, and has similar activities elsewhere in Latin America. When asked about the legality of this move in Colombia, an individual familiar with the project said that the clinic was indeed illegal, but that prosecution was unlikely, if only because the children of public figures were using its services. A staff member further commented: "Where abortion is culturally acceptable we don't think that the law is restrictive in an ethical sense. We are also concerned at the practical level—will it be enforced or not?" He likewise raised a crucial point about legality: the difference between the laws on the books and the laws as interpreted by the government. In Bangladesh, abortion is still technically illegal in most cases, but the government has instructed medical schools that by 1981 the country's 420 local health centers should offer "menstrual regulation" services. There is thus a difference between legislative law and executive law, with the latter taking preponderance in Bangladesh.

The Pathfinder Fund, which receives over 90 percent of its funds from AID, has been hard hit by the Helms Amendment. The net effect has been to force the organization to choose between providing family planning services without abortion or abortion without broader services. If Pathfinder wants to help establish a family planning unit without abortion, AID will cover all or most of the costs. But if abortion is included, AID will provide only the contraceptives necessary. As a Pathfinder official put it, "The Helms Amendment has disastrously affected population programming by destroying all the linkages between abortion and contraceptive recruiting." Pathfinder has also been forced to change its accounting and auditing system in order to convince government monitors that no federal funds are being spent for abortion.

One of the most influential and yet anomalous organizations in this field is the *Population Crisis Committee* (PCC). Long known as a powerful lobbyist for birth control in Washington, this organization has been very much "up front" on the domestic scene. With its board made up of retired ambassadors and generals, prominent businessmen, and other notable public figures, it would seem an unlikely supporter of illegal abortion activities overseas. And yet that is precisely what it does outside the United States, though never under its own name. A recent United Nations document on population programs and projects contains this description of the Population Crisis Committee/Draper Fund:

> PCC/DF works to generate support for reducing world population growth in two basic ways: through high-level advocacy at home and abroad to increase government commitment to strong, effective family planning programmes; and through its highly selective support of innovative, cost-effective private family planning projects in developing countries. . . . Through arranging private support of special projects overseas, PCC makes possible indigenous activities that can be readily expanded or replicated.[8]

While abortion is not specifically mentioned in this description, closer checking reveals that this is its major form of "innovative, cost-effective, private family planning projects." Abortion activities account for about one-half of the committee's "Special Projects" and about one-fourth of its international budget. The organization works as follows:

> PCC has no overseas operations. Instead, it funds or finds funding for selected high-leverage projects initiated by or recommended to PCC by IPPF and other family planning/population organizations that have a proven track record in overseas operations. Projects are undertaken in collaboration with indigenous leaders and groups. . . . Projects selected for support are those that promise exceptional return in lowered birth rates per dollar invested. Typically such projects involve one of the ten most populous Third World countries; they demonstrate or extend an approach to delivery of family planning services that has proven cost-effective in lowering birth rates in similar conditions elsewhere; they require private money because the government is not ready to accept a new approach until it has been proven successful; and they include a sensible plan for expansion or replication.[9]

At present the Population Crisis Committee leans strongly toward programs involving the participation of local businessmen. In abortion programs they speak of a three-legged stool involving the doctor, who provides the services, the woman, who receives them, and the businessman, who organizes them to generate a profit. In practice, PCC looks for projects in which a small amount of seed money can be used by local entrepreneurs to launch self-funding abortion activities on a much larger scale. PCC officials cite with pride an experience in Taiwan in which a loan for one clinic ultimately led to a total of nineteen, all patterned exactly after the first. PCC prefers projects in which abortion services are closely linked to contraception, so that the experience is not repeated. The following are some of its projects:

Philippines: Menstrual Regulation Training. To train and equip doctors to perform menstrual regulation on the island of Mindanao. $34,000 committed for two years beginning May 1978 to International Projects Assistance Services.[10]

Colombia: Bogotá Pregnancy Clinic. To provide inexpensive, humane treatment for incomplete abortions using the new technology developed for simple first-trimester abortion, clean-up techniques, and to reduce the incidence of abortion in Colombia by using the occasion of botched abortion to involve women in appropriate family planning practices.[11]

Bangladesh: (1) Abortion Training and Supplies. Training for doctors from government health centers, mobile camps and health districts in the use of the latest abortion techniques and supply of non-electrical vacuum aspirators. $8,356 committed for one year to International Projects Assistance Services. (2) Abortion Training. To train new doctors and qualified paramedics in early abortion, menstrual regulation and the treatment of incomplete abortions as well as contraceptive counseling in 6 regional and 2 Dacca medical colleges. $35,000 committed for one year to the Pathfinder Fund.[12]

The agencies most often chosen for project execution are the Pathfinder Fund and the International Projects Assistance Service. PCC officials feel that private abortion services have a bright future in the developing countries, mainly because they are profitable and thus appeal to the entrepreneurial instincts of local people. They also feel that the Helms Amendment may have been a blessing in disguise, for it has forced abortion advocates to rely less on large donors and the public sector and make productive explorations into abortion as a commercial venture. Beyond its catalytic role in stimulating abortion activities, the PCC is the U.S. purchasing agent for the IPPF and supplies it with vacuum aspiration kits manufactured by the International Projects Assistance Service. Though unobtrusive in its international operations, the PCC is undoubtedly one of the most influential agencies in this field. And besides its own indirect funding of abortion and other projects, PCC takes an active role in raising money from others for worthwhile activities, including abortion.

The most aggressive organization in this arena is the *International Projects Assistance Service* (IPAS), formerly known as the International Pregnancy Advisory Service. This is an organization that is disreputable and proud of it. Its policy is to move in wherever it can to promote abortion. As a former staff member said, "Our policy is that the more abortion is illegal, the more attractive it is because it is necessary. If it is legal other organizations can handle it." At present IPAS works in three areas: (1) providing loans for the establishment of abortion clinics; (2) manufacturing vacuum aspiration equipment for sale to other organizations, such as Pathfinder and the IPPF; and (3) direct abortion services. Their strategy on this last front is to identify doctors who are interested in abortion, whether it is legal or not, and then help them to initiate new services. They are now supporting clinics in some twenty countries, including Mexico, Brazil, and Indonesia, where abortion is illegal. They are also training midwives in the Philippines to use the vacuum aspirator, even though this technique is specifically banned by the government. In Bangladesh, Pakistan, Sri Lanka, Thailand, and Mexico, IPAS also offers vacuum aspirator kits through a direct mail program and provides training in their use. They find themselves handicapped in raising funds, mainly because their direct action tactics leave potential donors uncomfortable about supporting a "pariah." Foundations such as Ford and Rockefeller are unwilling to support them, while AID is unable to do so. Hence they must depend on grants from the Population Crisis Committee and other private sources as well as on the revenues generated by their loan program and manufacturing operations. Although, as they put it, "our response is always yes," the executive director claims that the funds available are much smaller than the interest they find in expanding abortion services.

Other organizations involved in some aspects of abortion

are Family Planning International Assistance, the international division of the Planned Parenthood Federation of America; Population Services International; and Johns Hopkins University, which provides training in techniques of abortion. But the most critical actors are IPPF, Pathfinder, the Population Crisis Committee, and IPAS.

TOWARD NEW GROUND FOR ETHICAL DEBATE

Foreign aid for abortion raises a host of ethical questions. The most basic is, of course, the morality of abortion itself. Debate on this issue is not simple within the United States, but it becomes immensely more complicated when the scene of action involves two or more nations. The root problem is that there is no universally accepted ethic, nor is there even a common language for debating moral issues across countries and cultures. Thus when we ask what ethical principles should guide the United Nations in aid for abortion, we quickly stumble over the questions of what and whose moral views should prevail. Should we opt for a frank national relativism, allowing each country to determine its moral standards and then having the United Nations respect those judgments? This position is appealing in its simplicity, but it clashes with the concept of universal human rights also endorsed by the UN. And where governments have unequivocally stated their opposition to abortion on religious, moral, or political grounds, should prochoice advocates try to claim that their conceptions of individual rights take precedence over national sovereignty? These are tough questions that will not be resolved with instant absolutes or ready relativisms. And the debate is not likely to progress very far without much more systematic work on a cross-cultural and cross-national ethics. At this time our poverty of principles is outdone only by the richness of rhetorical flourishes in the abortion debate.

While the morality of abortion will remain the paramount question in evaluating foreign aid for that purpose, it is not the only issue at stake. Other questions arise from the objectives, processes, and composition of international assistance in this field. There may well be situations in which the most staunch prochoice advocate would concede that certain kinds of foreign aid for abortion are unjustified, and where equally ardent prolife representatives might grant that aid for problems related to abortion is ethically acceptable. To stake out some new ground for ethical debate, it will be helpful to begin with three working principles.

The first is that *the overarching goal of foreign aid should be the individual and family welfare*. All assistance to the developing countries should aim to promote such universally sought goods as health, education, a decent level of living, self-respect, and the ability to control significant aspects of one's existence. While this principle has been used by pro-choice as well as prolife groups to support their respective claims, there are questions transcending the usual debates. The broadest implication of the welfare principle is that foreign aid should be used to remove or reduce the conditions leading poor women to seek abortions in the first place. Boiled down to their basic ingredients, these conditions are poverty and ignorance. A welfare orientation would argue strongly against foreign aid for abortion that does nothing to change the socioeconomic conditions breeding high fertility. Thus the Population Crisis Committee has lobbied long and hard for action on birth control, but has not been equally firm in pushing for general assistance to reduce poverty. A single-minded concern with the fertility variable seems inconsistent with the promotion of individual and family welfare. The same criticism would apply to prolife groups that seem more intent on stopping foreign aid for abortion than on increasing the amounts spent on general development activities. Indeed, if prolife forces align themselves with anti-UN lobbies to cut off all U.S. funds to the World Bank and the United Nations Fund for Population Activities, as has been threatened in the past, they would join their antagonists in an obsession with fertility to the detriment of economic justice.

The welfare principle further suggests that foreign aid for abortion would not be justified if its sole or primary aim was to bring down the birth rate. It would seem a flagrant violation of welfare to use the desperation of women for population control while doing nothing to remove the conditions producing such desperation. Specifically, programs providing *only* abortion services, with no assistance for health or contraception, would be ethically suspect on welfare grounds, and doubly so when they yield a profit. The welfare criterion might also argue for foreign aid to treat incomplete abortions. Human compassion calls for helping women who incur the risk of death or serious illness from misconducted abortions, even if one disapproves of the source of that risk. Many physicians of prolife sympathies have no moral qualms about providing medical services in these circumstances, although they would reject the preventive step of medically supervised abortions. In short, raising the question of welfare may help to take the debate about foreign aid at least a few steps beyond the polarization that has been its hallmark to date.

A second working principle is that *foreign aid for population should respect national autonomy*. The World Population Plan of Action, approved in Bucharest in 1974, sets forth the following guideline: "The formulation and implementation of population policies is the sovereign right of each nation. This right is to be exercised in accordance with national objectives and needs and without external interference. . . . The main responsibility for national population policies and programs lies with national authorities."[13] Adherence to this principle would seem a prima facie obligation for international donors. According to the norm stated, the United Nations Fund for Population Activities and the World Bank would be justified, on procedural grounds, in supplying aid for abortion to countries requesting their help. By the same token, the clandestine activities reviewed earlier would be unjustified, particularly when abortion is not only technically illegal but directly contravenes a country's population policy.

Three overlapping arguments have been raised against respect for national autonomy. The first is that in many countries laws about abortion have no moral force since they are merely vestiges of colonialism and are not observed in practice. One prochoice physician compared them to the antiquated laws on the books in many states, such as those governing the positions of men and women walking together. A specific case cited was Bangladesh, where laws and executive edicts were patently inconsistent. This example does suggest that there are legitimate grounds for debate about what really constitutes a country's policies. Where the government itself openly requests aid for abortion, donor agencies would obviously not be violating its autonomy by providing such assistance. But where the government is manifestly and forcefully on record as being opposed to abortion, as in the Philippines, and assures its critics that abortion is not being practiced with the consent of national authorities, covert foreign aid for abortion to non-governmental recipients would violate autonomy.

A second argument is that foreign aid programs should honor, not the laws that are on the books, but the laws of cultural preference as expressed in citizens' behavior. Thus when large numbers of women show a clear preference for abortion by their actions, donors should respect their wishes rather than outmoded laws restricting safe abortions. Sometimes this argument is premised on the notion of universal human rights for women, sometimes on the principle that culture is a higher law than legislation. The problems with this argument are both substantive and procedural. On substantive grounds one would want to know if all cultural preferences, including the execution of minority groups, cannibalism, and female circumcision, should override a country's laws, or if a universal right to life of the fetus should be cited as a basis for subverting laws permitting abortion. From a procedural standpoint the critical difficulty lies in deciding who should make decisions about the relative merits of a country's laws vis-à-vis competing sources of legitimacy. It hardly seems justifiable for donor agencies to take it upon themselves to make this judgment, since their own bureaucratic or political interests are usually at stake in the decision. At the very least one would want the matter to be adjudicated by some neutral court of appeals.

A third argument against respect for laws restricting abortion is that governments themselves are often divided on this question. In such pluralistic settings some groups are in favor of action and others opposed. Under these conditions, donor representatives have argued, foreign agencies have a right to work with supportive officials, even if abortion is illegal and against the country's stated policy. In other words, when opinion is split on abortion policy, there is nothing wrong with donors taking sides since there will also be nationals on that side. But here, too, there are ethical difficulties. By taking sides, particularly when support is accompanied by a generous infusion of foreign monies, the donors are, in fact, infringing on national autonomy in a particularly delicate area. Foreign intervention becomes especially questionable when external financing is used as a bargaining chip in negotiating what is fundamentally a moral and political question on the national scene. Second, international agencies supplying aid for abortion under conditions of secrecy are themselves being hypocritical and aiding governmental double-dealing. This approach seems highly unjustified if the government simultaneously denies taking aid for abortion and accepts funds for that purpose. In such circumstances domestic critics of abortion, such as the Roman Catholic hierarchy in the Philippines, are being deliberately deceived about the government's intentions and the donor's actions, and are thus deprived of their right to comment on population activities. The ethical problems of covert intervention are compounded when, as is often the case, the donor's aim is to establish a beachhead of services which will be extremely difficult to dislodge even when they are made public. While such issues arise in other spheres of foreign assistance, they are of particular significance here because of the deep moral and religious values at stake in abortion.

A great drawback to violations of national autonomy is that they cannot be turned into a workable universal principle. One "categorical imperative" might read: Whenever a donor agency considers national autonomy subservient to its own conception of human rights or public policy, its conception should prevail. According to this criterion, foreign organizations opposing the U.S. Supreme Court's 1973 decision on abortion would have a moral warrant to use clandestine means in supporting the proposed constitutional amendment against abortion. Hence Saudi Arabia and other conservative Islamic countries would be justified in supplying the American Right-to-Life movement with, say, $100 million for undercover activities in support of this amendment. Most of us would find this highly inappropriate, yet this is very close to what is being done on a smaller scale to promote abortion in the developing countries.

A third guiding principle is that *foreign aid for abortion should not jeopardize foreign aid for socioeconomic development*. The great bulk of economic assistance today goes for activities other than population, including agriculture and nutrition, education, health, and public works. Most aid programs try to improve human welfare by finding better ways of producing rice and wheat, by increasing access to schooling for the rural poor, by experimenting with low-cost methods of delivering health care, and through similar means. To work well in promoting development, foreign aid requires an atmosphere of mutual trust and collaboration, not only between the donor agency and the government, but with other segments of the society as well. The greatest risk of covert aid for abortion is that it will pollute this environment and place all foreign assistance under a cloud of controversy and doubt. There are already suspicions in some quarters, particularly in Latin America and Africa, that donors bootleg as much birth control as possible into countries that do not want it. These suspicions are abetted by evidence that a decade ago, when family planning programs were coming into their own, donors imported the Lippes loop under the billing of "Christmas tree ornaments" and other contraceptives as "fungicides." The point here is that fears about hidden agendas and surreptitious activities on abortion can undercut the efforts of agencies that operate completely aboveboard, even in areas seemingly unconnected to birth control. And in the population field itself doubts about donor integrity can make a government reluctant to open the door for assistance to family planning services or even research. If an African minister of health fears that a family planning program will be infiltrated by agents of abortion and later cause a political explosion, he may be reluctant to move down that path at all. No program is an island in foreign aid.

In the end we must ask what constitutes ethical foreign

aid. Is assistance to other countries primarily a means to help governments attain their own purposes, or is it an instrument for subverting those purposes? The issues raised here can fruitfully be debated by persons who differ on the morality of abortion but who share a common commitment to the promotion of national development and international cooperation. It is a debate that is badly needed at this time.

NOTES

1. This paper is based on several interrelated sources: (1) the author's own research on foreign aid agencies conducted as part of the Hastings Center's Project on Cultural Values and Population Policies; (2) the country studies prepared for that project by scholars in several of the developing countries; and (3) recent interviews dealing specifically with foreign aid for abortion. Persons contacted included present or former staff members of the Population Council, the Office of Population of the Agency for International Development, the Population Crisis Committee, the Pathfinder Fund, the International Projects Assistance Service, the International Fertility Research Program, and the U.S. Senate.

2. H. R. Holtrop and R. S. Waife, *Uterine Aspiration Techniques in Family Planning* (Chestnut Hill, Massachusetts: Pathfinder Fund, 1976), p. 1.

3. Department of State, Agency for International Development, "A.I.D. Policies Relative to Abortion-Related Activities," Policy Determination, PD-56, 10 June 1976.

4. George Zeidenstein, "Future Directions of the Population Council," report prepared for the meeting of the Board of Trustees of the Population Council, 8–9 June 1976.

5. The information summarized here was obtained from an informal report on abortion prepared by IPPF in 1979.

6. Material describing this incident is contained in M. E. Lopez, A. M. R. Nemenzo, L. Quisumbing-Baybay, and N. Lopez-Fitzpatrick, *Cultural Values and Population Policy: Philippines, The Sociological Study* (Quezon City: Institute of Philippine Culture, Ateneo de Manila University, 1978).

7. The Pathfinder Fund, "Pathways in Population Planning," promotional flyer issued circa 1975.

8. United Nations Fund for Population Activities, *Population Programmes and Projects*, vol. 1, *Guide to Sources of International Population Assistance* (New York: 1979):297.

9. Ibid.

10. United Nations Fund for Population Activities, *Population Programmes and Projects*, vol. 2, *Inventory of Population Projects in Developing Countries Around the World 1977/78* (New York: 1979):303.

11. Ibid., p. 71.

12. Ibid., p. 31.

13. United Nations, World Population Conference, *Action Taken at Bucharest* (United Nations, New York: Center for Economic and Social Information / OPI for the World Population Conference, 1974), p. 10.

12

ABORTION: WHY THE ARGUMENTS FAIL

STANLEY HAUERWAS

Essays on the morality of abortion, whether they be anti or pro, have begun to take on a ritualistic form. Each side knows the arguments and counterarguments well, but both insist on asserting them afresh. Neither side seems to have much hope of convincing the other, but, just as in some rituals we continue to repeat words and actions though we no longer know why, in like manner we continue to repeat arguments about why abortion is right, wrong, or indifferent. It is almost as though we assume that the repetition of the arguments will magically break the moral and political impasse concerning the status of abortion in our society.

The intractability of the debate frustrates us and our frustration gives way to shrillness. Having tried to develop good philosophical, theological, legal, and social arguments, we find our opponents still unconvinced. In the heat of political exchange, both sides resort to rhetoric designed to make their opponents appear stupid or immoral. Thus we are besieged by slogans affirming the "right to life" or that every woman has the "right over her body;" or we are told to choose between being "prolife" and "prochoice." Some, concluding that there is no hope of conducting the public debate in a manner befitting the moral nuances of the abortion issues, have withdrawn from the field of battle.

Yet before anyone beat too hasty a retreat, it is worth considering why the arguments seem to have failed and why we have been left with little alternative to the oversimplifications of the public debate. There may be a moral lesson to be learned from the intractable character of the debate that is as important as the morality of abortion itself. And I suspect it offers a particularly important lesson for Christians. It is my contention that Christian opposition to abortion on demand has failed because, by attempting to meet the moral challenge within the limits of public polity, we have failed to exhibit those deep convictions that make our rejection of abortion intelligible. We have failed, then, in our first political task because we have accepted uncritically an account of "the moral question of abortion" determined by a politics foreign to the polity appropriate to Christian convictions. We have not understood, as Christians, how easily we have presumed the presuppositions of our "liberal" cultural ethos to be Christian. As a result, our temptation has been to blame the intractability of the abortion controversy on what appears to us as the moral blindness or immorality of pro-abortionists. By doing so, we fail to see how much of the problem lies in the way we share with the proabortion advo-cates the moral presumptions of our culture.

As Christians we have assumed that we were morally and politically required to express our opposition to abortion in terms acceptable in a pluralist society. To be sure, we did this with depth of conviction, for we assumed that those terms were the ones which should inform our understanding of the moral injustice involved in abortion. Hence we could claim that our opposition to abortion was not based on our special theological convictions, but rather founded on the profoundest presumptions of Western culture. All agree murder is wrong; all agree life is sacred; all agree that each individual deserves the protection of law; such surely are the hallmarks of our civilization.

We discovered that not every one agreed about when human life begins. This, we supposed, was the point of dis-pute. And no matter how earnestly we tried to document genetically that human life begins at conception, we found many accepting as perfectly intelligible Justice Blackmun's claim that the unborn are not "persons in the whole sense."[1] Philosophically we were told that our assumption that the fetus has moral status confuses the moral sense of being "human" or a "person" with the genetic,[2] and that we have to understand how the intelligibility of the concept of being a human or of being a person is anchored in our civilization's deepest moral values.[3]

Indeed, even as strong an antiabortion advocate as John Noonan has recently suggested that the issue of when human life begins is part of the public controversy that cannot be settled. "It depends on assumptions and judgments about what human beings are and about what human beings should do for one another. These convictions and conclu-sions are not easily reached by argument. They rest on par-ticular perspectives that are bound to the whole personality and can shift only with a reorientation of the person."[4] If that is true, then surely we Christians have already lost the battle by letting the enemy determine the terrain on which the battle must be fought.

When the issue is limited to the determination of when human life does or does not begin, we cannot prevail, given the moral presuppositions of our culture. Put more forcefully, where the debate is limited to the issue of when human life begins, it has already been uncritically shaped by the political considerations of our culture. The "moral" has already been determined by the "political"—something we fail to notice in the measure that we simply presume the moral presuppositions of our culture to be valid.

When the argument is so shaped, the very convictions that make us Christian simply never come up. Indeed, we have made a virtue of this, since some allege that appeals to religious convictions invalidate our views for the formulation of public policy.[5] As a result the Christian prohibition of abortion appears to them as an irrational prejudice of religious people who cannot argue it on a secular, rational basis.

But if Noonan is right that the convictions about human life rest on a perspective that is bound up with the "whole personality," then it seems that we Christians must make clear what we take such a "personality" to involve. For the Christian prohibition of abortion is a correlative to being a particular kind of people with a particular set and configuration of virtues. Yet we have tried to form our moral arguments against abortion within the moral framework of a liberal culture as though the issue could be abstracted from the kind of people we should be. How the moral description and evaluation of abortion depends on profounder assumptions about the kind of people we ought to be was thus not even recognized by ourselves, much less by those who do not share our convictions. As a result Christian arguments about abortion have failed. They have not merely failed to convince: they have failed to suggest the kind of "reorientation" necessary if we are to be the kind of people and society that make abortion unthinkable.

Of course it may rightly be objected that I am wrong; the arguments have not failed. Neither the fact that not everyone agrees that abortion is immoral nor the failure to pass a constitutional amendment is necessarily an indication that the antiabortion arguments have been invalid. Even at the political level there is still good reason to think that all is not lost, for there are political and legal strategies that are just beginning to have an effect on reversing our society's current abortion stance.[6] Yet even if such strategies succeed, our success may still be a form of failure if we "win" without changing the presuppositions of the debate.

To understand why this is the case, it is necessary to look more generally at the obstacles to moral agreement in our society. Only from such a perspective can we appreciate why the Christian stance concerning abortion may be a far more fundamental challenge to our society's moral presuppositions than even the most radical antiabortionists have considered.

ABORTION IN A LIBERAL SOCIETY

According to Alasdair MacIntyre, there is nothing singular about the failure of our society to reach a moral consensus concerning the appropriate manner to deal with abortion. He claims that the peculiar character of debate in our liberal, secular, pluralist culture derives from the absence of a rational method for resolving most significant matters of moral dispute. Any rational method for resolving moral disagreements requires a shared tradition about the nature of man and our true end.[7] But it is exactly the presumption of liberalism that a just society can be sustained by freeing the individual from all tradition.[8]

MacIntyre illustrates his argument by calling attention to three different positions concerning abortion:

> A: Everybody has certain rights over their own person, including their own body. It follows from the nature of these rights that at the stage when the embryo is essentially part of the mother's body, the mother has a right to make her uncoerced decision on whether she will have an abortion or not. Therefore each pregnant woman ought to decide and ought to be allowed to decide for herself what she will do in the light of her own moral views.
>
> B: I cannot, if I will to be alive, consistently will that my mother should have had an abortion when she was pregnant with me, except if it had been certain that the embryo was dead

or gravely damaged. But if I cannot consistently will this in my own case, how can I consistently deny to others the right to life I claim for myself? I would break the so-called Golden Rule unless I denied that a mother has in general a right to abortion. I am not of course thereby committed to the view that abortion ought to be legally prohibited.

C: Murder is wrong, prohibited by natural and divine law. Murder is the taking of innocent life. An embryo is an identifiable individual, differing from a new-born infant only in being at an earlier stage on the long road to adult capacities. If infanticide is murder, as it is, then abortion is murder. So abortion is not only morally wrong, but ought to be legally prohibited.[9]

MacIntyre suggests that, interestingly, each of the protagonists reaches his conclusion by valid forms of inference, yet there is no agreement about which premises are right starting points. And there exists in our culture no generally agreed-upon procedure for weighing the merits of the rival premises. Each of the above positions represents fragments of moral systems that exist in uneasy relation to one another in our culture. Thus position A, premised as "an understanding of rights which owes something to Locke and something to Jefferson, is counterposed to a universalibility argument whose debt is first to Kant and then to the gospels and both to an appeal to the moral law as conceived by Hooker, More, and Aquinas."[10]

The fact that these are "fragments" of past moral positions is particularly important. For as fragments they have been torn from the social and intellectual contexts in which they gained their original intelligibility and from which they derive such force and validity as they continue to possess. But since they now exist *only* as fragments we do not know how to weigh one set of premises against another. We do not know what validity to grant to each in isolation from those presuppositions that sustained their original intelligibility.

To understand the roots of our dilemma, MacIntyre argues that we must look to the moral presuppositions on which our society was founded. For in spite of the appeal to self-evident truths about equality and rights to life, liberty, and the pursuit of happiness, there was the attempt to provide some cogent philosophical basis for these "truths." The difficulty, however, begins when appeals such as Jefferson's to Aristotle and Locke in support of his position fail to acknowledge these to be mutually antagonistic positions. We are thus a society that may be in the unhappy position of being founded upon a moral contradiction.

The contradiction, in its most dramatic form, involves the impossibility of reconciling classical and modern views of man. Thus MacIntyre points out that "the central preoccupation of both ancient and medieval communities was characteristically: how may men together realize the true human good? The central preoccupation of modern men is and has been characteristically: how may we prevent men interfering with each other as each of us goes about our own concerns? The classical view begins with the community of the *polis* and with the individual viewed as having no moral identity apart from the communities of kinship and citizenship; the modern view begins with the concept of a collection of individuals and the problem of how out of and by individuals social institutions can be constructed."[11] The attempt to answer the last question has been the primary preoccupation of social theorists since the seventeenth century, and their answers to it are not always coherent with one another.

In the face of this disagreement the political consensus has been that the most nearly just social arrangement is one which requires no commitment to any good except the protection of each individual to pursue his or her interests fairly. Thus John Rawls says we ought to envisage the terms of an original contract between individuals on which a just society can be founded as one where they "do not share a conception of the good by reference to which the fruition of their powers or even the satisfaction of their desires be evaluated. They do not have an agreed criterion of perfection that can be used as a principle for choosing between institutions. To acknowledge any such standard would be, in effect, to accept a principle that might lead to a lesser religious or other liberty."[12]

Such a view can no longer provide a place for the classical insistence on the development of virtuous people. From the classical perspective judgments about virtues and goods are interdependent since the good is known only by observing how a virtuous man embodies it. But in the absence of any shared conception of the good, judgments about virtues and judgments about goods are logically independent of one another. Thus it becomes a political necessity, anchored in our society's profoundest moral convictions, that an issue such as abortion be considered on grounds independent of the kind of persons we would like to encourage in our society. The morality of the "act" of abortion must be considered separately from the "agent," for to take the character of the agent into account offends the basic moral and political consensus of our society.

We should be hesitant to criticize the moral achievement of political liberalism too quickly. By making the moral purpose of government the securing of the equal right of every individual to pursue his or her happiness as he or she understands it, liberalism was able to secure political peace in a morally pluralistic and fragmentary society. Its deepest advantage was to remove from the political arena all issues that might be too deeply divisive of the citizenry.[13] The ideal of liberalism is thus to make government neutral on the very subjects that matter most to people precisely because they matter most.

Of course our society has never acted with complete consistency on the principle of neutrality. Thus we ended slavery and outlawed polygamy. More recently, the modern welfare function of the state appears to require that certain beliefs about what is good for people be the basis of public policy. But it can still be claimed that the state leaves to individuals and groups the power to determine what private vision of happiness to pursue. "Hence governmental programs to assure full employment, to guarantee equal opportunity to enter the professions, to give everyone as much education as he wants, etc., imply no communal understanding of the good which is to be imposed on all. These programs aim only at establishing the conditions that enable everyone to pursue his own good as he understands it."[14]

One of the ironies, however, is that the liberal state so conceived has worked only because its citizens have continued to assume that the classical conception still held some validity for the regulation of their lives. Thus even though the virtues could not be encouraged as a "public" matter, they were still thought to be important as a private concern and to be of indirect benefit for our public life. Religion and the family institutions appropriate for the training of virtue were encouraged as necessary to sustain a polity based on the overriding status of the individual.

Thus, as Francis Canavan has argued, "liberal democracy has worked as well as it has and as long as it has because it has been able to trade on something that it did not create and which it tends on the whole to undermine. That is the moral tradition that prevailed among the greater part of the people. It is not necessary to pretend that most Americans in the past kept the Ten Commandments, certainly not that they kept them all the time. It is enough that by and large Americans agreed that there were Ten Commandments and that in principle they ought to be kept. The pluralist solution of withdrawing certain areas of life from legal control worked precisely because American pluralism was not all that pronounced. In consequence, many important areas of life were not withdrawn from the reach of law and public policy and were governed by a quasi-official public ethos."[15]

But in our day the moral consensus has disintegrated in a number of significant respects: we no longer have agreement on the value of human life, or on such basic social institutions as marriage and the family, or for that matter on the meaning of being human. "At this point, it is doubtful whether the typical response of the liberal pluralist society is any longer adequate, that is, to take the dangerously controversial matters out of politics and relegate them to the conscience of individuals. For this way of eliminating controversy in fact does much more. Intentionally or not, it contributes to a reshaping of basic social institutions and a revision of the moral beliefs of multitudes of individuals beyond those directly concerned. It turns into a process by which one ethos, with its reflection in law and public policy, is replaced by another. Liberal pluralism then becomes a sort of confidence game in which, in the guise of showing respect for individual rights, we are in reality asked to consent to a new kind of society based on a new set of beliefs and values."[16]

332

Perhaps this is nowhere better seen than in the phenomenon that Noonan has called the "masks" of liberty. By masks he means the linguistic conventions developed to redescribe the object and means of injustice.[17] Language such as "child," "baby," and "killing" has to be avoided for if it is used it will require a break with the moral culture we assume we wish to preserve.[18] "If all that has happened may fairly be described as 'termination of a pregnancy' with 'fetal wastage' the outcome, abortion may be accepted without break with the larger moral culture. If, however, such a description is a mask, if the life of an unborn child is being taken, it is difficult to reconcile the acceptance of abortion with the overarching prohibition against the taking of life."[19]

Thus we attempt to change our language so our commitment to greater individual liberty concerning abortion will not contradict our traditional views about what kind of people we should be to deserve to be free. The reason that our arguments concerning abortion are bound to fail is that we cannot resolve the morally antithetical traditions that form our society and our Christian ambitions for ourselves. The effort to resolve the issue as though the act of abortion could be separated from our convictions about character has been a futile attempt to settle a substantive moral issue on "objective" or procedural grounds acceptable to a liberal culture.

Thus Blackmun's opinion, while no doubt out of harmony with the majority of public opinion concerning abortion in America, might actually be in accordance with our deepest views if we were to apply them more consistently: an indication, perhaps, that we are better off as a people if we fail to think and act consistently! For the underlying presupposition of *Roe* v. *Wade* is consistent liberalism in assuming that the only entity with political standing is the individual. And the individual is understood to consist of characteristics sufficient to make him or her a "person." Of course, as Noonan points out, a liberalism so consistently applied also challenges some of our presumptions about the family,[20] but that may be but another price we have to pay in order to be "free."

Noonan has located the paradox of Justice Blackmun's opinion: "To invalidate the state abortion statutes it was necessary for him not only to ignore the unborn child but to recognize a liberty anterior to the state in the carrier of the child. The invocation of liberty which was the very heart of his opinion was the invocation of a standard superior to enacted law. His radical use of 'higher law' was only disguised by his claim that something in the Constitution supplied the standard by which the state laws on abortion were invalid. The ultimate basis of his decision was nothing in the Constitution but rather his readings of the natural law liberties of an individual."[21] Blackmun has based his opinion on the most cherished moral presumption of our society: the freedom of the individual.[22] Ironically, in the absence of a tradition, the ideal of a society constituted by individuals free of all tradition remains the sole moral basis we have for settling issues of moral significance.

CHRISTIANS AND ABORTION: THE PHILOSOPHICAL ISSUES

I have showed above how, in attempting to form their arguments against abortion in a manner that could be translated into public policy, Christians have accepted the moral limits imposed by our liberal heritage. As a result the reasons that Christians *qua* Christians should oppose abortion have not become a matter of public record. It should be noted that this was not just a strategy; rather, it witnessed to our standing conviction of a profound commonality between Christianity and liberalism. Christians have assumed that the liberal commitment to the individual carried with it the prohibition of abortion. Yet what they have found is that the "individual" whom liberalism has an interest in protecting does not, either conceptually or normatively (though perhaps legally), necessarily include the fetus.

Such a discovery is shocking in itself. Worse, it seems to leave Christians without further appeal. For we must admit that the fact and way that abortion became a matter of moral controversy caught us by surprise and unprepared. We were prepared to argue about whether certain kinds of abortion might or might not be legally prohibited or permitted. But that we would be required to argue whether abortion as an institution is moral, amoral, or immoral was simply unthinkable. As Christians we knew generally that we were against abortion, but we were not clear why. We assumed it surely had to do with our prohibition against taking of life, and we assumed that this was surely all that needed to be said.

There is nothing unusual about the Christian failure to know why abortion is to be prohibited. Most significant moral prohibitions do not need constantly to be justified or rethought. They are simply part and parcel of the way we are. When asked why we do or do not engage in a particular form of activity, we often find that it makes perfectly good sense to say "Christians just do or do not do that kind of thing." And we think that we have given a moral reason. But it is moral because it appeals to "what we are," to what kind of people we think we should be. Yet liberalism wishes to exclude such contentions from moral consideration in the interest of securing cooperation in a morally pluralistic society. Liberalism seeks a philosophical account of morality that can ground the rightness or wrongness of particular actions or behavior in a "theory" divorced from any substantive commitments about what kind of people we are or should be—except perhaps to the extent that we should be rational or fair.[23]

However, as Stuart Hampshire has argued, such theories falsify the way in which moral injunctions—such as those about life-taking, sexual relations, relations between parents and children, and truth telling—actually function. The meaning of and unity between such injunctions cannot be easily inferred from the axioms of a theory. Rather, "taken together, a full set of such injunctions, prohibiting types of conduct in types of circumstance, describes in rough and indeterminate outline, an attainable and recognisable way of life, aspired to, respected and admired: or at least the minimum general features of a respectworthy way of life. And a way of life is not identified and characterized by one distinct purpose, such as the increase of general happiness, or even by a set of such distinct purposes. The connection between the injunctions, the connection upon which a reasonable man reflects, is to be found in the coherence of a single way of life, distinguished by the characteristic virtues and vices recognized with it."[24]

Of course ways of life are complicated matters marked out by many details of style and manner. Moreover, the "connectedness" for any set of injunctions often has the character, not of "rational" necessity, but rather of a "reasonableness" that derives from the history of a community's moral experience and wisdom. Such a community may well have prohibitions that have an almost absolute character, such as the Christian prohibition of abortion, but such prohibitions need not be categorical, in the Kantian sense, nor based on principles of rationality. Rather, they are judgments of conditioned necessity, "in the sense that they imply that what must be done is not necessary because it is a means to some independently valued end, but because the action is a necessary part of a way of life and ideal of conduct. The necessity resides in the nature of the action itself, as specified in the fully explicit moral judgment. The principal and proximate grounds for claiming that the action must, or must not, be performed are to be found in the characterisation of the action offered within the prescription; and if the argument is pressed further, first a virtue or vice, and then a whole way of life will have to be described."[25]

But I am suggesting that this is exactly what we as Christians failed to do when it came to explaining why abortion is to be avoided. We failed to show, for ourselves or others, why abortion is an affront to our most basic convictions about what makes life meaningful and worthwhile. We tried to argue in terms of the "facts" or on the basis of "principles" and thus failed to make intelligible why such "facts" or "principles" were relevant in the first place. We spent our time arguing abstractly about when human life does or does not begin,[26] and as a result failed to challenge the basic presuppositions that force the debate to hinge on such abstractions.

Hampshire suggests that the best means to avoid the kind of abstract thinking encouraged by moral theories given birth by liberalism is to tell stories. For "telling stories, with the facts taken from experience and not filtered and at second hand, imposes some principles of selection. In telling the story one has to select the facts and probabilities which, taken together, constitute the situation confronting the agent. Gradually, and by accumulation of examples, belief that the features of the particular case, indefinite in number, are not easily divided into the morally relevant and morally irrelevant will be underlined by the mere process of story-telling. One cannot establish conclusively by argument in general terms the general conclusion that the morally relevant features of situations encountered cannot be circumscribed. One can only appeal to actual examples and call the mind back to personal experience, which will probably include occasions when the particular circumstances of the case modified what would have been the expected and principled decisions, and for reasons which do not themselves enter into any recognized principle."[27]

In a like manner I am suggesting that if Christians are to make their moral and political convictions concerning abortion intelligible we must show how the meaning and prohibition of abortion is correlative to the stories of God and his people that form our basic conviction. We must indicate why it is that the Christian way of life forms people in a manner that makes abortion unthinkable. Ironically, it is only when we have done this that we will have the basis for suggesting why the fetus should be regarded as but another of God's children.

For, as Roger Wertheimer has shown, arguments concerning the status of the fetus's humanity are not factual arguments at all, but actually moral claims requiring the training of imagination and perception. Wertheimer suggests that the argument over the status of the fetus is a "paradigm of what Wittgenstein has in mind when he spoke of the possibility of two people agreeing on the application of a rule for a long period, and then, suddenly and quite inexplicably, diverging in what they call going on in the same way. This possibility led him to insist that linguistic communication presupposes not only agreement in definitions, but also agreement in judgments, in what he called forms of life—something that seems lacking in the case at hand (i.e., the fetus). Apparently, the conclusion to draw is that it is not true that the fetus is a human being, but it is not false either. Without agreement in judgments, without a common response to the pertinent data, the assertion that the fetus is a human being cannot be assigned a genuine truth value."[28]

Wertheimer suggests that there seem to be no "natural" responses, no clear forms of life, which provide the basis for why the fetus should be regarded one way rather than another. Thus failure to respect the fetus is not analogous to failure to respect blacks or Jews since we share forms of life, common responses, with them that make the denial of their humanity unintelligible. Thus the forms of life that lead some to see and treat blacks and Jews as less than human can be shown to be perverse by appeal to factual counter claims based on our common experiences.

Wertheimer may be right that the case for respect for blacks and Jews is more immediately obvious than the case for the fetus, but I hope to show that the Christian form of life provides powerful reasons for regarding the fetus with respect and care. Moreover, such respect is as profoundly "natural" as our current belief that blacks and Jews have moral status. What we must understand is that all "natural" relations are "historical" in so far as the natural is but what we have come to accept as "second nature."[29] The recognition of blacks and Jews was no less dependent on a history than was the recognition of the status of the fetus. Both are the result of the experience of communities which are formed by the substantive convictions of the significance of being open to new life. Because such an "openness" has become so "natural," and often so perverted, we have forgotten what profound moral commitments support and are embodied in the simple and everyday desire for and expectations of new life that appear among us through and after pregnancy. Such a desire is obviously not peculiar to Christians, but by attending more directly to the Christian form of life, I hope to show why and how the Christian desire for children makes it imperative that the fetus be regarded with respect and care.

CHRISTIANS AND ABORTION: THE NARRATIVE CONTEXT

If my analysis has been correct, we should now have a better hold on why arguments concerning abortion have failed in our society. At one level I have tried to show that they must fail, given the moral presuppositions and language offered by our liberal ethos. But I have also tried to suggest that failure at this level is but an indication of a deeper failure for Christians. Christians have failed their social order by accepting too easily the terms of argument concerning abortion offered by our society. If we are to serve our society well, and not on alien terms, our first task must be to articulate for Christians why abortion can never be regarded as morally indifferent for us. Only by doing this can we witness to our society what kind of people and what kind of society is required if abortion is to be excluded.

Such a suggestion may sound extremely odd, since it seems to ask that we reinvent the wheel. Surely that is not the case, for both anti- and proabortion advocates know that, rightly or wrongly, Christians have had their minds made up about abortion from the beginning. It is certainly true that Christians, drawing on their Jewish roots, have condemned abortion from the earliest days.[30] Yet this condemnation does not come from nowhere; it is a correlative of a way of life that must be constantly renewed and rethought. The task of each new generation of Christians is to rediscover that way of life and to understand why prohibitions such as that against abortion are critical reminders of what kind of life it is that they are called to lead. The Christian way of life, though often lived simply, is no simple matter, but rather involves a complex set of convictions that are constantly being reinterpreted as our understanding of one aspect of the tradition illuminates another. What we must do is show how this process makes a difference for our understanding of the prohibition of abortion.

It is important, furthermore, to distinguish my argument in this respect from those who make the often unfair criticism that the church must rethink its position on abortion because it allows life taking in other contexts. Though I do not wish to deny that Christians have often been inconsistent, especially in practice, about the protection and taking of life, there is nothing conceptually inconsistent about the prohibition of abortion as the unjust taking of life and the permissibility of just war and capital punishment. My call for the church to rethink her understanding of abortion involves the more fundamental concern that the church perceive why abortion is incompatible with a community whose constitution is nothing less than the story of God's promise to mankind through the calling of Israel and the life of Jesus.

Such a discussion must be both theological and political. One cannot be separated from the other. Our beliefs about God are political in that they form the kind of community that makes the prohibition of abortion intelligible. But the discussion is also political in that it must be carried on in a way that allows Christians to listen and learn from one another concerning their different understanding of what is at stake in abortion. Only as we proceed in this manner can we be a paradigm—perhaps even a witness—to our society of what a genuine moral discussion might look like.

I do not mean to imply that such a discussion has been missing entirely in recent Christian history. Yet I think it is fair to say that we have not paid sufficient attention to how Christians as Christians should think about abortion.[31] Indeed, I suspect many are not even sure what a call for this kind of discussion entails. Therefore I will try to suggest the kind of theological concerns that any discussion of abortion by Christians should involve.

To begin with, the first question to ask is not, "Why do Christians think abortion is wrong?" To begin there already presupposes that we know and understand what abortion is. Rather, if we are to understand why Christians assume that by naming abortion they have already said something significant, we have to begin still a step back. We have to ask what it is about the kind of community, and corresponding world, that Christians create that makes them single out abortion in such a way as to exclude it.

For we must remember that "abortion" is not a description of a particular kind of behavior. Rather, it is a word that teaches us to see a singular kind of behavior from a particular community's moral perspective. The removal of the fetus from the mother's uterus before term can be called an "interruption of pregnancy," the child can be called "fetal matter," and the mother can be called a "patient." But from the Christian perspective, to see the situation in that way changes the self and the community in a decisive way. The Christian insistence on the term "abortion" is a way of reminding the faithful that what happens in the removal of the fetus from the mother in order to destroy it strikes at the heart of their community. From this perspective the attempt of Christians to be a community where the term "abortion" remains morally intelligible is a political act.

In this respect the proabortion position has always been at a disadvantage.[32] For its advocates have had to carry out the argument in a language created by the moral presuppositions of the Jewish and Christian communities. "Abortion" still carries a sinister nuance. Thus to be "proabortion" seems to put one in the embarrassing position of recommending a less than good thing. It is not without reason, therefore, that proabortion advocates seek to redescribe both the object and the act of abortion. What we must remind them, however, is that by doing so they not only change the description of the act; they also change themselves.

Christians attest to the significance of such a change by refusing to live in a world that rejects abortion as a moral description—a world which admittedly will, as a result, involve deep tragedy. Doubtless, to insist that termination of pregnancy be called abortion has to do with our respect for life, but that is surely too simple. Jews and Christians are taught to respect life, not as an end in itself, but as a gift created by God. Thus life is respected because all life serves God in its way. Respect for human life is but a form of our respect for all life.

But note that just as no life can claim highest value, except as it exists for love and service of God, neither can human life be thought to have absolute value. The Christian prohibition against taking life rests, not on the assumption that human life has overriding value, but on the conviction that it is not ours to take. The Christian prohibition of abortion derives, not from any assumption about the inherent value of life, but rather from the view that as God's creatures we have no basis to claim sovereignty over life.

And we cannot forget that this creator is also our redeemer. The life that lies in the womb is also a life that has come under the lordship of Jesus Christ. As Karl Barth has said: "This child is a man for whose life the Son of God has died, for whose unavoidable part in the guilt of all humanity and future individual guilt He has already paid the price. The true light of the world shines already in the darkness of the mother's womb. And yet they want to kill him deliberately because certain reasons which have nothing to do with the child himself favor the view that he had better not be born! Is there any emergency which can justify this? It must surely be clear to us that until the question is put in all its gravity a serious discussion of the problem cannot even begin, let alone lead to serious results."[33]

The temptation, in this secular age, is to ignore this kind of rhetoric on the assumption that all it really amounts to is that Christians also believe in the value or sacredness of life. But from the perspective of Christian convictions about life as the locus of God's creating and redeeming purpose, claims of life's "value" or "sacredness" are but empty abstractions. The value of life is God's value and our commitment to protect it is a form of our worship of God as a good creator and a trustworthy redeemer. Our question is not, When does life begin? but, Who is its true sovereign? The creation and meaningfulness of the term "abortion" gains its intelligibility from our conviction that God, not man, is creator and redeemer and thus Lord of life. The Christian respect for life is first of all a statement, not about life, but about God.[34]

Yet the way of life of Christians involves more than the conviction of God's creating and redeeming purposes. We also believe that God has created and called us to be a people whose task it is to manifest and witness to his providential care of our existence. Thus to be a Christian is not just to hold certain beliefs; it is to be part of a historic community that has the task of maintaining faithful continuity with our forebears. To be a Christian is to be part of a people who live through memory, since we know how to face and create our future only by striving to be as faithful and courageous as our forebears. The necessity of memory for our continued existence is but a form of worship of our God, who wills to be known through the lives of his followers.

Christians are thus a people who have an immense stake in

history. We look neither to escape nor to transcend history. We are determined to live with history, faithful to the memory of our founder. There is no conviction, therefore, more significant for Christians than our insistence on having children. For children are our anchors in history, our pledge and witness that the Lord we serve is the Lord, not only of our community, but of all history. The family is therefore symbolically central for the meaning of the existence of the Christian people.

From a Christian perspective children represent our continuing commitment to live as a historic people.[35] In the Christian community children are, for those who are called to be married, a duty. For the vocation of marriage in part derives its intelligibility from a couple's willingness to be open to new life. Indeed, that is part of the test of the validity of their unity as a manifestation of "love" in the Christian sense. It must necessarily be open to creation of another.

The Christian community's openness to new life and our conviction of the sovereignty of God over that life are but two sides of the same conviction. Christians believe that we have the time in this existence to care for new life, especially as such life is dependent and vulnerable, because it is not our task to rule this world or to "make our mark on history." We can thus take the time to live in history as God's people, who have nothing more important to do than to have and care for children. For it is the Christian claim that knowledge and love of God is fostered by service to the neighbor, especially the most helpless, for that, in fact, is where we find the kind of Kingdom our God would have us serve.

It is the Christian belief, furthered by the command of Jesus that we must learn to love one another, that we become more nearly what we were meant to be through the recognition and love of those we did not "choose" to love. Children, the weak, the ill, the dispossessed provide a particularly intense occasion for such love because they are beings we cannot control. We must love them for what they are, rather than for what we want or wish them to be, and as a result we discover how to love. The existence of such love is not unique or limited to Christians. Indeed, that is why we have the confidence that our Christian convictions on these matters might ring true even for those who do not share them. The difference between the Christian and the non-Christian is only this: what is a possibility for the non-Christian is a duty for the Christian.

But the Christian duty to welcome new life is a joyful duty because it derives from our very being as God's people. Moreover, the language of duty is correlative to the language of gift. For because children are a duty they can also be regarded as gift. It is duty which teaches us to accept and welcome children into the world, not as something that is "ours," but as a gift which comes from another.[36] As a result Christians need not resort to destructive and self-deceiving claims about the qualities they need to have or the worldly condition that must exist before they can decide to have children. Perhaps more worrisome than the moral implications of the claim "no unwanted child ought ever be born" are the ominous assumptions about what is required for one to "want" to have a child.

Christians are thus trained to be the kind of people who are ready to receive and welcome children into the world. For they see children as a sign of the trustworthiness of God's creation and of his unwillingness to abandon the world to the powers of darkness. The Christian prohibition of abortion is but the negative side of their positive commitment to welcome new life into their community: life that they know must challenge and perhaps even change their own interpretation of their tradition, but also life without which the tradition has no means to grow.

It is, of course, true that children will often be conceived and born under less than ideal conditions, but the church lives as a community which assumes that we live in an age which is always dangerous. That we live in such a time is all the more reason we must be the kind of community that can receive children into our midst. Just as we need to be virtuous, not because virtue pays, but because we cannot afford to be without virtue where it does not pay; so we must learn how to be people open to new life. We can neither protect our neighbors from that suffering nor deny them the joy of participating in the adventure of God's kingdom.

For Christians therefore there can be no question of

whether the fetus is or is not a "human being." That way of putting the matter is far too abstract and formal. Rather, because of the kind of community we are we see in the fetus nothing less than God's continuing creation destined in hope to be another citizen of his kingdom. The question of when human life begins is of little interest to us, since our hope is that life will and does continue to begin, time after time.[37]

This is the form of life that brings significance to our interaction with the fetus. Our history is the basis for our "natural" sympathies, which have been trained to look forward to the joy and challenge of new life. Wertheimer may well be right that there is in our society no corresponding "natural" welcome for life that would make intelligible the recognition of the fetus as having moral status. Yet I suspect that the expectation of parents, and in particular of women, for the birth of their children remains a powerful form of life that continues to exert a force on everyone. Such an "expectation," however, in the absence of any more substantive convictions about parenting, too easily becomes a destructive necessity that distorts the experience of being a parent as well as that of being a child. Particularly repugnant is the assumption that women are thus primarily defined by the role of "mother," for it leads us to forget that the role of being a parent, even for the childless, is a responsibility for everyone in the Christian community.

Nor should it be thought that the Christian commitment to welcome new life into the world stems from a sentimental fondness for babies. For Christians the having of children is one of their most significant political acts. From the world's perspective, the birth of a child represents but another drain on our material and psychological resources: children, after all, take up much of the energy that we could use in making the world a better place and our society a more just one. But from the Christian perspective, the birth of a child represents nothing less than our commitment that God will not have this world "bettered" through the destruction of life. That is why there is no more profound a political act for the Christian than taking the time for children. It is but an indication that God, not man, rules this existence, graciously inviting us to share in his adventure and his kingdom through the simple action of having children.

CHRISTIANS AND ABORTION: THE IMMEDIATE POLITICAL TASK

To some it may seem that I have argued Christians right out of the current controversy. For my argument has made appeal to religious convictions that are inadmissible in the court of common morality. But it has certainly not been my intention to make it implausible for Christians to continue to work for the protection of all children in the public arena; nor do I think that this implication follows from the position I have developed. Of course Christians should prefer to live in societies that provide protection for children. And Christians should certainly wish to encourage those "natural" sentiments that would provide a basis for having and protecting children.

Moreover, Christians must be concerned to develop forms of care and support, the absence of which seems to make abortion such a necessity in our society. In particular, Christians should, in their own communities, make clear that parenthood is a role that we all share. Thus the one pregnant and carrying the child need not be the one to raise it. We must be a people who stand ready to receive and care for any child, not just as if it were one of ours, but because in fact each is one of ours.

As Christians we must not confuse the political and moral strategies we adopt to get the best possible care for children in our society with the substance of our convictions. Nor should we hide the latter in the interest of securing the former, for when that is done we abandon our society to its own limits and our arguments fall silent in the most regrettable manner. We must, therefore, remember that our most fundamental political task is to embody and to point to that truth which we believe to be the necessary basis for any life-enhancing and just society.

In particular, I think that we will be wise as Christians to state our opposition to abortion in a manner that makes clear our broader concerns for the kind of people we ought to be to welcome children into the world. Therefore, rather than concentrating our energies on debating whether the fetus is or is not a "person," we would be better advised to show by example and then by argument why we should hope it *is* a child. We must demonstrate that such a hope— involving much more than just the question of the status of the fetus—is indeed the very basis upon which our sharing in God's creation becomes such an extraordinary and interesting adventure.[38]

NOTES

1. *Roe* v. *Wade*, 410 U.S. 113, 153–54 (1973).

2. For example, see Mary Anne Warren, "On the Moral and Legal Status of Abortion," in *Contemporary Issues in Bioethics*, eds. I. Beauchamp and L. Walters (Encino, Calif.: Dickenson Publishing Co., 1978), pp. 222–25. Warren's argument in this respect is common in current philosophical literature. Perhaps the most celebrated form of it is Michael Tooley's article, "Abortion and Infanticide," in *The Rights and Wrongs of Abortion*, eds. M. Cohen, T. Nagel, and T. Scanlon (Princeton: Princeton University Press, 1974), pp. 52–84.

3. Thus Warren argues that "the moral community consists of all and only *people*, rather than all and only human beings," and the characteristics of the former she takes to be consciousness, reasoning, self-motivated activity, the capacity to communicate whatever the means, and presence of self-concepts (pp. 223–24). For an extremely interesting article dealing with the ambiguity of deciding whether a class of beings is human, see Edmund Pincoffs, "Membership Decisions and the Limits of Moral Obligation," in *Abortion: New Directions for Policy Studies*, eds. E. Manier, W. Liu, and D. Solomon (Notre Dame: University of Notre Dame Press, 1977), pp. 31–49. I have argued elsewhere against the significance of "person" as a moral ascription, but it is hard to deny its significance in a society such as ours, for the idea of "person" embodies our attempt to recognize that everyone has a moral status prior to any role they might assume. It therefore represents the profound egalitarian commitment of our culture. The difficulty, of course, is that the notion of being a "person" seems to carry with it psychological implications that simply exclude certain beings from being treated with respect. See Stanley Hauerwas, *Truthfulness and Tragedy* (Notre Dame: University of Notre Dame Press, 1977), pp. 127–63.

4. John Noonan, *A Private Choice: Abortion in America in the Seventies* (New York: Free Press, 1979), pp. 2–3. In his earlier essay, "An Almost Absolute Value in History," Noonan had argued that conception is the decisive moment of humanization because "at conception the being receives the genetic code. It is this genetic information which determines his characteristics, which is the biological carrier of the possibility of human wisdom, which makes him a self-evolved being. A being with a human genetic code is man" (in *Ethical Issues in Modern Medicine*, eds. R. Hunt and R. Arras [Palo Alto: Mayfield Publishing Co., 1977], p. 137). Noonan obviously no longer regards such empirical claims as decisive for establishing the moral status of the fetus though they may certainly be suffi-

cient for claiming that the fetus is a human being. Underlying the issue of the relation between the moral and descriptive status of the fetus may be the larger assumption that the distinction between facts and values, or how values include factual claims, makes sense. Thus the claim that the antiabortionist is confusing a "moral" claim with a "factual" claim may involve the unwarranted assumption that such "facts" are not moral.

5. Thus Roger Wertheimer suggests that the antiabortionist "realizes that, unless he uses religious premises, premises inadmissible in the court of common morality, he has no way of categorically condemning the killing of a fetus except by arguing that a fetus is a person" ("Understanding the Abortion Argument," in Cohen, Nagel, and Scanlon, eds., *Rights and Wrongs of Abortion*, p. 37). But, as we shall see, the assumption that there is a common morality with an agreed content can hardly be accepted in our society. Moreover, I hope to show that theological convictions play a role quite different from what Wertheimer and many others seem to assume. Indeed, a Christian understanding of the morality of abortion should make such a question irrelevant.

6. Noonan has made a strong case, for example, for a constitutional amendment that would not prohibit states from protecting unborn life if it is the will of their legislatures to do so. Such an amendment would at least provide the possibility of a more refined moral debate on this issue in our society. Moreover, it might result in laws that do not have the negative effect on other of our institutions, such as the family, that the current abortion rulings seem to involve. See Noonan, *A Private Choice*, pp. 178–88.

7. Alasdair MacIntyre, "How Virtues Become Vices," in *Evaluation and Explanation in Biomedical Sciences*, ed. H.T. Englehardt, Jr., and S. F. Spicker (Dordrecht: Reidel, 1974), p. 104.

8. Ironically, the antitraditional stance of liberalism results in self-deception, since liberalism is only intelligible in the light of its history. It is, of course, true that liberalism is an extremely complex phenomenon that is not easily characterized by even the most sophisticated forms of political theory. I associate liberalism, however, with the political philosophy of Rawls and Nozick, the political science of Dahl, and the economics of neocapitalism. There often appear to be deep disagreements between the advocates of liberalism in America, but such disagreements are, finally, arguments between brothers.

9. Alasdair MacIntyre, "How to Identify Ethical Principles," in *The Belmont Report: Ethical Principles and Guidelines for the Protection of Human Subjects of Research* 1 (Washington, D.C.: DHEW Publication no. (OS) 78-0013, 1978):9–10. For an extremely able development of Argument C, see Philip Devine, *The Ethics of Homicide* (Ithaca: Cornell University Press, 1978). Devine argues "that acts of homicide are prima facie seriously wrong because they are acts of homicide, and not for any supposedly more fundamental reason, such as that they tend to produce disutility or are unjust or unkind, and that this prima facie wrongness cannot be overridden by merely utilitarian considerations" (p. 11). He correctly refuses to try to give a further theoretical account for why unjustified homicide is wrong, since such an account necessarily has the effect of qualifying the prohibition.

10. MacIntyre, "How to Identify Ethical Procedures," p. 10. Garry Wills's recent study of Jefferson certainly requires a reconsideration of

Jefferson's position vis-à-vis Locke. Wills makes clear that Jefferson's position owes more to the communitarian strains of the Scottish Common Sense philosophers, such as Hutcheson, than had been suspected. An indication of the power of Locke and the general liberal-contractarian tradition in America is that, in spite of what Jefferson's own views might have been, they were simply interpreted through the eyes of Locke. See Garry Wills, *Inventing America: Jefferson's Declaration of Independence* (Garden City: Doubleday, 1978).

11. MacIntyre, "How to Identify Ethical Principles," p. 22. The change in perspective also makes clear why there are so many attempts to form all moral arguments in the language of "right."

12. John Rawls, *A Theory of Justice* (Cambridge: Harvard University Press, 1971), p. 327. One of the difficulties with Rawls's assumption that the meaning of justice can be separated from a conception of the good is that he ends up endorsing an understanding of the good to which he would object on other grounds. For, in spite of Rawls's richer view of the relation of individual and community in the last sections of *A Theory of Justice*, methodologically his position does not exclude the economic man enshrined in liberal theory.

13. Francis Canavan, "The Dilemma of Liberal Pluralism," *Human Life Review* 5 (Summer 1979):7. The social and political experience of the American people has often contained more profound moral commitments than our commitment to liberal ideology could express. As a result we have often been unable to give political standing to some of our most significant achievements.

14. Ibid., p. 9. Nowhere is this illustrated better than in the Bakke case. For Bakke is quite right: from a liberal perspective, he has been the victim of reverse discrimination. But that does not mean he has been treated unfairly if we had the means of politically recognizing that blacks should receive preferential treatment, given our history as a country of slavery and discrimination. On a liberal view, we cannot give blacks standing as blacks, but only as individuals who now have the opportunity to compete within the rules of fair play.

15. Ibid., p. 14.

16. Ibid., p. 15.

17. Noonan, *A Private Choice*, pp. 153–69.

18. It is interesting, however, that women undergoing abortion often continue to describe the fetus as a baby or child. See, for example, Linda Bird Francke, *The Ambivalence of Abortion* (New York: Random House, 1978), and my "Abortion: Once Again" (forthcoming).

19. Noonan, *A Private Choice*, p. 175. Warren's attempt to deny that her arguments imply infanticide are interesting in this respect. She says that infanticide would be wrong for at least two reasons: it would be wrong "in this country and in this period of history, and other things being equal, to kill a new-born infant, because even if its parents do not want it and would not suffer from its destruction, there are other people who would like to have it, and would, in all probability, be deprived of a great deal of pleasure by its destruction. Thus, infanticide is wrong for reasons analogous to those which make it wrong to wantonly destroy natural resources, or great works of art. Secondly, most people, at least in this country, value infants and would much prefer that they be preserved, even if foster parents are not immediately available" ("Moral and Legal Status," p.

227). Warren seems to feel no difficulty in making the prohibition against infanticide depend on whether someone might want a child. Moreover, she is rigorously consistent and clear that if an "unwanted or defective infant is born into a society which cannot afford and/or is not willing to care for it, then its destruction is permissible" (p. 228). It does not seem to occur to her that we ought to be the kind of society, no matter what our material appetites, that is able to receive children, even retarded children, into our midst. Her argument is a clear example, therefore, of the assumption that the rightness or wrongness of acts can be abstracted from the kind of people we ought to be.

20. Noonan, *A Private Choice*, pp. 90–96. See also my "The Moral Value of the Family," *Working Paper Series: Center for the Study of American Catholicism* (Notre Dame: Center Publication, 1978).

21. Noonan, *A Private Choice*, p. 17.

22. The abortion decisions of the current Supreme Court can in some ways be interpreted as the further extension of the arguments of the laissez-faire capitalist applied to issues of personal morality. Indeed, there has always been an uneasy tension between our legal tradition and the ideology of liberalism. It may well be, however, that as liberalism has become an increasingly self-fulfilling prophecy in so many other aspects of our life, so it will ultimately transform our legal tradition.

23. It is my contention that current ethical theory involves an attempt to write about "morality" in a manner required by a liberal society. Indeed, the very assumption that "ethics" can be a "discipline" separate from political theory and economics seems to me to be an indication of the power of liberalism over our imagination. Such moral philosophies attempt to provide highly formal accounts of the conditions of moral argument and judgment separate from the beliefs of actual agents. One cannot help but admire their attempt to find a way to make moral argument work between people who share no common values, but they fail to see that such accounts too easily become ideologies for the status quo.

24. Stuart Hampshire, "Morality and Pessimism," in Stuart Hampshire, ed., *Public and Private Morality* (Cambridge: Cambridge University Press, 1978), p. 11.

25. Ibid., p. 13.

26. Ironically, Christians have often tried to construct their arguments by using moral theories, especially the more deontological theories, that make rationality the basis for any moral claim. Though these theories often provide powerful accounts for why everyone deserves a minimum of respect, by their very structure they exclude the fetus from their account.

27. Hampshire, "Public and Private Morality," in Hampshire, ed., *Public and Private Morality*, pp. 38–39.

28. Wertheimer, "Understanding the Abortion Argument," p. 42. See also Wertheimer's fine article, "Philosophy on Humanity," in Manier, Liu, and Solomon, eds., *Abortion: New Directions for Policy Studies*, pp. 117–36.

29. I suspect that Wertheimer would not deny this point. He is not using "nature" in a theory-laden sense but simply means by it "what is common." Thus, whereas we have many everyday experiences with blacks, we do not encounter the fetus in the same manner. Yet, as I will argue below, there are powerful forms of life which are unintelligible apart from the existence of the fetus.

30. See John Connery's excellent history of moral reflection on the

subject, *Abortion: The Development of the Roman Catholic Perspective* (Chicago: Loyola University Press, 1977).

31. In a sense Christian discussion of abortion has been too ethical and insufficiently theological. In effect, we became the victim of our own highly refined casuistry on the subject and failed to rethink the theological context that made the casuistry intelligible in the first place. Thus considerations of whether certain acts of abortion might be permissible were abstracted from the community's narrative that made the prohibition of abortion intelligible. No community can or should avoid casuistical reflection, but it should always remember that the function of casuistry is to help the community save its language and judgments from distortion, through analogical comparisons. And the control of the analogies ultimately depends on paradigms rooted in the community's experience as interpreted through its central narratives.

32. There is a broader issue involved here that can only be mentioned. For just as liberalism has often "worked" only because it could continue to count on forms of life that it did not support and even worked against, so current ethical theory has often seemed intelligible because it continued to be able to rely on moral language and descriptions for which it can give little basis. Thus contemporary ethical theory tends to concentrate on questions of decision and justification and avoids issues of how we learn to see and describe our experience morally.

33. Karl Barth, *Church Dogmatics*, trans. A. T. MacKay et. al. III/4 (Edinburgh: T. and T. Clark, 1961):416.

34. There is nothing about this claim that requires that all abortions are to be prohibited. Indeed, when abortions may be permitted will depend on the experience and discussion of a community formed by the conviction of God's sovereignty over life. The broad theological claims I am developing here cannot determine concrete cases, though they can determine how abortion as a practice can and should be understood and evaluated.

35. In his *The Culture of Narcissism* (New York: Norton, 1978), Christopher Lasch suggests that a people's sense of historical time and their attitudes toward children are closely interrelated. Thus "the narcissistic personality reflects among other things a drastic shift in our sense of historical time. Narcissism emerges as the typical form of character structure in a society that has lost interest in the future. Psychiatrists who tell parents not to live through their offspring; married couples who postpone or reject parenthood, often for good practical reasons; social reformers who urge zero population growth, all testify to a pervasive uneasiness about reproduction—to widespread doubts, indeed, about whether our society should reproduce itself at all. Under these conditions, the thought of our eventual suppression and death becomes utterly insupportable and gives rise to attempts to abolish old age and to extend life indefinitely. When men find themselves incapable of taking an interest in earthly life after their own death, they wish for eternal youth, for the same reason they no longer care to reproduce themselves. When the prospect of being superseded becomes intolerable, parenthood itself, which guarantees that it will happen, appears almost as a form of self-destruction" (p. 211).

36. For a fuller presentation of this theme see my *Truthfulness and Tragedy*, pp. 147–56.

37. The issue of when life begins will, of course, come up in considering

hard cases. Connery, for example, provides a good overview of the history of such reflection in his book. Yet just as hard cases make bad law, so hard cases can distort our moral reflection if, in the process of our reflection on them, we forget the more positive commitments that make the casuistry intelligible. As Connery makes clear, the question of when life begins has always been a side issue for Christian casuistry. Rather, the concern has been whether the taking of the life of the fetus under particular circumstances is analogous to other situations where it is unavoidable or permissible that life be taken.

38. I would like to thank Rev. David Burrell, Rev. James Burtchaell, and Dr. David Solomon for criticizing an earlier draft of this paper.